OTTOMAN IZMIR

OTTOMAN IZMIR
The Rise of a Cosmopolitan Port, 1840–1880

Sibel Zandi-Sayek

UNIVERSITY OF MINNESOTA PRESS
MINNEAPOLIS · LONDON

The University of Minnesota Press gratefully acknowledges the financial assistance provided for the publication of this book from the College of Arts and Sciences at the College of William and Mary.

Portions of chapter 3 were published in "Struggles over the Shore: Building the Quay of Izmir, 1867–1875," *City and Society: An Annual Review of the American Anthropological Association* 12, no. 1 (Spring 2000): 55–78. Portions of chapter 4 were published in "Orchestrating Difference, Performing Identity: Urban Space and Public Rituals in Nineteenth-Century Izmir," in *Hybrid Urbanism: On the Identity Discourse and the Built Environment,* ed. Nezar AlSayyad (Westport, Conn.: Praeger, 2001), 42–66.

Every effort was made to obtain permission to reproduce material in this book. If any proper acknowledgment has not been included, we encourage copyright holders to notify the publisher.

Copyright 2012 by the Regents of the University of Minnesota

All rights reserved. No part of this publication may be reproduced, stored in a retrieval system, or transmitted, in any form or by any means, electronic, mechanical, photocopying, recording, or otherwise, without the prior written permission of the publisher.

Published by the University of Minnesota Press
111 Third Avenue South, Suite 290
Minneapolis, MN 55401-2520
http://www.upress.umn.edu

Library of Congress Cataloging-in-Publication Data

Zandi-Sayek, Sibel, author.
Ottoman Izmir : the rise of a cosmopolitan port, 1840–1880 / Sibel Zandi-Sayek.
pages cm
Includes bibliographical references and index.
ISBN 978-0-8166-6601-0 (hc : alk. paper)
ISBN 978-0-8166-6602-7 (pb : alk. paper)
1. Izmir (Turkey)—History—19th century. 2. Harbors—Turkey—History—19th century.
I. Title.
DS51.I9Z36 2012
956.2′5—dc23
2011040862

Printed in the United States of America on acid-free paper

The University of Minnesota is an equal-opportunity educator and employer.

18 17 16 15 14 13 12   10 9 8 7 6 5 4 3 2 1

To
Alin *and* **Remon**

Contents

Author's Note / ix

Introduction
A World in Flux / 1

1. **Defining Citizenship**
   Property, Taxation, and Sovereignty / 47

2. **Ordering the Streets**
   Public Space and Urban Governance / 75

3. **Shaping the Waterfront**
   Public Works and the Public Good / 115

4. **Performing Community**
   Rituals and Identity / 151

Epilogue
The View from Izmir / 187

Acknowledgments / 197

Notes / 201

Bibliography / 235

Index / 261

Author's Note

The maps in this book are intended as historical guides. The three that precede the text are key maps for readers to orient themselves within Izmir's spatiotemporal layout. Map 1 presents the city in the mid-1830s and sets it in relation to surrounding sites mentioned in the chapters. Maps 2 and 3 offer snapshots of the city's extraordinary expansion in the 1850s and 1870s and indicate the location of close-up maps included in each chapter.

Throughout the book, I overlay my annotations on historical maps instead of redrawn base maps. Like other documentary evidence, historical maps open an invaluable window into the mindset of the particular groups who commissioned them. The maps reveal how they conceptualized the boundaries, structures, and patterns of urban expansion; how they prioritized different kinds of information regarding the changes in the city; and how they came to understand their ever-changing environment. Retaining and conveying these diverse voices and experiences is a central concern of this book. All annotations on maps and figures are mine, unless otherwise indicated.

The different names local residents used to refer to the same places are a testimony to Izmir's fluid, multilingual character. Linguistic variations of the same name (for example, Fassolah, Fassula, Fasulya) or names of completely different provenance (such as Frank Street and Sultaniye Street) were simultaneously used until the early twentieth century. The city was variously known as Izmir, Ismeer, Smyrna, Smirni, or Smyrne, eluding a standard nomenclature. For the sake of simplicity and consistency throughout this book, I use Izmir—both the city's current designation in international parlance and its official designation in Ottoman Turkish records. In quoted passages, all city and place names are retained as they appear in the original source.

To designate the city's native residents, I use the English form "Smyrniot." I also use the Anglicized version closest to the modern Turkish spelling for Ottoman Turkish or Arabic words that have entered into the Oxford English Dictionary; hence *pasha, bey, khan, molla* instead of *mollah, efendi* instead of *effendi, kadı* instead of *cadi*. In the text and notes, I avoid all diacritics associated with transliteration, except for the circumflex to indicate long vowels in Ottoman Turkish, such as *râya*. All English translations and paraphrases are mine, unless otherwise indicated. Some Turkish letters do not appear in the English alphabet, and others are pronounced differently from their English counterparts:

C, c: j as in "jam"
Ç, ç: ch as in "chin"
Ğ, ğ: the soft g slightly lengthens the preceding vowel; it has no sound, like the silent gh in "weight"
I, ı: e as in "target"
İ, i: i as in "fit"
Ö, ö: u as in "fur"
Ş, ş: sh as in "sharp"
Ü, ü: ew as in "few"

The dates in the main text are given according to the Gregorian calendar. Islamic hicri (H) or the Ottoman malî (M) dates are supplied only in note citations when they appear in the original document.

MAP 1. Izmir and its surroundings, by Captain Richard Copeland, 1834. Bibliothèque nationale de France.

LEGEND: 1 = Caravan Bridge; 2 = Kadifekale (Mount Pagus); 3 = Değirmentepe; 4 = slaughterhouses; 5 = The Point (Tuzla Burnu); 6 = Meles River; 7 = Halkapınar (Diana's Bath); 8 = aqueduct.

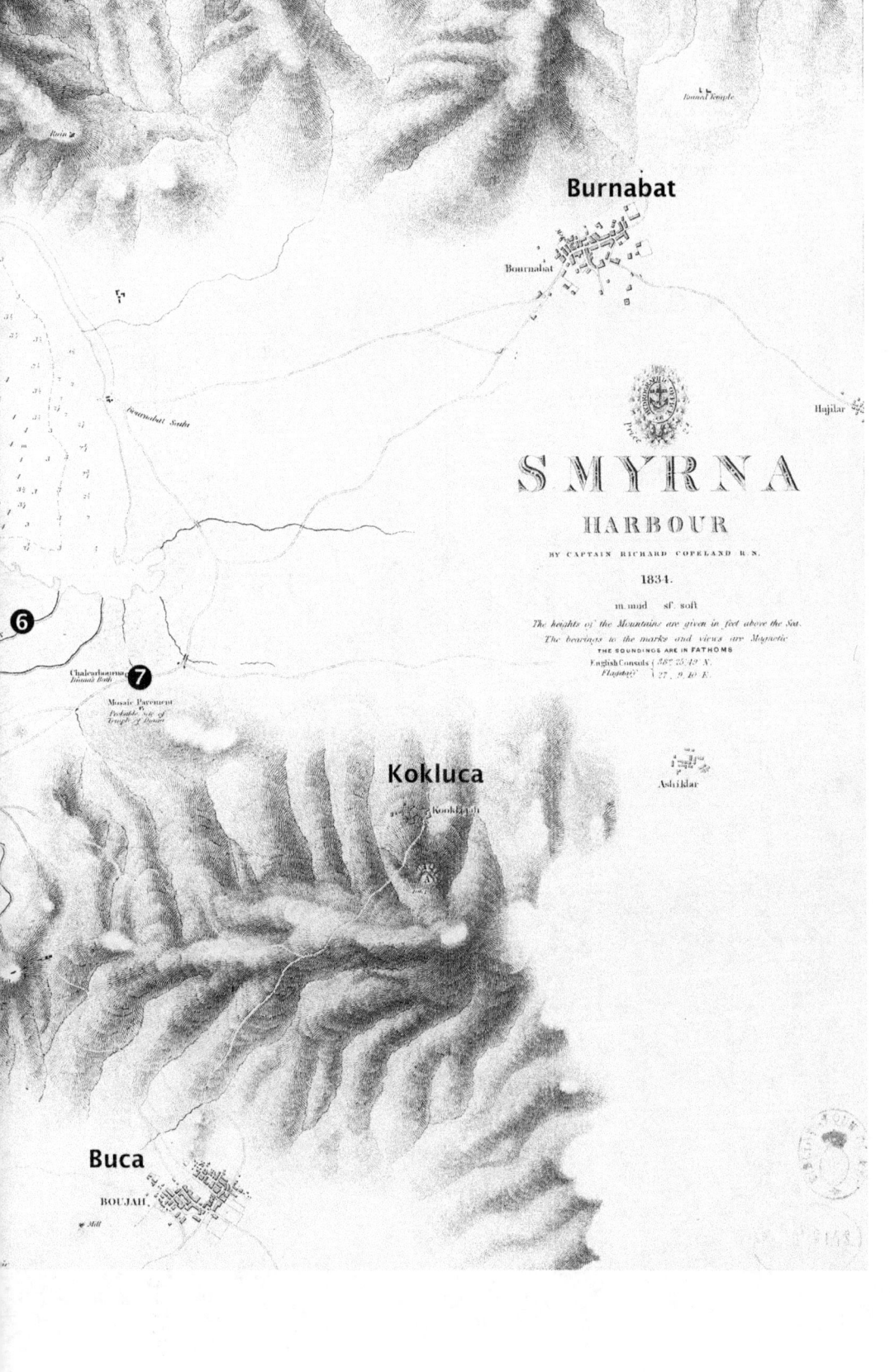

MAP 2. Plan of Izmir by engineer Luigi Storari, dedicated to Sultan Abdülmecid, 1854–56. Bibliothèque nationale de France.

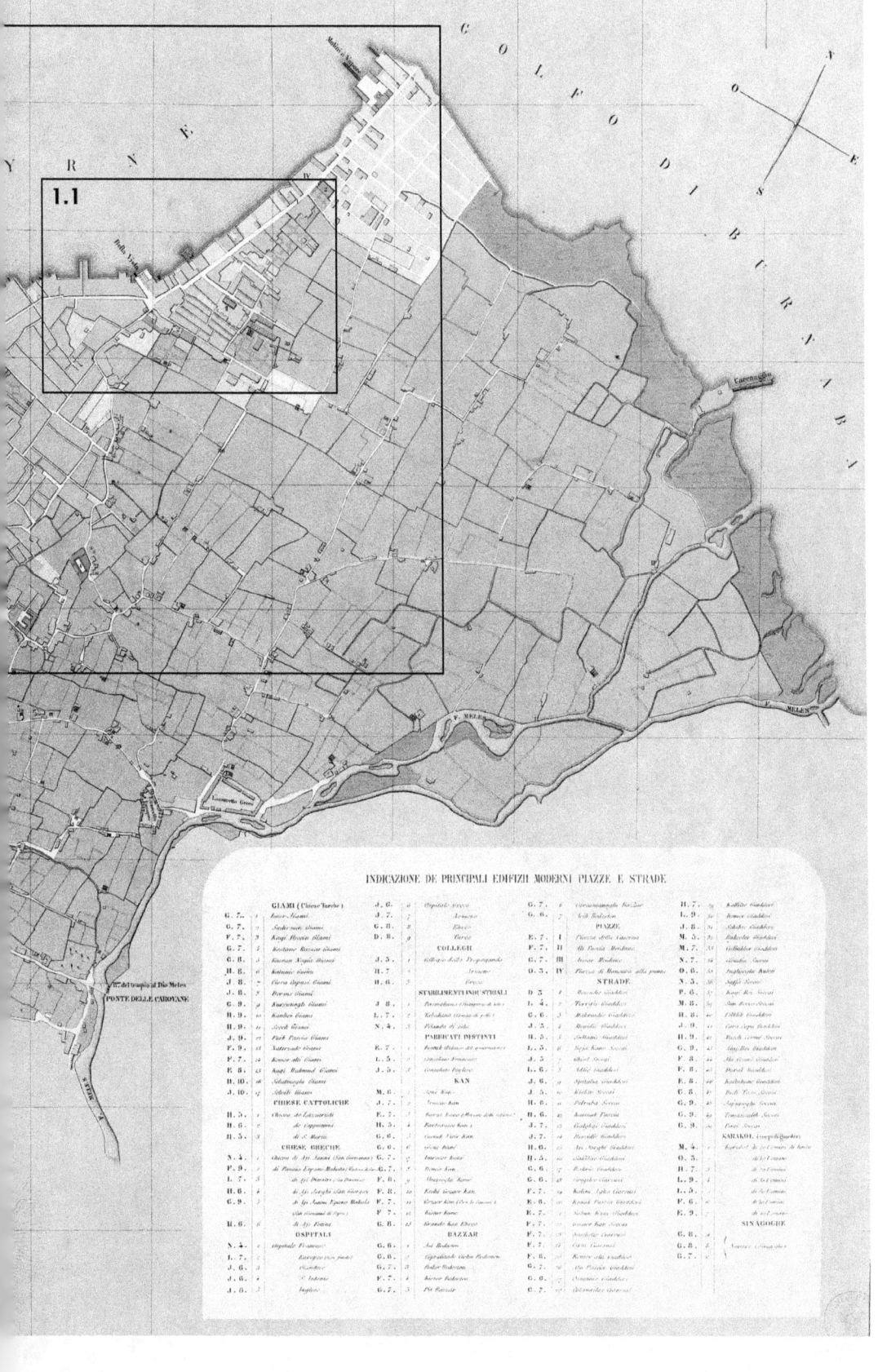

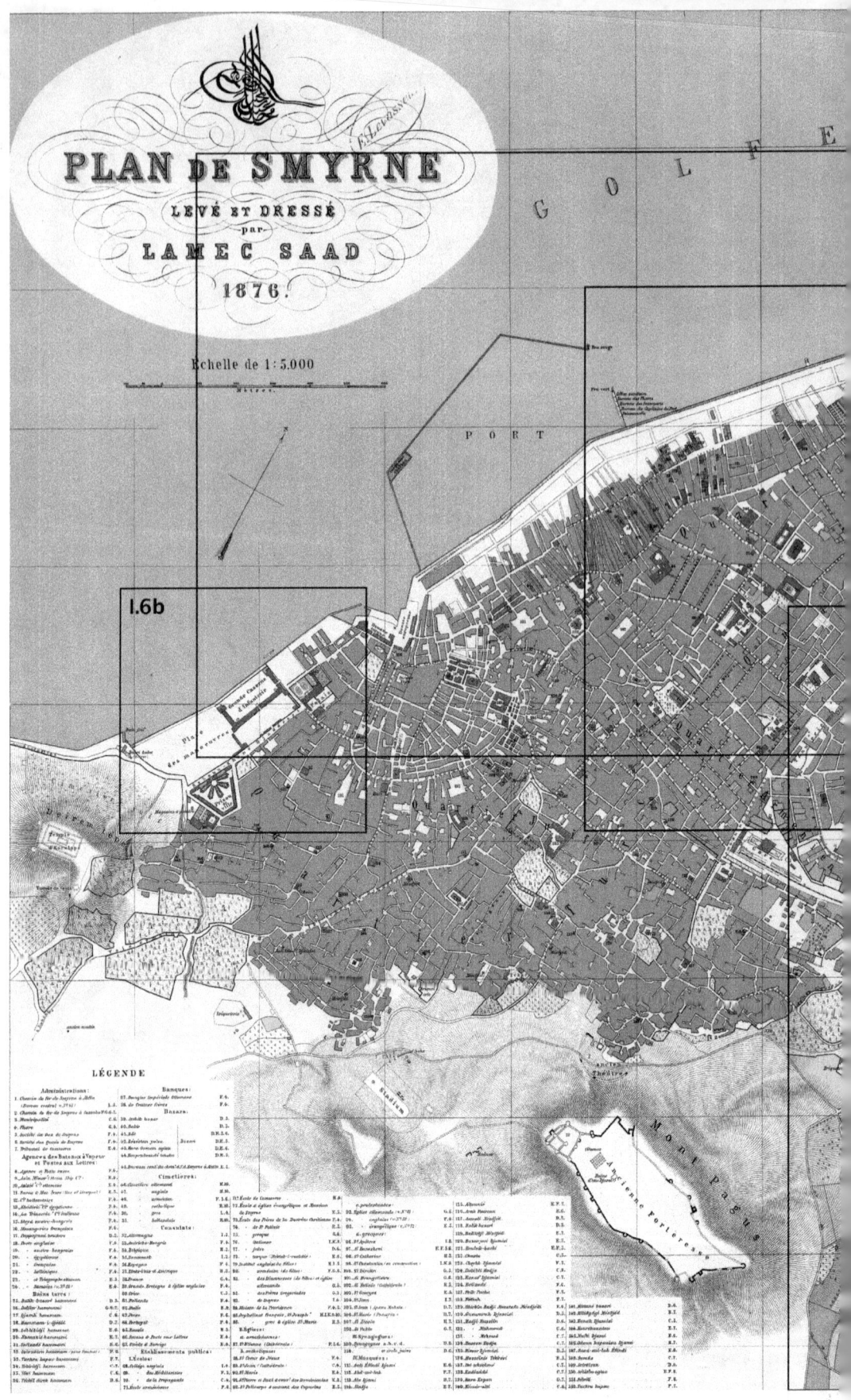

MAP 3. Plan of İzmir by Dr. Lamec Saad, 1876. Courtesy of the Regenstein Library, University of Chicago.

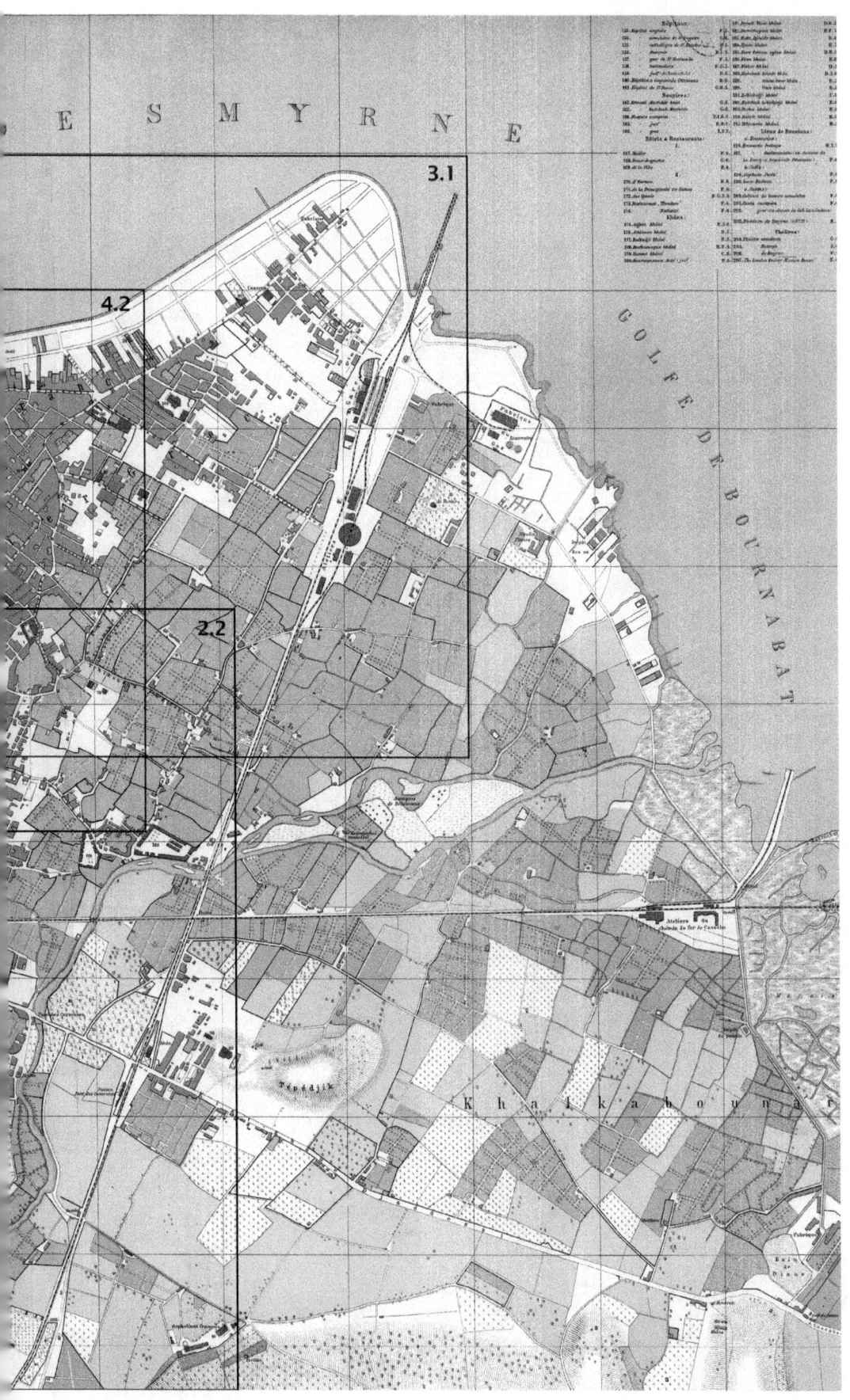

Introduction

A World in Flux

IN THE MID-NINETEENTH CENTURY, the Ottoman seaport of Izmir, the gateway to Asia Minor on the Eastern Mediterranean, was in the throes of tremendous physical change. A modern harbor equipped for international steamship traffic and railway lines linking the city to its rich hinterland dramatically transformed the nature and volume of commercial activity. Migrants, seasonal workers, and transient sailors thronged into a city already home to communities of diverse ethnic, religious, and national origins, more than doubling the population to two hundred thousand between the 1840s and the late 1880s.[1] Banks, postal services, insurance companies, brokerage firms, commercial packing and storage warehouses, dry-goods stores, hotels, commercial clubs, theaters, cafés, printing houses, and similar types of modern establishments dotted the urban landscape, serving as visual markers of a radical economic and cultural boom. While hastily built working-class neighborhoods developed on the urban fringes, grand villas rose up in garden suburbs to house those who were making new fortunes. A two-mile-long waterfront promenade lined with attractive buildings gave a new face to the city; it also offered increased possibilities for cross-class, cross-religious, and cross-national encounters. Expanded and renovated communal institutions such as churches, mosques, synagogues, schools, and hospitals exhibited the wealth of an emerging class of patrons. Similarly, newly built governmental quarters and an imposing military barrack block, prominently fronting the bay, provided evidence of the Ottoman state's bureaucratic expansion.

Simultaneously, the administrative and legal mechanisms governing this thriving environment were subject to continual reform and negotiation that profoundly transformed the character and experience of the city. A modern city government sought to reconfigure and consolidate the provision of urban services previously handled privately, patchily, and more informally by local communities. Modern urban infrastructure, building codes, sanitary ordinances, and other types of regulations imposed more uniform and clear-cut conceptions of public and private, safety and danger, and hygienic and unhygienic on a city historically shaped by a wide range of discrete regulations and circumstantial arrangements. Newly standardized laws about property ownership, taxation, and citizenship cut across established legal categories that defined personal status and granted rights of residence and business, eventually restructuring prevailing modes of participation in the urban polity. This was uncharted territory. As a result, the process was tentative and contentious, often developing in fits and starts and necessitating constant modification.

The city's motley actors—from local merchants to foreign consuls to Ottoman civil servants—astutely used a range of tools and strategies to promote urban improvements, while also striving to hang onto their stakes in their rapidly changing city. Thanks, in no small measure, to living in an international port that allowed for a continuous flow of people, goods, commodities, and ideas from different localities, they were informed about changes taking place well beyond their immediate territorial confines. Moreover, by residing in a multiethnic, multiconfessional, and multilingual polity, they had become well versed in dodging conventional communal boundaries and forming coalitions of shared interest across communal lines when it suited their needs. At times, business leaders and merchants proficient in conducting both European and local transactions could turn the tide in their favor, and even subvert or direct government measures and international actions. They exerted pressure through ad hoc committees, petitions, signature campaigns, and other available methods of interaction with the Ottoman state and foreign governments. They also forged new civic channels, using the empire's newly established newspapers, publishing pamphlets in various languages, and deploying contemporary arguments of equity, progress, and justice to further their interests. Local communities also retooled familiar religious feasts, public events, and other forms of collective expression to realign themselves with emerging ideas of nationhood and identity at a time when ethnoreligious communal concerns were moving to the center stage of Ottoman politics and culture. In 1852, French parliamentarian Charles Rolland, who had visited Izmir for the second time in three years, found the city to be in an "unaccustomed" state of agitation. "This city," he wrote, "which for centuries saw no other turmoil than fires, seems transformed into an arena of debates and experiences ... past and future, Reformists and Conservatives are warring; and I find among all my acquaintances, Turkish or Christian, an excitement, even an asperity of speech when interests are at stake."[2]

This book foregrounds Izmir's built environment as a crucible in which various local actors vied to shape urban policies and practices and assert or preserve their relative positions of influence during a time of rapid change, centered around the mid-nineteenth century. The book spans roughly from the 1840s to the 1880s, a formative period when major transformations—some of which began earlier, and some of which continued beyond the 1880s—were taking place in multiple spheres, both within and outside the empire. I explore how people from a wide spectrum of society, Muslims and non-Muslims, subjects and foreigners, newcomers and long-term residents, merchants, investors, civil servants, and press reporters, engaged in the reorganization of the city's physical space. In the process, they formed alliances, waged resistance, and negotiated interests. As people developed strategies to address issues related to their built environment, they also activated certain aspects of their identity and made choices about their relationship to their city and to those with whom they shared the same urban territory. They stretched and flexed existing institutions, defined new forms of political participation, and reconfigured or undermined the boundaries of social power and authority, ultimately revealing how the physical and the political are indissociable.[3]

Izmir offers an excellent site to investigate the complex interrelatedness of urban space, institutional practices, and civic culture in the context of multiethnic and multinational imperial polities. In addition to its good harbor and crossroads location between Asia Minor and the Mediterranean, Izmir owed its prosperity to its diffuse yet remarkably dynamic structures of power. Ottoman Greeks, Muslims, Armenians, and Jews, and colonies of Venetian, French, Dutch, and British merchants, who had made the city their home since at least the seventeenth century, coexisted as separately governed communities. Premised on diversity, the Ottoman social order allowed them to preserve their identities and the differential customary rights, duties, and privileges associated with those identities. Hence, migrants and traders from across the Mediterranean and interior districts, lured by the city's prosperity, shared the same territory, mixed and mingled, without necessarily assimilating. Together they forged in Izmir a distinctive polyglot enclave, marked by differences but also conducive to creative forms of interdependence, exchange, and initiatives. That the city's various power holders, including European consuls, Ottoman provincial agents, communal leaders, and notables, had stakes, but none could claim full control, gave Izmir a vibrant political climate—at once cooperative and competitive. At the same time, this modus vivendi, which entailed all sorts of balancing acts, often mediated through everyday spaces and interactions, makes Izmir all the more illuminating for understanding processes of urban change.

What makes mid-nineteenth-century Izmir particularly fascinating is the window it opens into the dynamics of urban modernization and their tentative, contingent, and conflicted character. Initially, the bureaucratically led Ottoman reforms—the Tanzimat-ı Hayriye inaugurated with the 1839 Gülhane Edict and reconfirmed with the 1856 Hatt-ı Hümayun—were piecemeal, uncertain, based on compromises, and implemented unevenly. Uniformly applicable rules, standard jurisdictions, and modern state institutions brought innovation, but they did not categorically erase existing practices. Instead, discrepant and partially overlapping laws and governance regimes coexisted and competed, creating both conflicts and pressures for further institutional negotiations and openings for people to insert themselves opportunistically. At the same time, the world-historical context within which these developments were taking shape was fluid and unstable. As Eric Hobsbawm put it, the question of which nation would acquire a state and which of the nonnational states would be recognized as sovereign nation-states by their peers was yet to be settled.[4] Global geopolitical balances and alignments were volatile as was the place of the empire within them. The launching of the Ottoman reforms themselves were in no small part a recognition that the empire's territorial integrity depended on alliance with leading European powers without letting these allies interfere in the empire's internal affairs. In this context of instability, Izmir's property regime, streets, waterfront, feasts, and rituals—the city's material infrastructure and practices—became a battleground for the reformist state, rival foreign powers, and various local groups to stake their claims and articulate their priorities, both directly and by proxy.

Battles over the ownership, use, and representation of urban spaces were certainly not exclusive to Izmir. The pressures nineteenth-century Izmir contended with and the challenges it addressed were widely shared, even if their particular forms were shaped by Izmir's economic, social, and political conditions and its unusually diverse set of actors and interests. Congestion, poor sanitation, safety, and repeated epidemics pressured fast-growing cities in many parts of the world to improve their infrastructure, modernize their institutions of governance, and reorder their material resources. Moreover, whether in "Western," "non-Western," or colonial cities, this process was never purely technical, but inevitably political.[5] The provision of large-scale urban infrastructure and the management practices associated with it offered various concerned parties fertile ground for formulating and legitimizing their particular understanding of the public good and who the benefiting public ought to be. Similarly, the creation of new local government structures, responsible for urban services and civic improvement, necessarily altered the rights and obligations of local residents, potentially shaping the modes of participation in the public sphere. Studying Izmir in this light not only draws attention to issues critical to all modernizing cities—and, in particular, to the constitution of a modern public and emerging forms of civic engagement and citizenship; it also inscribes the Ottoman experience in a world-historical context of nineteenth-century urban transformation.[6] Consequently, in this book, I selectively probe the conflicts and controversies engendered by Izmir's urban spaces to provide an analytic framework that could be fruitfully used to interpret modernizing cities elsewhere.

Nineteenth-century Izmir also brings into sharp focus the experiences of Eastern Mediterranean seaports, especially those that modernized under Ottoman rule. As has been widely recognized, the expansion of trade with industrializing Europe was a major force in transforming many seaports around the Mediterranean into bustling, international commercial and cultural centers.[7] Given their deepwater harbors suitable for long-distance vessels, resource-rich hinterlands that could be exploited for export, and remarkably adaptable mercantile classes with local know-how and far-reaching commercial networks, port cities like Alexandria, Izmir, Thessaloniki (Salonika), or Beirut were indeed poised to attract increased flows of capital, investors, and migrant workers. Moreover, the decisive opening of these ports to free trade, particularly after the 1838 Anglo-Ottoman commercial treaty, further spurred urban growth and development, turning them into vibrant regional nodes within emergent global networks of exchange.[8] The rapid advances in Izmir's commercial infrastructure and institutions and the creation of new local constituencies empowered by wealth were some of the powerful manifestations of this broader economic restructuring affecting port cities throughout the Mediterranean and beyond.

Equally important in shaping the urban character of these fast-growing seaports was the simultaneous expansion of Ottoman state bureaucracy by a leadership eager to assert its sovereignty at home and in the international arena. As recent scholarship has shown, beginning in the mid-nineteenth century, Ottoman reformers deployed the tools and technologies of modern statecraft to bring under their jurisdictions areas that formerly eluded their control and keep European expansionist ambitions in check.[9] They focused on the empire's chief commercial centers and provincial capitals to implement more standardized laws, administrative procedures, and a taxation system. Sometimes years before reformed codes were institutionalized across the empire, Ottoman seaports boasted new commercial and criminal courts that tried cases under reformed legal codes. Izmir, like Thessaloniki, was in the forefront of modern cadastral efforts that provided a basis to enforce a new real-estate and income tax.[10] Similarly, several major seaports acquired new local governments before empire-wide municipal regulations were established, making these centers important sites of innovation, but also of greater institutional uncertainty.[11] How the Tanzimat reforms played out in different localities, especially in major Ottoman centers, has recently commanded attention from historians, revealing, on the one hand, an empire that was far more dynamic and flexible, striving to affirm its place in an increasingly state-centered international order, and, on the other, numerous local groups and actors who actively participated in and engaged with the changes affecting their world.[12]

This book joins this rapidly growing literature on nineteenth-century Eastern Mediterranean and Ottoman cities, but it also charts a new historiographic and methodological terrain. I use urban space and spatial practices as a lens to investigate the dynamic nature of identity and belonging in a rapidly modernizing and centralizing, multinational and multireligious state. If some aspects of social identity were shaped by existing, and changing, institutional categories used by the Ottoman state, others, I argue, were actively produced and reconfigured through living within the confines of a fixed urban territory and sharing the resources and pressures associated with it.[13] The ethnoreligious organization (or the *millet* structure) through which the Ottoman state had historically granted communal privileges and tax obligations to the diverse peoples living within its territories certainly informed social behavior and reinforced a sense of group identity at the local level, but it neither confined nor totally defined social life and city dwellers' actions. Individuals from across religious, ethnic, and linguistic boundaries frequented spaces outside the sphere of their community. They crisscrossed the town to get provisions at the market, to go to work, or to engage in leisure activities, and they entered into commercial transactions with one another. In mid-nineteenth-century Izmir, newly emerging governance, business, and consumption practices demanded a much wider range of interactions and exchanges than those conventionally afforded by communal networks or localized neighborhoods. People from various walks of life participated in and shaped this increasingly complex socioeconomic environment and its power hierarchies, aligning and realigning their interests as they saw fit and, in the process, reinforcing or undermining perceived (or assumed) communal identities and boundaries. The battles engendered by the rapid reorganization of Izmir's physical space are brimming with fascinating information on how social groups organized themselves and how interest groups formed and split in relation to different priorities and issues. They lay bare how urbanites construed their relationship to the city, showed support or opposition to particular policies and measures, and expressed allegiance to different and sometimes competing sources of power and authority.

By focusing on the multilayered, fluctuating, and contingent identities of Izmir's plural society, this book provides an important corrective to studies of Ottoman cities, which have too often been conditioned by assumptions of clear-cut ethnoreligious boundaries and national divides. While scholars acknowledge how social, economic, and linguistic factors complicate Ottoman ethnoreligious categories, these categories continue to frame and inform the study of Ottoman society.[14] This is not to say that these boundaries and divides were false or unreal, or that Izmir provided the setting for a seamless and harmonious coexistence. Quite to the contrary, religious, ethnic, national, and linguistic differences were becoming enormously powerful in the mid-nineteenth century as administrative and legal reforms gave greater fixity and uniformity to existing institutional categories and cast them in mutually exclusive terms as never before. Rather, local groups and actors strategically exploited these differences, sometimes selectively activating a particular aspect of their layered identity when expedient or desirable. In particular, I show how people negotiated and maneuvered between institutional boundaries at a time when the reformist regime was actively drafting more effective measures to close the loopholes within its system of rules. By recognizing the dynamic context of everyday urban politics, and the pragmatic actions and temporary alliances spawned in the process, this study highlights people's agency and opens up the possibility of observing the fluid and constructed nature of identity. It offers an empirically grounded reading of Tanzimat reconfigurations of identities and institutional norms that complicates and expands narrowly conceived interpretations of plurality in Ottoman cities.

How we view Ottoman plurality has a direct and important bearing on how Izmir's Ottoman past—especially the century that preceded the tragedy that beset the city—has been construed. As myriad historical and more contemporary studies have documented, in the early twentieth century Izmir was the scene of one of history's most tragic humanitarian catastrophes, which decimated its plural society, its established institutions, and most of its physical structure.[15] In 1922, the retaliation of Turkish troops to the three-year-long Greek military occupation of Western Asia Minor culminated in a devastating fire and the persecution of large numbers of Izmir Greeks and Armenians. A year later, the compulsory population exchange between Greece and Turkey forced Ottoman Greeks to leave their homeland permanently, eventually reducing Izmir's urban population to half. These events have profoundly marked historical memory, giving Izmir a highly symbolic significance in rival ideologies and agendas. They also hopelessly prejudiced historical writings, presenting the Ottoman imperial past through a framework that sought to justify the categories of nascent nation-states. That the bulk of modern studies has focused on the discrete histories of Ottoman Greeks, Jews, or Armenians—often uncritically adopting and extending the fault lines used in forging nation-states onto the peoples of the past—has further impaired our capacity to comprehend urban transformations in their own historical context. Significantly, they have obscured the very processes by which institutional and communal boundaries had been continually challenged, regenerated, and modified by virtue of people sharing the same territorial basis—what I view as fundamental and vital to the workings of any plural society.

Although the events leading to the dismantling of Izmir as a plural society, and the Ottoman Empire as a political entity, are far beyond the scope and time period of this book, this book indirectly addresses some of their historiographic repercussions. Rather than starting with stable categories and divides, it probes how institutional and interest-group boundaries were porous, constituted and reconstituted through struggles and debates over the control, management, and meaning of material assets and resources. As a result, it reveals a world in flux, hinged on delicate balances, fraught with competing and intersecting priorities and interests, wherein groups, factions, and alliances are continually changing. Viewing mid-nineteenth-century Izmir on its own terms, as opposed to a prelude to its demise, this book elucidates the Ottoman Empire's most often studied and, arguably, least understood century.

A City Betwixt and Between

In the eyes of most nineteenth-century European observers, Izmir did not readily fit preconceived notions of the Orient. Its domes and minarets interspersed with cypress trees, its narrow winding streets, its heaving bazaar, and the variety of physiognomies and costumes encountered on the streets, indeed, epitomized what the Orient was supposed to be (Figure I.1). And yet, the city did not present a full cultural separation from "Christian Europe." Its population included a large proportion of Christians and sizable and influential communities of European settlers. Its shops were stocked with "most of the luxuries and comforts of France and England," and its casino (or clubhouse) was supplied with European newspapers.[16] Travel accounts of the period regularly referred to the city as "le petit Paris du Levant" (little Paris of the Levant).[17] Muslims popularly called it "gâvur Izmir" (infidel Izmir), alluding to its majority non-Muslim population—and possibly to the absence of a pronounced Muslim character.[18] Izmir was the West of the East or the East of the West, a city betwixt and between, home to an astoundingly diverse population and molded by a large repertoire of languages, creeds, and customs. In the words of George Rolleston, head physician of the city's British hospital in 1856, there were "few other towns in the world with a *fixed* and *resident* population consisting of so many distinct and distinguishable elements."[19] Above all, Izmir was a significant breeding ground for the mixing, crossing, and redefinitions of ideas and identities integral to the Eastern Mediterranean experience. It was part of a broader, established Levantine/Mediterranean world with combined communities of Arabic, Greek, Italian, Judeo-Spanish, and French speakers, including Christians, Jews, and Muslims, that had for centuries been connected through trade.[20]

Izmir owed its distinctively plural character as much to its crossroads position on the Mediterranean as to the relative stability and openness it enjoyed under Ottoman rule. Lying at the head of a long and well-protected bay, approximately halfway down the western coast of Asia Minor (or Anatolia) in present-day Turkey, Izmir had occupied a prominent place in history long before coming under Ottoman rule (Maps 1 and I.1). It was a prosperous and attractive trade center during Roman times, boasting such honorific titles as "*Protos Asiæ*" (First of Asia) and "the Jewel of Ionia."[21] It was also the seat of a large archbishopric after the official recognition of Christianity, and the celebrated site of one of the Seven

FIGURE I.1. View of Izmir from the bay highlighting the city's mosques and minarets and its wooden piers and structures lining the bay front, ca. 1840. Lithograph. From Eugène Napoléon Flandin, *L'Orient*, vol. 1 (Paris: Gide et Baudry, 1853).

Churches of the Apocalypse. Beginning in the eleventh century, Izmir became part of a fiercely contested territory at the intersection of the Latin, Byzantine, and Muslim worlds as its repeated siege, conquest, and reconquest by Greek, Turcoman, Genoese, Rhodian, and Mongolian rulers indicate. Eventually, its incorporation into the Ottoman domain in 1424 exempted it from the scourges of war, allowing for a comparatively long period of tranquility. Despite occasional local uprisings, outbreaks of plague, frequent fires, and two devastating earthquakes in 1688 and 1778, all of which temporarily arrested urban growth, Ottoman Izmir flourished into a major trade and shipping center linking the Anatolian markets to the Mediterranean world and beyond.[22] Its phenomenal boom in the seventeenth century anchored its identity as "the modern capital of Asia Minor"[23] and "the chief emporium of the Levant."[24] In addition, Izmir sustained a multilayered historical identity. Although much of the physical evidence of its earlier history had been erased by the seventeenth century, incidental fragments scattered through the Ottoman city continued to hint at a rich heritage, making Izmir a major destination for antiquarians, missionaries, and pilgrims through the following centuries.

The broad contours of Ottoman Izmir's plural society were established in the late sixteenth and early seventeenth centuries when the city grew from a regional port supplying the capital, Istanbul, to a principal Eastern Mediterranean center for export trade with Europe. Waves of migration, both from Ottoman provinces and from around the Mediterranean, brought the population from a few thousands

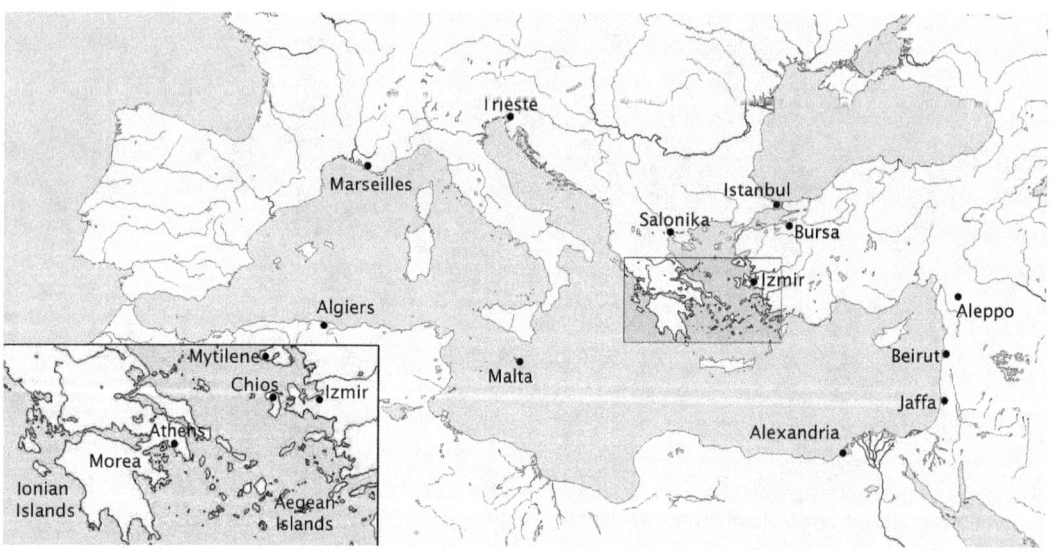

MAP I.1. Izmir and the Mediterranean. Interactive Ancient Mediterranean.

to about thirty thousand and significantly diversified its ethnic and religious composition.[25] Cotton, raisins, and other agricultural products of the region's rich hinterland attracted scores of European traders. Dutch, French, Genoese, and Venetian merchants set up a core of trading houses, factories, and consular representatives, and the English Levant Company established itself there as early as the 1610s (Figure I.2).[26] Concurrently, Jews from Thessaloniki, who fled the crisis that beset the Ottoman textile industry, migrated to Izmir in search of more favorable opportunities, often serving as translators, customs house officials, and tax farmers. Armenians from Aleppo, Bursa, and Isfahan came principally because of the silk trade with Persia that linked Izmir to an already extensive trade system stretching from China to Europe. By the seventeenth century, Greeks from Chios (Sakız or Scio), other Aegean islands, and the Morea had already established a small community, and with continual migration, they far outgrew other communities.

Izmir's plural social makeup had a counterpart in the city's physical organization. Since the seventeenth century and to almost the end of the nineteenth, residential neighborhoods exhibited a spatial sorting consistent with established social hierarchies within the empire. Muslim, Jewish, Armenian, Greek, and Frank (European) quarters intimately interlocked with one another, spreading over an urban area built to the north of the port on a maritime plain and to the south on sloping ground between the sea and a commanding hill rising up dramatically behind it (Figure I.3). The majority of the Muslim population lived on the acclivity of this hill known as Kadifekale (or Mount Pagus), distinctly crowned by the remains of an ancient castle. Jewish areas lay adjacent to the Muslim quarters, extending down onto the plain, and next to them, on level ground, was the Armenian quarter, adjoining the road leading to the Caravan Bridge—the major entry point to the city from inland. Greek neighborhoods occupied the northern sections of the city, lying between a ribbon-like section along the shore known as the Frank quarter and the vast orchards and green fields along the Meles River. The presence of distinct quarters, however, did not compel a pattern of religious or national segregation. To begin with, residential quarters were not as homogeneous as might be imagined. They were usually subdivided into smaller units that consisted of a few streets centered on and sometimes named after a church, a mosque, or a synagogue. In the midst of the Muslim quarters on the hill were small Greek neighborhoods, such as the Apano Mahalle (Upper Quarter), clustered around the small Greek Orthodox church of St. John, and the Panagia (Virgin Mary), centered on the church of St. Mary. Several Jewish and Muslim families lived in the same neighborhood while blocks of houses

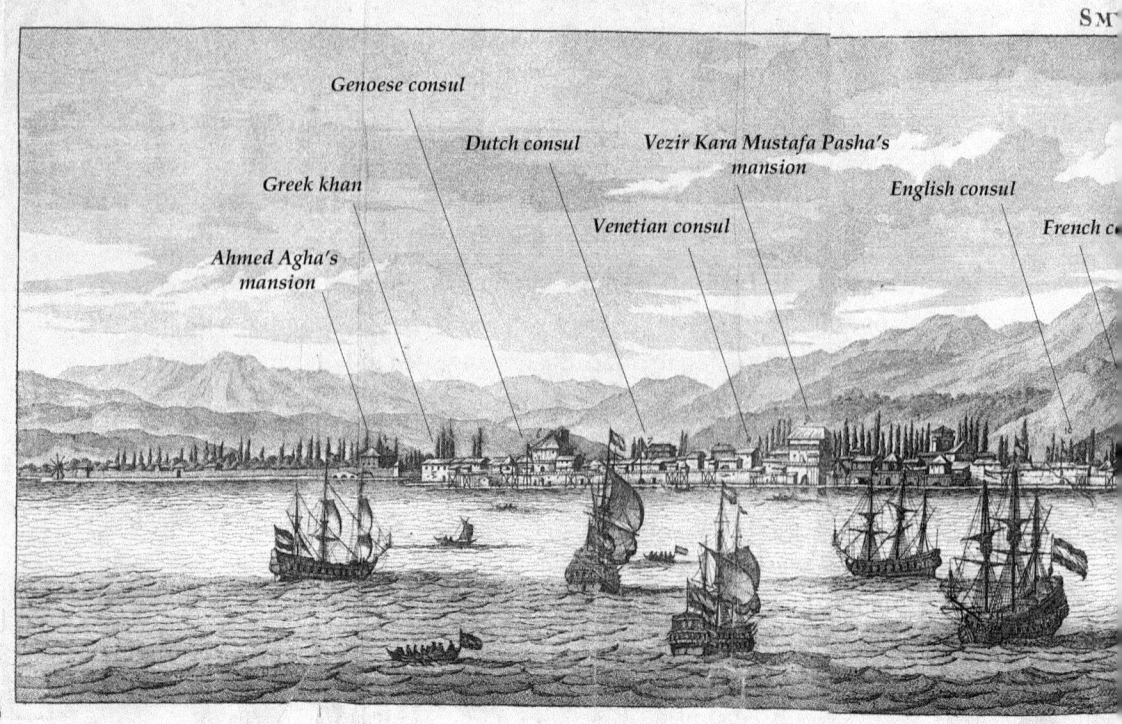

Figure I.2. Izmir as seen from the bay, by Cornelius de Bruyn, ca. 1680. The frenkhanes of foreign merchant-consuls and mansions of prominent Muslim notables are located along the shore to the left. The bazaar, inner harbor, and commercial functions extend to the right. From Cornelius de Bruyn, *Voyage au Levant* (Paris: J.-B.-C. Bauche le fils, 1725).

FIGURE I.3. Izmir as seen from the bay, by Benjamin and Pierre de Combes, 1686. Muslim quarters lay along the slope of Kadifekale, while Armenian and Jewish quarters were closer to the coast. Greek quarters occupied the flat plain behind the Frank quarter. Bibliothèque nationale de France.

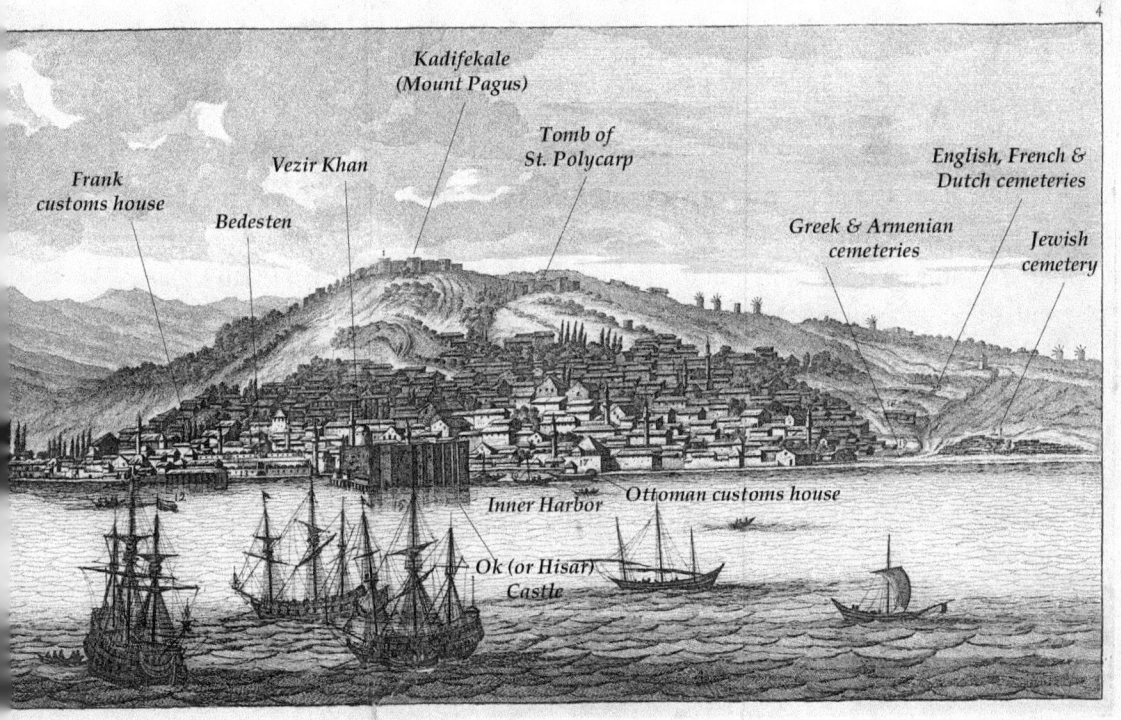

Veue de la ville de Smirne d'un mil au large

occupied by Greeks and Maltese wedged in between sections of the Frank quarter along the shore.[27]

Izmir's seventeenth-century boom also created a distinctive commercial structure that prevailed through the nineteenth century and centered on two particular areas, the bazaar *(çarşı)* and the Frank quarter *(mahalle-i efrenc)* (Map I.2). As with other cities in the Ottoman domain, the bazaar was at the heart of economic life and activities. Located to the south of the city, Izmir's bazaar conveniently lay between the port and the residential neighborhoods it served. It also constituted the terminus of the long-distance road that linked Izmir through the Caravan Bridge and outlying cemeteries, orange groves, and gardens to its hinterland, and to the Anatolian markets beyond (Figure I.4). Peasants from nearby towns with heavily laden carriages, donkeys, and oxcarts came through this road to sell their crops to local merchants and supply the city with daily provisions. Long-distance camel caravans, carrying bales of goods, followed the same path to reach the bazaar where they stored or exchanged merchandise to be shipped to different

FIGURE I.4. View of Caravan Bridge set against outlying cemeteries shaded by cypress trees, ca. 1830. Drawing by Thomas Allom; engraved by W. J. Cooke. From Thomas Allom, *Constantinople, the Scenery of the Seven Churches of Asia, and the Shores and Islands of the Mediterranean* (London: Fisher, Son; New York: R. Martin, 1838–41).

parts of the Mediterranean (Figure I.5). The bazaar area developed in a horseshoe of dense and narrow streets around a former inner harbor that was eventually drained and filled in in the mid-eighteenth century. Artisans and dealers clustered in small shops along the same streets, each of which was dedicated to a single trade, while large, mainly seventeenth-century commercial khans centered around courtyards anchored the area, providing secure temporary lodging for long-distance traders, depositories for goods to be traded, and office space for local merchants. Numerous coffee shops, mosques, and bathhouses interspersed in the marketplace served the daily needs of the commercial population while small groceries and chandler shops provided workers with daily supplies. This arrangement largely conformed to the general practice of sorting vocational groups and types of goods and of separating home from workplace common to Ottoman cities.[28]

In contrast, the Frank quarter to the north of the bazaar developed primarily in response to the needs of international trade and combined both commercial and residential functions from the outset. The quarter started out in the seventeenth century as a seaside enclave for European merchants, whose sojourn in the

Figure I.5. Ali Pasha Fountain located in the heart of the bazaar, ca. 1840. Lithograph. From Eugène Napoléon Flandin, *L'Orient*, vol. 1 (Paris: Gide et Baudry, 1853).

empire was viewed, at least from an official standpoint, to be temporary and whose commercial activities were protected under special treaties. These merchants were not required, as they were in many other Ottoman commercial centers, to reside in khans. Instead, they leased private and secured stone buildings, commonly known as *frenkhanes* (Frank houses), with stores and warehouses on the ground level and residences surrounded by spacious terraces above. They also paid their dues at a separate Frank customs house or *efrenc gümrüğü* (Figures I.2, I.3).[29] Set amid orchards and gardens, these merchant houses opened on one side to the water and had private piers or wharves for merchandise to be shipped directly to and from them. On the other side, they faced a long street, known in English sources as Frank Street, that ran parallel to the shore and provided access to it through a series of perpendicular, privately held, vaulted passageways that could be locked at night or in times of epidemics and other perils.[30]

The Frank quarter may have originated out of host- and home-state regulations to monitor foreigners' residences in the empire and to regulate their relationship

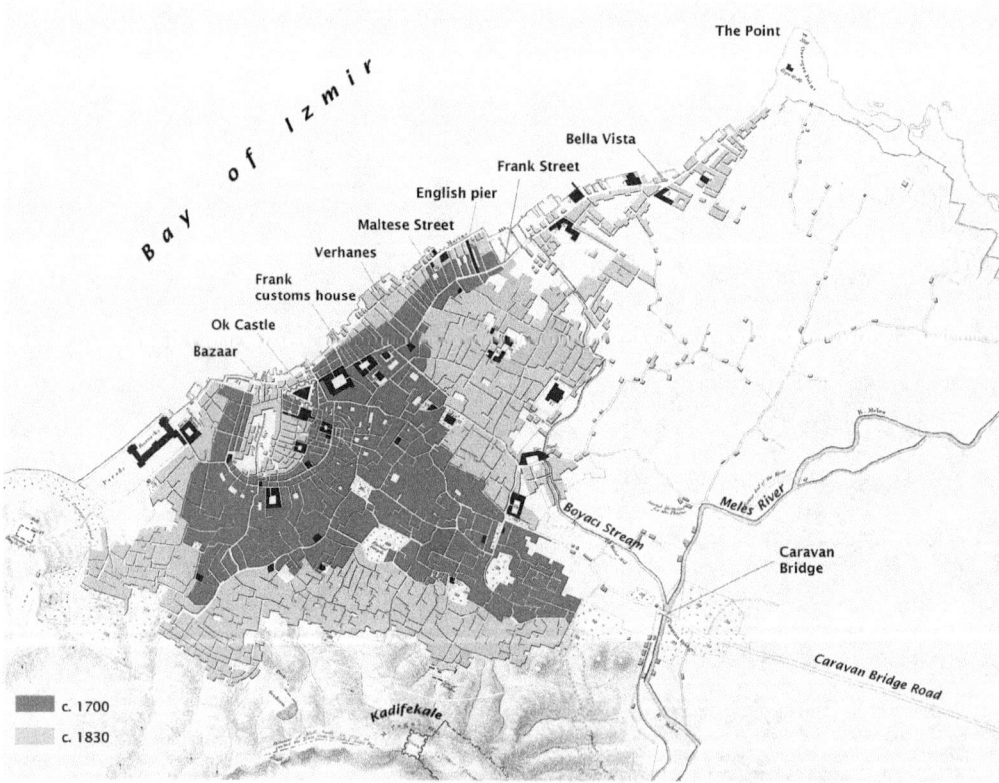

MAP I.2. Urban expansion, ca. 1700–1830. Based on the map of the city by Lieutenant Thomas Graves, 1836. Bibliothèque nationale de France.

with Ottoman subjects, but with sustained commercial growth over the next two centuries, the area steadily expanded, merging with the rest of the city, both physically and functionally. Properties along Frank Street gradually lost their vast gardens. New private passageways—popularly known as *verhanes* or *ferhanes* after the contracted form of frenkhanes—were cut through an increasingly tightly knit row of elongated houses that gave a larger number of leaseholders access to the sea. The filling in of the inner harbor and the relocation of port functions onto the bay also created additional pressure for shorefront land. Properties to the southern end of Frank Street began to extend onto reclaimed land, eventually forming a new strip along the waterside that stretched from the Frank customs house all the way to the wooden-pile English pier *(İngiliz iskelesi)*, the new landing place for all overseas passengers. Shipping and warehousing functions, formerly handled through the frenkhanes, moved to this new street, varyingly referred to as Maltese, Sahiliye (Shore), and Bahriye (Maritime) Streets, whereas frenkhanes themselves became subdivided into small stores, offices, and apartments to accommodate the city's growing need for housing and commercial services (Map I.2).[31] By the 1850s, Frank Street had developed into Izmir's foremost north–south artery. Lying four hundred to five hundred feet from the sea, it ran for about half a mile from the bazaar to Fasula Place and continued for another mile, first as Fasula Street and then as Bella Vista Street, to the then largely vacant northernmost tip of the city, the Point (also known as Tuzla Burnu, Darağaç, and Punta).[32]

As Frank Street lost its relative proximity to the shore, its role shifted from a street geared toward the specific needs of European merchants to one that served as the public hub of the newly emerging and expanding neighborhoods along the maritime plain. Offices, business establishments, foreign consulates, hotels, boarding houses, commercial and social clubs, specialty stores, neighborhood shops, as well as churches of various denominations and their ancillary educational and residential facilities concentrated on Frank Street. While the western side of the street led to the comb-like pattern of *verhanes* with numerous services and commercial activities occupying every nook and corner, its eastern side opened onto a series of cross-streets and neighborhoods serving different social classes (Map I.3). A few blocks north of the bazaar end of Frank Street, between the prominent Greek Orthodox cathedral of St. Photini and the Catholic church of St. Polycarp, was the Street of the Great Taverns (Megalas Tavernas or Kaymak Pasha), a working-class market street with numerous coffee shops and drinking places that attracted scores of locals and newcomers of modest means as well as sailors looking for a quick meal. Branching off this street was Dilruba Street, the

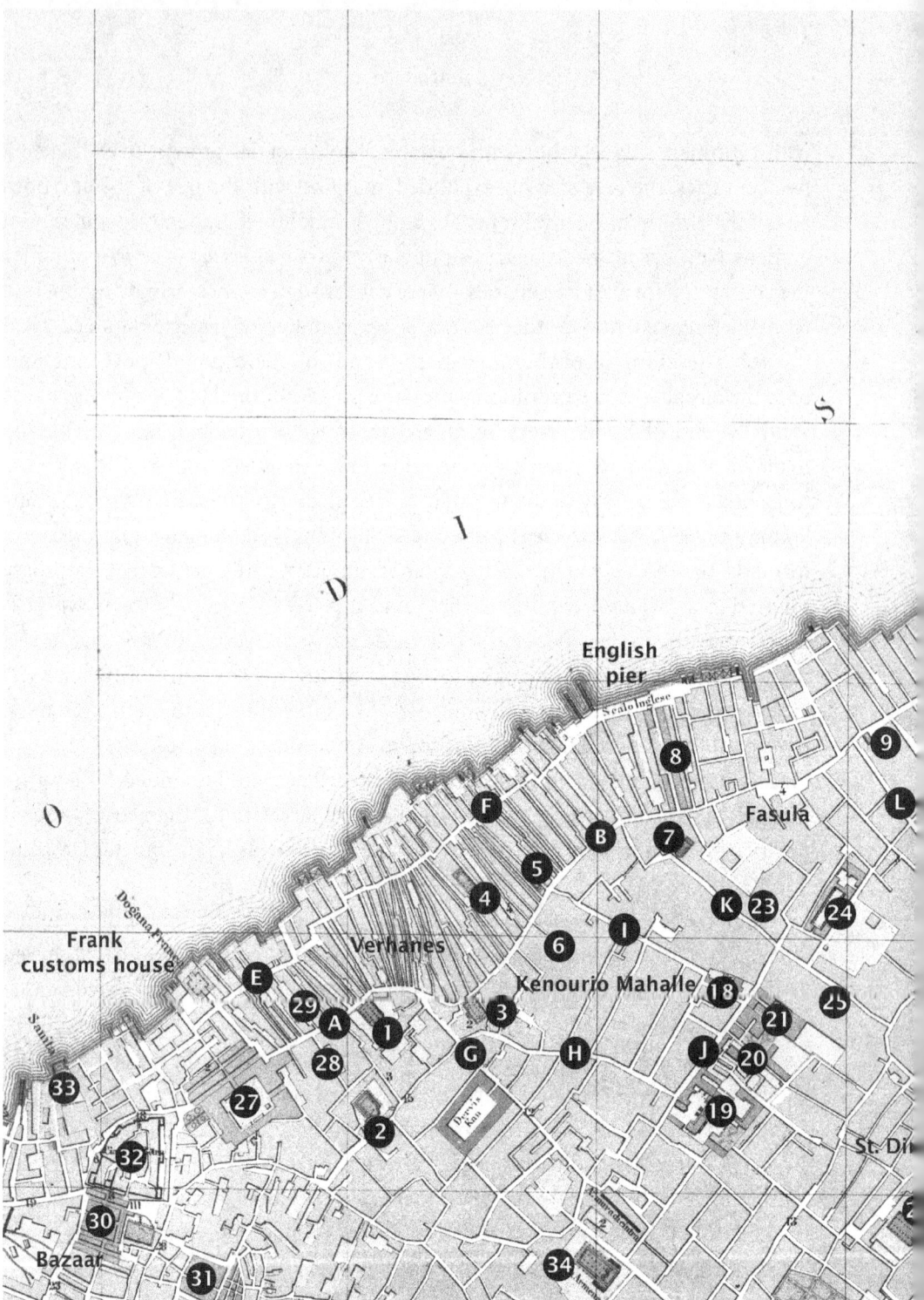

MAP I.3. Frank Street and environs, ca. 1850s. Based on the plan by Storari (Map 2).

LEGEND: 1. St. Photini (Greek Orthodox); 2. St. George (Greek Orthodox); 3. St. Polycarp (Catholic); 4. St. Mary (Catholic); 5. Lazarist Church (Sacré Cœur); 6. Establishment of the Sisters of Charity; 7. Euterpe Theater; 8. English Consulate and Chapel; 9. Guardhouse for 30 men (Karakol); 10. French Consulate; 11. Guardhouse for 40 men; 12. Military Parade Grounds; 13. Guardhouse for 40 men; 14. Steam Mill; 15. Cousinéry's Silk Factory; 16. St. John (Greek Orthodox); 17. French hospital; 18. British hospital; 19. Greek hospital; 20. Hospital of St. Antoine (Austrian); 21. Dutch hospital;

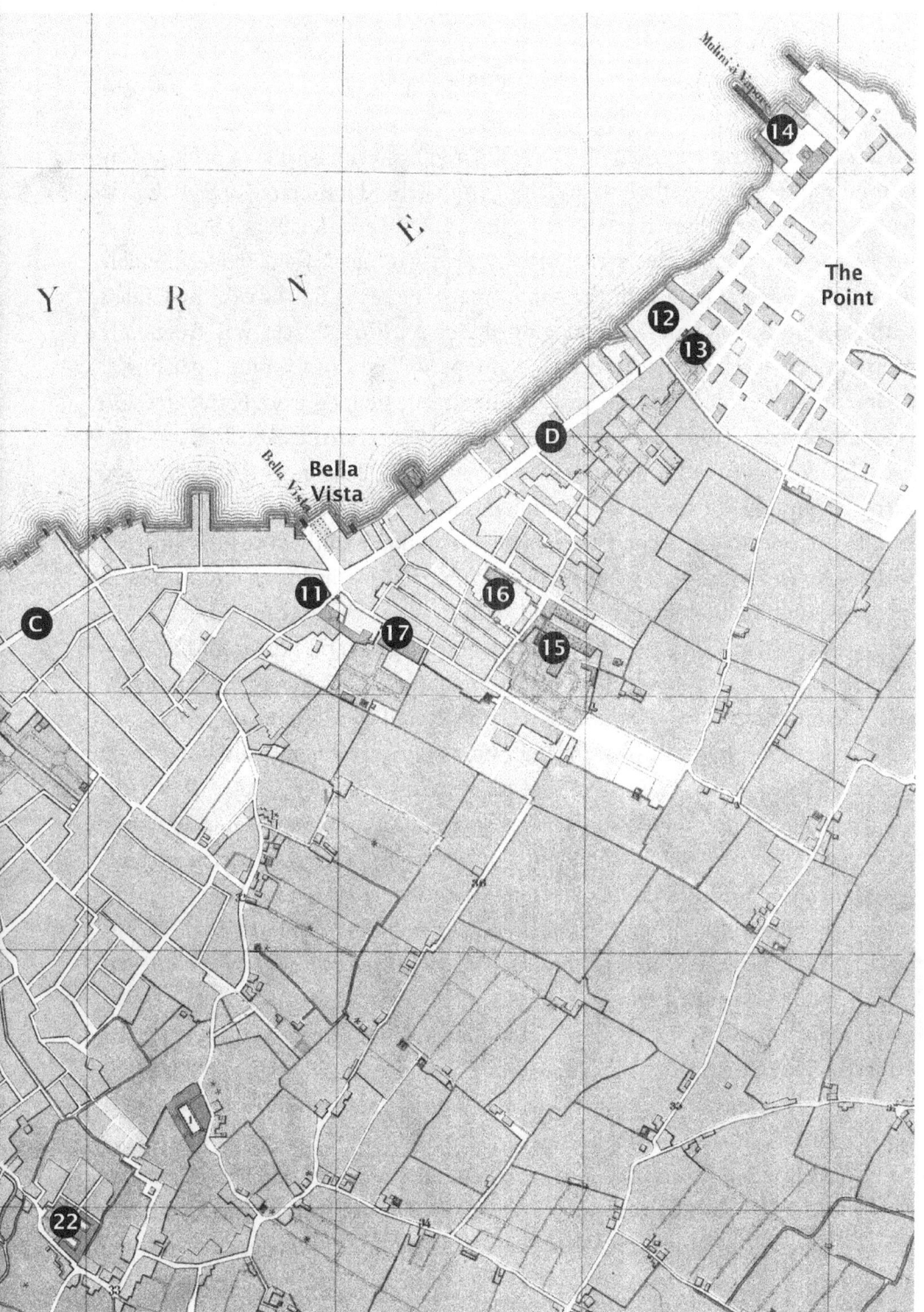

22. Hospital of St. Roch; 23. Christian Brothers Boys' School ; 24. College of the Propaganda; 25. Deaconesses (Girls') Institute; 26. St. Dimitri (Greek Orthodox); 27. Büyük Vezir Khan; 28. Küçük Vezir Khan; 29. Coya Khan; 30. Kızlarağası Khan; 31. Demir Khan; 32. Castle (Ok or Hisar Kalesi); 33. Sanitary Offices; 34. St. Stephen (Armenian); A. Frank Street (Mahmudiye); B. Frank Street (Sultaniye); C. Fasula Street (Teşrifiye); D. Trassa Street (Mesudiye); E. Bahriye or Sahiliye Street; F. Maltese Street; G. Street of the Great Taverns (Kaymak Pasha); H. Dilruba Street; I. Kızlar Street; J. Hospital Street (Ispitalia); K. Rose Street (Gül); L. Tanners Street (Boyahane).

main street of Kenourio Mahalle (New Quarter), a residential area occupied by Ottoman and foreign Catholics, stretching from behind the church of St. Polycarp to Hospital Street, where the Greek, English, Dutch, and Austrian hospitals and their respective chapels clustered. Further north was the pleasant and fashionable Rose (Gül) Street. Lined with the handsome stone mansions of wealthy Greeks with projecting balconies overhanging the street, Rose Street was frequently praised as an excellent place to catch a glimpse of "beautiful women, pausing at their windows, like flowers in a vase."[33] The street extended from Frank Street to Hospital Street, leading on one side to two newly created establishments—the French College of the Propaganda and the Prussian Deaconesses' School. From there, it continued, through a circuitous route, to St. Dimitri and other Greek neighborhoods on the urban fringe, made up predominantly of tightly clustered wooden houses with overlapping roofs and inhabited by the lower-middle classes (artisans and small shopkeepers) and daily wagers.[34] Eventually, Frank Street opened onto Fasula Place, a busy square where wagons and horses for hire congested the area at all times, and an assortment of butchers, grocers, fishmongers, coffee shops, taverns, and gambling parlors catered to migrants who occupied nearby neighborhoods, thrown together hurriedly over green fields and market gardens.[35] Beyond Fasula, Frank Street turned mostly residential. A row of well-built merchant houses and consulates led to Bella Vista Point, forming a favorite promenade for locals and visitors alike. At the small waterside square of Bella Vista, anchored by the French hospital and a Turkish guardhouse, boats could be hired for excursions on the bay and several coffee shops with terraces extending out to the sea provided European newspapers and, some evenings, held comedies and musical performances.[36]

Despite its prestige and prominence in the life of the city, and its international outlook, Frank Street was neither grand nor wide. Its winding shape followed the historical shoreline, and sections of it could barely accommodate the two-way traffic of animal transport (Figures I.6, I.7). In the words of French writer Alexis de Valon, who sojourned in Izmir in the 1840s, the street had "much character, but correspond[ed] in no way to expectations." Like other commercial streets in Izmir, Frank Street was roughly paved, with houses of all sizes and shapes abutting on it and a deep channel running down its middle to carry off the rainfall. During the daytime shopkeepers extended their canopied stalls and counters, crowding the street. And, as with other commercial spaces in Izmir, Romaic Greek, Turkish, and dialects of French and Italian were heard at all times of the day.[37] Businesses and shops in the area were run by a wide spectrum of Ottoman and foreign subjects. Every day all classes of people in every description of attire crossed the street to

FIGURE I.6. Frank Street during a funeral procession crowded with awnings and pedestrians of all classes, by Rubellin Père & Fils, 1884. Courtesy of the Suna & İnan Kıraç Research Institute for Mediterranean Civilizations.

FIGURE I.7. Frank Street, ca. 1890. Although the street had been repaved and partially widened over the years, throughout the nineteenth century it retained its narrow and winding shape and its commercial character. Postcard. Courtesy of Petros Mechtidis.

get to work or buy food and other necessities. Mid-nineteenth-century observers repeatedly described Frank Street as a multiethnic, polyglot, and commerce-oriented space that exemplified the cultural confluence and mixing that lay at the very root of the Levantine, Ottoman city. Fezzes, European hats, and caps mingled with turbans and other traditional headgear while imported consumer goods and specialty articles—from Parisian hats to European factory-made textiles—lay next to stalls filled with scores of regional and local wares, edibles and otherwise.[38]

A Mid-Nineteenth-Century Port in the Remaking

This snapshot of Frank Street corresponds to a time when Izmir was in the midst of momentous changes that affected almost every aspect of urban life. In the mid-nineteenth century, Izmir's international trade was growing dramatically, as was its population. The city's built-up areas were expanding into surrounding fields and orchards as piecemeal efforts to improve infrastructure, rebuild areas damaged by fires, and renovate the administrative quarters were steadily refashioning the urban core. Ottoman military and technical modernization efforts—under way for half a century and culminating in the wide-ranging bureaucratic reorganization of the Tanzimat (1839–76)—were further restructuring the property and citizenship regimes, and reorganizing the administration of justice, finance, and security in the city. New institutions connected to an emerging consumer society, governmental buildings suited to the needs of a modern bureaucracy, and newspapers in a range of languages were transforming public life, social relations, and thought patterns in unprecedented ways. The decades surrounding the midcentury, which constitute the focus of this book, were remarkably vibrant. Izmir was in a constant state of flux, coping with experimental policies and an unsettled institutional context while reshaping itself into an international commercial center and the administrative capital of the province of Aydın. Of course, the pace of urban change did not abate afterward. Izmir's population and economy continued to grow, European powers' expansionist policies deepened, and Ottoman state centralization and legitimation efforts intensified during the post-Tanzimat, Hamidian era. But the enthusiasm and volatility of the midcentury decades illustrate particularly well a modern city in the making. This book is concerned with this formative moment, zooming in on its dynamics, excavating short-lived experiments and untaken paths to reveal the untidy ways in which Izmir was reshaped into a cosmopolitan city par excellence.

Following an economic slowdown during the Napoleonic Wars (1799–1815) and the Greek War of Independence (1821–29), Izmir's foreign trade began a new course of rapid growth. Between the 1840s and the 1880s, not only did the total volume of trade increase over fourfold, but trade patterns and consumption habits changed significantly as the empire participated more deeply in a global economy centered on Europe, especially Britain, which took over France's long-held position as the empire's major trade partner. The Anglo-Ottoman commercial treaty and similar agreements signed with European powers abolished the age-old system of trade monopolies in the empire and lowered customs tariffs, boosting imports nearly sixfold.[39] In addition to the traditional imports of French woolens and such staples as coffee, sugar, and rice, an ever-growing quantity of European manufactured goods, including cotton, silk, and woolen textiles, fashion wares, hardware, and leather goods, began to flood local markets, dealing a severe blow to traditional artisanal products.[40] Simultaneously, Izmir continued to enhance its role as a center of export trade, with exports increasing threefold within the same period.[41] Agricultural crops and raw materials comprised the bulk of export commodities. Figs and grapes, by far the most valuable crops at the time, were grown in neighboring vineyards and cured in Izmir. Natural dyes used in textile production, such as madder, were picked, packed, and pressed locally. Valonia and similar tanning agents for leather processing were collected from the hinterland, then were cleaned and sorted in the city. Other articles such as silk, cotton, opium, rugs, and carpets as well as emery and chromium were brought from interior districts and towns to the port where they could at once be assembled, packed, and shipped to various European destinations.

Whereas other cities and towns in the region remained relatively stable in size, beginning in the 1840s Izmir's population increased steadily and much faster than the empire as a whole.[42] In the 1880s the city passed the two hundred thousand mark, firmly securing its position as the largest city in the Ottoman Empire next to Istanbul. The lack of complete census figures for the first half of the nineteenth century and the different criteria used in delimiting the urban extent and breaking down the urban population makes it impossible to determine exact growth rates. That fierce outbreaks of bubonic plague in 1809, 1812–15, 1826, and 1836–38 claimed tens of thousands of lives lends additional difficulty in gauging population size. Assessments for the 1840s differ significantly—from around 40,000–50,000, as evidenced in Ottoman counts, to anywhere from 80,000 to 130,000 according to numbers given by travelers.[43] Despite large variations, these estimates suggest a considerable population increase of at least twofold, if not three- or fourfold, which was, evidently, largely due to immigration, rather than natural growth alone. They also agree on the relative ethnic and national split of the population, with Muslim Turks forming the predominant group (45–55 percent), closely followed by Orthodox Greeks (25–35 percent), and roughly equal proportions of Jews, Armenians, and foreign subjects (each within 4–10 percent). Judging from the 1890 Province of Aydın *Salname,* or administrative yearbook, these proportions remained relatively stable, with a slight decline in the percentage of Muslim Turks.[44] What most dramatically changed, however, was the proportion of foreign subjects, who now amounted to a quarter of the total population. To be sure, immigrants came not only from within the empire—especially Western Anatolia and, later on, parts of the lost Balkan territories—but also from outside the imperial borders. Mid-nineteenth-century Izmir hosted an increasingly diverse society, from Maltese, Ionians, and other subjects of the British government, to Greeks with Hellenic nationality, and Hungarian and Italian exiles from the failed political revolutions of 1848. Even so, the radical increase of foreign subjects in Izmir cannot be understood without taking account of mounting numbers of non-Muslim Ottoman subjects, predominantly but not exclusively Greek Orthodox, who placed themselves under the protection of one or another of the powers that had a stake in the Ottoman Empire.[45] As I discuss in chapter 1, nationality became a highly fungible category in the mid-nineteenth century, complicating and confusing individual status and the criteria by which local residents were counted and classified.

While up until the first decades of the nineteenth century population rise was largely absorbed within the limits of the existing city, unrelenting growth thereafter resulted in the hasty conversion to urban uses of orchards and vineyards on the urban periphery. Already by 1845 over twenty new quarters emerged around Fasula to contain Greek, Maltese, and Ionian immigrants.[46] The Boyacı (Tanners') Stream that used to run through this area, and had long defined the city's northern limit, had to be covered up and turned into a street drain to mitigate the dearth of infrastructure.[47] Sites that lay at a discreet distance from the city, like the French hospital at Bella Vista, were surrounded on all sides by newly built merchant houses.[48] By the 1850s new building allotments were being opened at the Point while small industrial plants, including a silk-winding factory, a distillery, a modern olive and sesame oil press, steam-powered flour mills, a paper mill, and gasworks, were spurting up between the Point and the estuary of the Meles River.[49] In the following decades, the marshes in the area were drained and additional working-class neighborhoods, inhabited largely but not exclusively by Greek-speaking Orthodox populations—such as Tepecik, Murtakya, and Çikudya—were laid out around the belt of cemeteries adjoining the Caravan Bridge.[50] Likewise, beginning in the 1880s Muslim refugees from the Balkans set up new quarters at the southernmost slopes of Kadifekale. Construction activity was all the more frenzied as a higher population density had made the city more prone to fire hazard. Indeed, in 1834, 1841, 1844, 1861, and 1882 devastating fires consumed vast swaths at a time, necessitating a constant renewal of existing buildings and urban spaces, at times with far more stylish structures and realigned streets. Moreover, further efforts to clear cluttered areas were underway, including the removal of the old crusader's castle (Hisar or Ok Kalesi) by the bazaar and the tidying up of the Fasula area in the 1860s (Map I.4).[51]

Although additions to the city and piecemeal reworking of the existing urban core significantly altered the physical landscape, it was infrastructure projects that had the greatest impact on Izmir as a whole. Owing to its remarkably enterprising merchants and dominant position as a transshipment hub, Izmir was the first Ottoman city (outside Istanbul) to acquire a broad range of public works, from railroads and port facilities to streetlights. Like urban infrastructure projects

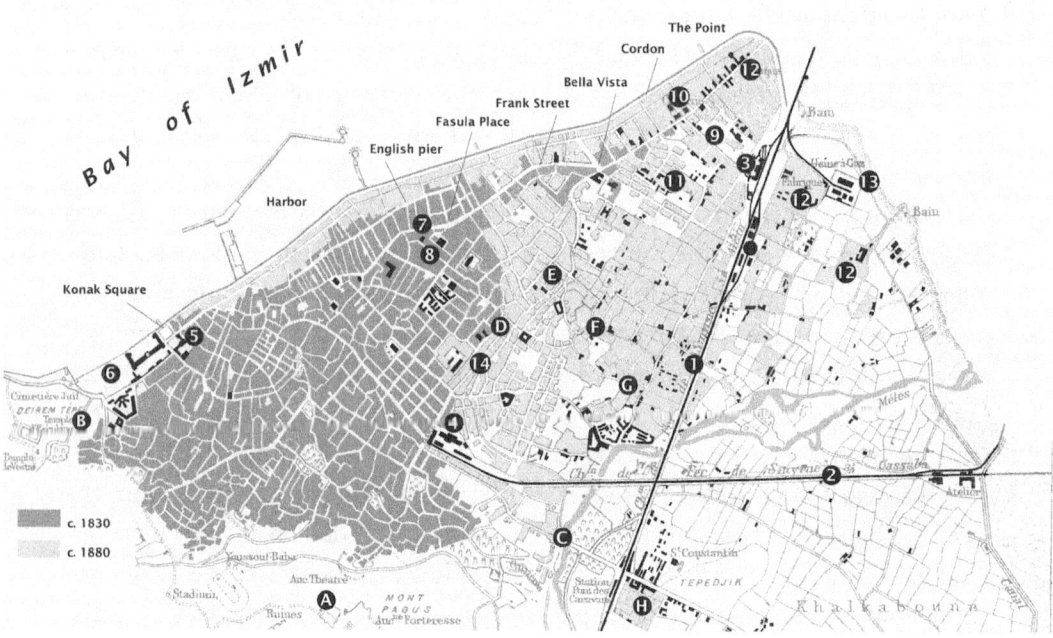

MAP I.4. Urban expansion, ca. 1830–80. Based on map of the city by Demetrios Georgiades, 1880s. From Demetrios Georgiades, *Smyrne et l'Asie Mineure du point de vue économique et commercial* (Paris: Chaix, 1885).

LEGEND: 1. Izmir-Aydın Railway; 2. Izmir Kasaba Railway; 3. The Point Station; 4. Basmahane Station; 5. Governor's Palace; 6. Barracks and Maneuver Ground; 7. Euterpe Theater; 8. Cammarano Theater; 9. Smyrna Gardens; 10. Barracks at the Point; 11. Silk-Winding Factory; 12. Factories/Mills; 13. Gasworks; 14. Tannery; A. Kadifekale; B. Değirmentepe; C. Caravan Bridge; D. St. Dimitri; E. St. Catherine; F. Çikudya; G. Murtakya; H. Tepecik.

elsewhere, these works raised all sorts of questions about private rights and the public good, turning Izmir into a significant test site for mediating and reconciling the divergent interests of private and public stakeholders. That these projects were backed by an uneasy partnership between the Ottoman government (in the form of state concessions) and private capital (mostly foreign)—as I detail in chapter 3—made their implementation even more contentious and protracted. Despite the tensions and controversies that beset them, infrastructure projects shaped Izmir in powerful ways. First, improvements in transport and communications better linked the city to emerging webs of international trade, further spurring economic growth. In the mid-1860s two railroads (the Izmir–Aydın and Izmir–Kasaba lines) accelerated the flow of agricultural and mineral wealth from the interior to Izmir's year-round harbor, reducing several days of caravan trips to a mere few hours and minimizing seasonal disruptions due to the weather (Maps I.4, I.5). In addition, submarine and overland telegraph lines brought Izmir in closer contact with Istanbul and major domestic and international centers. In the mid-1870s, expanded harbor facilities serviced a growing number of steamship lines, which connected the city on a regular basis with London, Liverpool, Marseilles, Trieste, Alexandria, and other Mediterranean ports.[52]

Second, modern infrastructure offered new comforts and conveniences, significantly improving the conditions of urban life in beneficiary areas. Newly built carriage roads to Buca (1858) and Burnabat (1861), followed later by suburban railway lines, brought these outlying villages within daily commuting distance from the city (Figures I.8 and I.9), contributing to the proliferation of suburban estates favored by the city's prosperous merchants. In 1865, a system of gas conduits and streetlights replaced the faint glow of makeshift kerosene lanterns, enhancing the appearance of Izmir's major arteries and changing people's experience of the night. A decade later, the Cordon—a nearly two-mile-long and sixty-foot-wide granite quay, complete with an underground sewer system, a tramway line, and a scenic promenade—created prime development frontage along the entire bayside, opening the waterfront to the larger public (Figure I.10).

The businesses, shops, and recreational spaces that sprung up around Izmir's improving infrastructure—especially its remarkable Cordon—offered Smyrniots new kinds of urban experiences that were markedly different from what they had before. In the words of Grattan Geary, editor of the *Times* of India, who visited Izmir in 1878, the "splendid quay" was both a "great centre of commerce" with "a line of palatial edifices ... intended for hotels and business premises" and "a sort of marine Champs Elysées" with "no less than nine café chantants of considerable size ... nearly all on the model of the Parthenon." What made the space even more

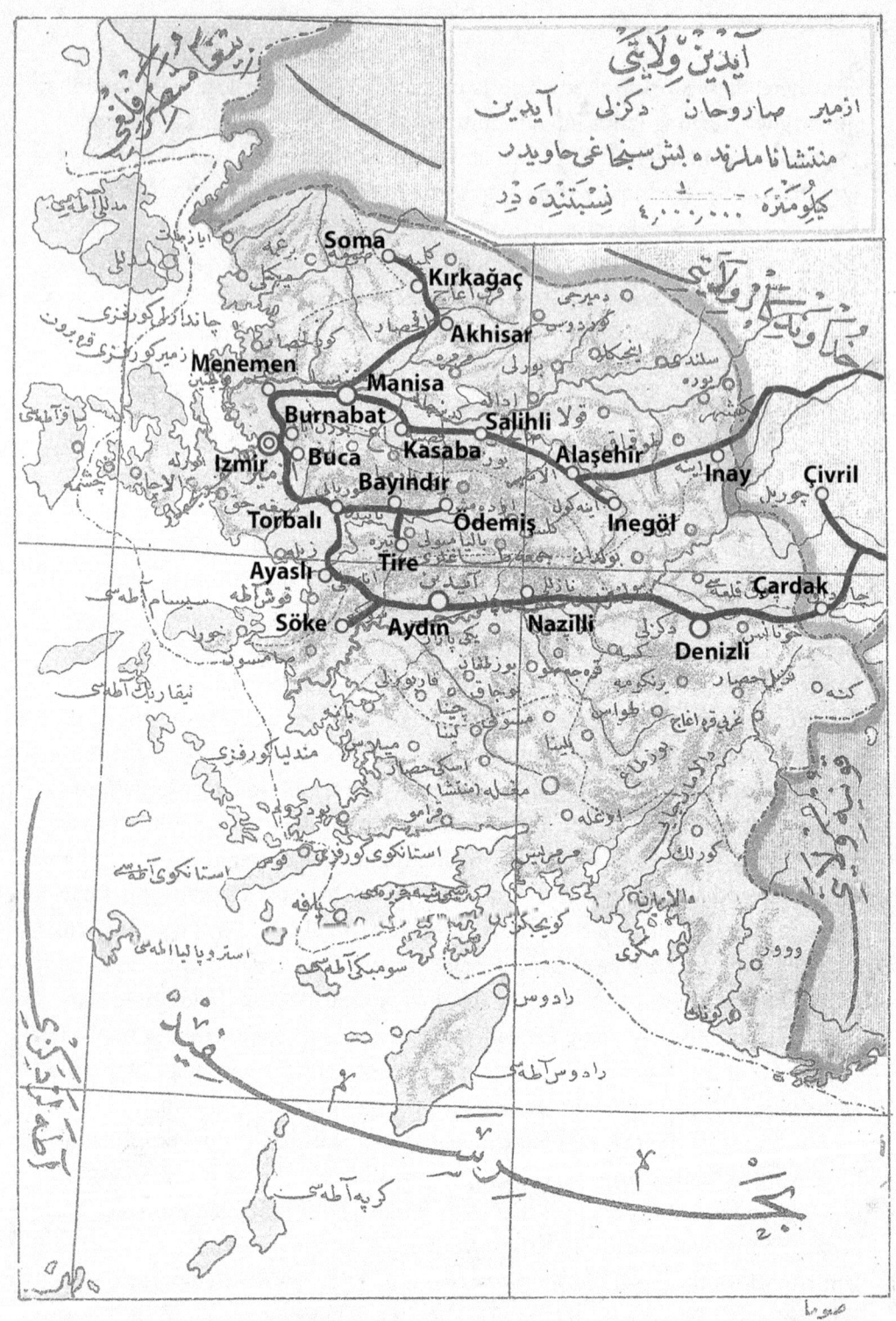

MAP I.5. Map of the *vilayet* of Aydın, showing the Izmir–Aydın and Izmir–Kasaba railway lines and branch lines, ca. 1890. Postcard. Courtesy of Petros Mechtidis.

spectacular was its arresting mix of sights, sounds, and people. The "profuse gas illuminations" that shone from the cafés "light[ed] up the quay and turn[ed] night into day."[53] "Motley costumed crowds" swarmed the promenade and "strains of oriental as well as European music and the bubbling of *nargilehs* [were] heard on all sides."[54] Indeed, while the numerous hotels, maritime agencies, insurance companies, national post offices, and modern warehouses lining the Cordon attested to the energy of Izmir merchants who were actively modernizing their business practices and linking up with expanding international commercial networks, the host of brasseries, beer gardens, and cafés, many with open-air orchestras, revealed an appetite for a consumer-oriented lifestyle shared by a growing number of Smyrniots across the social spectrum (Figure I.11).

To be fair, however, many of these trends predated the Cordon. New retail, business, and leisure establishments had been reconfiguring social and consumption practices for over a quarter century. Already by the 1840s men and women

FIGURE I.8. Izmir–Aydın railway station at the Point, main entrance with classicizing details, ca. 1890. The station was also the terminal point of the suburban line to Buca. Courtesy of Istanbul University, Rare Books Library (90641/10).

FIGURE I.9. Izmir–Kasaba railway station at Basmahane, main entrance, ca. 1890. The station was also the terminal point of the suburban line to Burnabat. Courtesy of Istanbul University, Rare Books Library (90641/14).

from the prosperous classes, especially but not exclusively non-Muslims, began to partake in an ever-expanding world of commodities, as evidenced by the emergence of new types of shops and marketing techniques. By then, milliners and specialty fashion shops carrying newly arrived European goods were doing brisk business on and around Frank Street. In 1850, P. Xenopoulo, a native of Chios, opened his modern dry-goods store, P. Xenopoulo & Cie., selling masses of imported textiles and related merchandise. He was followed in the next decades by branches of Istanbul- and Cairo-based department stores such as Orosdi-Back and Salomon Stein, as well as French *grands magasins,* including Au Bon Marché, Au Louvre, and La Samaritaine (Figure I.12).[55] At the same time, new sites of entertainment—some privately run and limited to members—were expanding the types and range of encounters afforded by the city. By the 1850s, Izmir boasted lively casinos, fashionable commercial clubs where merchant families could mix business and pleasure. Both the European casino and the Greek

FIGURE I.10. View of the Cordon, looking north from Bella Vista, with buildings laid out on regular lots, ca. 1890. Postcard. Courtesy of Petros Mechtidis.

FIGURE I.11. Hotel Kraemer Palace on the Cordon, ca. 1890. The glass building to the left housed the hotel's brasserie. Postcard. Courtesy of Orlando Carlo Calumeno and Birzamanlar Yayıncılık.

casino (or commercial club) included a series of social rooms where members played cards, read the news, or conducted business, and a ballroom for musical performances and charity balls that offered Izmir's elite a place to see and be seen.[56] In 1841, the purpose-built Euterpe (or Efterpi) Theater, located off Frank Street, followed in 1861 by the spacious, three-story Cammarano (or Kamerano) Theater, fitted with the most recent improvements, provided primary venues for staging itinerant opera troupes, actors, and musicians traveling around the Mediterranean.[57] The Smyrna Gardens (Jardin de Smyrne), located off the busy road to Burnabat by the spacious and alluring new train station at the Point, opened its doors in 1865, featuring live music five days a week.[58] Beyond the city center, the annual public horse races held since the 1850s in Buca combined sports and entertainment. Organized by the Smyrna Jockey Club and funded by an imperial grant, they attracted Smyrniots from all walks of life. These leisure spaces and practices spawned novel and more varied social experiences, also rendering emergent patterns of class distinction and group consciousness more conspicuous.

Especially after the 1840s, the periodical press became an integral part of this changing urban consciousness, simultaneously shaping how people perceived their city and expanding the ways they engaged with it and what lay beyond it.[59] Although Izmir's newspapers—like others in the empire—needed official permits to operate and were closely monitored to prevent the publication of content that conflicted with the interests of the Ottoman government and its allies, they had a freer hand in covering and presenting local affairs. Business news, appointments of local officials, philanthropic and charity work, visiting dignitaries and public celebrations, as well as local gossip and crime stories were a staple of Izmir's dynamic press. These papers, initiated by private individuals and published in the many different languages spoken in the city, took divergent stances on events and issues, promoting specific group interests depending on the audiences they targeted.[60] Despite their differences, however, Izmir's print media collectively played a key role in generating and disseminating ideas about urban life at a time when access to books, pamphlets, and street literature and functional literacy in a range of local languages and scripts were on the rise. By engaging their readers with the events, spaces, and goings-on of daily life in their city, they raised awareness of those with whom they inhabited the same urban territory. They fostered a shared sense of purpose and responsibility for the city while maintaining and even highlighting the linguistic, religious, and ethnic differences and social hierarchies that separated its residents. In other words, newspapers cultivated a consciousness of being a Smyrniot, even if people had very different understandings of what it meant to be one. Izmir's vibrant and multilingual print media also offered remarkably

FIGURE I.12. Consumer-oriented businesses established in the mid- to late nineteenth century. (a) Print advertisement for P. Xenopoulo & Cie., from Jacob de Andria and G. Timoni, *Indicateur des professions commerciales et industrielles de Smyrne, de l'Anatolie* (Smyrna: Imprimerie commerciale Timoni, 1894). (b) Letterhead of the Orosdi-Back store; courtesy of Petros Mechtidis. (c) Print advertisements in different languages for the Stein store, from Jacob de Andria and G. Timoni, *Indicateur des professions commerciales et industrielles de Smyrne, de l'Anatolie* (Smyrna: Imprimerie commerciale Timoni, 1895).

a

GRANDS MAGASINS
DE LA RUE FRANQUE
Connus pour Vendre le Meilleur Marché

P. XENOPOULO & Cⁱᵉ

Maison Fondée en 1850

50, Rue Franque, 52

SMYRNE

Soieries et Lainages, Spécialités de Garnitures pour Robes et Confections, Rubans, Dentelles, Broderies, Corsets, Ombrelles et Parapluies, Couvertures de voyage, Bonneterie et Draperie, Rideaux et Tapis.

Grande variété de Mouchoirs Fantaisie,
Articles de Ménage et Toilette
Spécialité de Toiles et Blancs.

Comptoir Spécial de Tissus pour ameublement, etc.

DÉPOT DE GROS
DANS LE LOCAL

Vente à prix fixe

b

detailed coverage of events beyond Izmir. Their editors exchanged routine dispatches with client newspapers in Istanbul, major provincial centers, and Mediterranean ports of interest to their readers, forging a shared regional consciousness and establishing Izmir's distinctive place within it.

Most important, newspapers opened up new platforms for public discourse and collective action for local audiences, expanding already existing civic mechanisms, be it petitions, signature campaigns, or ad hoc committees and boards.[61] Recognizing the political potential of their medium, editors and reporters acted as brokers in a range of civic, economic, and cultural affairs. They selectively covered ongoing developments to lobby on behalf of local interests, and through their regular dispatches, they also advanced these interests beyond Izmir, engaging external players in local matters and drumming up support from relevant quarters. During the period under consideration, Izmir's print media acted as an important catalyst for change, helping constitute and coalesce new interest groups and offering an important site for forging and legitimating new civic discourses.

In concert with these changes, the new buildings and institutions, which housed the modernizing imperial bureaucracy, were further refashioning people's experience of the city. A salient example was the creation of modern military and police organizations to replace the Janissary corps, the long-standing organ of municipal control and revenue collection, dissolved in 1826. The U-shaped barracks, set up in 1829 in the southernmost end of the city, and the additional maneuver field, laid at the opposite end near the Point, bespoke the permanent presence of the *nizam-ı cedid* (new order) troops in Izmir (Map I.4, Figure I.13). Built on grounds created in part by expropriation and in part by landfill, the imposing masonry barracks, known as Kışla-i Hümayun or Sarıkışla, could shelter five to six thousand soldiers, outdoing in scale all other urban structures and rendering central state power ever more visible.[62] In addition, by the 1850s several police stations *(karakolhane)* holding twenty to forty officers were positioned along Frank Street and the Caravan Bridge Road leading to the bazaar, introducing new surveillance mechanisms along the city's major traffic arteries.[63] These institutions were the Ottoman state's new tools for overseeing public order and security, even if, as I discuss in chapter 2, in its early years the local police remained chronically short-staffed and ill-equipped to deal with the problems of an ever more diverse population.

Perhaps most important, the central government also established new offices in Izmir to accommodate the fundamental changes it was making to provincial administration. Generally, existing premises were converted and expanded, and when the spatial demands of the bureaucracy increased, purpose-built structures

FIGURE I.13. Panoramic view of Izmir from Değirmentepe, ca. 1865. The military barracks and maneuver grounds are in the foreground. Beyond the barracks to the right is the old governor's house, the Kâtipzâde mansion. Courtesy of the Suna & İnan Kıraç Research Institute for Mediterranean Civilizations.

were erected. A case in point was the governor's mansion or Konak by the barracks, originally built in 1804 by the Kâtipzades—the local magnate family *(âyân)* who had long dominated Izmir's political scene and assumed governorship positions through the first quarter of the nineteenth century.[64] In the 1840s, the mansion was taken over and repurposed when the central government began to appoint its own civil servants to undercut the authority of the âyâns and bring the empire under a single administrative order.[65] Eventually, in 1867, when the old timber-framed structure could neither comply with newly issued building codes nor contain the expanding bureaucratic and ritual functions of the Tanzimat state, it was demolished and rebuilt. Completed in 1872 in a markedly classicizing style and with a formal layout, the new government palace formed the centerpiece of

a larger cluster of public institutions that remained in the works through the second half of the nineteenth century, physically exemplifying the incremental and rather contingent course of state power consolidation (Figure I.14).[66]

Imperial institutions anchored the governmental character of the Konak-Sarıkışla area as much as Izmir's status as administrative capital within the provincial hierarchy. To begin with, additional public buildings helped consolidate the expanding functions of the modern state within the same area. In the early 1850s, the Gureba-i Müslümin, the imperial Ottoman hospital built to the south of the military parade ground adjoining the barracks, served all subjects regardless of origin, enhancing Izmir's already extensive array of communal hospitals.[67] The massive prison, erected behind the parade ground in 1873, replaced the ad hoc facility formerly housed in the Cezayir Khan in the bazaar and supplemented the small jail within the newly overhauled government palace. Moreover, in 1875, the open space between Konak and Sarıkışla was enlarged and reorganized into

FIGURE I.14. The new governor's palace with a neoclassical facade, ca. 1890. Postcard. Courtesy of the Suna & İnan Kıraç Research Institute for Mediterranean Civilizations.

a formal square, as part of the construction of Izmir's monumental quay, ultimately adding to the area's prestige and revealing an Ottoman state eager to promote its authority (Map I.6).[68] Indeed, in its sheer scale and the classical uniformity of the facades framing it, this was a space fit for the ceremonial displays and rituals that were becoming ever more necessary to expressions of modern state sovereignty (Figure I.15). In addition, the substantial construction in the Konak-Sarıkışla area permanently fixed the provincial capital in Izmir. The center of the Sığla district *(sancak)* since the mid-sixteenth century, Izmir temporarily served as provincial seat in place of Aydın in the early 1840s before assuming this role more definitely in 1850.[69] While the Tanzimat restructuring of provincial administration in 1864 and 1867 confirmed the city's prominence within the imperial geography, the reconstruction of the Konak—the financing of which required the treasury to sell considerable property—rendered Izmir's new bureaucratic standing palpable.[70]

Notably, at a time when Izmir was being rapidly incorporated into international trade networks, the imperial state was actively constructing an urban image that was at once distinctive and recognizably Ottoman. The collective massing of Izmir's public buildings articulated a new civic monumentality, amply corroborated in

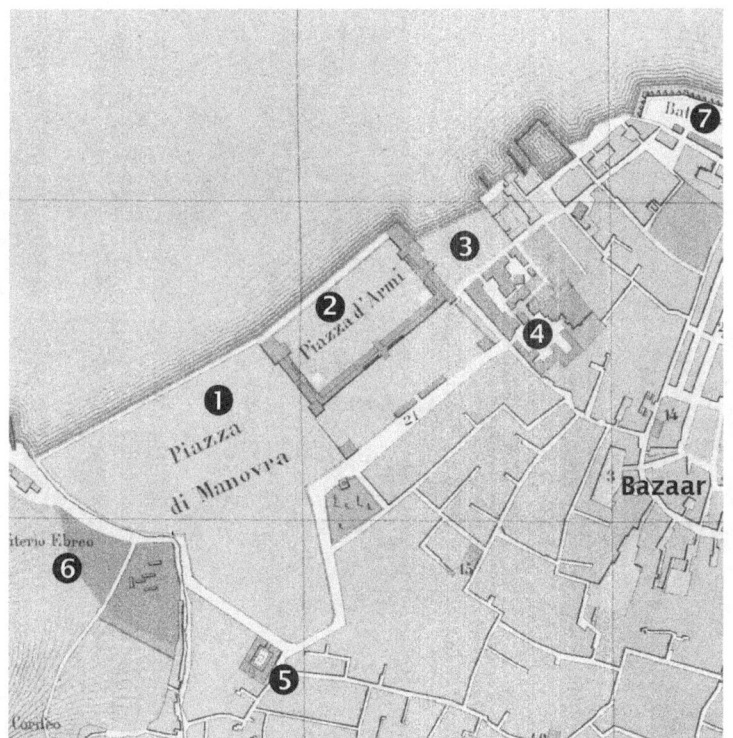

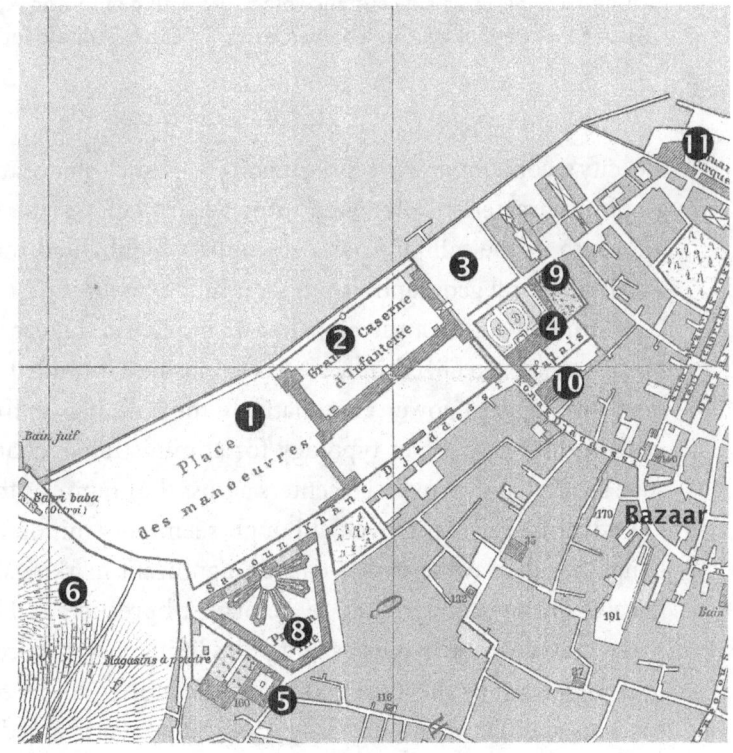

MAP I.6. (a) Konak-Sarıkışla area in 1854, based on the plan by Storari (Map 2).
(b) Konak-Sarıkışla area in 1876, based on the plan by Saad (Map 3).

LEGEND: 1 = maneuver grounds; 2 = military barracks (Sarıkışla); 3 = Konak Square; 4 = governor's palace (Konak); 5 = Ottoman hospital (Gureba-i Müslümin); 6 = Jewish cemetery; 7 = battery; 8 = prison; 9 = Konak Mosque; 10 = municipality; 11 = Ottoman customs house.

FIGURE I.15. Sarıkışla side entrance block projecting onto Konak Square, ca. 1890. Postcard. Courtesy of the Suna & İnan Kıraç Research Institute for Mediterranean Civilizations.

the city's contemporary representations. Izmir's panoramic prints and photographs, characteristically taken from Değirmentepe (the small mound rising to the south of the military parade ground), highlighted the Konak-Sarıkışla area within the local geography, framing it in the foreground of a busy port or setting it prominently against the city's low-rising fabric (Figures I.16, I.17). State interventions, albeit realized in a piecemeal fashion, branded Izmir's landscape with marks of imperial power. Cumulatively, the buildings in the Konak-Sarıkışla area ushered in a new urban typology for administrative quarters that the Ottoman state replicated in provincial centers across the empire as the hallmark of its modern governance.[71] Moreover, although seemingly minor, insignias, symbols, and temporary displays served as equally significant markings, signaling the comprehensive changes undertaken by reformist bureaucrats. The small Ottoman imperial crescents above the gaslight poles lining major thoroughfares, the standard uniforms worn by the local police pacing through the streets, or the profuse decorations and illuminations that periodically accompanied state ceremonies were some of the material means through which the Ottoman state made its presence increasingly more conspicuous in the everyday experience of the city.

Perhaps less visible but even more powerful in organizing public life were the structural changes that brought local transactions more directly under state control, ultimately forging a new relationship between state and subjects. The Tanzimat government initiated major reforms to shore up Ottoman sovereignty against internal and external challenges that threatened the empire's territorial integrity. Building on a loose pattern of modernizing efforts that had begun in the late eighteenth century to adapt indigenous institutions to changing domestic and geopolitical circumstances, Tanzimat bureaucrats called for a far more systematic use of European models as a basis for restructuring. Although implemented unevenly and without always phasing out existing structures—which often led to parallel arrangements that caused complications—the reforms were

FIGURE I.16. Sarıkışla as seen from Değirmentepe, by Rubellin Père & Fils, 1878. Library of Congress.

FIGURE I.17. Izmir as seen from Değirmentepe, ca. 1865. Drawing by J. Schranz; engraved by L. Sabatier. Bibliothèque nationale de France.

far-reaching, covering nearly every aspect of society from legislation, education, and intercommunal relations to governance and political processes.[72]

Most consequential for Izmir were the newly constituted courts, land-registry offices, and administrative councils. In a rapidly growing international port like Izmir, litigations involving parties under different jurisdictions were becoming increasingly common, often generating conflicts about Ottoman officials' and European consuls' respective areas of oversight, and cutting deeply into the Ottoman state's ability to govern people within its territories. In 1840, as a critical first step in mitigating these problems, the Tanzimat regime introduced a mixed commercial court *(ticaret meclisi)*, presided over by a Muslim judge and comprising non-Muslim Ottoman and foreign panel members, followed in the 1860s by other secular courts for criminal and correctional cases *(temyiz-i hukuk meclisleri)*.[73] While these initiatives formed part of a broader scheme for drawing Ottoman laws closer to international practices, in Izmir they also enabled Tanzimat bureaucrats to bring more effectively under their supervision individuals who had previously eluded their control. At the same time, in 1850, to tap more systematically into the city's dynamic real-estate market and generate revenue with a pioneering property and income tax, the central government established within Izmir's cadastral bureau *(defterhane)* a new office for the registry of freehold land *(emlak dairesi)*. Applied to proprietors of all classes regardless of status and levied at a uniform rate, the new tax turned a collective responsibility into a direct obligation between individual taxpayers and the state. Moreover, in 1864, assuming a more active role in monitoring participation in local governance, Tanzimat bureaucrats enacted new laws that set the ground rules for membership composition and activities of provincial and municipal councils *(vilayet ve belediye meclisleri)*. Participatory forms of governance based on consultative meetings had long existed, but these new arrangements allowed state officials to structure more closely the exchanges between the city's various stakeholders on a regular basis and in a more methodical way.

Tanzimat reforms also recalibrated the relative status of local communities within the empire's social ordering. Especially significant for the purposes of this book were state efforts to fix the boundaries of Ottoman subjecthood and the rights and duties associated with it. In the Ottoman Empire, as in other modernizing states, clear-cut and stable identity categories that rendered society more legible to central bureaucrats were becoming ever more necessary to enhance state control over the empire's subjects and resources.[74] As I elaborate in chapter 1, the ambiguous legal status of increasing numbers of individuals holding some form of foreign protection papers was severely thwarting the central state's ability to keep tabs on local populations. In response, Tanzimat bureaucrats adopted a mixture of planned and ad hoc measures, gradually replacing what had historically been a permeable subjecthood regime, based on accommodative practices, with one of modern citizenship that, like its emergent European counterparts, was far more rigid and exclusive. For example, mixed commercial courts not only delineated a new sphere of justice for trying cases between Ottoman and foreign subjects, but also bolstered the distinction between these categories, casting them as mutually exclusive. The 1869 Ottoman Nationality Law (Tabiyet-i Osmaniye Kanunu) further reinforced this divide, categorically denying property and inheritance rights to Ottoman subjects acquiring foreign naturalization. In addition, the central government closely tied the rights of election and representation in municipal councils to Ottoman subjecthood, thus excluding by fiat foreign subjects from formal participation in local political processes.[75]

Concurrently, to defuse secessionist tensions that were threatening the integrity of the empire, Tanzimat leaders tried to establish a more egalitarian polity.

The Ottoman social organization had long comprised multiple groups—ethnic, religious, national, professional—that had differentiated rights and duties. However, at a time when post-Enlightenment ideas of justice and equality were becoming ever more prevalent, this two-tiered system that granted Muslims privileges over non-Muslims emerged as a point of contention. New statutes sought to abate, if not always eliminate, the constitutional differences between Ottoman subjects. Hence, reformed legal codes and procedures granted all subjects equal standing in secular courts, even if Muslims continued to hold privileges over non-Muslims in Islamic courts. Local councils, although still largely dominated by elite groups, became more representative of each locality's demographic makeup than it had ever been before. In addition, the Tanzimat leadership reorganized the governing structures of its three main non-Muslim communities—Greek Orthodox, Gregorian Armenian, and Jewish millets—and granted constitutional status to newly formed ones. Most visibly, it increasingly included millet leaders in formal state ceremonies as a deliberate expression of a new notion of Ottoman subjecthood *(teba-i Osmaniye)*, premised on an imperial identity that comprised various ethnoreligious subject communities.

The trends outlined above, spurred in part by increasing integration with the global economy and in part by a centralizing state bureaucracy, converged in reshaping Izmir and the ways people associated themselves with it. Together, these developments introduced new urban technologies, refashioned public spaces and institutions, and reconfigured the modes of local governance. They also radically transformed how people articulated their membership in the urban polity, claimed a right to the city, and maneuvered between normative identities and those produced through social practices. That different actors and discrete agendas prompted these developments made the midcentury decades a rich and contentious period of debates over the control and meaning of the city's material resources. Who should be given rights to property and under what conditions, who should pay for urban infrastructure and services, what activities constitute public nuisance, who should use the streets of the city and subject to what rules, and what the public good is and how it is to be achieved were some of the issues that local stakeholders fought over and negotiated as they grappled with the day-to-day realities of a changing present. Rivalries and dissent could lock various parties in conflict while converging interests could push different actors to coalesce around a single goal.

The diverse and dispersed material traces left by these processes reveal both the distinctive dynamics among the various players in the city and the common challenges shared by Izmir and other modernizing cities elsewhere. Archival sources and contemporary publications provide valuable clues for reconstituting aspects of Izmir's now largely lost physical environment and the ways people engaged with it. Although the 1922 fire eradicated many of the city's municipal records and much of its core urban fabric, thus greatly frustrating urban historical analysis, a range of sources in different languages pertaining to everyday life and practices still survives, if scattered in locations outside Izmir. Newspapers, Ottoman administrative and bureaucratic records, consular reports, geographic surveys, travel and missionary accounts, citizen petitions, and trade directories, as well as historic guidebooks, insurance and city maps, photographs of street views and principal buildings, and tourist postcards, which are used in this study, are themselves the telltale signs of the modernizing practices of communication and information collection.

Evidently, these sources were produced by a variety of actors and for distinct audiences, disclosing the priorities and intentions of their makers. For instance, whereas provincial *salnames* (yearbooks), surveys, and city maps sought to create stable and totalizing representations to fix fleeting and complex social realities into orderly categories, journalistic accounts, consular dispatches, and citizen petitions *(arzuhal)* tended to convey events as they were in flux, sometimes without closure, rendering visible the tentativeness of changes under way. Despite divergences in their provenance, these sources often speak of the same urban environment. They offer perspectives on the same material infrastructure and spaces, cumulatively portraying the range of experiences, exchanges, and discourses sustained by Izmir's urban spaces at a time of rapid growth and expansion. When critically played off against each other, these sources importantly elucidate the anxieties and contentions that animated urban life. They show how myriad stakeholders perceived the problems and promises of their city, and how they framed their complaints and negotiated power and position in relation to specific sites and projects, eventually laying bare the complex and fluid interactions among the various groups who were shaping the city.

In sum, a critical reading of the evidentiary sources, both for their physical and discursive content and for the incongruities they reveal, brings to the fore the trials and errors, the premeditated actions and improvisations, and the manifold conflicts and compromises involved in Izmir's modernization. That Izmir was changing simultaneously with its better-studied Western counterparts—which were also grappling with similar pressures of urban growth, questions of inclusion and exclusion in the urban polity, considerations of the public good, and class and communal identity formation—makes it hard to speak of one being a derivative of the other or an import of a fully formed model. Rather, this synchronism firmly positions Izmir as a comparable site, albeit with its own peculiarities, for examining key issues central to cities across the modernizing world.

In what follows, I probe representative projects and practices that illustrate the reciprocity between the processes of institutional and economic modernization and the material structures and conditions in Izmir. These reciprocities also determine the structure of the book. Each chapter is framed in terms of the articulation of a major theme in the history of modern urbanism as a field of study. Chapter 1 focuses on modern regimes of property rights and citizenship, examining the tensions that arose when the Ottoman state enforced such means to bring under its control individuals and groups whose vestigial privileges enabled them to step outside its jurisdictions. Chapter 2 turns to the emergence of modern organs of local government. It analyzes the contentious process of constituting a municipality to replace the range of urban services—street maintenance, policing, and sanitation—historically provided by motley local institutions, highlighting attendant problems of political representativeness and of realigning state and local jurisdictions in this new configuration. Using the construction of Izmir's modern quay, the city's most remarkable infrastructure project at the time, as a case in point, chapter 3 explores Smyrniots' divergent interests and priorities in relation to this large-scale, capital-intensive venture, establishing at the same time that the rival notions of the public good underpinning the architectural modernization of the waterfront were equally valid and modern. Chapter 4 considers emergent spectacles of nationhood and statehood in Izmir. It investigates how various religious communities, consular legations, and central state officials simultaneously used public feasts and rituals to promote their respective political agendas, exposing not only the challenges of creating a unified Ottoman polity in the face of secessionist threats but also the ability of the built environment to generate and sustain divergent social and political identities.

Clearly, in these chapters, the built environment constitutes both an agent and an object of change.[76] Not only was Izmir's physical environment radically transformed as a result of various internal and external interventions, but the organization of the city's physical spaces, the ground rules that governed these spaces, and the power structures, jurisdictions, and social norms associated with them facilitated certain transactions while constraining others. Significantly, they informed people's perceived priorities, how they pursued their visions and organized themselves to improve their city and boost its competitive position in relation to its peers. This book highlights the material city as a creative force—as an agent in its own right, intervening as a factor in all forms of contestation and negotiation, imposing its material substance, and producing in turn specific social and political relations.

1

Defining Citizenship
Property, Taxation, and Sovereignty

REAL-ESTATE TRANSACTIONS AND TRANSFERS offer a valuable lens to examine Izmir's entangled legal regime. As with other multinational and dynastic polities developed through conquests and incorporation of diverse territories, in the Ottoman Empire legal pluralism and differential legal statuses—accorded on the basis of subjecthood, religion, or social rank—were the norm. Hence, the Ottoman system comprised a complex array of judicial spheres and jurisdictions. Civil matters and contractual disputes were handled in different courts depending on the status of the litigants. The *mahkeme,* the local court presided over by the *kadı* (both an Islamic judge and a civil administrator), lay at the heart of the Ottoman-Islamic legal system, and its jurisdiction was largely unbounded, extending over Ottoman subjects regardless of religion. Cases among Christian or Jewish subjects of the empire could also be settled in ecclesiastical or rabbinical tribunals respectively, according to their own laws and customs.[1] Moreover, disputes between foreign subjects in the empire were adjudicated in consular courts, which applied the laws of their respective country and whose competence was confirmed by extraterritorial agreements *(ahd)* granted by the sultan. In contrast, all disputes concerning real (immovable) property came under the jurisdiction of the Ottoman state.[2] Buildings, roads, land, and attachments to land like trees were conceived as physically and legally inseparable from Ottoman territories; therefore, litigations over such property involved procedures that applied to everyone residing in the empire regardless of their creed or status. Consequently, real-estate sales, purchases, and transfers, rental contracts, inheritance and division of property, acquisition of building permits, or conflicts over easements, title deeds, and property tax regularly brought together actors who were otherwise governed by distinct jurisdictions and compelled them to work within shared legal frameworks, forged by mutual negotiation.

While the relative legal autonomy granted to non-Muslim communities, whether subject or foreign, enabled their members to maintain their distinctive religious and institutional structures and cultural practices, shaping the character of urban life, it certainly did not preclude individuals across communities from entering into all sorts of everyday exchanges.[3] In a highly diverse and commercialized city like Izmir, people of different status or ethnoreligious background encountered one another in the streets and regularly interacted in the workplace. They also entered into legally binding transactions, many of which involved property. Smyrniots bought and sold property frequently. Buildings and stores constituted more than a shelter for their daily activities; they provided rental income, had a liquidity that was comparable to cash, and comprised a substantial share of the assets of individuals and families. People of all descriptions used property as a vehicle for securing credit and raising capital or as collateral to increase their financial resources for doing business. And when formal laws got in the way, they found ways around it. They maneuvered the legal processes and navigated between judicial spheres to circumvent obstacles. Hence, according to Izmir's cadastral records, foreigners held over one third of the taxable property in the mid-1850s.[4] This was staggering considering that Ottoman laws at the time did not allow foreign subjects to hold property in their name, unless exceptionally authorized by special decree of the sultan.[5] Yet, clearly, through a variety of consensual and pragmatic arrangements, people had managed to reconcile legal norms with the local needs of a commercial society and create a class of foreign property owners—achieving de facto what they were denied in de jure rights. Such property transfer strategies often go unrecorded in official histories of the Ottoman property regime, yet they provide highly illuminating evidence on how formal legal structures can be adapted and reworked to meet everyday exigencies and facilitate shared living and collective viability in plural urban societies.

Mid-nineteenth-century changes triggered by Ottoman state centralization and global trade capitalism severely undermined the possibilities for such circumstantial arrangements. On the one hand, Tanzimat bureaucrats began to deploy new spatial technologies to enhance state control over the empire's variegated territory, assets, and people. Population censuses (1831), income registers (1840 and 1844), and cadastral surveys that tracked population distribution and resources; a new Land Code (1858) that streamlined landownership patterns; and new citizenship laws that fixed the parameters according to which people were officially considered to be Ottoman citizens were some of the most salient manifestations of this process in Izmir. On the other hand, European powers were competing with one another to expand their influence within the empire, while also trying to maintain the region's stability within the context of the "Eastern Question." To broaden their economic and political sway in the empire, they tacitly permitted their legations to extend protections and immunities to various local groups, thereby expanding a privilege that had historically been available exclusively to foreign nationals, consular and diplomatic staff, and certain monastic establishments.[6] Indeed, as mentioned earlier, the four- to fivefold increase in the number of foreign subjects in Izmir between the 1840s and the 1890s attests not only to massive in-migration, but also to growing numbers of individuals, mostly non-Muslims, placing themselves under the protection of an interested European power to gain immunity from certain tax liabilities and local police control. In short, while Tanzimat statesmen territorialized their authority more systematically, various European legations pushed back by expanding their long-standing extra-territorial treaties—popularly known as the capitulations—within the empire, both parties seeking to enforce their respective jurisdictions in uncompromising and exclusionary ways.

Nowhere were these competing processes more evident than in the protracted battles over property rights and taxation in Izmir. As I expound in this chapter, while the reformist state began to enforce new ownership rights and tax responsibilities to bring more uniformly under its jurisdiction the diverse peoples who inhabited its territories, various liable parties claimed exception using the system of foreign immunities and privileges and pleading foreign governments to leverage their extraterritorial agreements. Measures devised in one context triggered countermeasures in the other, ultimately escalating into an international crisis. Although the question was never fully resolved, it generated a series of provisional settlements whereby the rights and duties that defined foreign residents' membership in the urban polity were defined and contested.

In this chapter, I focus on these provisional settlements to investigate the dynamic relationship between property and urban citizenship. I use citizenship in a broader sense to mean a particular relationship between individuals and their polity, governed by more or less codified rights, obligations, and principles of exclusion and inclusion. In the past few decades, sociology, anthropology, and political theory have provided considerable insight into the concept of citizenship by dissociating it from the exclusive domain of nation-state to which it has been tied for the past two centuries. Theorists of citizenship are now turning their focus toward the city as a locus for political belonging and a place where the meaning, content, and extent of citizenship is made and continually renegotiated.[7]

A key consideration in this debate is the distinction between the formal (legal) dimension of citizenship governed by institutional categories imposed from without and its informal (sociocultural) dimension acted and experienced in all sorts of daily practices. In other words, urban citizenship is premised not only on legal status but also on active participation in and appropriation of the city's economic, social, and cultural spheres by virtue of residing in an urban territory.[8] Above all, it is a process, mediated by the built environment and its sociospatial relations, through which a sense of individual and collective belonging is forged and social boundaries are articulated.

With these considerations in mind, I begin with a brief outline of legal pluralism in the Ottoman Empire and lay out the complex interplay between legal norms and daily practices as evidenced through property transactions involving foreign subjects. Against this fluid background, I first examine the controversies that erupted when Ottoman bureaucrats used property tenure and ownership rights as a political instrument to undercut the long-standing yet increasingly disputed question of foreign privileges. Next I turn to the central government's new property-tax scheme, tracing how its preconceived tax requirements had to be modified and fine-tuned repeatedly as they met specific opposition on the ground. The resulting exchanges reconfigured the modes of participation in city politics, informing the scope and boundaries of urban citizenship, and importantly revealing the significance of property—one of the city's major assets—as both a site and a means for complex identity politics.

Legal Pluralism

A salient feature of Ottoman legal pluralism was the simultaneous existence of personal and territorial laws, each governing certain categories of disputes.[9] Personal laws applied on the basis of religious identity or appointment to court and army service and were, so to speak, portable. They had their origin in a once commonly observed principle that status rather than place of residence determined the law under which an individual lived.[10] In contrast, territorial laws indiscriminately governed all inhabitants in a distinct spatial unit. While they could vary from one location to another depending on local practices, they brought together individuals of diverse status residing in a bounded area. As a result, depending on the category of the transaction or class of dispute, separate sets of laws could apply to one individual.

Personal laws were an integral aspect of Islamic law and evolved in response to the pragmatic demands of Ottoman imperial conquest and the incorporation of diverse people within its fold. Jews and Christians who lived under Muslim rule were entitled to *zimmi* protections, which allowed them to regulate their internal affairs according to their own laws, customs, and institutions in return for the payment of a poll tax *(cizye)* and the acceptance of certain restrictions that marked them as a class inferior to their fellow Muslim subjects.[11] In the early days of Ottoman expansion, Ottoman sultans officially recognized the Greek Orthodox, Gregorian Armenian, and Jewish communities, investing their religious leaders with deeds or *berats* that codified the privileges of their office as both spiritual and secular leaders of their community. Patriarchs and rabbis were thus incorporated into the imperial administration, establishing the multireligious and multiethnic basis of the empire. They presided over their respective religious courts, arbitrated civil cases between members of their communities, performed marriages, recorded births and deaths, and divided inheritance. They were also entrusted with extensive authority over matters of communal governance and taxation.[12]

Similarly, foreign communities residing in Ottoman territories enjoyed considerable autonomy in administering their internal affairs under the supervision of their diplomatic agents. According to Islamic law, foreigners or *müstemins* residing temporarily in Muslim territories were exempt from taxation up to a period of one year, after which they were placed on the same footing as zimmis and were subject to the cizye.[13] Ottoman sultans who wanted to encourage economic relations and trade with other parts of the Mediterranean overrode canonical precepts, extending these exemptions and immunities more permanently to European merchants who settled in Ottoman lands. Initially modeled after the commercial and judicial privileges accorded by medieval Muslim leaders to Italian traders, the various capitulations, signed between successive Ottoman sultans and European monarchs, granted foreign merchants the right to trade and the freedom to profess their religion in the empire. These arrangements, which were remarkably accommodating at the time, attracted enterprising tradesmen from around the Mediterranean, helping create diverse and robust ports of trade within the empire's territory.[14] In some ways, the capitulations were comparable to zimmi protections. Like the spiritual heads of non-Muslim communities, consuls and diplomatic agents received a berat from the Ottoman government that gave them jurisdiction over the members of their respective communities. They also had the power to settle all civil and criminal cases in their place of residence according to their own laws and customs, provided all parties were members of the same foreign community. The capitulations, however, provided far more extensive privileges than zimmi protections. They exempted their holders from the cizye, offered other important tax immunities (such as taxes on exported goods and local customary taxes), and guaranteed the inviolability of a foreigner's residence.[15] Such extraterritorial provisions—which may seem odd from the perspective of the nation-state present where jurisdictions throughout have become primarily territorial and states have claimed exclusive sovereignty over their territory—were widely used in Europe until the decline of the city-states of the late medieval age and continued to exist through the early twentieth century in various dynastic and multinational states.[16]

While the Ottoman imperial center gave some degree of jurisdictional autonomy to officially recognized constituencies, it retained all matters related to ownership and use rights of real property, taxation, security, city and district government, and intercommunity disputes within its own territorial jurisdiction and courts. At the top of the local judicial hierarchy stood the kadı court. It handled civil and criminal cases between Muslims and between non-Muslims litigating with Muslims or with non-Muslims of different communities. It also heard the cases of parties belonging to the same non-Muslim community who chose to litigate before the kadı court.[17] Importantly for the purposes of this study, the kadı court was the clearinghouse for all kinds of disputes dealing with property. Spouses, heirs, neighbors, business partners, creditors, and debtors brought grievances, complaints, and other matters related to their property before this court. Additionally, the kadı court served as a kind of notary registering and legalizing deeds and agreements and issuing to all classes of Ottoman subjects—Muslims and non-Muslims—documents that served as legal proof of property rights.

This brief outline provides only the normative contours of the Ottoman legal system. In practice, neither was kadı court justice exclusively derived from canonical Islamic law, nor were the various local courts discrete in the way they handled cases. To begin with, the constant interaction and accommodation of various sources of jurisprudence, including Islamic law *(şeriat)*, sultanic decrees *(kanun)*, and customs *(örf)*, made the kadı court a particularly dynamic and flexible institution.[18] In addition, the mechanisms that kept Islamic doctrine in continuous dialogue with practices such as legal opinions issued by Islamic jurists *(fetvas)* and mediation for maintaining communal harmony *(sulh* or *musalaha)* further contributed to the evolving character of Ottoman laws while maintaining them within the framework of a broadly Islamic legal tradition.[19] Moreover, the kadı court played an indispensible part in dispute resolution under the capitulatory regime. It had competence over cases involving Ottoman and foreign parties, although in such cases the capitulations required the presence of a consular dragoman at the court, whose approval was necessary to complete the verdict.[20] Equally important, in an increasingly commercial and plural city like Izmir, wherein individuals of different legal status entered into all sorts of dealings and exchanges, Ottoman and various European consular jurisdictions frequently intersected and partially overlapped, sometimes even converging on the same person or applying to parts of the same dispute. In such cases, the jurisdictional boundaries between the kadı and consular courts had to be negotiated and adjusted, creating a highly fluid legal environment of unpredictable outcomes.

Property and Entangled Legal Spheres

Property transactions involving foreign subjects reveal the complex dynamics between legal norms and day-to-day practices. Although foreigners in the empire did not have rightful access to freehold property until 1867, through a careful manipulation of existing laws, many of them did find ways of holding property. The prevailing method was to register the titles in the name of an Ottoman subject that the kadı court recognized as the actual owner. In Izmir, this front person was usually a female relative of the foreigner—the wife or the mother-in-law. For the purpose of conveyance, she would agree to be considered an Ottoman subject or *râya* since in the eyes of the kadı court, despite marrying a foreign man, a râya woman retained her original subject status; therefore, she could be a legitimate property owner.[21] When the front person was not an immediate relative, the title deeds were supplemented with yet another contract, made before either the consular authority of the foreigner or the religious court of the Ottoman subject, in which the front person declared that he was not the rightful owner but had only lent his name to complete the required paperwork before the kadı court.[22]

Property registration under borrowed names profitably met the demands of all concerned parties, which may explain its frequent adoption as a favored tactic. Indeed, it became a widespread de facto practice in Izmir, as in cities like Alexandria, Istanbul, and Thessaloniki, frequented for generations by foreign merchants.[23] For one, this arrangement allowed foreigners to invest their money without compromising their foreign status and the important personal and tax immunities that came with it. It also worked to the satisfaction of Ottoman officials as it retained real-estate transactions within the laws of the empire, attracted investment, and generated revenues through transfer fees and construction permits. Moreover, it conformed to the formal tenets and procedures of the kadı court and maintained the superiority of this court in the overall hierarchy of the legal system. In some instances, property registered in the name of the wife offered additional advantages to the foreign husband, including a way around property seizure if he went bankrupt. In Izmir's highly commercialized milieu, it was not uncommon for foreign merchants to declare bankruptcy. In such cases, the uncertain status of a wife's property with respect to her husband's debts posed an important challenge. Consular courts generally considered such property as part of the husband's assets on the basis that the wife was merely a nominal owner and insisted that it should be seized for the benefit of the creditors. For the kadı court, however, property registered in the name of a râya woman was not necessarily liable for the foreign husband's debts. As the registered proprietress, her consent was necessary if the property had to be sold to pay off the husband's debt or transferred to the creditor.[24]

These differences caused considerable concern to consular courts when disputes that presumably fell within their scope could not be settled without the concurrence of the kadı court.[25] In principle, contractual obligations between foreign litigants were within the jurisdiction of the consular court. Meanwhile, territorial claims affecting ownership or use rights—such as acquisition, alienation, and various forms of leasing that determined or limited the extent of rights to a real property—were matters for the kadı court and had to be carried out in conformity with the information recorded on the title deed.[26] Yet certain categories of contractual disputes, such as those related to the use of real property as collateral or to bankruptcy, could also involve territorial rights, requiring such cases to be settled in two courts. The consular court judged the personal obligation, ordering either the seizure and auctioning off of the property to pay the debt or its transfer to the creditor, while the kadı court completed the actual transfer and registration. In 1861, litigations resulting in favor of bankrupt proprietors due to wives withholding their assent at the kadı court took alarming proportions, driving the British consular judge in Izmir, Donald Logie, to wage an open attack on the kadı court's procedures for perpetuating "the grossest and most mischievous frauds."[27] Such moments of crises provide illuminating glimpses of the legal entanglements that could occur around property transactions. As I discuss later, the sheer scale of this particular problem compelled foreign and Ottoman authorities to bring greater definition to the question.

Consular courts provide some useful insight into the process of settling property disputes between litigants bound by different rules. Generally, complications arose out of the necessity of coordinating the settlements pronounced at each court and forging convergence between different legal norms and procedures. In one case that began in 1845, for example, a property mortgaged by a French subject residing in Izmir, Firmin Guys, to the Swiss commercial firm Geilinger &

Blum could not be seized. Upon Guys's bankruptcy the French court authorized the expropriation and proceeded with a public auction. In addition, the potential buyer, Abraham İnebekoğlu, made the necessary deposit at the French consulate toward the purchase, and even the kadı informed the consul that his court would authorize the transfer to the party chosen by the consulate. However, the transaction eventually fell through because, once at the court, the title deed *(temessük)*, on the basis of which the kadı court had agreed to make the transfer, turned out to be in the name of Guys's mother-in-law, Sara de Hochepied, who was not present at the proceedings. De Hochepied, a Dutch subject, had previously bequeathed the property to her daughter with a contract signed before the Dutch consular court.[28] The kadı court, however, recognized only the person whose name was on the original title, the presence and consent of whom was necessary for the transaction.

Ambiguity about the division of labor between courts added further hurdles to property cases. For instance, when Sara Karcher, Dutch protégé, petitioned the French consular court to gain possession of a house mortgaged to her by a French proprietress, the court declared itself incompetent. Instead, it referred the litigants to the kadı court because "the question fell under the exclusive jurisdiction of territorial authorities."[29] For his part, however, the *molla* of Izmir (the senior judge in the hierarchies of kadıs) also refused to deliver the written sentence *(ilâm)*, requesting that the debt be initially settled at the consular court. To be sure, these back-and-forth moves between courts indicate the impracticalities of coordinating legal actions, which, more often than not, had to be effected through bribery and enticement, since corruption was a chronic vice of various courts that was integral to running the legal machinery. Above all, these moves pointed to the agency of these courts and to the range of maneuvers they could perform to direct the case in favor of a specific party.

The imprecision in consular court procedures and the variations across different consular courts and in the degree of competence courts claimed in a given case provided leeway for such manipulations, ultimately making property disputes a convenient instrument for reciprocal arm-twisting. At times, consulates framed the issue so as to assume competence over all personal matters related to the case, leaving only the actual writing of the title deed to the kadı court.[30] At others, they categorically refused to interfere with any aspect of the question. This was the case with the Austrian court during the division of a house and warehouse complex (known as Frenkhane Fisher) between the British heirs of J. K. Fisher and the Austrian heirs of Mrs. Kramer, widow of Fisher. The British plaintiff, C. Fisher, opposed the division requested by the kadı court, maintaining that the molla's jurisdiction "ceased when the question of ownership was decided by him" and that "division of property of whatever kind among European heirs should be made by their own authorities."[31] In contrast, the Austrian court, which generally played a more active role in similar cases, chose to declare itself incompetent and recognize the molla's pronouncement, which dovetailed all too conveniently with the interest of its own subjects.

Gaps and blind spots in legal procedures also offered openings that allowed litigants to sway the case in their favor. A case in point was the provision of having a dragoman accompany the foreign litigant at the kadı court. In cases with "mixed" litigants, the capitulations called for the presence of a dragoman. Property suits, however, were premised on the assumption that all parties to the litigation were Ottoman subjects. Hence the presence of a dragoman was a contradiction in terms. This was, at least, the perspective of Ottoman authorities in a suit brought in 1851 by an Armenian zimmi, Hripsima, against Manoli Vapopoulo, a British subject, who refused to appear at court without the presence of his dragoman. A few days prior to declaring bankruptcy, Vapopoulo had his friend, a Greek Ottoman subject under whose name he had formerly bought the warehouse, promise the property to Hripsima who had already paid the purchase price. Meanwhile, unaware of this deal, the British consulate authorized Vapopoulo's creditors to seize his warehouse, making the same property subject to multiple claims.[32] Although the eventual settlement of the case remains unknown, clearly Vapopoulo's insistence on bringing his dragoman was a delaying tactic that postponed an unfavorable sentence against him for over a year.

Men and women, plaintiffs and defendants, judges and clerks, and consuls and local authorities exploited the openings and loopholes available to them and circumvented the legal obstacles standing in the way. Contrary to prevailing views of Ottoman pluralism, people did not necessarily inhabit insular judicial spheres. They often had to navigate a permeable legal regime in which rules and normative designations were far from given or fixed. As they responded to everyday challenges and changes through their practical and personal dealings and disputes, they also negotiated and reconfigured legal boundaries, ultimately exposing a highly enmeshed world of multiple parties, discrete interests, and interconnected issues. Moreover, that property exchange connected diverse social actors around a shared legal landscape did not necessarily mean that these parties construed this landscape and its workings the same way. The kadı court had a procedural cast of mind. It saw and settled property cases and transactions insofar as they could be framed in a language compliant with the principles and precepts of Islamic legal tradition. However, consuls' penchant for codified, rather than accumulated, rules meant that they attributed the frequent holdups and setbacks in property transactions to the imprecision and flexibility of local laws. "All difficulties would come to an end," wrote the acting French consul of Izmir, L. Béchard, in 1847, "if only Islamic law, rather than functioning on the basis of subtle tolerance, granted or prohibited in *absolute* terms property ownership rights to Europeans."[33] Notwithstanding divergent understandings, the rewards seem to have far exceeded potential frustrations, enticing people to invest in property, hence creating sufficiently stable and lasting, albeit repeatedly negotiated, arrangements that acquired the legitimacy and authority of bylaws.

Parallel Courts, Ambiguous Identities

Soon after the pronouncement of the 1839 Gülhane Edict, the central government embarked on a series of legal reforms, promulgating new laws and codifying existing ones to establish the empire as an equal member in the Concert of Europe and reinforce its sovereignty over its territories. The 1840 and 1858 Penal Codes, the 1850 Commercial Code, the 1858 Land Code, the 1863 Maritime Code, and the 1876 Civil Code were important manifestations of this reformist current. In some areas, this was done through a wholesale adoption of European codes such as the Penal and Commercial Codes, largely derived form the French model. In others, it was achieved through a systematization of existing local laws. The Civil Code (or Mecelle) codified particular domains within Islamic law, primarily those dealing with transactions, contracts, and obligations, whereas the Land Code classified all imperial land according to categories of tenure derived from Islamic principles and previous Ottoman practices.[34] Moreover, to bring larger areas of jurisdiction under its direct rule and create a more unified legal space over which to exercise more effective control, the Tanzimat government introduced a secular court system—the *nizamiye* (or regular) courts—comprising a hierarchy of courts, ultimately linked to central administrative units.[35] Although the widespread implementation of these courts across the empire came only in the 1880s, the demands of international trade and the presence of diverse religious and national groups accelerated their introduction in Izmir, placing the city at the forefront of Ottoman legal modernization. Beginning in the 1840s mixed commercial courts and later other secular courts for hearing criminal, correctional, and civil cases sought to insure impartiality by means of new judicial procedures, including the recognition of the testimony of Muslims and non-Muslims as equals and the appointment of a mixed panel of judges consisting of Ottoman (Muslim and non-Muslim) and various European judges.

Tanzimat courts and laws added more intricacies to the skein of legal practices complicating Izmir's already carefully negotiated legal regime. Although the reforms were meant to streamline and limit kadı court jurisdiction primarily to matters of personal status and pious endowments that fell within the realm of Islamic law, the demarcation of the domains of kadı and nizamiye courts were drawn-out processes, riddled with complications and contradictions.[36] Throughout the second half of the nineteenth century, kadı courts continued to operate, often retaining competence over the same cases that were referred to the nizamiye courts. Disputes at the interface between private and public rights, like questions of easement or the opening or widening of roads, are particularly illuminating as they could potentially be settled in either court with divergent outcomes. The kadı court, which retained jurisdiction on all claims pertaining to *mülk* (freehold) or *vakıf* (endowed) property commonly based its judgment on Islamic precepts that prioritized the protection of private rights, allowing, under certain circumstances, a proprietor to block a public easement going through his/her property.[37] The nizamiye courts, which by and large arbitrated cases related to the public domain and the joint rights of a collectivity of users to public spaces, however, founded their ruling on the new Penal and Land Codes that emphasized public convenience and necessities.

A case in point was the contentious dispute in 1858 between a Frenchman, Auguste Cousinéry, owner of a silk factory and Constantino Zadé, an Ionian/Greek Orthodox subject and British protégé, who blocked a sewer easement running through his own property, thus preventing the discharge of the silk factory waters (Map 1.1).[38] Zadé asked to settle at the kadı court, insisting that questions pertaining to his mülk were within the exclusive jurisdiction of Islamic laws. Cousinéry, however, demanded a trial based on the *nizamname*s (secular regulations) that the municipal council had been using in its arbitrations, arguing that this was the only competent body of law for questions of public easement.[39] In a manner akin to what legal anthropologists term "forum shopping" or the selective use of legal systems, both parties tactically framed the issue in a manner that was most advantageous to them to steer their cases to a court that was likely to provide more favorable treatment.[40] That divergent yet equally valid legal understandings of private and public rights could converge in settling claims over the same property or space, a question I develop in the following chapters, significantly shaped the direction and scope of urban interventions in the public domain, informing Izmir's mid-nineteenth-century transformation.

Arguably the most salient source of legal ambiguity and shiftiness in Izmir were individuals who claimed extraterritorial exemption by obtaining foreign

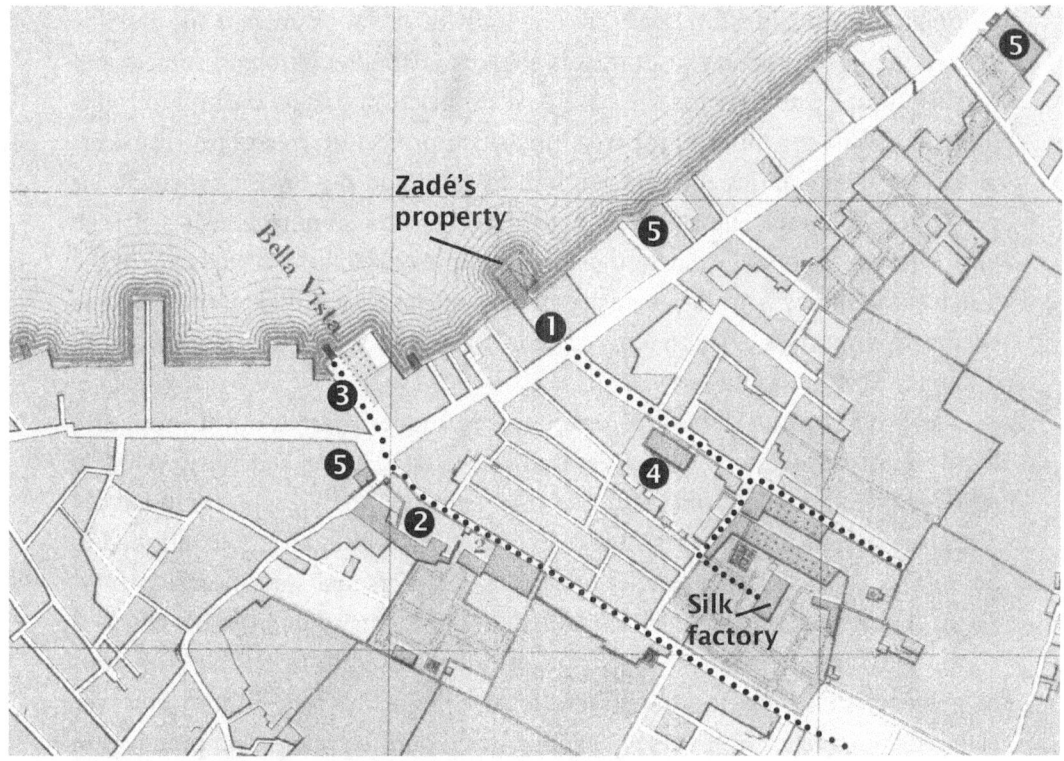

MAP 1.1. Location of Cousinéry's silk factory, Zadé's property, and the gateway blocking the sewer, based on the plan by Storari (Map 2).

LEGEND: 1 = Zadé's gate blocking the sewer; 2 = French hospital; 3 = quay of French hospital; 4 = St. John (Greek Orthodox); 5 = guardhouses (*karakol*).

protections. Historically, such protection was limited to a small group of native agents, translators, and guards employed by foreign consulates. But as European powers pressed claims on entire non-Muslim Ottoman communities and granted protection papers with relative ease, the privilege became available to larger segments of the local population. Commercial expansion and the presence of large numbers of foreign residents, intermarrying and engaging in business partnerships with natives, further expanded the means for acquiring protégé and foreign statuses.

Acquired through diverse mechanisms, including naturalization, purchase of consular protections, intermarriage, and European investments and business partnerships, foreign immunities enabled wider groups of non-Muslim actors to enjoy personal and tax exemptions and shield themselves from liability to Ottoman laws.[41] In some cases, they also generated exceptional legal complications due to the convergence of inherently conflicting personal statuses—that of an

Ottoman subject and a foreigner—in one individual. For example, Zadé, the litigant in the 1858 property dispute, was a Greek Orthodox Ottoman subject and a British protégé at the same time. While his subject status allowed him to rightfully own, lease, or inherit property, his British protection freed him from certain tax responsibilities and enabled him to call upon the British consulate for personal protection. The ability to hold these statuses simultaneously—at least until Ottoman nationality laws officially came into effect in the last quarter of the nineteenth century—produced an ever more fluid landscape that permitted some groups to transgress existing legal categories and use privileges associated with different identities as they saw fit.

The protégé status is hard to translate into modern terms, but it presents a highly illustrative example of a carefully negotiated formal identity. While it released the individual from the duties that defined Ottoman subjecthood, it did not give the person another political identity. Generally, a protégé continued to be an Ottoman subject in matters related to his personal status, such as marriage, divorce, and death, which remained under the jurisdiction of his religious community. Indeed, some consuls categorically refused to intervene in matters of personal status, leaving the task to local religious leaders. Others, however, claimed competence over these questions based on the policies and practices of their respective governments, performing, for instance, the marriage contracts of their protégés. In some cases, consuls within a given locality developed some shared rules for handling specific questions, as in the case of inheritance for which they based themselves on Islamic law.[42] Hence, variances among the procedures were not uncommon, making the protégé status an utterly unstable and relational identity category that swayed between the jurisdictions of different authorities.

While the origin of the protégé status goes back to the establishment of regular diplomatic representation at the Ottoman court in the sixteenth century, the system of exemption itself was rooted in the domestic practices and social hierarchies of the empire. The division between the *askeri* and râya—the former referring to the tax-exempt military-administrative class and the latter comprising all tax-paying nonbureaucratic subjects—was the primary determinant of status in the empire.[43] Major officers of the court and army could exempt their servants and agents from taxes and grant rights and privileges on the basis of appointment to an office.[44] In a similar vein, the Sublime Porte issued a limited number of berats, allowing foreign merchants to provide immunities to their clerks, dragomans, guards, and other local agents who facilitated their daily transactions with Ottoman authorities.[45]

As with any exemption system, the protégé *(beratlı)* system was prone to abuse by both the individuals who sought them and the foreign states that granted them. Locals coveted the benefits it extended and began to purchase these privileges from a local consulate for a fee, using their confessional ties or business relations. Already by the late eighteenth century, in major cities where foreigners and subject non-Muslims lived and worked side by side, berats became commercialized, passing from appoint agents to third parties. Foreign powers for their part cited their role as guardians of Ottoman Christians as a pretext and used the protégé system as a means of exerting pressure on the empire. Consuls no longer limited themselves to selling berats handed out by the Porte. They also began to issue protections on their own authority, extending these privileges in a general way over specific religious groups—as in the case of France over the Catholics and the Russians over the Greek Orthodox.[46] The moral justification for issuing these protections was rooted in the belief that multinational empires such as the Ottoman treated their "national minorities" unjustly—a common tenet in nineteenth-century liberalism.[47] Claiming people through protection enabled foreign powers to further their political influence in the region not only vis-à-vis the Ottoman government, but also vis-à-vis their European counterparts, with whom they found themselves in a relentless competition. These conditions aggravated the abuse of the protégé system. In a vibrant and diverse commercial center like Izmir, commanding the attention of several European nations vying for influence, ambiguous legal identities proliferated. Hence, for example, a Greek Orthodox subject might obtain either Russian or British protection or become a national of the recently established Greek state, while a Catholic Ottoman subject might be a French, Austrian, or Sardinian (and later Italian) protégé.

To be sure, individuals manipulated these mechanisms opportunistically, switching between them according to need and the prospects available. Similarly, consuls engaged in various maneuvers by granting and withdrawing these protections as they saw fit. Several court cases reveal the variability of status and the tactical machinations that went with it. For example, during a bankruptcy case that lingered for over a decade, the defendant, Marcozade, appeared before the court in 1832 as a subject of the Ionian British Islands. The islands having come under British rule in 1815, Ionian subjects could claim British consular protection. As a result, when Marcozade's property had to be seized and sold for the benefit of his British creditors, the British consular court declared itself competent for the case. But when Marcozade's mother-in-law appealed the same case in 1846, British consul Brant refused to intervene on the pretext that he discovered of late that Marcozade was a native of Thessaloniki and consequently an Ottoman râya who was passing himself off as an Ionian subject. Meanwhile, divested from his British protection, Marcozade had already acquired an alternative status, appearing before the court in 1846 as a subject of Greece.[48]

Although the number of Ottoman subjects claiming foreign privileges is difficult to assess, existing evidence points to the pervasiveness of the practice. In Ottoman censuses, protégés were largely conflated with non-Muslim subjects, or with foreigners, if they held some form of foreign naturalizations.[49] The absence of consistent institutional categories to classify these groups or the various ways in which they obtained protection further confused the issue. During Izmir's 1844 census, for instance, the central government appointed Ahmed Vefik Pasha to assess whether the claim of over 1,500 persons of Maltese and Ionian origins was entitled to British protection.[50] At the top of the Porte's concerns were the losses in anticipated revenues, as in the late 1840s when two thirds of the cizye tax in Izmir could not be collected.[51] Periodic governmental query to investigate dubious claims to foreign protection and nationality indicate the persistence of the problem through the nineteenth century. Considering that consular protections extended not only to individuals but also to their entire household and, until 1863, were transmitted through inheritance, the number of protégés must have increased rapidly and steadily—at least in the course of the first half of the nineteenth century. Moreover, because protégés included wealthy and influential merchants, their impact must have been greater than their numbers would suggest.

While the Porte eventually succeeded in limiting the further expansion of the protégé status, the legitimacy of individual claims to foreign protection continued to foment strife between consular and local authorities, at times even sidetracking court cases. Since the late eighteenth century, the Porte had been adopting measures to mitigate the proliferation of protégés, creating disincentives by issuing new imperial patents that gave Ottoman merchants comparable advantages to their foreign counterparts and pressuring European governments to add restrictive clauses to the capitulations. These efforts met with mixed success depending on location, but on the whole they did not eliminate the propensity among non-Muslims to seek a protégé status. Finally, in 1863, as a result of international negotiations, the Porte managed to restrict the benefits of the status to a specific individual for the duration of his appointment, contingent on its approval. But it grandfathered those who had acquired it prior to the 1863 measure, resulting in two classes of protégés: permanent and temporary.[52] More importantly, it triggered a considerable surge in the number of Ottoman subjects pursuing foreign naturalizations, kindling Ottoman authorities' resentment of native-born subjects who had shifted status, even in nonterritorial disputes.[53] For example, in a civil suit that the American A. S. Macropoderi brought against an Ottoman subject, Adem Konciyan, Macropoderi's changes of status turned the case against him. Macropoderi was born in Chios, an island only a few miles away from Izmir. According to American consul E. S. Smithers, he was rightfully entitled to American protection. Formerly holding a Sardinian passport, Macropoderi had become a naturalized American after going to the United States in 1853, and on his return to Izmir in 1862 had registered himself at the local United States consulate. But Izmir's governor, Süreyya Pasha, to whose attention the issue was brought, had a different opinion. Not persuaded by this evidence and evidently irritated by foreign consulates shielding native subjects, he ordered an investigation to ascertain Macropoderi's identity, throwing the proceedings off course.[54]

Although the reformers at the Porte earnestly attempted to codify legal procedures and simplify the unwieldy status categories, they eventually generated more jurisdictional entanglements and status classes than they initially began with. As existing structures proved impossible to expunge, the mid-nineteenth-century legal regime became ever more complicated by the tensions and gaps arising from the incongruities between new and old practices. For Smyrniots, who were quick to grasp legal loopholes and activate their business and family ties or linguistic affiliations, the city's plural and unstable regime offered additional opportunities to exploit. For the bureaucrats at the Porte, however, the volatility of this legal regime was what undercut the empire's sovereignty and caused revenue shortfalls.

Ownership Rights and Citizenship

Against this background, property tenure took on an undeniably political significance. Tanzimat bureaucrats were determined to bring within the remit of Ottoman jurisdictions all individuals whose extraterritorial immunities undercut tax revenues and impeded local police action. At the Congress of Paris in 1856, where the Ottoman Empire was finally inducted into the Concert of Europe, Âli Pasha, minister of foreign affairs and zealous advocate of modernization reforms, declared that such privileges were incompatible with the norms of modern sovereignty and European public law and constituted an "intractable obstacle to any kind of improvement."[55] In a memorandum he sent in 1860, he announced to foreign legations that the Ottoman government categorically refused to recognize new protégés, asking such individuals either to leave the country within three months or to accept being treated as Ottoman subjects. He also required such individuals to sell their property prior to their departure and underlined that hereafter they would be denied the right to inherit from their Ottoman parents.[56]

While these drastic measures were impossible to implement in full, they ushered in a series of crucial provisions that linked real property to Ottoman sovereignty in unprecedented ways.

In Izmir, Âli Pasha's pronouncement stirred, most immediately, the question of third-party tenure, especially the widespread practice of using foreign female fronts. Ottoman authorities took an uncompromising stance and began to treat all proprietresses as bona fide Ottoman subjects. This procedure, wittingly or not, shielded foreign women from liability in the consular court, creating undeniable hurdles for these courts when, for example, they had to issue a property-repossession order in the case of the male relative's bankruptcy.[57] In tandem, the central government introduced more stringent identity checks for property transfers and sales. Those who wished to purchase property had first to obtain from their religious leader a certificate *(ilmuhaber)* that established their Ottoman subjecthood and their membership in that particular religious community (or millet). Following successive official orders sent from Istanbul in 1862, the measure was enforced unequivocally, tightening the screw on property registration in Izmir. Thereafter, all real-estate-related purchase and sale contracts effected through private agreement or before a foreign authority, such as a consul, would be considered null and void.[58]

Within a matter of weeks, the measure suspended the registration of scores of transactions, making it clear to foreign subjects and protégés that their hold on property was at the mercy of the Ottoman state. It also categorically closed a vital loophole in Izmir's property market, cutting deeply into the interests of a significant portion of the population. In response, affected property owners forcefully argued their case in the local press to ensure the Porte heard their claims, insisting that the measure would inevitably lead to the collapse of the real-estate market in the empire's second city. The consuls implored their respective governments to intervene on behalf of their subjects. They claimed that the Porte was acting arbitrarily by halting a practice that it had "admitted and acknowledged for nearly two hundred years," thus in effect denouncing the clear-cut procedures they had been demanding all along.[59] As Etienne Pisani, dragoman of the British embassy in Istanbul, declared, however, the Ottoman government had never knowingly admitted or sanctioned property ownership by foreign parties. The many foreign women who held property in their own names were "allowed to hold it under the fiction that they are subjects of the Porte."[60] By abstaining from using their surnames in the title deeds, foreign-born women had willingly confounded themselves with their Ottoman-born counterparts, further sustaining this legal fiction.[61] Moreover, the Tanzimat regime countered Izmir's affected property owners' attacks by mobilizing Istanbul's foreign-language press. James Carlile McCoan, founder and editor of the semiofficial weekly the *Levant Herald,* commended the measure for rectifying a fraudulent practice and doing away with large numbers of "sham protected subjects," blaming instead European subjects and protégés.[62]

Beyond its impact on Smyrniot proprietors, the measure changed the terms of the debate. Not only was a long-held property tenure practice recast as a legal fiction and an evasion of the law, but more importantly, it was also presented as a legitimate act of sovereignty by a modern state over its internationally recognized territories. Before long the issue escalated into an international crisis, forcing foreign missions to address what they had already been seeing as a difficult and complex question.[63] Eventually, in 1867, following long-drawn-out negotiations between the Porte, which wanted to sap extraterritorial jurisdictions, and foreign governments, which refused to relinquish them, an imperial decree recognized foreigners' right to own land in their own names on the condition that they submitted to Ottoman laws and accepted to be considered as an Ottoman subject in all matters concerning land and property.[64] In other words, foreign owners would give up their privileges and comply with Ottoman territorial jurisdictions except for the immunities attached to their person and their movable goods.

Although granting foreign subjects the privilege of owning real estate may seem to be yet another concession to foreign powers, the circumstances within which this decree was issued suggests that it was proactive. First, the decree was a tactical move by the Ottoman government that unmistakably asserted its territorial sovereignty. As mentioned earlier, prior to 1867 foreign subjects could not officially own property, although in practice they did. In contrast, by overtly granting them this right, the decree brought foreign property owners and their property under greater state control. Compliance with police regulations, tax obligations, and Ottoman laws (article 2) was now uniformly enforceable on foreign subjects—albeit for issues pertaining primarily to their property. Second, in explicitly denying property rights to native-born Ottoman subjects who had acquired foreign naturalization (article 1), the decree also closed a loophole created by the aforementioned 1863 measure. It deterred Ottoman subjects from acquiring foreign nationalities at a time when European and neighboring states, which were concurrently refashioning their own naturalization laws, were enrolling people by the hundreds, sometimes even granting certificates of naturalization without residency requirement.[65] As a result, the 1867 decree constituted a strategic first step in imposing a more uniform and exclusive jurisdictional control that modern territorial rule demanded. It brought foreigners on a more even footing with Ottoman subjects by granting them ownership rights in return for certain citizenship duties, and by the same token, it categorically deprived Ottoman subjects who renounced their nationality in favor of another country from sharing similar benefits.

What made the protocol perhaps most remarkable was the distinctive, if not unique, legal position in which it placed Izmir's foreigners. During the protracted negotiations that led to the signing of the 1867 protocol—a process that took up to seven years for some signatory states—European nations made explicit claims over those they considered their own subjects, each government ensuring that, except on questions of property and land, the protocol did not undermine their rights and control over their subjects.[66] After all was said and done, the standing of foreign subjects in the overall Ottoman imperial hierarchy was cleverly adjusted, even if this reconfiguration did not entirely eliminate frictions and concerned parties often interpreted its provisions differently.[67] By virtue of the property they owned, they became Ottoman subjects and were made to conform to its obligations. Yet these new ownership rights and duties did not undo their foreign nationality. For other matters related to their person and movables, they retained their foreign privileges and immunities and, by extension, the rights and duties they held toward their respective governments. In short, they became part-Ottoman and part-foreign subjects, or in the language of Istanbul's French-language press, "sujets Ottomans étrangers"—that is, foreign Ottoman subjects, as opposed to foreign subjects.[68]

This hybrid category, through which both Ottoman and various foreign states made claims, is telling in a number of ways. First, it articulated a new relationship between property, citizenship, and modern sovereignty. Accordingly, property was not only a source of socioeconomic power for its possessor or a source of revenue for the state. It was a quintessential instrument through which the Ottoman state sought to fix and stabilize its permeable legal regime that had enabled certain groups to elude its jurisdiction and extend more uniformly its sovereignty over those who occupied its territory. Second, this category illustrates how property tenure and ownership rights became a fundamental arena for constructing and negotiating the boundaries of modern citizenship. That the status, privileges, and duties of foreign subjects as modern citizens were shaped through social actors variously interacting at and sometimes moving between the local, domestic, and international levels reveals the complex and multiscale character of the identity processes in question. Last, this elaborately negotiated category points to the difficulty of arriving at the kinds of clear-cut boundaries that modern state rule assumes. Through most of the nineteenth century, the Ottoman regime remained remarkably resilient, accommodating multiple claims, even over the same assets and individuals, and in the face of the obvious asymmetry of power, wherein foreign states were chipping away at its territorial sovereignty.

Taxation and Citizenship

Ottoman judicial reforms coincided with a wide-ranging fiscal reorganization that introduced, among others, an unprecedented real property tax in Izmir, further transforming the meaning of property and the rights and obligations attached to it. Soon after the proclamation of the Gülhane Edict, Tanzimat bureaucrats began to consolidate the various market and household dues that had historically made up the bulk of urban revenues and replace them with an equitable and universal tax levied on property *(emlak)* and professional income *(temettü)*.[69] In Izmir, the new tax, which was announced in 1841 and further detailed in 1843, was to yield a preset annual sum of 1,200,000 piastres and be enforced on all those who held real property, exercised a trade, or engaged in local commerce.[70] Not only did this formulation reposition these groups as equals before the law, but the taxation of urban property constituted a significant departure from existing practices. To be sure, land taxes in the form of tithe *(aşar)* or tribute *(haraç)* were an integral aspect of the Ottoman fiscal regime as in other agrarian empires. But urban property was generally viewed as the extension of one's residence and was, therefore, tax exempt.[71] Although during periods of crisis, certain forms of house- and household-based customary taxes, known as *tekalif-i örfiye,* provided additional funds to the treasury, never had such taxes been based on the market value of urban properties or the income they generated. Notably, the new tax made the person, rather than the community, liable for the tax, thus putting the state in more direct control of individuals, which in itself was a radical categorical shift. Even long-held individual taxes in the Ottoman Empire, such as the cizye collected from all male non-Muslim subjects, had generally been paid directly by the communities as a lump sum.

Fiscal restructuring, as with changes in the legal domain, was tentative, experimental, and riddled with conflicts and logistical problems, marking the midcentury decades as a period of continual search for effective methods of taxation and delaying the adoption of a modern property tax law across the empire until the late 1880s.[72] The taxation of urban property, first introduced in Izmir just before the Tanzimat proclamation, was a case in point. In 1831, new census reports increased the state's awareness of the distribution of resources among the empire's population, also highlighting urban wealth and, particularly, the urban real estate market as an important source of revenue.[73] A year later, to offset its budget deficits, the Porte issued a *firman* to impose a radical one-time tax on all of Izmir's proprietors, regardless of status, even stating that their failure to pay could result in the confiscation of their property. Strangely enough, the firman recognized that many of the potential taxpayers would be foreigners—tacitly admitting the widespread practice of property tenure by foreign subjects more than three decades before it was formalized. To preempt possible frictions, Tahir Bey, the new tax commissioner appointed by the Porte, proposed including foreign proprietors in the valuation process. Izmir's consular corps, which could not overtly deny the Porte's right to exact real-estate taxes, refused to get involved, deferring the matter to their embassies in Istanbul, hence avoiding becoming the target of complaints from their notoriously litigious citizens and protégés.[74] Property owners, who for their part saw in the tax all the makings of a permanent annual charge, feared that if it continued to be implemented only in Izmir, it was likely to become an onerous and unfair burden for the city's residents.[75] Invoking both established and emerging notions of justice, they argued that the firman was the product of an extortionist scheme, the real intention of which was to satisfy tax collectors rather than implement a fair and equitable tax, eventually asking the Porte to revoke it. In the end, the lack of consistent guidelines for allocation and apportioning, a general sense of unfairness among the people, and the state's concern about a negative backlash left the question unresolved.

The government's second attempt at real-estate taxation in Izmir met with similar local resistance. To begin with, efforts to collect the relevant data as the basis of taxation proved futile as the two surveys ordered by the central government in 1840 and 1844 rendered unreliable and incomplete information due to the lack of public cooperation.[76] Consequently, Tanzimat bureaucrats found themselves reverting to the familiar yet outmoded practice of requiring preset lump sums *(maktu)* from a given locality or community—the very practice they had set out to eradicate.[77] Moreover, the tax provision raised procedural questions as to whether owner-occupied houses and certain types of leasehold property were liable for the tax.[78] As with many premodern and early modern states, in the Ottoman Empire property tenure and use rights were not uniform, comprising both freehold property (mülk) and various forms of leasehold property (such as *gedik*) subject to specific conditions.[79] That the state had to continue working with these complex and customary forms of tenure and create new procedures to accommodate them in this process further complicated the implementation of the tax. Eventually, by 1849, after lengthy contested negotiations and pressure by the Porte on foreign governments regarding the internationally recognized right of a sovereign state to tax property within its territorial limits, local authorities and foreign consuls arrived at an accord. They would form a permanent, mixed cadastral commission *(emlak komisyonu)*—comprised of both Ottoman and foreign proprietors—to organize and oversee the taxation scheme.[80] Unlike earlier refusals to assist with the taxation scheme, as during Tahir Bey's tenure, foreign consuls almost unanimously nominated delegates from among their subjects to serve in the commission. A year later, even the Austrian consul, whose predecessor had repeatedly rebuffed attempts to reach some kind of compromise for nearly a decade, consented to this arrangement.[81]

Modern property taxation called for an unequivocal identification of each property with a specific individual, who could then be held directly responsible for the relevant payment. It also required greater standardization in determining taxable revenues to ensure equitability among taxpayers. Recognizing these exigencies, in 1850 the central government dispatched imperial commissioner Ali Nihad Efendi to Izmir to form the cadastral commission and ensure the continued support of the various local constituencies in the property evaluation process. A seasoned bureaucrat in the foreign office *(tercüme odası)*, Ali Nihad was expected to secure, in particular, the backing of the consuls. Between 1850 and 1854, with the assistance of the commission, he undertook a new cadastral survey, produced new registers, and set the methods and procedures for apportioning the tax, establishing the basis for modern taxation in Izmir. As Istanbul's French-language press extolled, this ambitious endeavor was a pioneering achievement that was first being tested in Izmir and Thessaloniki with an eye toward its broader implementation throughout the empire.[82]

Ali Nihad Efendi and the cadastral commission initiated two important changes. First, they regularized the urban nomenclature to make real estate more legible to the official eye. Customary and ad hoc naming conventions used at local courts for property identification may have achieved a level of precision and clarity suited to the needs of knowledgeable locals, but they would have been incomprehensible to state officials examining such records in Istanbul. To facilitate the identification of urban property, Ali Nihad proposed to have all major streets named and each house, shop, store, and vacant lot numbered. The name and nationality of the owner (or leaseholder) and the assessed value and annual income yield of the property were then recorded according to these numbers.[83] Although no cadastral (parcel-by-parcel) map was produced, Ali Nihad hired Italian engineer and exile Luigi Storari to create a new city map showing all streets and major roads, urban blocks, prominent landmarks, and surrounding fields, thereby providing a consistent basis for identifying property (see Map 2).[84] Second, the commission developed standard bureaucratic procedures to clarify taxable revenues by means of preprinted forms *(varaka-i matbuat),* which in itself was a novelty, and various categories of licenses *(patenta* or *ruhsatiye tezkeresi)* distributed according to income level. It also established the property tax on a uniform 0.4 percent of the assessed value of the real estate. Hence, the lump sum requirement of 1,200,000 piastres was broken down into different taxes with different bases and collection mechanisms.[85] Even if the conventional Ottoman practice of lump-sum taxation could not be abandoned, these developments ushered in key codifications associated with modern taxation systems, making taxation an individual obligation.

Perhaps most notably for the purposes of this chapter, the cadastral commission opened up a new way of entry in the city's political sphere, distinct from national and religious origins that had conventionally defined membership in the Ottoman polity. Although consuls and affluent foreign merchants had always wielded power and swayed local decisions by forming ad hoc committees or using diplomatic channels, they could not officially participate or be represented in administrative and advisory councils. In a special meeting held with Governor Salih Pasha in 1843 to discuss the property tax, a committee of French proprietors argued that their exclusion from the council apportioning the taxes was a major setback on the way to just taxation.[86] Such arguments found a receptive audience at a time when Ottoman reformers were trying to create a more participatory governance structure based on popular consent to mitigate potential abuses of power and evasion of responsibility.[87] Indeed, the very composition of the cadastral commission proclaimed residency and property-tax payment in the city as a legitimate basis for inclusion in local governance. The 1856 regulation *(nizamname),* which provided the charter for the commission, explicitly stated that the inhabitants *(sekene)* of the city should elect commission members from among its taxpayers *(eshab-ı vergi).* It further stipulated that the commission—which had to be composed of six foreign and eight Ottoman members—represented on the whole an "indigenous" body *(yerli bir heyet).*[88] Consequently, by extending political representation to foreign subjects, the commission acknowledged them as an integral part of the urban polity—an important step in making foreign subjects into citizens of Izmir.

The cadastral commission also established a new demand for reciprocity in terms of taxes in return for urban services. In addition to administering the land registry *(emlak dairesi)* and managing tax collection, the commission was entrusted with the task of implementing urban improvement. According to the 1856 regulation, the cadastral commission would annually collect a supplemental two hundred thousand piastres over the 1.2 million already required by the central government to fund these improvements. While this provision bestowed Izmir with one of the empire's earliest modern municipal bodies—contemporaneous with the creation of Istanbul's first modern municipal district—it also advanced a new understanding of tax obligation akin to modern practices of citizenship. As Izmir's correspondent to Istanbul's semiofficial press underlined in 1857, "Europeans would be taxed from now on; this is fine; but the intent of the governor should not be to impose taxes for the mere purpose of collecting funds. We feel that he owes something in return." Significantly, taxation was no longer the obligation of the subject as traditionally conceived in Islamic and Ottoman polities. It was a sacrifice that could only be justified by corresponding benefits. "The authorities should at least maintain the roads; they should allocate funds to remove the refuse that accumulates in neighborhoods, to prevent our streets from turning into pools, then into muddy marshes during rainy days, and to create an effective police service," he added, underscoring this exchange of taxes for urban improvement.[89] Similar complaints raised in the press as well as calls for greater accountability of municipal activities and for publishing cadastral revenues and expenditures corroborated this new reciprocity.

While the cadastral initiative offered foreign subjects the opportunity to press the government for representation and urban improvement, it fell short of raising the state's expected yearly returns and generated among local constituencies a great deal of skepticism about its viability as a municipal body. Within the first five years of its operation, the commission managed to collect more than 80 percent of the property taxes. But income taxes—which were more easily hidden from the official eye and subject to competing provisions granted by the capitulations—produced about 77 percent arrears and intractable resistance.[90] Even if the cadastral commission set up new rules, regulations, and bureaucratic standards for fair taxation, its ability to enforce these rules was at best limited and uneven. Local actors—including the committee members who were asked to run that machinery—needed to adjust to these changes, and more often than not, they continued to operate according to the more familiar informal and personalized transactions. As one commentator remarked, "the officers of the government of Smyrna have been in the habit of swindling it by taking less than the regular dues and returning still less, and the Smyrniots have profited by the system and wherever they could have not paid at all."[91] Moreover, the local press frequently called into question the competence of the commission as a municipal body, charging it with inaction regarding the poor condition of the streets while continuing to exact property taxes.[92] Above all, what made the commission problematic was the influence of the consular body on its decisions.[93] In newspaper commentaries, Izmir was often depicted as being "strewn with obstacles because of the various foreign authorities creating unwarranted difficulties for the local administration."[94]

These concerns compelled the central government to dissolve and reconstitute the commission according to the new principles formulated in the aforementioned 1867 protocol about foreign subjects' property tenure, thereby bringing these subjects under more direct state control. As discussed earlier, what made the protocol significant were not the property rights it granted to foreigners—already tacitly admitted long before the protocol—but the obligations and duties of citizenship it demanded through property. In all matters related to property, foreigners were henceforth required to obey and conform to the laws of the Ottoman state without the mediation of their consuls. In a memorandum to the consular corps, Governor İsmail Pasha explicitly stated that consulates would no longer be represented in the commission. Foreigners could only participate in the commission as individuals if they agreed to be treated as Ottoman nationals for property taxation purposes.[95] In 1869, the minister of foreign affairs, Âli Pasha, reiterated that the Porte was willing to admit foreigners in the commission insofar as their membership was based on terms equal to those of native Ottoman subjects. Further he insisted that the foreigners' representation at the commission had to be proportional to the size of their population in Izmir, not to the value of their property. This was an important amendment to the 1856 regulation intended to decrease the number of foreign subjects in the cadastral commission and by extension limit their leverage in municipal affairs.[96]

These provisions were not so much about excluding foreign subjects as devising new institutional frameworks through which to include them without compromising the practices and logic of modern state sovereignty. Accordingly, participation and inclusion in local politics was granted only to those that the sovereign state directly governed. In Izmir, bringing all property-related rights and obligations directly under state control required a decisive elimination of the loopholes that permitted continued consular infringements over domestic matters. Tanzimat bureaucrats were persistent in their demands. For example, in 1869, the governor entirely bypassed the consulates and invited foreign proprietors directly to the commission's elections, making their status closer to Ottoman subjects. Some governors also repeatedly expressed indignation at the use of *mixed* commissions, which they argued contradicted the principles of the 1867 protocol, further supporting the assimilationist line pursued by the central government.[97]

Not surprisingly, not all state amendments could be implemented as intended. Foreign subjects waged a forceful resistance as these new rules would limit their influence in municipal affairs and deprive them from the benefits of consular representation and foreign government intervention. Mobilizing all official channels that historically had worked for them, they pressured the Ottoman government to stay with the terms granted in the 1856 agreement. In 1870, they also formed a voluntary committee, known as the Commission for the Defense of Property.[98] Foreign proprietors were effective in manipulating the range of discourses at their disposal. They argued that since they had already long enjoyed customary property rights, the 1867 protocol merely gave them "an illusionary and quite unnecessary right" while robbing them of an "indisputable right" of representation, granted with the 1856 regulation.[99] This opposition allowed them to mitigate both the Ottoman government's encroachment and what they perceived as their own respective governments' complicity with the Ottoman state. The eventual resolution reached in 1874 took into account both the demographics and the value of property owned by foreigners, also permitting the consuls to oversee the election of foreign delegates serving on the cadastral commission.

The settlements reached in 1856, 1867, and 1874 constituted salient milestones in a long, conflicted, and largely unresolved process of defining foreign subjects' right to the city at a time when the central government was deliberating the rules of inclusion and exclusion in the imperial polity. As exemplified by the repeated changes to membership requirements in the cadastral committee, each time government officials and civic groups reached an agreement, new points of contention emerged, triggering yet another round of negotiations. This fluid state of affairs provided myriad tactical openings for foreign residents to position themselves as legitimate players in the city's governance. For example, in a memorandum addressed to Governor Hamdi Pasha in 1872, a delegation of twenty spokesmen of Izmir's foreign colonies regarded it as their "imperative duty" to inform him of the "complaints of the public" and pressed for urban improvements in various areas. The delegation, led by M. A. Edwards, the former editor of the local newspaper *L'Impartial*, introduced itself as follows:

> Although of foreign *nationality*, we do not feel any less tied to the country than the natives. Among us are families that have *resided* here for several generations, and we all have considerable *vested interests in real estate and trade*. It is on this basis that we believe to have the right to speak, both on our behalf and on behalf of our co-citizens, and we hope that you would like to hear us in the same spirit and in the same feeling; that of the public good, which brings us to you.[100]

This was a peculiar formulation that eluded both easy categorizations of native/foreign and a reductive understanding of Izmir's society in terms of ethnic and religious affiliation. It was rather an identity selectively derived from established forms of belonging based on residency and participation in the economic spheres of urban life and from emerging state-sanctioned forms of identity, premised on the equation of citizenship with nationality.[101]

Notably, the members of the delegation cleverly exploited the ambiguity created by the coexistence of both old and new forms of association with the city to justify their entitlement to urban services and goods. They demanded, among other things, improved sewers, the draining of the unhealthy marshes at the Point, the relocation of the quarantine facility at a safe distance from the city, an effective police force to deal with increasing assaults and crimes, and the removal of fishmongers' and other street vendors' encroaching on Fasula and Frank Street and blocking circulation. Above all, they insisted on making Izmir's municipal body from which they had recently been excluded more responsive to their concerns as taxpayers.[102]

As I expound in the next two chapters, during the midcentury decades, the scope, boundaries, and zones of contention of urban citizenship—as the rights and duties that defined inclusion in the urban polity—were unstable, yet profoundly intertwined with the built environment. Not only were they constituted through real property, but they were also enacted through people's ability to participate in the decisions that shaped their material environment. The provision of key urban services and infrastructure and the construction and control of these modern sites and services enabled people to forge new rights, new forms of exclusion, and political hierarchies, articulating, in the process, diverse understandings of who Izmir's public was, what it should be involved in, and how it should be represented.

2

Ordering the Streets
Public Space and Urban Governance

"OUR CITY OFFERS A SAD CONTRAST," wrote a correspondent to the *Journal de Constantinople* in 1861, alluding to the stark difference between Izmir's stylish new buildings and their unkempt surroundings.

> While new edifices are built with as much riches as elegance, marble is used unsparingly, the most coveted furniture is that of the most fashionable style, and while luxury is making astounding progress, our streets exhibit a truly shameful spectacle. The surroundings of Smyrna are in an even more appalling state.... In the past, we could make a promenade to the Point. Now we are barred from it because of the sheer quantity of puddles on the road. The same goes for the Caravan Bridge.... Hence, we have admirable weather, but cannot enjoy it, unless we are willing to sink in the mud up to the knees.[1]

The new mass media of the mid-nineteenth century dedicated considerable attention to the dreadful conditions of Izmir's streets. Commentators on Izmir's urban life constantly bemoaned the narrow and poorly paved streets, the absence of sidewalks, the open sewers, and the mounds of trash piling up along the roads. They also lamented the glaring absence of police that created an open field for all sorts of disorder. "Where are these sinister figures, who are freely walking our streets for over two months, coming from? Why [are] all these robberies [occurring] in broad-daylight on the streets, at the theater, and in the most busy coffeeshops?" questioned an Izmir reporter in 1856.[2] The perils of the urban environment—from losing one's footing to the risk of disease and of being attacked by the ruffians infesting the streets—were the staple of journalistic reports. If some of these images mobilized familiar orientalist tropes of dirt, chaos, and terror, they were intended, above all, to pressure Ottoman authorities to make improvements befitting Izmir's rising importance as the empire's second city by playing into the government's anxiety about being perceived as backward.

The unprecedented growth that mid-nineteenth-century Izmir experienced had palpable consequences on the material conditions and the social life of its streets. New transport technologies not only transformed the nature and volume of commercial activity but also severely strained the city's existing infrastructure. The arrival of steamship lines and shipping companies, followed by the construction of railroads, resulted in ever-increasing cargo traffic crossing the city and congesting its streets. Newly established small-scale urban industries, including calico-printing shops, silk-winding and soap factories, distilleries, and flour and paper mills, taxed existing water and drainage systems, making water provision and waste disposal a chronic problem.[3] Moreover Izmir's rising commercial importance and expanded work opportunities brought an influx of new migrants to the city, ranging from entrepreneurs and merchants to menial workers, seasonal laborers, and sailors. While many nameless migrants were housed in hastily laid-out neighborhoods on former orchards and marshlands, lacking proper roads and infrastructure, the wealth they generated funded the construction of lavish urban homes, new European-style institutions, and handsome suburban mansions for the rising mercantile classes.[4] Widening social and economic disparities also transformed the character of Izmir's public spaces. A diverse mix of people from a much wider range of backgrounds, occupations, and experiences than ever before had to share Izmir's streets. New rules, repeatedly posted in public spaces, listing the punishments for expressing religious prejudices and harassing passers-by, as well as the upsurge in pickpocketing and street assaults, were important indications of the kinds of tensions that characterized day-to-day urban life.[5]

Alarmed by these changes, both government officials and local leaders and merchants sought to reform the management of streets and public spaces, making repeated attempts to devise new regulations and a more effective municipal apparatus to respond to the city's pressing needs. Historically, in Ottoman cities, a patchwork of autonomous and often unconnected local institutions provided the necessary urban services. Charitable endowments *(vakıf,* pl. *evkaf)* supplied public fountains, road construction, cleaning services, and public parks. Various agents tied to the Janissary corps—the elite troops of Ottoman soldiers—assisted the kadı in supervising the markets and in matters of police duties, firefighting, building activity, and public order.[6] The collective initiative of neighborhoods *(mahalle),* religious groups *(cemaat),* and guilds *(esnaf)* also contributed to meeting the needs of urban communities, providing funds for communal institutions and hospitals and relief to indigent populations.[7] In a dramatic shift from such pre-existing institutions and their discrete provisions, state and local actors envisioned rationalizing urban services by consolidating them under one management and control. Accordingly, the cleaning, paving, lighting, regularization, and policing of the streets would become the exclusive province of a single, more centralized municipal authority.

In many rapidly growing commercial cities around the globe, streets and public spaces became increasingly subject to conflicting claims and differing views on use rights. They had to respond to emerging health and safety demands, accommodate heavier loads and more traffic, and facilitate the quick and easy flow of goods and people. At the same time, as public property, they had to balance complex sets of individual rights to serve the common interests of urban dwellers. Although these challenges were experienced throughout the modernizing urban world, they produced distinctive responses in each case as new measures had to be weighed against existing practices.[8] To begin with, in Izmir and other Ottoman cities, Islamic codes and customary practices that had historically informed the production of urban public space gave greater protection to private property than legal systems based on Roman law. If a temporary encroachment on the street benefited the owner of an adjacent property, without presenting a substantial obstacle to people's right of passage and shared use-rights to the street, it could eventually acquire legitimacy and become a permanent right. Given this more negotiated relationship between public and private rights, modern street regulations, which rested largely on a uniform and unequivocal conception of public rights and obligations, had to be reconciled with individual proprietors' equally plausible private claims over the street. In addition, Izmir's streets brought together people divided not only by class, language, and culture but, as examined in the previous chapter, also by legal status. While new police measures were repeatedly pronounced, they could not be evenly enforced on a population governed by different, partially overlapping, and sometimes conflicting jurisdictions. When a suspect claimed foreign protections, extraterritorial provisions hampered police action, further complicating the supervision of the streets and the everyday power relations within them.

In what follows, I begin by laying out some of the urban anxieties that prompted government officials and local groups to develop new institutional and practical measures to regulate Izmir's streets. Although these measures often yielded mixed results, they were highly revealing of the political processes at play and of the particular constraints under which urban improvements had to take place. Next, I turn to repeated efforts made at creating a modern municipal apparatus, highlighting how institutional configurations and the material conditions of the streets were intimately interrelated, mutually shaping and inflecting one another. The delineation of state and local powers, the allocation of already limited funds, and representation and election procedures directly informed the nature and scope of urban improvements. At the same time, the deplorable state of the streets and public spaces legitimized new political hierarchies and new claims for inclusions in and exclusions from the municipal body. Finally, I focus on the actual challenges of improving the streets, illustrating how relational understandings of public and private, and diverging yet often equally modern views of public nuisance, appropriate street use, and rights to public spaces converged in Izmir's streets, resulting in a negotiated modus vivendi.

Urban Anxieties: Fires, Epidemics, and Ruffians

Fires, epidemics, and brigandage were three great fears endemic to everyday life in nineteenth-century Izmir. Their pervasiveness and inherent unpredictability lent a certain precariousness to social and economic life, while also impeding urban dwellers' sense of a safe and secure urban environment. To be sure, these were different types of threats, each brought on by specific material conditions, and affecting people differentially. Whereas fires and epidemics had far-ranging destructive effects, brigandage and robberies were generally more contained, often targeting specific groups and individuals. But in the minds of locals, these threats shared an important quality. Their effective containment demanded better control over streets and street life. Hence, in a rapidly growing commercial city dependent on greater environmental stability, these chronic anxieties drove local groups and authorities to adopt radical new measures for supervising the streets.

Consuming fires, some accidental, others arson, erupted periodically, ravaging the city's mostly timber-built structures and opening swaths of land for redevelopment.[9] Following a major fire in 1834, most of the Frank quarter had to be rebuilt. Another disastrous fire in 1841 destroyed about four thousand houses and public buildings and twenty-five hundred stores, resulting in the extensive reconstruction of Muslim and Jewish neighborhoods.[10] Four years later, in 1845, a catastrophic fire burned down the Armenian quarter, several hospitals serving various segments of the Christian population, large sections of Frank Street, and the Greek neighborhoods of St. George and St. Dimitri, driving an even more extensive redevelopment.[11] Within the decade between 1835 and 1845 much of the city's building stock was destroyed and re-created (see Maps I.3 and I.4).

Despite their calamitous aftermath, fires offered an important opportunity for renovating old institutions, particularly in prospering non-Muslim neighborhoods. Old regulations prevented the erection of new buildings for non-Muslim worship and required government authorization for the renovation of old ones.[12] Fires, however, facilitated the granting of such permission. Coupled with the financial support of a new moneyed class, they encouraged the creation of more prestigious churches, bringing in significant changes to the cityscape and making the prosperity of the community visually more prominent. In the years following the 1845 fire, for example, the Armenian Church of St. Stephen (Figure 2.1) was reconstructed, the Orthodox Church of St. George (Figure 2.2) was entirely demolished and rebuilt, the Catholic hospital of St. Antoine moved to a new building, the hospital of St. Roch was established, and the Greek hospital was considerably expanded (see Map I.3).[13] In each case, the new buildings that went up were of a far more elegant style than the originals (Figure 2.3).

Above all, the 1845 fire provided an important impetus for introducing new measures related to the form and dimensions of streets, constituting the earliest known effort in Izmir at bringing geometric regularity to the urban fabric. Unlike former postfire reconstructions that maintained preexisting land-use conditions and followed the same footprint, the 1845 fire resulted in redesigning the Armenian quarter and nearby commercial streets on a new grid plan (Map 2.1). New postfire development guidelines issued by the central government mandated that streets two to five pics wide (5–12.5 feet) be enlarged to a minimum width of six to eight pics (15–20 feet), balconies and overhangs conform to specific sizes, and fire walls be erected between every three to four houses (Figure 2.4).[14] Widening and realigning the streets constituted a radical departure from established postfire reconstruction practices. They required house owners to surrender a portion of their property for a wider street—an idea that often met with resistance. During the rebuilding of the Armenian quarter, a consensus was reached when each owner was allowed to encroach on the immediate neighbor's property for the amount of land he or she gave up for public use, thus compensating for individual loss. Meanwhile, owners of corner lots, who had to relinquish land to their neighbors in both directions, received a monetary compensation.[15]

Wider and straighter streets not only alleviated the risk of fire and devastation but also facilitated movement between critical elements of the city's commercial landscape, namely the Caravan Bridge, the bazaar, and the nearby harbor area. The realigned Tilkilik Avenue or the newly created Reşidiye and Haliliye Avenues, which cut through the existing fabric (Map 2.1b), permitted easier connection between the Caravan Bridge and the port. Moreover, these measures gave an

FIGURE 2.1. Central dome and bell tower, Armenian Church of St. Stephen, rebuilt after fire in 1845. Postcard. Courtesy of Orlando Carlo Calumeno and Birzamanlar Yayıncılık.

Figure 2.2. Greek Orthodox Church of St. George with Kadifekale in the background, to the left, by Rubellin Père & Fils, ca. 1880. Courtesy of the Suna & İnan Kıraç Research Institute for Mediterranean Civilizations.

appearance of geometrical order, progress, and modernity to the neighborhood, raising property values. Soon after the rebuilding, the regularity of the streets of the Armenian quarter and "its charming new houses" were used as an example to encourage other improvements.[16] In 1860, following another fire that destroyed the St. Dimitri neighborhood, *Journal de Constantinople* announced that the government intended to widen the streets of the neighborhood on the Armenian model.[17]

Epidemics, like fires, produced devastating effects, destroying a considerable percentage of the urban population. Although the plague receded by the mid-nineteenth century, a major occurrence in 1812 decimated about 20 percent of the population. Another outbreak between 1836 and 1838 resulted in the deaths of at least 7 percent of the population.[18] In addition, cholera, which made its first appearance in Izmir in 1831, continued to erupt in the city throughout the nineteenth

FIGURE 2.3. View framing the major churches, by Rubellin Père & Fils, ca. 1870. In the background from left to right are the tower of St. Photini, the dome of St. Stephen, and the Church of St. George. Courtesy of the Suna & İnan Kıraç Research Institute for Mediterranean Civilizations.

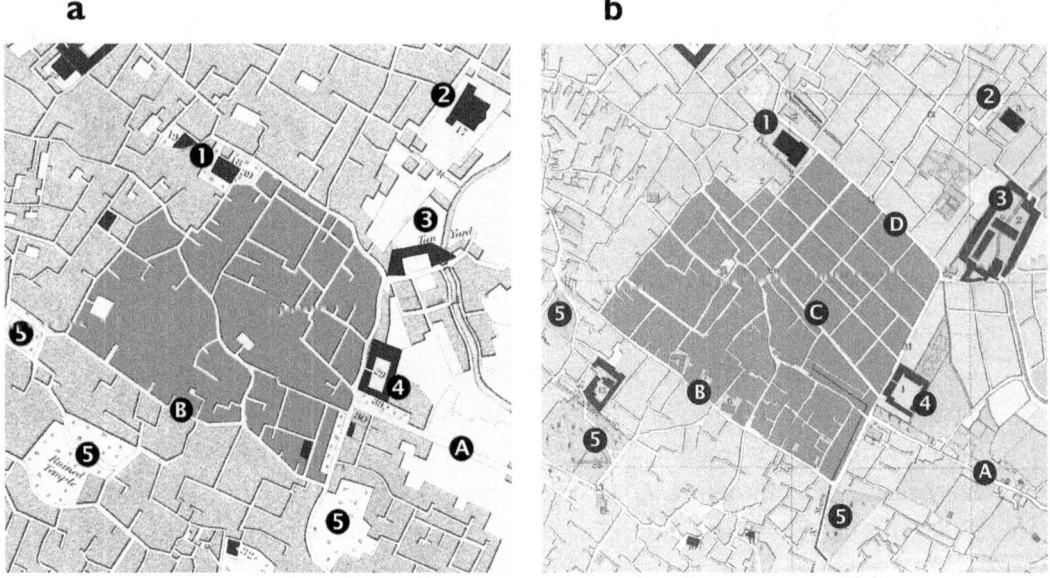

MAP 2.1. (a) Armenian quarter before the fire; based on the map by Lieutenant Thomas Graves (Map I.2). (b) Armenian quarter after the fire; based on the plan by Storari (Map 2). The heart of the Armenian quarter lay between St. Stephen, the calico factory, and Reşidiye and Haliliye Avenues.

LEGEND: : 1 = St. Stephen (Armenian); 2 = St. Dimitri (Greek Orthodox); 3 = tannery *(tabakhane)*; 4 = calico factory *(basmahane)*; 5 = cemetery; A = Kemer Avenue (or Caravan Bridge Road); B = Tilkilik Avenue; C = Haliliye Avenue; D = Reşidiye Avenue.

century.[19] Severe outbreaks in the summers of 1831, 1849, and 1865 took thousands of lives, producing in 1865 over four thousand deaths within less than three months.[20] Up until the early nineteenth century, a fatalistic understanding of disease, based on religious attitudes that viewed epidemics as the will of God and thus unavoidable, had discouraged organized efforts for preemptive measures. Responses were at best reactive and individual, ranging from the avoidance of bodily contact to temporary exodus from the city. The rich escaped to the nearby villages of Buca, Burnabat, and Kokluca (see Map 1), where they held secondary houses, or shut themselves in their homes for the duration of the epidemic, sealing themselves against outside elements. Although Izmir recovered time and again from the ruinous effects of such scourges—owing, in large part, to extensive communal relief efforts and private charity in their aftermath—epidemics caused significant recession in trade.[21] Soon after the cholera epidemic was confirmed in 1865, over a quarter of the population fled, halting commercial activity and severely crippling the local economy.[22]

In an economy increasingly reliant on international trade and shipping, ravages caused by epidemics became a greater concern. Coupled with new knowledge about preventive measures, they prompted new urban regulations for keeping

FIGURE 2.4. View of a regulated street facade, ca. 1910. All facades are aligned and regular second-story bays project over the street. From Frédéric Boissonnas, *L'image de la Grèce: Smyrne* (Geneva: Editions d'Art Boissonnas, 1919).

contamination away from the streets. Soon after the 1836–38 plague, new public health procedures imposed quarantine on ships and required health passes from incoming passengers.[23] Beginning in 1840, those suspected of contagion were detained in a new, purpose-built lazaretto at a safe distance from urbanized areas to prevent the spread of disease within city borders. Originally located on the shore, at some distance from the slaughterhouses to the southwest of the city (see Map 1), in an area that eventually bore its name, Karantina, Izmir's lazaretto was spacious enough to accommodate four to five hundred individuals.[24] By the 1860s the city's southwesterly growth infringed on the lazaretto's *cordon sanitaire*, making the building obsolete and necessitating its relocation to an island at the entrance of the Gulf of Izmir. But on the whole, quarantine practices proved effective in shielding the city from future plagues.[25]

Similarly, the 1865 cholera epidemic prompted a series of precautionary and palliative measures. These measures, however, targeted specifically the hygiene of the streets. Soon after the epidemic erupted, Governor Reşid Pasha endorsed, and further promoted, the efforts of the Committee of Hygiene and Relief—a voluntary association initiated by doctors, sanitary officers, consuls, and leading merchants and assisted by the Committee of Ladies—to mitigate the inroads of the epidemic.[26] Presided over by British consul Robert Cumberbatch, the committee ordered a large-scale cleaning and treatment of open sewers in several neighborhoods suffering from poor drainage and provided street-sweeping and refuse-removal services.[27] These actions were informed by contemporary theories that viewed miasma, the noxious exhalation of decomposing organisms infecting the air, as the main agent for the propagation of disease.[28] The mounting anxiety of sickness and fever in Izmir, when stagnant lakes formed in the heart of town during seasons of rain and extreme heat, indicates the strength of such convictions. For example, in summer months, streets were seen as "little better than cesspools, whose nephitic exhalations place the health of the residents in direct jeopardy."[29] At times, shops were even closed because "sewers spread such an infection."[30] Apart from eliminating the dirt that piled up on the streets and the stench of sewers, the committee also posted instructions in various languages in public spaces, asking residents to follow personal hygiene recommendations and helping them identify early symptoms of the disease.[31] Whether or not such warnings could evenly penetrate the various segments of urban society, they reveal how city leaders and authorities perceived the relationship between streets, public health, and individual bodies.

The 1865 cholera epidemic also led to sanitary measures that affected the built environment in more permanent ways. A government order issued in 1865 forbade interment within urbanized areas, requiring instead the creation of extramural cemeteries.[32] Until then, burials took place in small urban cemeteries next to mosques, churches, and hospitals. Muslims and Jews also had larger cemeteries on the outskirts of town, next to the Caravan Bridge and to the south of the city on the slope of the Değirmendağı, which also provided recreational outdoor areas for the local population. Within a decade, new interment measures, based on considerations of public health *(hıfz-ı sıhhat-ı umumiye),* resulted in the formation of a number of extramural cemeteries. Local Greek and Armenian communities established large general suburban cemeteries.[33] The Catholic community, on the recommendation of its archbishop, built a private cemetery on the road to Buca next to the tracks of the Izmir–Aydın railway. Meanwhile, the cemetery of the British community having been expropriated for the construction of the Izmir–Kasaba railway and the newly allocated Protestant cemetery being subject to continual floods, the central government, after long deliberations and discussions, eventually offered a new piece of land for Protestant burial to be shared by local British, Dutch, and Prussian (later German) subjects (Map 2.2).[34]

While efforts at controlling fires and epidemics brought about new ways of setting up and maintaining the streets, the necessity of ensuring the security of property and person made the streets the focus of new disciplinary measures. With the availability of new wealth to plunder and more potential victims, brigandage, which had long been a way of life in the Western Anatolian countryside, gained a new force and notoriety in the mid-nineteenth century. In the local press, as in government and consular reports, it was depicted as "the plague of the province."[35] Imagined in a similar way to disease, it erupted time and again, causing a significant threat to public safety in the region. Gangs, comprising tribesmen of the Western Anatolian mountains *(zeybek)* or Greek and Albanian migrants from the Aegean Islands and Balkan provinces, periodically caused public alarm in Izmir and its immediate countryside.[36] In the early 1850s, the gang of Katırcı Yanni and his associate Nicoli were responsible for numerous assaults in Izmir and its environs.[37] Having gained a foothold in the village of Buca—the suburban retreat for Izmir's mercantile elite—they frequently kidnapped affluent residents for ransom. "At this time, the city of Smyrna offers no more security than the countryside," explained a group of British residents in a petition directed in 1852 to the Sublime Porte through their embassy.[38] "Soon after sunset, walking on the streets has become a danger, even in the most crowded neighborhoods. In the past days, several individuals, men and women, have been robbed of their belongings, and every morning we hear news of homes and stores, broken in by night."[39]

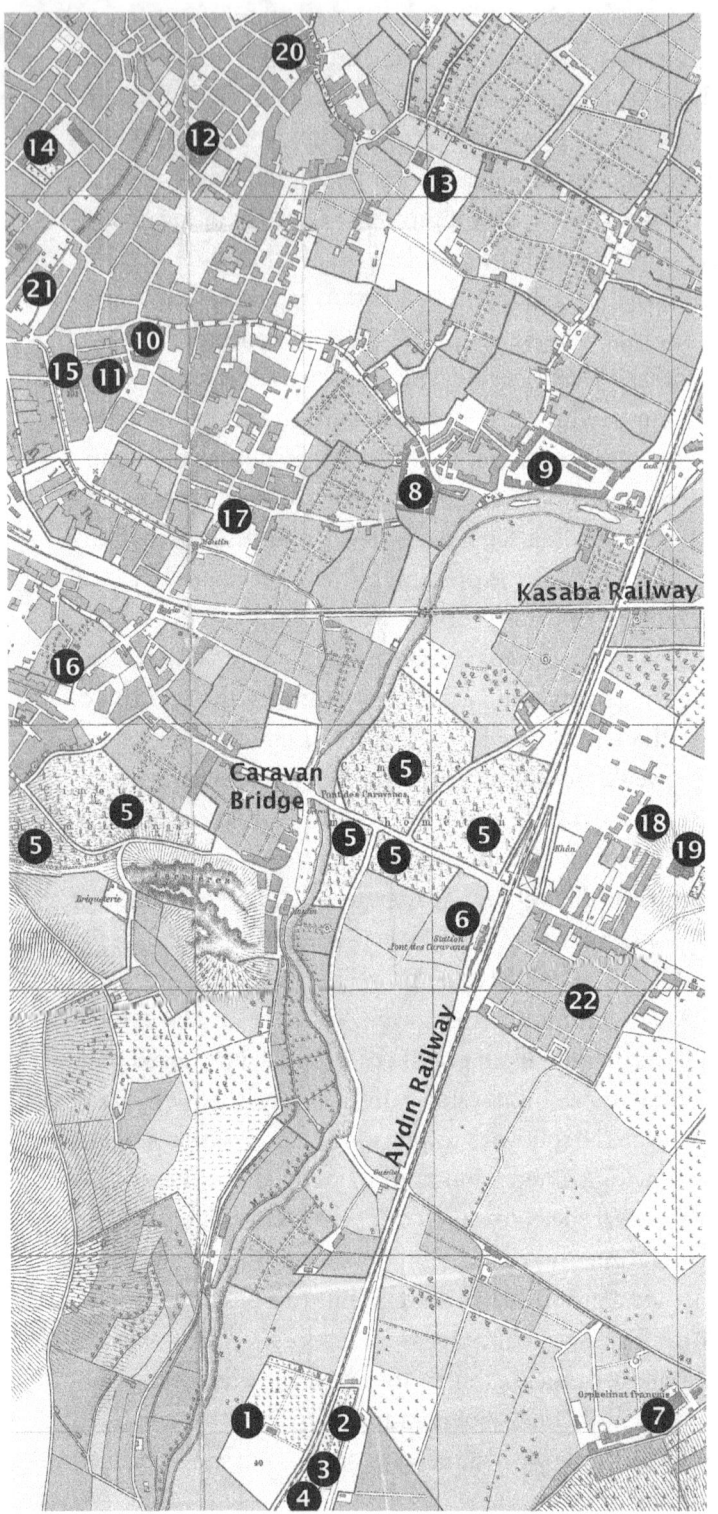

MAP 2.2. Relocation of the Catholic and Protestant cemeteries to the urban fringe, based on the plan by Saad (Map 3).

LEGEND: 1. Catholic cemetery; 2. Protestant cemetery (British); 3. Protestant cemetery (Dutch); 4. Protestant cemetery (Prussian); 5. Muslim cemetery; 6. train station at Caravan Bridge; 7. French orphanage; 8. European hospice; 9. Greek hospice; 10. Armenian hospice (Murtakya Khan); 11. Armenian hospice (Küçük Murtakya Khan), 12. Hospital of St. Roch; 13. British (Girls') Institute; 14. St. Dimitri (Greek Orthodox); 15. St. Evangelistra (Greek Orthodox); 16. St. Vukla (Greek Orthodox); 17. St. Nicola (Greek Orthodox); 18. St. Apostles (Greek Orthodox); 19. St. Constantin (Greek Orthodox); 20. Çikudya Khan; 21. tannery; 22. Tepecik.

While anxieties about security were not new, they were exacerbated by the unprecedented demographic changes, which included the proliferation of dense neighborhoods with increasingly restive populations, the influx of sailors and transient workers through the port, and the movement of irregular troops and war refugees. Daily brawls and drunken provocations took place in heavily populated neighborhoods, particularly near taverns and coffeehouses. Sailors passing through the city were frequently reported to be intoxicated, reeling through the streets, and were eventually detained in consular prisons.[40] Poorer Greek neighborhoods on the urban fringe—which lay in close vicinity to the more affluent quarter, around the Point—remained outside the range of local authorities and were notorious as the sites of "murderous assaults."[41] In sum, the increased and more diverse working-class populations were regarded as closely linked with the manifold threats of the streets. What made the streets even more treacherous— at least in the minds of Izmir's polite society—were the neighborhood toughs *(palikaraki)*, whom the Izmir correspondent for the *Levant Herald* declared to be the city's worst plague in the last quarter century. "This lawless class mostly of the offspring of the laboring population leads, from very childhood, a life of dissipation, passing their existence in the myriad of coffeehouses and drinking shops."[42] Moreover, political instability at the fringes of the empire periodically brought army irregulars from neighboring regions to Izmir, whence they were dispatched to war zones, triggering weeks of unrest in the city. Wars and defeats also brought over thirty thousand refugees from the Balkans, a large proportion of whom were resettled in rapidly laid-out neighborhoods in Değirmendağı, on the southern slopes of Izmir.[43]

In response, the government sought to improve security on the streets through a combination of familiar and innovative measures. In 1850, Governor Halil Pasha forbade individuals from carrying firearms in the street under penalty of fine and imprisonment. He also ordered the early closing of coffeehouses and taverns to limit drinking and to prevent thieves from gathering in coffeehouses, where they were believed to plot their schemes. To keep migration in check, he required incoming migrants to find a job and a sponsor *(kefil)* within two weeks of their arrival, or risk deportation.[44] He also established a neighborhood watch, particularly in nearby suburbs, making all residents, native or foreign, sign a mutually binding pledge to not host, feed, or help robbers, and to denounce neighbors who did otherwise.[45]

In addition to these commonly accepted measures enforced during periods of crisis, enterprising governors also introduced new street-surveillance techniques of a preventive and more sustained nature, each bringing his personal twist to a process that continued through the first decades of the twentieth century. At the beginning of their terms, governors usually instituted a night watch, recognizing the importance of effective police supervision. In 1860, governor Osman Pasha asked for foot soldiers of the regular army *(nizami)* to make the rounds, bringing greater order and efficiency to street watch.[46] In 1862, when the chief of police, Emin Bey, reconstituted the police department—which had been established in 1845 as a specialized agency directly under central government authority—he also extended the range of patrols all the way to the Point.[47] In the following years, fifteen to twenty gendarmes *(zaptiye)* were assigned to the Frank quarter and surrounding neighborhoods to watch the streets at night. The local press even called for instituting regular beats for these gendarmes, expressing a desire for more systematic forms of surveillance.[48] During his tenure in 1881, Governor Midhad Pasha, who took exceptionally stringent measures to restore order after a period of intense banditry, also set up more effective modes of street patrol. Officers walked the beat in pairs to reduce the risk of being attacked and, at times, were followed by an additional two to three gendarmes.[49] Although Izmir's police force remained numerically insufficient and underpaid, beginning in the second half of the nineteenth century, its recruitment process, duties, appearance, and mode of patrolling were modernized.[50] More significantly, a permanent police force always on duty, rather than intervening only during crises, brought about more routinized forms of street surveillance.

In the mid-nineteenth century, the provision of street lighting followed a similarly incremental and patchy process that ultimately made nighttime illumination a default condition of the street. Until then, most streets were lit up by the casual glow of paper lanterns that passersby were required to carry when they went out at night. During the tenures of Halil Pasha in 1850 and Kayserili Ahmed Pasha in 1863, the carrying of lanterns was further enforced, violators risking arrest by night patrols.[51] Occasionally, collective efforts by homeowners also helped brighten the streets. For example, in 1862 the residents of the Point provided individual kerosene lamps for lighting the area and the adjoining streets, often described as the "sanctuary of thieves and bravos."[52] In the following year, similar lamps were placed along major thoroughfares and paid for by house owners.[53] Eventually, beginning in 1864, gas lamps introduced more systematic street lighting, charting safer routes through specific sections of town (Figure 2.5). At first, gas lamps supplied a frail light and were placed only along a triangular path, linking the Point, the bazaar, and the Basmahane railway station (Map 2.3). Even in these initial phases, they helped create a space through which residents felt they could move more freely after dark.[54]

In sum, Izmir's new material and demographic conditions, which drove urban groups to demand a healthier, safer, and more secure environment, brought about important changes in the ways streets were managed, controlled, and supplied with amenities. From the 1840s on, the central government created new institutions such as quarantine offices and police departments to address questions of public health and public security at the local level. But several pressing problems remained uncovered by the newly formed and inherited administrative structures. In particular, the provision and maintenance of sewers, roads, and similar amenities required institutional mechanisms beyond the scale and capability of individual neighborhoods and communities. In addition, the abolition of the Janissary corps in 1826, during Mahmud II's centralizing reforms, had already deprived towns and cities of an important organ of market control and revenue collection. The Ministry of Ihtisab (or market inspection), founded shortly afterwards to fill

FIGURE 2.5. Street lighting around Bella Vista, by Rubellin Père & Fils, ca. 1880. Courtesy of the Suna & İnan Kıraç Research Institute for Mediterranean Civilizations.

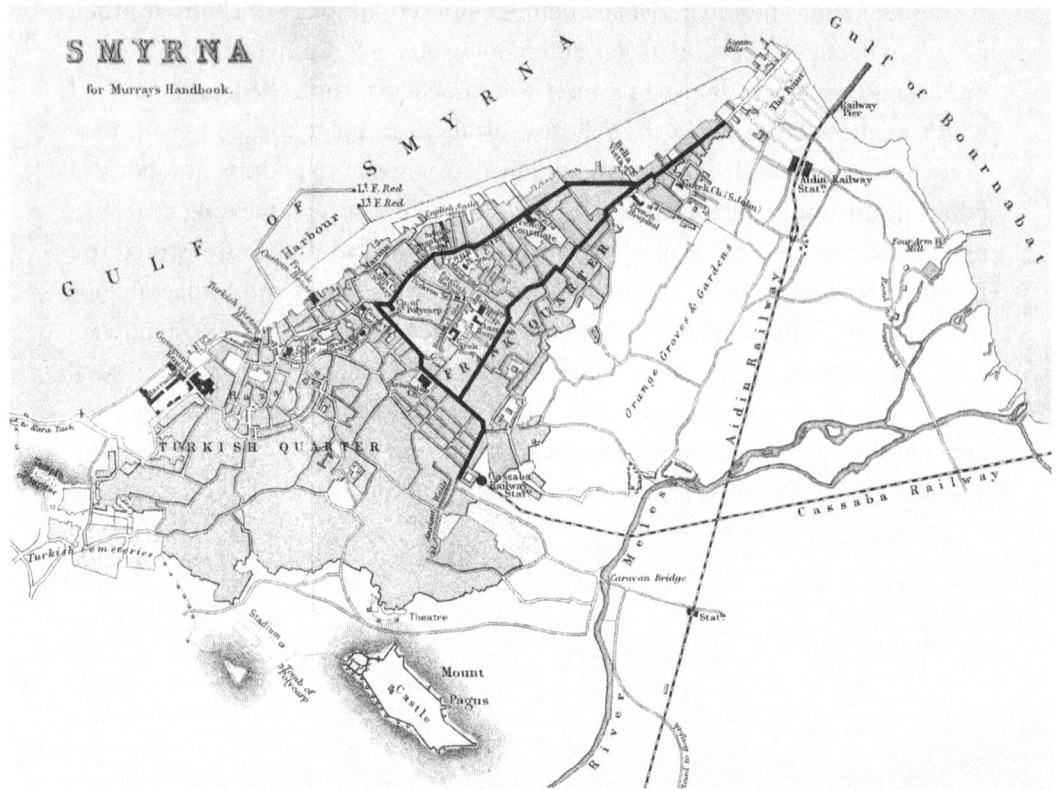

MAP 2.3. The path of street lighting in 1864, based on *Murray's Handbook for Travellers in Turkey in Asia including Constantinople, the Bosphorus, Plain of Troy, Siales of Cyprus, Rhodes, &c., Smyrna, Ephesus, and the Routes to Persia, Bagdad, Mosool, &c.* (London: John Murray, 1878), facing page 247.

this gap, was chiefly concerned with fiscal matters rather than delivering actual services.[55] Its eventual elimination in the early 1850s signaled not just another vicissitude of reformist policy, but a new will on the part of both central government agents and urban interest groups to devise municipal organizations more attuned to the provision of modern street services.

Articulating a Municipal Apparatus

The street measures discussed above coincided with the diffusion of modern fields of knowledge and practices related to urban planning and management. The mid-nineteenth century was a time when new urban standards were reformulating both the form of the streets and the social life within them.[56] In many parts of the world, the jumble of house signs and house fronts was tidied away to provide clear sight lines, new illumination technologies eliminated dark corners, and new forms of surveillance placed the street under the direct gaze of public authorities. In the United States and in Europe and its colonies, streets had become necessary objects of reform, the foci of new disciplinary technologies, and showcases for an idealized modern urban order. Regular pavements, maintenance services, night lighting, prohibitions against encroachment onto the streets, and the introduction of street signage not only made urban outdoor spaces more orderly, hygienic, and inoffensive environments, but were also seen as the tangible manifestations of a civilized and progressive urban society.

Ottoman bureaucrats recognized the importance of urban improvements in conferring prestige and distinction to their capital. Ottoman military alliance with France and England during the Crimean War opened the door to unprecedented foreign capital investment, bringing much wealth to Istanbul's business elite who began to demand modern amenities and institutions found in contemporary European cities.[57] Taking advantage of this favorable environment, the central government introduced reforms in Istanbul's municipal organization. These reforms did not chart a single linear process by which a municipal government gradually assumed a set of predetermined responsibilities for urban improvement. Rather, city officials and government agents engaged in a flurry of institution building, often scrapping or modifying their recently developed creations. The short-lived Istanbul Prefecture (Istanbul Şehremaneti) in 1854, the Advisory Board for Ordering the City (Intizam-ı Şehir Komisyonu) in 1855, and the model municipality for the district of Galata two years later—all envisioned as agencies capable of providing the urban improvements urgently needed in the capital— were important indications of the ad hoc nature of institutional formation.

The effective provision of modern urban services was also behind the 1864 Provincial Code (Vilayet Nizamnamesi) aimed at reconfiguring municipal government and jurisdictions in the provinces. A year later, a long article in the *Levant Herald* announced that the duties of municipalities in Ottoman cities, hitherto very varied and limited to the judicial sphere, soon would encompass the characteristic duties of municipalities in Europe—that is, "cleansing, paving, and lighting the streets."[58] In Izmir, for over two decades, the local press had been calling attention to the city's urgent environmental needs. In an article devoted to the issue in 1845, the founder and editor of *Écho de l'Orient,* Th. Bargigli, underlined that it was the business of the local administration to repair the roads, upgrade the underground drainage system, and clean the streets. He also blamed the haphazard urban developments that exacerbated existing flooding problems on the northern urban fringe to the lack of effective management. "Twenty new neighborhoods have been built within the last fifteen years. If a capable architect had planned the layout at the outset, we could have enjoyed the benefits of having wide, open, well-ventilated, and well-paved streets."[59]

At Izmir residents' behest, the central government initiated a series of efforts to establish a municipality that could deliver modern urban services. The repurposing of the cadastral commission into a municipal body in 1856, the formation of an autonomous municipality following the Galata model in 1868, and the creation of two municipal districts according to the provisions of the Provincial Code in 1879 attest to the trial-and-error nature of institutional formation. However short-lived these municipal experiments, a closer look at their functions, their perceived shortcomings, and the roadblocks they experienced reveals how Izmir's municipal institutions were simultaneously connected to local politics, national restructuring, and international interests. Moreover, these municipal institutions were not mere outcomes of these broader processes; the specific street improvements and amenities (or lack thereof) that they provided shaped the nature of municipal politics, the content of state reforms, and the course of international investment. In other words, the material conditions of Izmir's street inflected broader political and institutional processes. In essence, then, these municipal experiments reveal the inextricable links between the physical and the sociopolitical.

The cadastral commission was the first in a number of attempts to provide municipal functions. As discussed in the previous chapter, the central government had initially formed the commission as a local agency for registering property and levying income taxes derived from property and trades. Ultimately, negotiations between the central government and taxpayers resulted in assigning a portion of these taxes to the commission to fund needed improvements in Izmir. Consequently, the commission's tasks came to embrace several urban-planning and management duties characteristic of modern municipalities, including the regulation of private construction through building licensing and inspection, the alignment of streets, and the control of encroachment to public ways.

For most of its decade-long existence, however, several obstacles stalled the commission's work. To begin with, resistance to taxation resulted in several years' arrears owed to the state, ultimately undercutting the commission's returns. Moreover, the commission's ability to proceed with urban improvements depended on local government agents. Although local taxpayers constituted the governing board, the commission was presided over by the governor, who held the power to enforce regulations and execute the works. Instabilities within the central government and the relatively rapid turnover of Izmir's governors, whose tenure rarely exceeded one year, often hindered the commission's performance. Also, although the commission appeared to imply collaboration between Ottoman state agents and consuls in dealing with local questions, it was, in fact, an embattled alliance. On the one hand, government agents sought to set limits on consular interference in internal affairs—even if they periodically had to call on the consuls for assistance in controlling and taxing local groups who claimed foreign protections. On the other hand, consuls strove to increase their influence to sway local decisions that could advance their business interests or win their conationals contracts and concessions in the region.

Against all these odds, the commission implemented some modern urban-planning measures, particularly with the backing of reform-minded governors. Especially after fires, the cadastral commission drew up new plans, aligning the streets as regularly as possible and allocating them the minimum width prescribed in the 1845 government order.[60] It tried to reorder densely built commercial areas to create more room for public circulation. For example, on the initiative of Kabuli Mehmed Pasha in 1864, the commission succeeded in demolishing encroachments by shops on public thoroughfares, easing the flow in several bazaar areas. It also relocated the market, improvised on Sundays and holidays along Frank Street, further north to Fasula Place to improve circulation on the town's main artery.[61] Also under the auspices of the commission, the provincial government decided to undertake such projects as the demolition of the old crusader's castle near the bazaar and its replacement with orderly stores, the relocation of the slaughterhouses and the quarantine facilities at a safe distance from urban areas, and the building of a prestigious government palace in place of the dilapidated Kâtipzade mansion.[62]

Nonetheless, the cadastral commission suffered fatal flaws. Since its inception, the influence of the consular body on its operations had called into question its legitimacy as a representative organ of the city. The issue gained momentum in 1864, when the central government assigned the commission to negotiate the cost of lighting Izmir's streets with the Smyrna Gas Company. Two years earlier, the Smyrna Gas Company, a London-based firm, had obtained from the Porte the concession for building a gas plant at the Point and illuminating the city with (piped) gas. According to the concession, the gas dues, imposed by the company, would be assessed and collected in agreement with Izmir's representative. Given the consuls' clout in the commission and perceived conflict of interest, many taxpayers refused to recognize the commission as qualified to uphold local interests against international contractors. Although the commission succeeded in dropping the cost that the gas company had initially asked, taxpayers found the price excessive compared to what they had formerly paid for kerosene lamps, street sweeping, and cleaning.[63] The legitimacy of the cadastral commission as a municipal body remained at the heart of the conflict over the cost of gas, pitting taxpayers, the Smyrna Gas Company, and the cadastral commission against one another. The resulting gas strike, during which the company cut off the supply to the street lamps for over three years, dealt a final blow to the commission's municipal functions, visibly confirming its shortfall as a local governing body.

As the cadastral commission fell out of favor, Izmir's enterprising mercantile elite began to lobby for a municipal organization with more revenues and autonomy. Already in 1859, some of them had been promoting the achievements of the recently created municipality in Galata, soliciting the support of Governor Muammer Pasha in establishing a similar institution in their city. In a petition drafted to the grand vizier with over two hundred local signatories of all nationalities, they argued a similar institution in Izmir would be beneficial to both the state and the city. In addition to contributing to the "comfort and beautification" of cities, a modern municipality, they maintained, would "simplify the relationship between citizens and the governing authority by relegating to a special committee the responsibility of everyday affairs and relieve the Treasury from expenditures that pertain to cities only."[64] Similarly, the local press presented the creation of a municipality as the panacea for urban problems. By addressing "a myriad of issues associated with urban improvement and beautification, which are beyond the responsibility of the central government," a municipality would place Izmir "among the most beautiful cities of Europe."[65] Eventually in 1867, recognizing the size of the city and the neglected state of its streets and marketplaces, the Porte authorized Governor İsmail Pasha to form a municipal council *(belediye meclisi)* on the Galata model.[66]

Like its forerunner, Izmir's new municipal organization had a rocky history, reconstituting and repurposing itself repeatedly through its decade-long existence (Figure 2.6). A pervasive impediment to effective urban improvements was the difficult alignment of state and local priorities. The allocation of funds to street lighting and similar services, which continuously strained the interaction of government agents and municipal councilmen, illustrates this problem particularly well. Municipal regulations stipulated the levying of a street-lighting duty from individual proprietors to cover expenditures. In 1869, however, after three years of homeowners' stiff opposition to the cost of gas lamps, Governor Veli Pasha used the municipal *kantariye* (weighting tax) revenues to make up the difference and stop the gas strike, diverting funds formerly devoted for road construction and urban sanitation.[67] While the beneficiaries of street lighting regarded this

FIGURE 2.6. Inauguration ceremony for the relocation of Izmir's municipality to a new building, ca. 1890. Courtesy of Istanbul University, Rare Books Library (90854/19).

arrangement as a de facto settlement, successive governors considered it a provisional measure, striving to reverse the situation—albeit to no avail. In return, the state periodically staked claims on various local funds it had formerly handed over to the municipality. Originally, Izmir's new municipality, like the Galata municipality, was to benefit from an expanded tax base, deriving its revenues from property taxes; fees on deeds, contracts, and building repairs; market taxes (*rüsumat*); and miscellaneous dues as those levied on carriages. In 1876, however, fees on rental contracts were redirected to the central treasury, while in 1888, market taxes were transferred to the state, depriving the municipality of its principal source of income.[68]

The difficulty of balancing state control with local autonomy was most patently manifested in the conflict over the location of Izmir's municipality. In 1876, in view of increasing efficiency, Governor Hurşid Pasha ordered the recently reconstituted municipal council to leave the rental premises that it occupied on the third floor of a building on Frank Street and relocate its offices to the governor's palace. This, he argued, would not only help alleviate the budgetary pressures, but also prevent people from wasting an entire day on insignificant transactions. The cadastral office and the police department were both located at the governor's palace. To get a simple building permit, a person had first to go to the municipal office, next obtain a certificate ascertaining the payment of property tax from the cadastral offices, and finally return to the municipal offices. Similarly, for a straightforward contravention, a detained person was first taken to the municipal office then to the police department.[69] Foreign members of the municipality, however, saw the relocation of the municipality as a major attack on the institution's autonomy. They denounced Hurşid Pasha for robbing the municipality of the privileges and freedoms guaranteed by Izmir's municipal regulation and relegating councilmen to minor government agents.[70] Hence, autonomy, authority, and similar assertions of political power were played out through control over locational decisions within the city.

Controversies over major urban development schemes also affected the performance of the municipality. The creation of the 1868 municipality coincided with the redevelopment of Izmir's urban foreshore into a monumental quay—one of the most contentious infrastructure projects in the city. As I elaborate in the next chapter, the project drew both strong supporters and detractors among local merchants and landed proprietors. Consequently, for these groups, the municipality provided an opportune instrument to advance their respective interests. As Governor İsmail Pasha's report indicated, a key problem in constituting the 1868 municipal council was the different factions striving to hold sway over the quay project.[71] Although the municipal council was eventually constituted, many councilors were less interested in addressing the pressing problems of the city than in controlling the course of specific projects.[72] "What to expect from individuals whose principal motivation is private interest and unique concern is the success of their business?" bemoaned the Izmir correspondent to the *Levant Herald*.[73] In the end, the crisis triggered by the quay scheme pitted the governor, who supported the project, against Muslim councilors and some of their foreign counterparts, who had allied themselves in opposition to the development, eventually resulting in the dissolution of the first municipal council within less than a year of its constitution.[74]

A parallel concern that further eroded the legitimacy of the 1868 municipality was the much-debated question of who constituted Izmir's citizenry and by whom this citizenry should be represented. During the formation of the municipal council, newspaper commentators critiqued the creation of a privileged class of councilmen, who "would have no contact point with the peoples, would know nothing of their real needs [and] would vote for what they like."[75] They also denounced the electoral base used in Izmir for violating the provisions of the 1864 Provincial Code, which had recently been enacted for implementation in all established settlements, villages, towns, and cities within the Ottoman domain. Indeed, voters and candidates in Izmir consisted exclusively of landed proprietors paying a yearly tax of five hundred piastres and above. In contrast, the Provincial Code was premised on a broader electoral base, allowing all Ottoman subjects paying fifty piastres and above to vote and those paying one hundred and above to be elected as representatives (or *muhtars*).[76]

These debates recall familiar trends of expanding popular political participation in contemporaneous modern states, but in Izmir they were further complicated by contentions over whether or not to involve foreigners in local affairs. Despite its limited electoral base, the 1868 municipality included all proprietors of Izmir, regardless of origin, religion, or status. The central government had approved this exceptional principle in its effort to bring foreign proprietors within the fold of state jurisdictions. Such inclusion was regarded as a way of creating broader points of convergence within the larger urban community and mitigating consular meddling, a danger had foreign residents been left outside the municipal council.[77] As discussed in the previous chapter, however, despite the central government's repeated efforts, Izmir's foreign residents could not be satisfactorily assimilated into the Ottoman state framework.

Meanwhile, in government circles, foreigners' involvement in the domestic affairs of the empire was increasingly perceived as a threat to national interests. In a long article published in 1861, entitled "What Is Regarded as Public Opinion in Turkey," the semiofficial *Journal de Constantinople* scathingly portrayed the empire as a "peculiar" place where "foreigners think they should get more than their share and natives believe they should receive less than their due!"

> Who speaks of politics, criticizes the government, gives it advice, meddles with its business, spread news and rumors, approves or disapproves?—The foreigner. The government, however, is an OTTOMAN government: Turkey is a free power, autonomous and sovereign. It is an Empire by treaties and by European public law.[78]

Such arguments called for the exclusion of foreigners from local political processes. Ultimately, the amended 1877 Provincial Code, passed in the first Ottoman Parliament, gave a legal basis to such requirements, mandating Ottoman nationality (*teba-i Osmaniye*) as an absolute requirement for voters and electable councilmen.

As a result of these compounding issues, Izmir's municipality was revamped in 1879. The new provisions radically shaped the contours of citizenry and the ways the city was experienced and imagined by its users. First, the new municipal elections, held in conformity with the 1877 Provincial Code, introduced radical shifts in the electoral base, expanding participation, but also instituting new forms of exclusion.[79] By lowering the five hundred piastres voting franchise to fifty, they opened the political process to the lower classes of tradesmen and artisans, representing more closely the composition of the population. At the same time, by enforcing Ottoman nationality, they undercut the property and residency qualifications that had thus far offered foreigners membership in the polity, categorically eliminating this group from local political processes either as candidates or as voters. Hence, while property and wealth had been envisioned as the primary voting and election criteria since the creation of the cadastral commission, nationality became the decisive factor with the 1879 municipality.

Second, the 1879 municipal reorganization reconfigured the relationship between Izmir's political and geographical structures. Given its size and the growing needs of its population, Izmir was divided into two municipal districts, one serving the upper town, the other the lower town. The boundary between the two districts ran on a roughly east–west axis, starting at the northern part of the bazaar at the shore and continuing into the city in the direction of the Basmahane train station and the Caravan Bridge Road (Map 2.4).[80] To the south of this line was the first municipal district, which included Muslim and Jewish neighborhoods, the administrative-military quarters, customs clearing and warehousing facilities, and the older commercial center, comprising artisanal trade and suppliers of agricultural goods and traditional consumer items. To the north of the line lay the second district, which encompassed the Greek, Armenian, and European neighborhoods, the consulates, and newer types of businesses, including hotels, banks, brokerage firms, dry-goods stores selling imported goods, and modern entertainment establishments such as European-style cafés, clubs, and theaters. This arrangement, which lasted a decade, was intended to create municipal councils more attuned to the needs of the peoples it served.[81] Although both appointed mayors belonged to the Muslim bureaucratic elite, the councils they headed comprised both Muslim and non-Muslim Ottoman members, reflecting more closely, if not proportionally, the social composition in these districts. Hence, whereas Muslim councilors prevailed in the first district, non-Muslim councilors were the majority in the second district.[82]

The municipal division recognized existing geographic and economic hierarchies, reinforcing them with ethnoreligious divisions. Since the inception of the

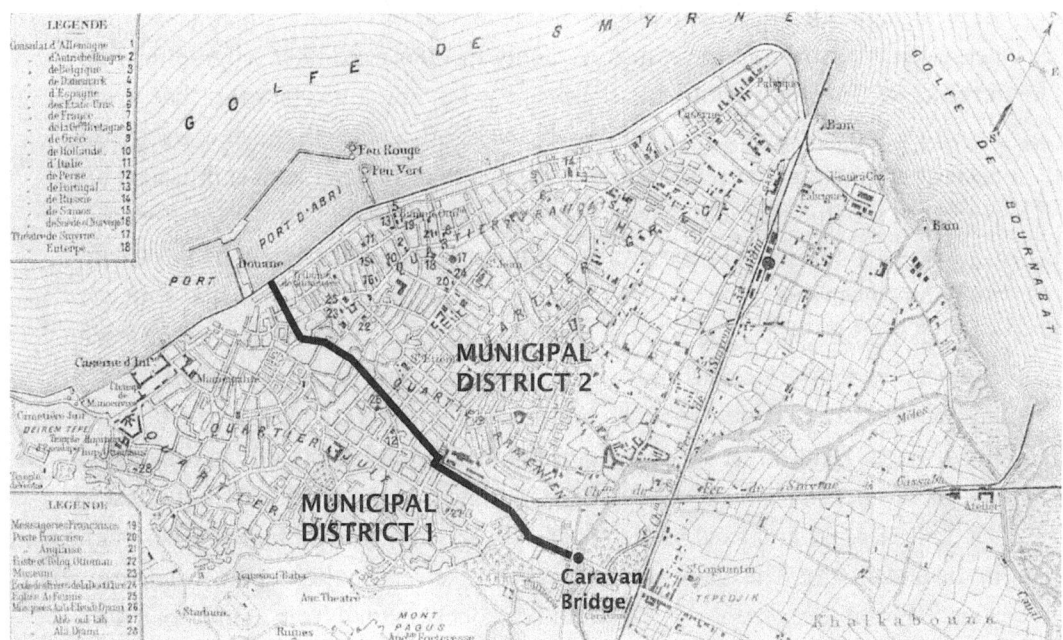

MAP 2.4. Izmir's two municipal districts, layered on a map of the city by Demetrios Georgiades, 1880s.

two-district arrangement, commentators presented the division along ethnoreligious lines. For example, objecting to recent municipal changes, *La Réforme* wrote that "We are changing things around and creating a bifurcation that is as contrary to political economy as to established practices. Hence, there will be a Muslim section and a non-Muslim section."[83] Similarly, other commentators referred to a municipal division between the Turkish and Christian quarters, or the Turkish and European sections.

Moreover since both municipal districts were underfunded, executing improvements largely depended on residents' capacity to help finance them. Indeed, a considerable portion of the second district was equipped through resident contributions. In 1888, for example, half of the paving and infrastructure expenses were collected from district residents.[84] That most large retail stores, prestigious institutions, and affluent residential neighborhoods were within the boundaries of the second municipal district gave this area a clear economic advantage. In addition, the new waterfront development, completed in the late 1870s and well integrated with the existing street structure of the second district, drastically increased the already high property values of surrounding areas. In contrast, the areas within the first municipal district were on the wrong side of the tracks, suffering a significant drop in real-estate values and receiving comparatively meager resident contributions for improvements. In 1880, to counter geographical disadvantage, Governor Midhad Pasha proposed opening new arteries that would directly connect the Muslim and Jewish neighborhoods with the new waterfront and the Basmahane railway station—a project that was met with enthusiasm but could not see the light of day with the removal of Midhad Pasha from office.[85]

These economic and geographic conditions affected the extent of infrastructural improvements in each district, further articulating class hierarchies with ethnoreligious differences and making them tangible. The Ottoman Turkish biweekly *Hizmet* (literally Service), whose primary readership was the inhabitants of the first municipal district, devoted much attention to the significant disparities between the districts. Tying street improvements to the pride and prestige of an urban society, *Hizmet* periodically compared the amount of pavement and the length of sewers built, cleaned, and fixed in each district in an effort to elicit more development in the first district. The quality of pavement and sewers further set the two districts apart. The affluent sections of the second district benefited from a smoother, more durable, and more costly pavement called Neapolitan *(napoli taşı)* and from vaulted sewer conduits *(tonoz lağım)* whereas the streets of the upper town were of cobblestone *(arnavut kaldırımı)* and equipped with common sewers *(âdi lağım)*.

Exacerbating the visible divisions in the physical landscape was the type and availability of street lighting, a marker of prosperity and influence. Between 1879 and 1890, although the number of gas lamps more than doubled, increasing from 750 to 1,600, these mostly illuminated the neighborhoods in the second municipal district.[86] Most major streets of the upper town had kerosene lamps, which had been frowned upon as outdated "dirty petroleum makeshifts" since the advent of gas to the city.[87] Unlike gas lamps connected to the gasworks through a system of underground conduits that exemplified a rational production of space, kerosene lamps were self-contained and had to be lit and extinguished individually. Only in 1873, a decade after its introduction to the Frank quarter and with the energetic support of Governor Süreyya Pasha, were the first 146 gas lamps installed on the major thoroughfares leading to the bazaar area.[88] And even then, their light remained comparatively dim. Appealing to municipal agents, *Hizmet* complained that "lamps in the Frank quarter are illuminated right at twelve [sunset] and their piercing and bright glow dazzles the eye; whereas in our part, except a few conspicuous streets, lamps are lit much later and their glow is frail and pale."[89]

The perceived neglect of the streets, which presented undeniable inconveniences to many, validated larger institutional and organizational demands particularly well. As a discourse produced in the press and governmental documents, the problems of the street offered a powerful tool to condemn or praise ongoing municipal experiments. They also helped certain groups claim membership in the polity. For example, foreign nationals, when they were decisively excluded from the municipal council in 1878, protested the decision, demanding inclusion on the basis of "the dangerously dilapidated pavements and filthy state of the principal thoroughfares," "the abominable condition of the public sewers," and "the miserable and disgusting shambles pertinaciously maintained as public slaughterhouses."[90] Consequently, arguments over the streets and their amenities were as much about formulating and legitimizing institutional bodies to deal with environmental questions and deciding how and by whom to run them as they were about immediate physical nuisance.

Streets as Objects of Reform

Implementing street improvements and effective surveillance remained controversial and ridden with legal challenges. Modern street amenities presupposed a vastly streamlined public property regime with uniform public access and use rights and clear-cut public–private boundaries. In Izmir, as in other Ottoman cities, however, the simultaneous operation of parallel, often overlapping, legal systems—one based on Islamic law, another on state regulations *(nizam)*—laid public property open to multiple interpretations and appropriations. Broadly speaking, Ottoman jurisdictions viewed streets, marketplaces, and other shared urban property as abandoned land *(arazi-i metruke)*, that is, state-owned land given for the collective use of the entire population or a community of users.[91] Although such land was explicitly dedicated for public use, it could be the subject of various forms of private claims.

Islamic law, as codified in the 1870s in the Ottoman Civil Code (Mecelle), relied on negotiable rather than absolute conceptions of private and public, admitting certain forms of appropriations, albeit conditionally.[92] So long as the public's right of passage *(hakk-ı murur)* was not violated, a proprietor could have an overhanging balcony over a public way or a connector bridge between two houses on either side of the street.[93] Similarly, he or she could alienate an unessential portion of the street or temporarily put it to private use, granted public passage *(marre)* was not obstructed.[94] A proprietor could also block a public easement crossing his property, if the detriment caused to private property exceeded the benefits accrued to the public.[95] In contrast, a period of uncontested public usage of the easement would imply a grant from the private owner. Moreover, Islamic law distinguished between through streets *(tarik-i âm* or public way) and dead-end streets *(tarik-i hass* or private way), attributing to each type different access and use rights that expanded and contracted depending on local circumstances. Through streets were open to the circulation of all inhabitants, whereas dead-end streets were considered the joint property of those whose houses abutted on them. If they wished, proprietors on a dead-end street could restrict outsiders or deny the opening of new access doors onto it.[96]

These relational considerations attest to the greater emphasis that Islamic law and customary practices put on protecting private property rights rather than collective rights to public property, shaping the physical environment in distinctive ways and permitting some degree of "privatization of public space."[97] Hence, public ways were often relegated to functional access-ways, cut to the minimal necessary width for pedestrian and animal traffic (Figure 2.7). In the commercial sections of town, small shopkeepers used a portion of the street as an immediate continuation of their store, extending their stalls to display their goods and sustain their trade (Figure 2.8). To be sure, these practices had parallels in many commercializing cities of the nineteenth century, but in the Ottoman context they remained within the permissible boundary of Islamic and customary legal behavior.

In contrast, Ottoman state regulations, which Tanzimat bureaucrats were expanding with new codes, placed emphasis on public property, delineating its boundaries and controlling and managing it as an entity of its own. The Building and Road Code (Ebniye ve Turuk Nizamnamesi), first enacted in 1848, assigned set widths to different categories of streets and stipulated new measures for ensuring their alignment and hygiene.[98] The Penal Code, largely drawn from French models, gave unequivocal priority to unobstructed flow, categorically restricting any private endeavors on streets and imposing a fine on anyone who encroached on them or littered them.[99] The 1858 Land Code underlined the inalienability of public property by private parties whereas new rules for expropriation for public purposes, passed two years earlier, permitted the public to acquire roads over private property with due compensation, further promoting public-interest uses.[100] These new codes, premised on a mutually exclusive notion of public and private, imposed a vision of the street as a space set aside primarily for flow, thereby challenging both the idea of the street as a commercial space and the practices derived from a relational understanding of public property.

To implement street improvements in Izmir was thus contingent on reconciling the inherent tensions built into public property and the various claims associated with it. Efforts at clearing and uncluttering the streets illustrate this conflict most explicitly. Demographic and commercial growth and the increased number

FIGURE 2.7. Thomas Allom, *A Street in Izmir*, ca. 1830. Lithograph. From Thomas Allom, *Constantinople, the Scenery of the Seven Churches of Asia, and the Shores and Islands of the Mediterranean* (London: Fisher, Son; New York: R. Martin, 1838–41).

Figure 2.8. Denis-Auguste-Marie Rafet, *Section of the Bazaar Known as the Old Fish Market*, ca. 1839. Bibliothèque nationale de France.

of people and goods circulating through the city produced ever-greater congestion. Stalls placed alongside public thoroughfares blocked the flow in several commercial areas (Figure 2.9). In his column, Bargigli called the attention of the authorities to Fasula Place, the commercial heart of the Frank quarter and a major route for a large part of the population going to work daily. "Besides dirt and overcrowding," he wrote, "the cluster of coffeehouses, butchers, *bakkals* [grocers], fishmongers turn this street into a scarcely navigable passage."[101] Congestion became more problematic after the reconstruction that followed the 1844 fire that destroyed the Frank quarter and Fasula Place. Several landowners who lost their houses had given up a portion of their land to widen the street and provide the area with more air, light, and relative security (Figures 2.10, 2.11). Given the sacrifice made by these residents, the blocking of circulation at the same location and the creation of a fish market, the "most disagreeable of all," in front of the church of the Lazarists produced even louder objections.[102] "Nobody easily gives away a tiny plot of land unless in consideration of public security and public good" wrote *L'Impartial*, asking authorities to amend the stalls, sheds, and other irregular buildings that encroached on the street.[103]

In addition to permanent retail stores, weekly markets were improvised along major commercial arteries. On Sundays, a market set with makeshift stalls slowed down circulation on Frank Street, which was also an important path for Christian worshippers, as it led to the parish churches of St. Mary and St. Polycarp, the

FIGURE 2.9. A Commercial Street *(The Street of the Great Taverns)*, with merchants encroaching on the sidewalk, ca. 1910. From Frédéric Boissonnas, *L'image de la Grèce: Smyrne* (Geneva: Editions d'Art Boissonnas, 1919).

Greek Cathedral of St. Photini, three Lazarist churches, and the British and Dutch chapels. The display of pork, lamb, beef, poultry, fruits and vegetables, fish, and other produce made the thoroughfare even more displeasing to polite eyes.[104] Despite efforts at relocating the market, persistent complaints in the press suggest that congestion created by small-time trade and traditional retail remained a matter of local concern through the second half of the nineteenth century. In the 1880s, *Hizmet* devoted ample space to such questions, denouncing the extensive traffic of carts and camels that turned the streets into swampy grounds. It also deplored the nuisance created by the trades that adjoined the streets, and in one case, condemned the heavy odor of oil that emanated from grocery stores that doubled in the back as eating places.[105]

Moreover, the uneasy mixture of old and new modes of transportation—from fancy carriages to street wagons and animal traffic—jammed circulation in unprecedented ways (Figure 2.12). Tanners had begun to haul their merchandise on heavy street wagons rather than on the backs of animals. Property owners loathed having these heavy carts on their street, complaining that their metal rims broke the pavement, sewers, and water pipes. In a petition drafted to the governor, they

FIGURE 2.10. View of Fasula Place after enlargement, ca. 1890. Through the nineteenth century, Fasula Place was a major hub for pedestrian circulation. Courtesy of the Suna & İnan Kıraç Research Institute for Mediterranean Civilizations.

FIGURE 2.11. View of Fasula Place, ca. 1890. Fasula Place also served as a station for horse-drawn carriages. Postcard. Courtesy of the Suna & İnan Kıraç Research Institute for Mediterranean Civilizations.

attacked the tanners' guild and demanded the termination of this harmful practice on the basis of public interest.[106] At the same time, affluent segments of the population began to use carriages—a practice regarded by many as an ill-suited pretense given the narrowness of the streets. As the reporter of *La Turquie* admitted, "these cars are totally useless," for their wheels damaged the pavement and their size obstructed circulation. "What is left for the pedestrian?" he added, reminding that the slow pace of camels and animal traffic already sufficiently obstructed free flow, making those on foot restless.[107]

These complaints provide insight not only into everyday experiences of the street but also into how the landscape of small commerce, scattered through shops, markets, and streets, came to be framed as a nuisance. Storefronts projecting onto the street and the guild of itinerant vendors exposing their goods for sale did so to the annoyance of walkers and to the hindrance of free circulation. Official orders published in newspapers, notices posted in public spaces, and initiatives taken by local authorities to remove shop fronts encroaching on public thoroughfares and otherwise regulate the streets further confirmed the invasiveness of

FIGURE 2.12. A satirical street scene from *Kara Sinan,* July 8, 1875, no. 2, 4. The original text read: "'What do we do now? Should the cart go over the camel or should the camel go over the cart?' 'Well, as long as we pass through the legs of the camel, I don't care how.'"

such uses. In 1864, Governor Kayserili Ahmed Pasha prohibited shopkeepers, peddlers, and any other individuals from stacking furniture, barrels, boxes, grain or produce, or other commodities intended for public consumption in the street.[108] Similarly, in 1875, *Aydın,* the official Turkish paper, published a notice setting a deadline for proprietors to demolish any structure they had built that extended onto a public thoroughfare.[109] Later, in 1878, the municipal commission posted another order that banned innkeepers and coffee-shop owners from placing chairs or tables in front of their stores for a period longer than one hour without prior approval of the authorities. Any object that potentially obstructed public circulation, blocked sunlight, or damaged the pavement—including wooden covers and signs projecting onto the street, outdoor frames and hooks for hanging produce, and carts and animals loaded above the limit set by a special tariff—were also prohibited.[110]

These measures did not eliminate proprietary claims over the street. Provisions to implement a space for unobstructed traffic were constantly opposed by less articulate but no less strongly held counterviews and practices of the street as a space for buying and selling. Shop-owners' long-held networks of solidarity through both guilds and informal interest alliances gave further weight to their claim to the street.[111] Indeed, fines seem to have been more strictly imposed on peddlers and itinerant vendors, who remained outside these occupational networks, than on shop owners who coopted public spaces in a more permanent manner and on a larger scale.[112] Comical scenes reported in the local press capture particularly well the pervasiveness of discordant demands placed on the street and their related rights of way. "As is often the case," reported *La Turquie* in 1866, "a passerby runs into the head or flank of a cow hanging in front of a butcher. The victim complains to the butcher who in turn insults him; as he retorts, people assemble, they argue, the police intervene; they speak Greek, Turkish, English, and French but fall far from agreeing."[113]

Considerations of public interest intersected and collided with the exercise of proprietary rights beyond the marketplace and commercial areas. A controversial shed, erected at Bella Vista on a lot serving as easement between the French hospital and the shore, illustrates particularly well how diverse local actors resourcefully exploited simultaneously operating legal principles (Map 2.5). In 1862, as real-estate pressures were increasing in the area, the French consul had used Ottoman state provisions to obtain an imperial firman prohibiting any construction on that lot. Although the firman was issued for concerns of public health and in anticipation of insalubrious uses that could harm the hospital, it was principally motivated by the consul's desire to prevent Sıvaslı Takvor, a local speculator, from taking over the lot and blocking the hospital's access to the sea. A decade later, in 1872, however, the consul had a shed built overnight on the lot in question, declaring that he had only renovated an existing shed to provide rental revenue to the hospital. This, he claimed, was a legitimate exercise of the hospital's rights to the property based on the deed granted in 1826/1241–42 by Izmir's molla and the recent reconstruction permit issued by the cadastral office.[114] In contrast, Governor Sadık Pasha regarded the property as a public way, given its uncontested usage as an easement for forty years, and the shed as a contravention to the firman. He requested its removal further arguing that the shed was detrimental to the city's interest, obstructing the projected widening of the street and blocking access to an existing public sewer on top of which the shed was built.[115] That equally valid legal principles backed both parties' claims further complicated the case. Although the shed continued to undercut the opening of a wider street for another decade, the controversy forced the consul to back off from his initial intention of erecting an entire row of rental sheds.[116]

This dispute is highly representative of the kinds of problems that stood in the way of clearing and widening the streets, exposing how modern streets had to mediate between proprietary claims and collective rights, movement and commerce. More importantly, it indicates the presence of equally modern structures

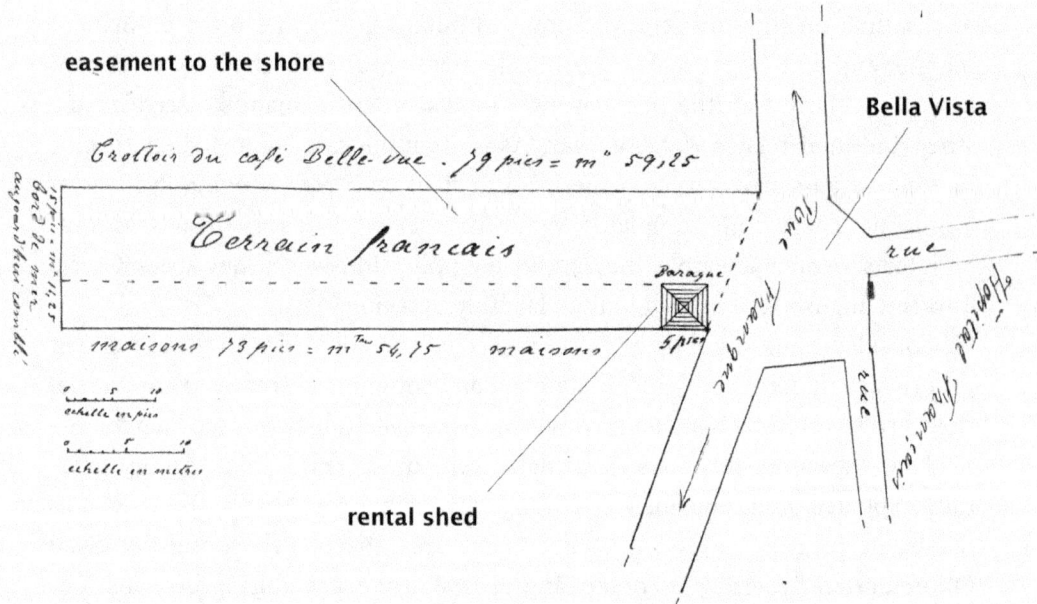

MAP 2.5. Location of the controversial shed, 1872. The shed stood across from the French hospital, along the easement leading to the shore. Courtesy of Centre des Archives Diplomatique de Nantes.

of significance that urbanites simultaneously exploited as opportunities arose. Rather than a clash between modern Western and traditional Islamic values—as Tanzimat reforms have generally been interpreted—such disputes reveal the contradictory demands of life that characterized the competitive and expanding commercial society of Ottoman Izmir, and the very tensions inherent to modern public space.

As with street clearing, the provision of a safe and secure street environment raised questions of legal character. Effective policing required an even enforcement of prohibitions and sanctions across the various segments of urban society. In Izmir, however, foreigners had historically enjoyed extraterritorial immunities, in particular exemptions from local jurisdictions and the inviolability of domicile, creating much discrepancy in police intervention and the prosecution of criminal offences.[117] As discussed in the previous chapter, these immunities were neither uniform nor complete. Their extent and practice depended on the treaty signed with foreign countries, the leverage a particular consular agent had, and the regard local authorities showed to these immunities at a given moment. But by the nineteenth century, as increasingly diverse classes began to acquire or indirectly benefit from foreign protections, extraterritorial immunities became a pervasive obstacle to police action, affecting the overall sense of public security.

The arrest of foreign protection holders was a troublesome matter that caused frequent disputes between government and consular agents. Extraterritorial rules stipulated that consuls be present each time local authorities seized or entered the home of a foreigner. Often, consuls manipulated these provisions, delaying their appearance to shield foreign offenders and making their arrest more difficult. Armed gangs, connected to or hired by foreign tradesmen to secure cargo transfers from inland, at times exploited these provisions, taking refuge in these wealthy merchants' residences to circumvent the police. When local authorities in pursuit of these gangs entered these suspected premises without the knowledge of the consul, their action was considered an infraction, providing sufficient grounds for a diplomatic crisis.[118]

The judgment and condemnation of foreigners further compromised the scope of judicial action since foreign offenders were tried according to their protecting country's penal system. Although crimes involving both foreign and Ottoman subjects fell under territorial jurisdictions, some European powers claimed jurisdiction for their consular courts whenever the accused was a foreigner.[119] Even after the creation of nizamiye courts in Izmir in 1851 to handle mixed cases, the judgment rendered by these courts against foreigners often remained unexecuted and challenged on procedural grounds, perpetuating the discrepancies.[120] Other perceived dysfunctions also frustrated the workings of criminal justice. For example, in 1876, despite efforts by Governor Sabri Pasha to double police measures and engage in massive arrests, abstaining witnesses caused undue leniency for offenders. As he complained in his letter to the consular body, "the condemnation of arrested people, among whom are particularly foreign subjects, require the witnesses and proofs demanded by law. Alas, witnesses fail to appear at court and since preventive arrests have limits by law, the detained are necessarily released and start again their mischief."[121] Moreover, criminals had means of evading justice by bribing parties in charge of the prison, further shaking local confidence in the penal regime. During a period of increased street assaults and robberies in 1862, the gendarme in charge of the Frank quarter, Deli Ahmed, admitted to the British consul that "it is useless to arrest thieves and send them at the Konak, for they are certain of being liberated, unless indeed they have no influence with some police spies, and means of escaping through their intercession."[122]

A parallel concern that damaged the sense of public security was the insufficient number of gendarmes, their poor pay, and, above all, the nature of the police corps. The established modus operandi of recruiting irregulars—generally Albanians and other outsiders to the province—as a police force was often seen as the root cause of growing disorder, for these "strangers" cared little about the population they were to protect, "their object being 'by hook or by crook' to make a little money and then return to their own homes."[123] Consuls insisted that the police corps should be enlisted from among properly trained troops by giving preference to reserve soldiers *(redif)*.[124] Similarly, newspapers called for a police corps who had local know-how and was more attuned to the social composition of the population. The Ottoman government too was cognizant that the effective control of a multireligious and multilingual population demanded a mixed police force, drawn from among both Muslim and Christian populations. A measure passed in the late 1860s for the admission of Christians into the police force eventually found application in 1876, during the term of the energetic Governor Sabri Pasha—praised for his familiarity with the traditions of the region.[125] Despite the vulnerability of these reforms to budget cuts, hence their brevity, Sabri Pasha's reorganization of the police received enthusiastic support in the newspapers for he "chose apt people … most Mussulmans spoke the language of the country and managed to communicate with people of all classes, while the others were recruited among indigenous of different nations [millet], who knew more or less the nest of prowlers."[126]

The immediacy of matters related to street security frequently drove government agents to seek a modus vivendi with consular agents. Especially during periods of repeated assaults, governors convened the consular body, asking for assistance and latitude to implement measures that would better protect the city or "cleanse the city from malefactors, who profoundly disturb public order."[127] A compromised sense of security also had obvious inconveniences to the life and commercial interests of foreign merchants. Hence, when public safety was at stake, consuls, who generally weighted any assistance on local matters against their mission of safeguarding extraterritorial privileges, were compelled to find ways of acting in concert with local authorities. In that way, the provision of a secure and orderly environment had a galvanizing effect on the various authorities who exerted influence in Izmir, periodically forcing them to renegotiate their difference.

⁓

The foregoing pages presented a snapshot of the sensorial realities of a rapidly growing city and how its inhabitants engaged with the changes in their urban environment. The perceived problems of the street—chronic congestion, epidemics, and street assaults—offered local residents a basis for demanding new institutional frameworks that could underwrite urban improvements and provide modern services. The creation of the cadastral commission (1856) was the first of a series of attempts to rationalize urban governance and formulate formal participation in it. However, as evidenced thereafter in the formation of a modern citywide municipality (1868), which was split into two separate districts (1879) only to be merged back into a single institution (1889), these efforts were often tentative and did not evolve along a linear trajectory. Competing public and private rights to the streets, the uneven extension of consular protections to certain individuals, and the ensuing complex tapestry of institutional remits generated frictions, hindering and delaying attempts to implement a rational order. That Ottoman governors were rotated frequently to prevent them from forming local ties and abusing their power, while foreign consuls held longer tenure and were also private stakeholders with personal interests on the line, further affected in no small measure the wavering character of Izmir's municipal reforms.

The processes I investigate in this chapter are illuminating on various counts. First, although continually contested and revised, efforts to tidy up the streets and provide urban services through the mechanism of a modern city government signal significant departures from neighborhood- or community-centered practices. The discourses that emerged in the press and the exchanges that took place in committees and councils reveal a growing collective sense of seeing and working with Izmir as a whole—a cohesive territorial and administrative entity, run by its tax-paying propertied members—rather than thinking of piecemeal interventions as previous institutions would have done. Second, contrary to interpretations of Ottoman modernity as a bureaucratically led effort, forced from above, street improvements reveal a dynamic interplay between the perceived urban problems of Izmir and the local institutional structures created to address them. Indeed, as both sites on which to project reformist agendas and instruments for giving these agendas a tangible form, Izmir's streets epitomize how physical and administrative structures mutually inform one another. Third, and in a broader sense, the specific conflicts arising in Izmir highlight processes common to modernizing cities across the globe; concerns over the deplorable conditions of the streets became a means through which to negotiate ownership of and rights to the city and the rules of conduct that regulate public spaces. In the next chapter, I delve more deeply into the intimate relationship between the physical and the political, focusing on the construction of Izmir's monumental quay—arguably the city's most ambitious urban intervention in the nineteenth century—as a prime locus for debating and formulating modern conceptions of the public good.

3

Shaping the Waterfront
Public Works and the Public Good

> Smyrna is a facade of European regularity tacked onto an Oriental confusion.... We land on a beautiful majestic quay, built by the French Company. We are still in Europe. We pass through a narrow street and cross a first block of houses. We reach Parallel Street, then Frank Street, and Europe grows increasingly distant... the most beautiful houses, western-style stores disappear; we have changed countries.
>
> —LOUIS DE LAUNAY, *La Turquie que l'on voit*

THE FRENCH GEOLOGIST AND TRAVELER Louis de Launay, who visited Izmir in 1887, was not exceptional in setting the space of the orderly quay apart from the irregular interiors of Izmir. Late nineteenth-century locals and outsiders alike remarked on the contrast between the open, long promenade on the shore and the narrow, cramped back streets of Izmir (Figure 3.1). Notwithstanding his reliance on orientalist tropes that defined Ottoman lands as lacking in European amenities, and his tendency to equate becoming modern and becoming European, de Launay's observations alert us to the striking novelty of Izmir's quay. Indeed, Izmir's new waterfront offered a distinctive urban experience. It was built on a long strip of land reclaimed from the sea that stretched over the two-and-a-half-mile bay front. The development added over 150 new urban lots, bounded by two avenues parallel to the water—the Cordon and the Second Cordon (or Parallel Street) (Map 3.1). Compared to the rest of the city, these avenues were remarkably wide, better paved, and better lit. They were lined with shops and cafés and defined by regular urban blocks and white-stone and stucco buildings, which together exhibited a uniform appearance. A tramway line, the first in Izmir, ran along the whole length of the Cordon from the Aydın railway station at the Point all the way to the customs house near the Konak (Figure 3.2). In sum, this orchestrated design effort endowed Izmir with a modern public space that soon became a favorite meeting place and promenade for a large part of the city's inhabitants.

FIGURE 3.1. View of the Cordon looking south from Bella Vista, ca. 1890. Postcard. Courtesy of the Suna & İnan Kıraç Research Institute for Mediterranean Civilizations.

Moreover, Izmir's quay was a massive technological and entrepreneurial feat that boosted the city's regional competitiveness. The project entailed difficult and costly embankments and a system of underground sewers. It also included a spacious and sheltered harbor with a monumental breakwater, a new customs house with roomy warehouses, as well as wharves, landing piers, and other essentials of an international shipping port. Improved loading and more reliable shipping facilities, coupled with two railroads that expedited the transfer of goods from the interior, ensured Izmir's standing as a major international port in an increasingly interconnected world, dominated by market economies. At the same time, this capital-intensive undertaking was a pioneering venture that combined private initiative and government incentive—a partnership model first adopted in the empire a decade earlier in the construction of two railways, again with Izmir as railhead. The Ottoman government gave incentives to attract private enterprise. It laid out the parameters of the works and provided legal and tax prerogatives to facilitate the project. Among other things, it enacted the eminent domain provision in 1856 to help acquire continuous strips of land necessary for large-scale public works and waived customs duties on imported machinery, pipes, and other equipment to be used in such projects. The organization, financing, and technical expertise, however, were left to private entrepreneurs, in this case the French firm of Dussaud Brothers (Dussaud Frères), who eventually brought the project to completion. Engineers with a first-class international reputation, they had recently built the jetties in Port Said and had considerable experience in undertaking similar ventures in port cities around the Mediterranean and beyond.[1]

While the quay accelerated Izmir's integration into an emerging global economy, its construction severely pitted French and British interests in the region against each other.[2] Initially, the Ottoman government granted the concessions to three local British entrepreneurs—John Charnaud, Alfred Barker, and George Guarracino—who established the Smyrna Quay Company and hired the renowned Dussaud Brothers as contractors to execute the project. Apart from a few select local investors, the company's funds were to be raised from London-based capital

FIGURE 3.2. New buildings and tramway line on the Cordon, by Rubellin Père & Fils, ca. 1890. Courtesy of the Suna & İnan Kıraç Research Institute for Mediterranean Civilizations.

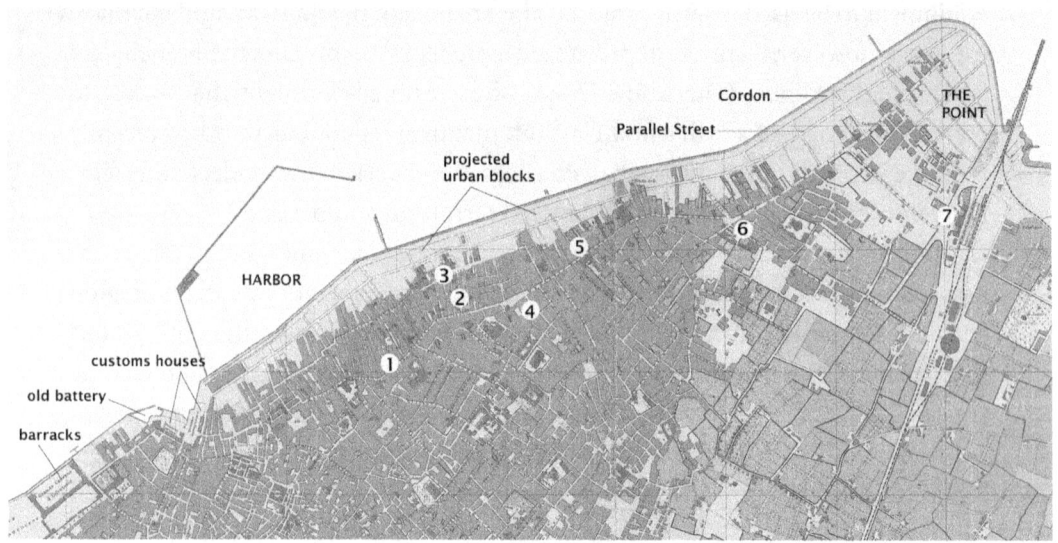

MAP 3.1. The Quay Project, showing urban expansion, the Cordon, and Parallel Street, based on the plan by Saad (Map 3).

LEGEND: 1 = Frank Street; 2 = English consulate; 3 = English pier; 4 = Fasula Place; 5 = French consulate; 6 = Bella Vista; 7 = train station at the Point.

markets, exciting, from the outset, a sense of distrust among local groups and making the project's completion and revenue-generation capabilities dubious. Unable to secure the high capital outlay required for construction and start-up operations, the entrepreneurs went bankrupt. The Dussaud Brothers, having already invested in the endeavor, stepped in, financed, and implemented the works between 1869 and 1875. This turn of events gave the Dussauds extensive control over the operation of the port facilities. But it posed a great challenge to British merchants, who resented the Dussauds for giving preferential treatment to French and Austrian companies on their quay dues and, in various ways, strove to undercut the project to gain back their influence in the region.

Most saliently, by completely dislocating existing property-ownership patterns and modes of handling trade and shipping on the shore, Izmir's quay offered a potent tool for debating the city's public good and welfare. Its wide and continuous span cut off direct water access for hundreds of shorefront properties. Moreover, the quay dues—which the Dussauds charged for loading and unloading merchandise in return for their investment costs—ended prior property owners' and merchants' free access to the shore. As I detail in this chapter, these changes generated some of the most contentious disputes in the city's history. They produced heated debates about real-estate value, environmental health, and sanitation as well as wharf taxes and tariff rates, leading to delays and negotiations among the Quay Company officials, government agents, and various local actors, ultimately shaping the course and outcome of the project. They also created rallying points that propelled residents to organize themselves into interest groups that did not necessarily line up with established ethnoreligious and national structures. Significantly, these exchanges and ensuing amendments provide rich evidence on the divergent meanings stakeholders attached to Izmir's shoreline and how they understood the idea of modern public works and the benefits associated with them.

Beyond their centrality to the functioning of modern cities, public works—like boulevards, underground sewer systems, street lighting, and similar infrastructure—are necessarily bound up with the public good. As goods that must be shared, if they are to exist at all, public works are the locus of divergent and often conflicting viewpoints and interests. At the same time, they offer opportunities for articulating and validating what the public good is and whom the public comprises. In that way, public works are profoundly political arenas, contested sites through which the boundaries and scope of the modern urban public are constituted and challenged. The construction of Izmir's modern quay and the complications surrounding its execution are illuminating on this count. From the outset, government officials and investors advanced the endeavor as a project of public utility, intended to benefit the general welfare of the city. But the protracted and sinuous process of implementation, with its shifting issues and coalitions, attested to the difficulty of reconciling a profit-driven venture with the discrete interests of local and government actors. In the end, if Izmir's quay effectively satisfied the demands of modern trade and offered a novel urban experience, its making brought about equally valid and modern yet incompatible definitions of the public good, ultimately revealing the impossibility of arriving at an all-encompassing definition of the public good and the public interest.

The Politics of the Old Shore

Although the construction of the new quay began only in 1869, the question of improving the docks had been on the table since the early 1850s. Newspaper pundits repeatedly deplored the state of the shore as they broached broader questions of urban improvement. They condemned the irregularity of the shore and the successive recesses forming along the shoreline wherein sewers and solid waste matter accumulated (Figure 3.3). By the middle of the nineteenth century the shoreline of Izmir had developed a very jagged layout (see Figure I.13). This

FIGURE 3.3. View of the old shore with wooden piers and properties abutting directly onto the water, by Rubellin Père & Fils, ca. 1860. Courtesy of the Suna & İnan Kıraç Research Institute for Mediterranean Civilizations.

rickety shape paralleled the legal and economic forces that regulated the waters adjoining the coastline. The waters of the bay of Izmir belonged to the imperial endowment of Bezm-i Âlem Valide Sultan (1807–53), the charitable trust of the wife of Mahmud II (r. 1808–39) and the mother of Abdülmecid (r. 1839–61). The endowment was established to turn inalienable state-owned *(miri)* land into a revenue-generating asset for the benefit of local mosques and their charities, and thus gainfully exploit the city's most important resource for commercial growth. Like other imperial trusts, Bezm-i Âlem's trust was administered by the new Ministry of Pious Endowments (Evkaf-ı Hümayun Nezareti), formed in 1826 to bring under direct state control the management of pious endowments, previously attached to the Janissary corps.[3] While, in theory, vakıf (endowed) property was outside the domain of private exchange and could only be rented for fixed periods of time to generate revenue for the endowment, in practice, as rental revenues became insufficient for the upkeep and rebuilding of vakıf buildings lost in fires and in other disasters, the government had devised sui generis rental contracts, such as *icareteyn* and *mukataa,* to raise more funds. These contracts offered perpetual use-rights and permitted transfers and even inheritance in exchange for a significant down payment and a preset monthly or yearly rent.[4] Mukataa contracts granted the most extensive use-rights, including mortgage rights, decisively restoring inalienable property to the economic cycle and making it almost akin to private ownership. Hence, in Izmir, since the early 1840s, the waters adjoining the shore had been parceled out and leased as mukataa to expand state funds, some of which were assigned to local Muslim charity. Aware of the high demand for shorefront properties, the ministry and its local branch office auctioned off these water lots to the highest bidder, basically introducing them to a competitive and speculative real-estate market. As lessees filled in their individual water lots at their discretion and extended existing wharves and plots into the bay, they also produced an increasingly irregular shoreline with long inlets and frequent breaks.

While the sale of water lots as speculative and developmental instruments was common to rapidly expanding British and American port cities in the eighteenth and early nineteenth centuries, in Izmir, the legal land regime and the specific method generated to sell the waters gave this process a distinctive course.[5] By placing the water lots on the market, the local office of the Evkaf compelled existing seafront proprietors to acquire the water rights fronting their property on penalty of seeing it acquired by another party. Moreover, it required lessees to fill in their water lot within a limited amount of time. If they failed, the lot would devolve to the Evkaf, which could resell it, eventually forfeiting the initial owner's purchase.[6] These stipulations triggered speculation, created opportunities for abuse, and occasionally generated conflicts. For example, in a petition submitted to the Sublime Porte in 1859, Polonie Aliotti, a shorefront property owner of Sardinian nationality, complained about Nişan Pişmişoğlu, an Armenian banker who had apparently bought the water lot in front of her property from the Evkaf and was trying to sell it to her. Aliotti claimed to have purchased that same lot from the Evkaf paying cash, though the permanent deed establishing her ownership—customarily issued and sent from the central office in Istanbul—had still not arrived.[7] Embezzlement of Evkaf funds, bribery, and the forgery of title deeds were rampant, despite various efforts, including the replacement of local officials with centrally made appointments. Indeed, only a few months before the dispute, central authorities had removed the director of the Evkaf office in Izmir, İbrahim Bey, from office.[8] Although this state of affairs might have generated some degree of anxiety among owners about the security of their tenure, it did not halt the rise in property prices. Between the 1830s and the 1860s, the price of seafront land had risen fourfold.[9]

A property map from the mid-1860s offers a visual snapshot of the increasingly commercialized nature of the bay front and the competitive forces at play.

The map exhibits a dense comb-like urban pattern consisting of several clusters of narrow shorefront lots separated by occasional alleys perpendicular to the bay (Map 3.2). The unusual narrowness of the lots in relation to their length and the multiplicity of proprietors further corroborate the high demand for shorefront lots and an ongoing tendency to subdivide these lots to maximize sea frontage. Registered lessees were almost entirely private individuals with the exception of a few institutions. Governmental structures such as the military barracks and the customs houses lay mostly to the southern end. Further north, the British and French consulates possessed two large lots fronted by private piers, and the Dominican and the Lazarist orders as well as the Armenian church held small lots. Judging from the names of individual proprietors, non-Muslim Ottoman and foreign subjects held a large percentage of the narrow lots, while Muslim notables possessed a few large parcels at the extremities of the shore. In addition, several lots were registered in the names of wives or daughters, attesting to their active role in the property market. Significantly, the map recorded not only shorefront proprietors but also the holders of the water rights. Although most shorefront proprietors had already acquired the water lot adjoining their lots either to

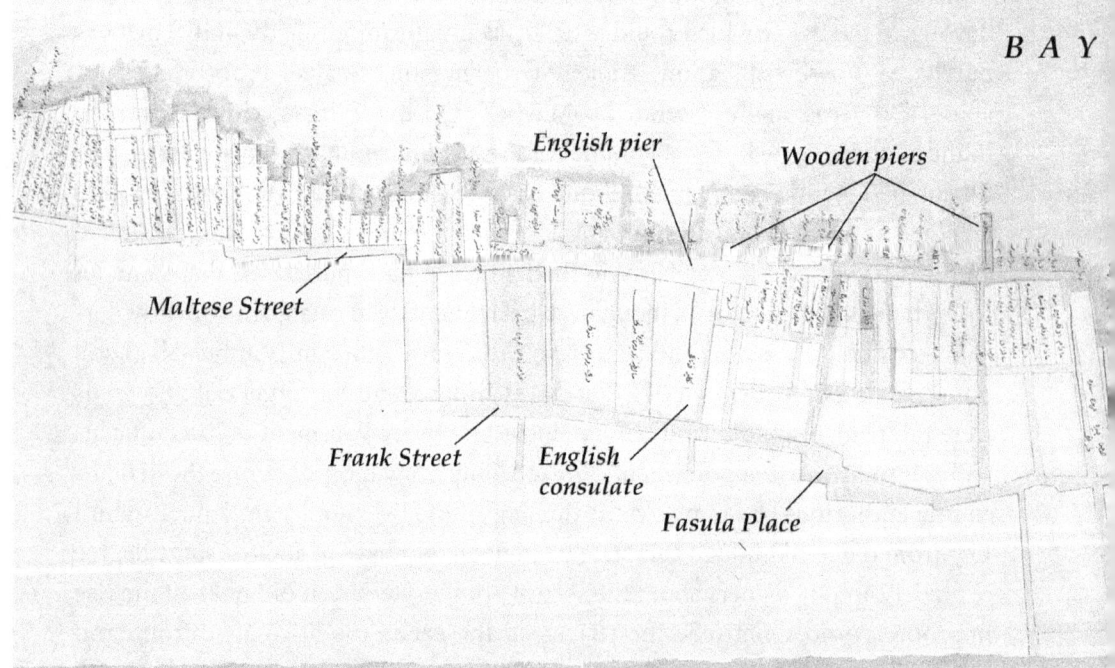

MAP 3.2. A portion of the shorefront property map, indicating individual proprietors of shorefront lots and water lots, ca. 1865. Courtesy of Başbakanlık Ottoman Archives.

extend their property or simply to prevent others from blocking them in the future, in some instances, as in the Aliotti versus Pişmişoğlu case, the shore and the water lots belonged to different individuals.

Aside from its complex and intricate ownership pattern, the waterfront exhibited a variety of uses, functions, and lifestyles. Anchoring the southernmost end was the city's most prominent state symbol, the massive Sarıkışla barracks, adjoining the vast military parade ground (see Map 3.1 and Figures I.13, I.16, I.17). Proceeding north and past the governor's house was a recently rebuilt battery with twenty-four embrasures. Next to it was the Ottoman customs house that was used for trade within the empire, including the North African seaports, and a short distance from there stood the sanitary office. After passing through a vegetable and a fish market, one came upon the Frank customs house used in international trade. The two customs houses, respectively adjoining the southern and northern extremities of the U-shaped bazaar, helped organized trade activity, sorting and monitoring the movement of goods in and out of the harbor according to destination. Next to the Frank customs house were the typical appendages of a seaport. Several marine shops, ship chandlers, and drinking houses extended

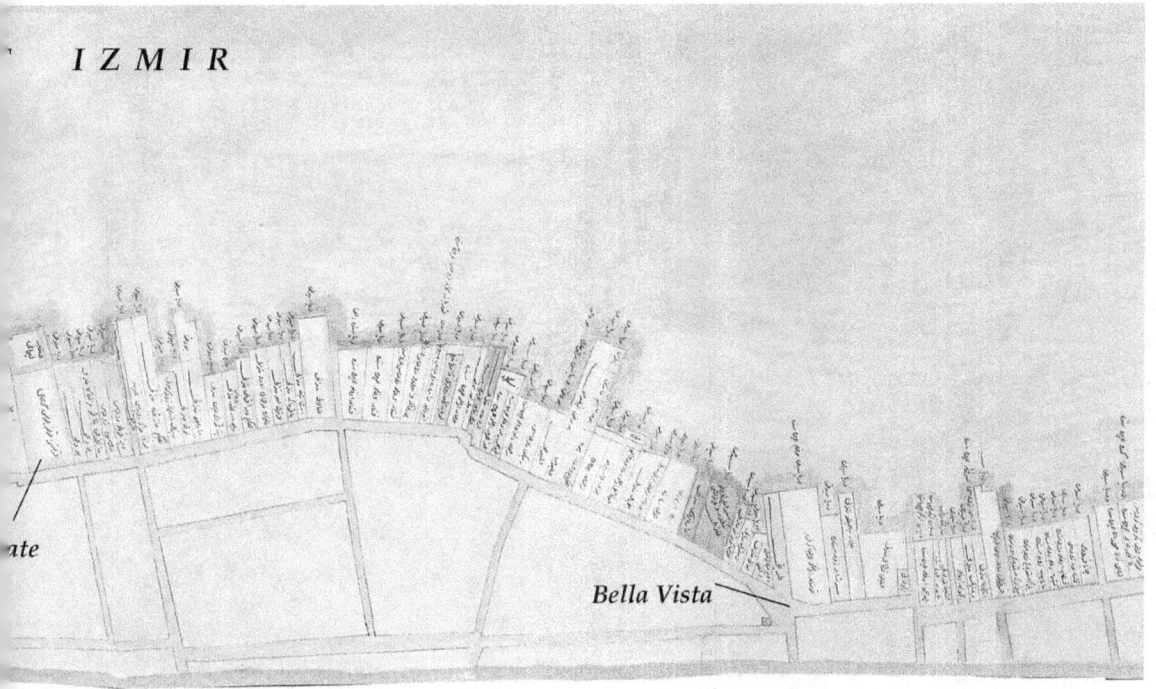

for over a third of a mile along the shore. These establishments were densely clustered and abutted directly on the water for easy access to shipping but left no public access to the water (Figure 3.4). Small boats, carrying goods, plied between them and the ships anchored at some distance. Further north the shore opened into the short esplanade of the English pier, where the British consulate and two steamship companies—the French Messagerie Maritime and the Austrian Lloyd, respectively headquartered in Trieste and Marseilles—were located (Figures 3.5, 3.6). At the end of this short esplanade, which also served as a landing for all overseas passengers, came a row of closely packed residences and drinking houses, operated by Greek and Maltese boatmen. This part of the shore had several wooden piers running out into the sea, suggesting private shipping activity. From there on was another stretch of European houses directly on the bay, among which were the French, Austrian, Prussian, Portuguese, and Greek consulates with the arms of each foreign consulate emblazoned on their seaward facade. On their marine front, most of these houses had private terraces, forming roofs to their warehouses, and upon which their owners commanded a view of the bay. The row

FIGURE 3.4. View of the old shore with cafés on piles and ship chandlers, ca. 1865. The large building in the background housed the Austrian Lloyd's Steamship Company (lower floors) and the Greek casino (top floor). Postcard. Courtesy of the Suna & İnan Kıraç Research Institute for Mediterranean Civilizations.

FIGURE 3.5. View of the English pier, ca. 1855. Courtesy of the Suna & İnan Kıraç Research Institute for Mediterranean Civilizations.

FIGURE 3.6. Maritime side of the British consulate on the English pier, ca. 1855. Courtesy of the Suna & İnan Kıraç Research Institute for Mediterranean Civilizations.

of houses terminated at Bella Vista corner near the French hospital and the Turkish guardhouse, which announced the limit of the built-up zone. Beyond this area, houses became sparser. Another military barracks stood on this end of the shore not far from a windmill that marked the northern tip of the shore, adjoining the Bay of Burnabat.[10]

Although the city extended for over two and a half miles along the bay, public access to the shore was possible only in a few designated locations since nearly all of the shore land was under private lease. Until the construction of the quay, there was no structured attempt at providing along the bay front a space for the collective use and enjoyment of city residents. Vakıf stipulations primarily focused on granting private rights to the water and stimulating development. They required private parties to comply with procedural matters and the basic servitudes that typically prevented one from obstructing a neighbor's light and air or from blocking an existing public way. But they neither obliged lessees to leave a public easement along the water nor imposed on these properties provisions to benefit the public good. As a result, the coastline had been incrementally developed and reconfigured through the aggregate interests of an ever-increasing array of private parties. Given these circumstances, any attempt to open a continuous public easement along the shore necessarily undermined owners' direct access to the water and was likely to generate contention. Presumably, central government bureaucrats recognized this tension when they began to set the parameters for the redevelopment of the waterfront. While the official report of the Council of State explicitly stated the public utility of the project and the importance of a modern and orderly harbor to "increasing the value and esteem" of the city, it did not enforce the adoption of the recently enacted eminent domain clause. Instead, following the standard practice of seeking the accord of shore owners, it declared that the project could go on only after the majority of the proprietors approved it.[11] Indeed, in Ottoman laws, actions that concerned any collective property required the preliminary consent of the community of abutting owners.[12] Whether government officials saw massive expropriation to contradict the existing statute of the shore or to be simply unwarranted, they insisted that the quay was to be developed in ways that would not generate hardship to the community of owners.

Debating the Public Good

A variety of actors voiced their desire to see a more orderly waterfront. Ottoman officials, merchants and businessmen, and newspaper owners and local correspondents, among others, brought up the pressing need of improving the shore in the general interest of the city. But how they articulated the public good to be derived from the shore and identified its benefiting public did not neatly align, placing different, at times conflicting, demands on what the space ought to be. To Ottoman authorities, the deformed and tortuous arrangement of the old shore was a problem because it allowed easy and constant smuggling. Ships often loaded and unloaded their goods at private piers and stored them directly in warehouses without paying customs dues. Rows of small coffee shops and drinking houses built on piles running out into the sea, numerous inaccessible inlets, and construction sites screened illegal activity along the seashore from the sight of customs officials and resulted in important losses of tax revenue (Figure 3.7). Access to the shore to seize smugglers was further impeded when these shops belonged to individuals who could claim foreign status and extraterritorial rights, allowing them to refuse, or at least delay, access to government officials. To remedy this situation, in 1862, the central government asked local authorities for studies and cost estimates to build an improved quay on piles.[13] The aim was to prevent losses in tax revenue by gaining better access, control, and an open line of vision along the wharves. This would help keep tabs on trade activity and facilitate revenue collection. It also had the added advantage of embellishing the shorefront with a regular facade that would represent the second city of the empire to the outside world. For the reformist government, which was trying to increase its control over the property market and police the shore, an orderly quay was of the highest priority. It would help secure state interest, and by extension would serve the interest of the public as a whole.

Izmir's business community perceived this development as an essential addition to the existing network of transportation. Already in 1857, as the first railway was projected, a mixed commission of merchants had studied the question of a new pier in conjunction with that of the railway station.[14] The proposals for railway piers, however, were limited in scope. They primarily sought to connect the railway terminal directly to the shore, rather than developing the entire waterfront. In addition, because storms periodically interrupted shipping activity at the landing facilities, a safe harbor that reduced the impact of variable weather became increasingly urgent. In 1865, forty-four of the most influential indigenous and foreign merchants in the city sent a memorandum to the governor of Izmir in favor of building new wharves and improving shipping conditions.[15] The merchants' appeal for order was based on a rationale that linked commercial improvement to the welfare and the livelihood of the entire population. Their views were couched in terms not of the discrete interests of the mercantile community, but of the well-being of an entire city and by extension of the state. As the argument went, improved infrastructure would improve trade—the most important sector of the city's economy. It would increase state revenues and provide employment for the working classes, thus benefiting large segments of the population. According to this rationale, the public good was the good of the economy—an idea that continues to have enormous power today.

That the development of the quay represented far more than commercial advantages was yet another view that received passionate support in newspaper columns (Figures 3.8, 3.9). For emerging classes of cosmopolitan residents, a modern waterfront was a fitting means of satisfying their social aspirations and bringing their city up to par with concurrent developments across the modernizing world. For example, the Izmir correspondent to the *Levant Herald* proposed turning the bay front into "a broad quay throughout its entire length" to "serve not only the purposes of trade, but . . . supply the want so much felt in Smyrna of a public promenade, where our carriages might roll . . . and our flaneurs might lounge."[16] At the time, the benefits that some European cities had derived from

FIGURE 3.7. View of the old shore with cafés on piles, ca. 1865. To the left are the flour windmill and Café Kivoto; to the right are the Austrian Lloyd's Steamship Company, the Greek casino, and Captain Paolo's café. Drawing by A. Deroy; engraved by A. Davdenarde. From *Le Monde Illustré* 32 (1873). Courtesy of University of Minnesota Libraries.

removing their historic fortifications and creating promenades were recognized well beyond their place of origin. Boulevards and esplanades were becoming part of a spatial vocabulary that had to be emulated both as model spaces for bourgeois entertainment and to ease circulation within cities. Indeed, in cities of the industrial and colonial worlds, there were concurrent efforts to create such spaces either on the fringes of the old urban fabric or by cutting through congested urban areas.[17] Taking his lead from such developments, Izmir's correspondent rose above commercial and utilitarian demands to advocate for a broad, orderly, and well-paved quay—a genteel space for recreation and promenade, for seeing and being seen—that would transform the experience of the city and of its citizens.

Similar calls, made a few years earlier in the *Journal de Constantinople*, stressed the potential public health benefits that would accrue from developing an esplanade. In this case, the correspondent urged for the creation of a wholesome environment around the shore. He condemned the continual encroachment on the bay and accused the few privileged property owners of depriving the city of its

FIGURE 3.8. View of the Cordon as a genteel space, ca. 1880. Courtesy of the Suna & İnan Kıraç Research Institute for Mediterranean Civilizations.

"fundamental pleasure" and of its "lungs."[18] Since the water lots had been placed on the market, the few narrow easements that formerly led to or adjoined the shore had been gradually blocked as owners extended their property straight down on the water "without bothering to substitute the portion of the quay that they blocked."[19] Owners, however, saw no obligation to compensate for the space they included in their property as the filling in of the water lot was in itself a taxing expense. The easements that led to the shore functioned as semiprivate spaces, much like dead-end streets that belonged primarily to neighboring property owners, who were entitled to regulate their use.[20] That until then the office of the Evkaf and the cadastral office (Emlak) had not challenged owners' doings may confirm the weight of proprietors' right to the shore or simply the inability of these offices to enforce such regulations. In his attack, the Izmir correspondent to the *Journal de Constantinople*, however, overtly reproached such practice for violating "all the rules of common sense and general interest." He asked owners to "advance onto the water, granted that (1) some order preceded such progressive movement, (2) at least 6 pics [15 feet] of quay is reserved to public use, and

(3) sufficient number of easements are opened not to prevent the flow between the shore and the town."[21] Demands of this nature received official support, in part because they corroborated the authorities' increasing desire to control trade on the shore. Indeed, a few months later, the Sublime Porte gave orders to the governor to take measures against shore owners who blocked sea views and to enforce a public easement on the seaside of such properties.[22] Regardless of whether such orders were implemented, they highlighted the role of the shore as a space of collective interest belonging to a more general public rather than to myriad discrete individuals.

In general, the anonymous Smyrna correspondents who supplied news to Istanbul's press promoted a notion of public good that transcended private interests. Using discursive strategies that had become a standard journalistic practice by the nineteenth century, they presented themselves as disinterested parties,

FIGURE 3.9. View of the Cordon with carriages and strollers, by Rubellin Père & Fils, ca. 1880. Courtesy of the Suna & İnan Kıraç Research Institute for Mediterranean Civilizations.

acting not as private individuals but as a "disembodied public subject."[23] Hence, they often spoke on behalf of the "population of Smyrna," denounced opportunism, and condemned endeavors that placed private interests above the general welfare. They also demanded responses to local problems by invoking themes of openness and political accountability. The owners and editors of Istanbul's French- and English-language press too went to great lengths to portray their papers' disinterested stance, sometimes publicly announcing to their readers that letters and commentaries on subjects that dealt with purely private interest, except as advertisement, would be declined.[24] Regardless of the specific issues at stake, newspapermen framed their opinions in terms of the public good, referring to an indivisible collective benefit in opposition to solely particular interests. To advance their arguments, some reporters also promoted conceptions of a more universalistic public that crossed cultural and class divides. During discussions of a prospective landing pier, for example, the reporter for the *Journal de Constantinople* remarked that "the golden dreams of such and such individual fades away, but in counterpart the Turkish, Greek, and Jewish quarters gain more value, the working class is better off and an entire population is not sacrificed for the interest of three or four speculators."[25] Although the reporters and editors of the empire's various newspapers were neither in agreement with one another nor as disinterested as they portrayed themselves to be, these rhetorical strategies helped cast them as neutral agents capable of political judgment and summon more effectively support for their arguments. Moreover, their familiarity with both domestic politics and the international context gave more legitimacy to their arguments, allowing them to reach broader audiences in the capital and beyond.

The local periodical press not only recorded and articulated divergent positions about the public good of the project; it also inaugurated a new type of platform for its audiences to discuss, contest, and shape the project's parameters. As the works progressed, different understandings of the public good were voiced through the press, ultimately directing and shaping the design of the waterfront.

Shaping the Shore

In 1864, three British subjects, John Charnaud, Alfred Barker, and George Guarracino, who resided in Izmir and in Istanbul submitted to the Sublime Porte a preliminary plan calling for the construction of a continuous straight boulevard along the shore. Building a straight boulevard along the uneven shoreline meant that some waterfront lots would end up as far as three hundred meters from the shore, creating important disparities in the amount of terrain to be reclaimed and bought by owners. Recognizing the multiple private interests at stake, and asserting that a new development along the shore required owners' approval, the central authorities asked Governor Kayserili Ahmed Pasha to form a committee of local notables and proprietors to evaluate the project.[26] Understandably, shore owners whose property would depreciate viewed the project unfavorably. The occupants of one part of the shoreline opposed the scheme by submitting a counterproject, which was disapprovingly described by one reporter as a "deformed and tortuous wharf," in place of the straight boulevard proposed originally.[27] Seeking to minimize the amount of land reclamation, the counterproject maintained the geometry of the existing shore. In the eyes of this reporter, however, dissenting shore owners were "conservative gentlemen," lacking any sense of public spirit, and their proposal was an "insult to the common sense and good taste of the Smyrna public as well as of the Turkish authorities." In addition, their hostility to the project was even less worthy because they lived in "an unsavory part of the shore line" and "lay claim to vested rights in the scum and sludge, which dampen the foundations of their tenements and which the broad straight quay, such as the projectors propose, would sweep away and clear up."[28]

For the opponents of the scheme whose land was further away, however, it was important to protect their water access without incurring vast expenses to purchase and fill in the land. More importantly, the proposal placed the less-affluent owners at the Point at a considerable disadvantage from their neighbors since their properties were the furthest from the proposed straight line. Two opposing views about the purpose of the development were behind this dispute. For the opponents the project was a private enterprise that threatened their individual rights and their livelihood for the sole purpose of serving the pecuniary interest of the three British entrepreneurs. For newspapermen who favored the quay, however, the new harbor was an enterprise of public benefit aimed at beautifying and transforming the city, providing employment to the working class, and improving general prosperity. Building a new quay was also a way of partaking in the spirit of progress, and its advantages easily offset private interests. These two convictions coexisted and competed throughout the project, producing delays and complications at various phases of the implementation.

Although the Sublime Porte gave priority to shore owners in developing their own scheme, it proved impossible to coordinate such a costly endeavor and reconcile each proprietor's interest. Taking up the more viable British proposal, but wanting to relieve shore owners' discontent, the central government asked Alfred Barker, who was living in Izmir at the time and was one of the promoters of the original plan, for suggestions for an alternate scheme. The proposed revisions broke the initial straight boulevard at four points according to the existing layout of the shore, thus regularizing the amount of land filled in without destroying the sense of a continuous avenue (Map 3.3). This arrangement also conformed to the desires of the customs and tax offices for it allowed easy control and good visibility for guards placed at the break points—a prime concern explicitly stated in official correspondence between the Porte and the governor of Izmir.[29] In November 1867, the Public Works Ministry approved the modified scheme, and the British entrepreneurs acquired the concession to build the quay with all required dependencies. The contract specified the construction of a twenty-five-pics (62.5-feet)-wide quay over a distance of four thousand meters, starting at the Point, the northern tip of the shore, and ending at Sarıkışla. It also included a tramway line, necessary sewers, and a jetty in front of the customs house. In return, the government granted the company privileges over reclaimed land and the right to operate the installation for a period of twenty-five years, after which the works would become state property. They also guaranteed that in order to protect the sea view of prospective owners they would prevent the sale of the sea beyond the limit of the quay.[30]

A month later, the concessionaires signed a contract with the Dussaud Brothers, who committed to build the works within a period of four years.[31] By January 1868, they launched the Smyrna Quay Company as a limited partnership with shares to be divided among select investors in the city and foreign industrialists in London.[32] The administrative council was composed of local and foreign

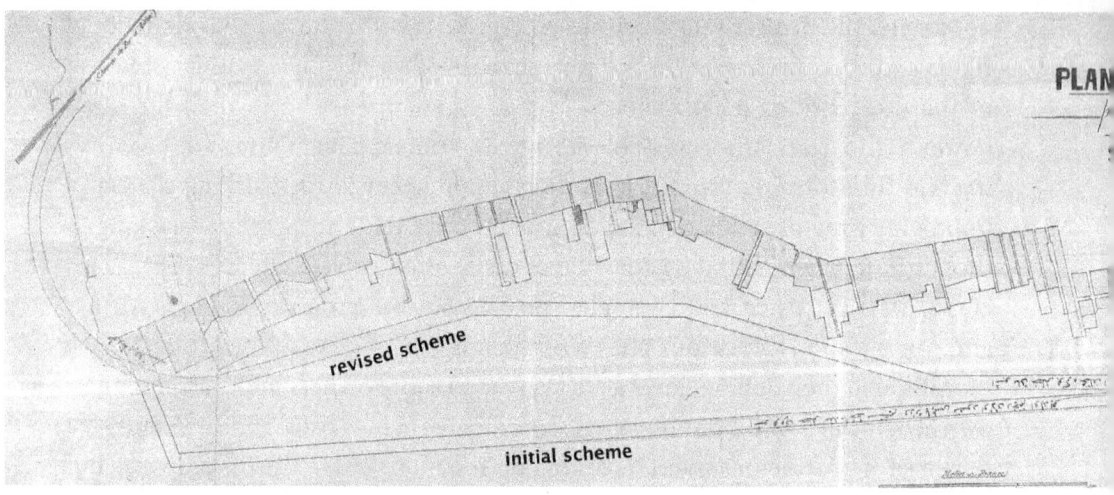

MAP 3.3. The quay scheme proposed and revised by J. Charnaud, A. Barker, and G. Guarracino, 1867. The lower part of the map is Izmir's Bay. Courtesy of Başbakanlık Ottoman Archives.

investors including, in addition to five British investors, Ange Cousinéry, a local French merchant, and K. Abro and A. Spartalı, two Ottoman merchants under British protection.[33] The company's capital was only 2.5 million francs, while the cost of construction was estimated to be 6 million, which was not so easy to raise for an enterprise perceived as having dubious prospects. At the beginning, the Dussaud Brothers invested four hundred thousand francs in the endeavor, becoming important shareholders in the enterprise. The entrepreneurs were hoping to raise additional funds as the works progressed, particularly through the sale of reclaimed land and the wharf tax.

Negotiating an agreement with the Porte did not guarantee local support for the project. To the contrary, the very stipulations of the contract produced general distrust about the endeavor. Shore owners perceived the privilege given to the company as a direct threat to their private property. The schedule of work granted the company substantial power over water lots, allowing it to fill in the water, to dispose of such land in the manner most advantageous to its interests, and to use the provisions of the imperial law of "expropriation for public utility." In case shore owners failed to fill in their portion of the water within a period ranging from one to three years—depending on how long they had owned the property—the company could expropriate the property by reimbursing the owners the purchase price shown on their title deeds.[34] Most water lots were privately registered in the name of individuals who now had to comply with the directives and deadlines of the company to maintain their water access. Owners whose properties

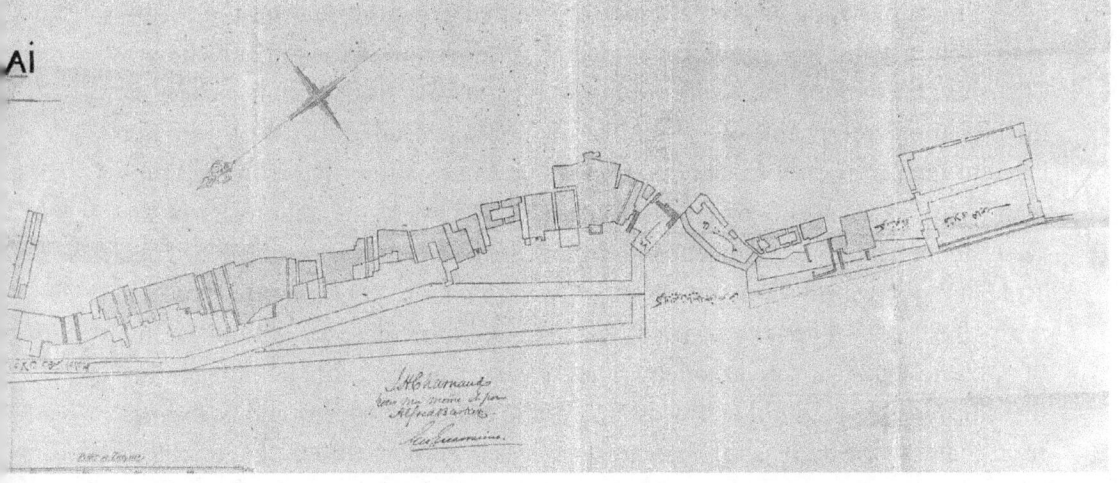

would be stranded inland saw their conditions deteriorate since they would not receive adequate compensation to balance out the loss of water view and free embarking and disembarking facilities. Not only would their property lose value, but the new parcel they would acquire, if they could afford to do so, would be subject to high property taxes without generating any revenue unless they spent substantially more money to build on it. The relationship of public works to private property created a major uproar among existing property owners, who argued that it was unfair to hurt a considerable number of private parties and their vested interests to develop public works. Proprietors were even more alarmed since they expected the entrepreneurs to place the largest possible amount of building sites on the market in order to maximize their revenue. This not only would harm them, but would negatively affect the real-estate market and by extension the general interest of the city. They denounced the enterprise as greedy and blamed it for promoting private business over general welfare. As an anonymous "Anglo-Smyrniote" observed in a letter to *La Turquie,* proprietors saw themselves as victims of the "appetite of a vampire public company aiming for lawless gain."[35] The letter also called for the attention of Ottoman officials by questioning whether notables in Istanbul would "consent to see their charming view and their fresh breeze of the Bosphorus be seized, to be relegated to a back street and have their magnificent property ruined in the personal interest of concessionaires."[36]

Stronger and more enduring objections against the scheme came from local merchants who questioned who should have control over the space and under what conditions. The imperial government conceded the company the privilege of levying duties upon all goods landed or shipped along the quay for the period of the contract with the condition of receiving 12 percent of the total revenues.[37] The wharf tax became the object of the longest and most heated public debate. At the beginning, merchants of foreign nationalities contended that they were not liable to the tax given the customs treaties that their nations had with the Ottoman state. Yet, according to the convention, regardless of the nationality of the vessel all merchandise landing at and shipped from the quay was subject to dues. Troubled by this provision, merchants of foreign nationality raised their protest to the Porte soon after the contract was signed. To mediate an agreeable solution, the minister of foreign affairs, Fuad Pasha, issued an official note stating that ships loading and unloading directly at the customs house would be exempt from charges. The ministerial note, however, was in conflict with the contract that allowed uniform taxation throughout the entire length of the works. New negotiations between the government and the Quay Company led to modifications in the agreement. An article added to the convention disengaged the company from any construction near the customs house, requiring it to allow a one hundred–pic (250-foot) zone on both sides of the customs house for free access (Map 3.4). In exchange, the government surrendered its 12 percent royalty to the company until the completion of the works.

This unexpected turn of events created a loophole in the rationale of the agreement. The Quay Company saw its anticipated revenues substantially diminished. Merchants, however, found one hundred pics to be too limited. When the company began charging wharf dues on the completed parts of the works, merchants continued to press for further extensions to the free zone.[38] In their appeal to the government and to newspapers, they referred to the quay works as a private affair, defined by a contract between Ottoman authorities and the Quay Company. They alleged that such a contract should not interfere with international treaties that protected shipping activity or become a threat to the "commerce of Smyrna" that they represented and upon which the prosperity of the entire city depended.[39] In addition to controversies related to private property and the control of management of the quay, *La Turquie* launched a new series of attacks on the negative effects of the works on Izmir's environmental conditions. As the

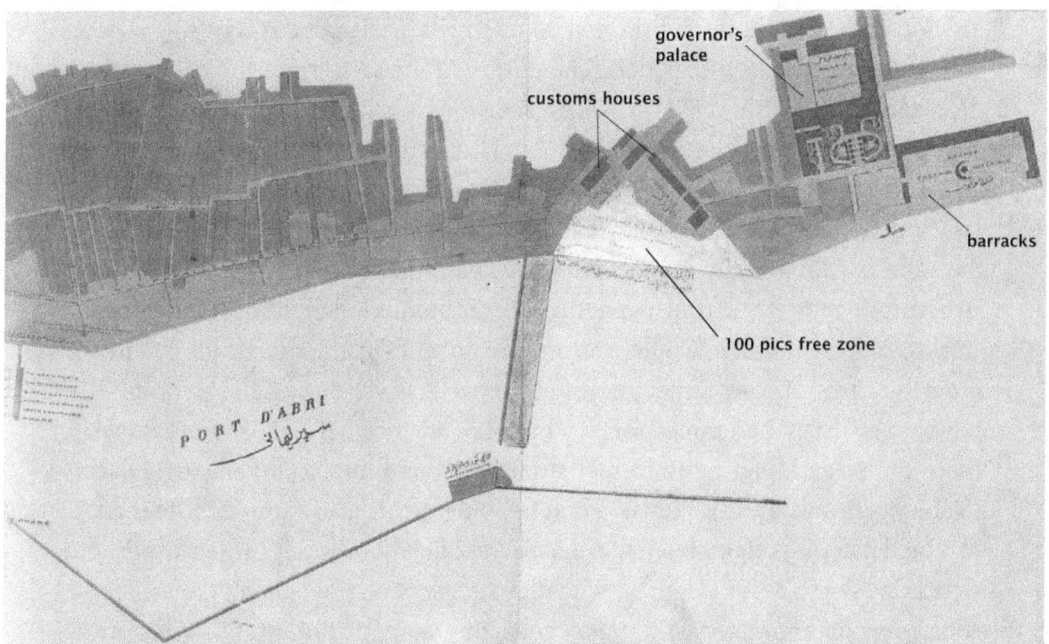

MAP 3.4. The negotiated one hundred pics free zone near the customs house. This section of the map was revised over and again to suit changing priorities. From *Osmanlı'dan Cumhuriyet'e İzmir Haritaları* (Ankara: Ajans Türk, 1998); original (1875) in Izmir Maritime Museum Archive.

one hundred pics free zone was negotiated, the paper deployed arguments that detailed the dangers the works inflicted upon public hygiene and public wealth, while also demonstrating the "uselessness" *(inutilité)* of the works with respect to shipping activity. The articles dedicated particular attention to the deleterious effects of the project upon urban sanitation and accused the promoters of imperiling the health of an entire city in exchange for maximum return on their investment.[40] The entrepreneurs were only responsible for extending the existing pipes to the new shore. This provision was found inadequate, for it would escalate actual sanitation problems experienced in the heart of town. Given the topography of the city, the discharge of refuse water had been a constant concern for inhabitants of the lower town. Part of the city, built on an acclivity, naturally drained itself. The lower parts, however, which had experienced a rapid population growth within the previous thirty years, had either no drain at all or poor drains kept open most of the year.[41] In addition, continual encroachment on the bay had only exacerbated these problems because the grade of reclaimed land was insufficient and typically, during rainstorms, sewers stopped flowing and winds drove the slops back, blocking the ducts and flooding the streets.

Concerns about public hygiene preceded the quay works. As discussed in the previous chapter, the insalubrious state of streets and public spaces was repeatedly mentioned in newspaper commentaries. At the same time, the relocation of the lazaretto and extramural burial had been looming large on the agenda of local government agents since the mid-1860s. This context of heightened sensitivity about urban hygiene measures gave greater currency to the attacks waged by *La Turquie* on the Smyrna Quay Company for compromising public health for the sake of filling a few private pockets. The articles maintained that the new structures on the waterfront, consisting of continuous tall buildings (three to four stories) along the water, would prevent the flow of fresh air from the sea to the inner quarters of town, infecting the city, particularly during hot periods. The newspaper used the opinion of the medical practitioners of Izmir to support these claims and referred to former studies that tied the lack of adequate drains to the death toll during the last cholera epidemic. It also reminded its readers of "the deleterious miasmas that infected vast neighborhoods," when winds and storms pushed refuse water back to the streets, "creating ceaseless pestilential sources" and announced with unprecedented gravity that all would be lost if the scheme was allowed to go on as suggested.[42]

If shore owners, merchants, and social activists were united in their antagonism against the enterprise, there was no immediate congruence in their conception of public good. Shore owners, most of whom were also part of the mercantile community, saw the protection of individual property and free-trade rights as a prerequisite and a necessary condition to general welfare. In their letter to the editor of *La Turquie,* the spokesmen of the "commerce of Smyrna" underscored that if their trade interests and rights perished, "those of the government would certainly not prosper."[43] While the business elite worked with the assumption that increased trade served the interest of the state and benefited the larger segments of the population, the reporter of *La Turquie* did not necessarily share this view. Instead, he saw excessive trade activity as contaminating the quay and spoiling the quality of a modern urban space (Figure 3.10). The company had to set aside a space three to six meters wide all along the quay for laying a tramway, running the full length of the quay with direct access to the customs house and serving the company as well as the general public.[44] In his attacks, the reporter disapproved of the idea of a tramway since it was to carry both freight and passengers (Figure

FIGURE 3.10. Commercial activity along the Cordon, by Rubellin Père & Fils, ca. 1880. The area was usually crowded with files of camels bearing bales of merchandise. Courtesy of the Suna & İnan Kıraç Research Institute for Mediterranean Civilizations.

3.11). He despised the idea that the tramway was to transport merchandise as it would prevent free circulation along the waterfront and crowd the whole area, ruining the quay and depriving all classes from enjoying the "beautiful public promenade."[45] As various parties debated the value of the works they produced new definitions of public good in relation to urban hygiene, private property, and trade rights. Public good was a flexible signifier that was capable of expressing different views and assumptions about what constituted progress and improvement and who the public of Izmir was.

Sites of Friction

With heavy dependence on the disposition of the business community for building its capital and unable to withstand local distrust, the British concessionaires could not raise the necessary funds and eventually went bankrupt. In the meantime, the Dussaud Brothers had already begun carrying out their agreement. Experienced in dealing with large-scale ventures and less dependent on the financial

FIGURE 3.11. Freight train along the Cordon, ca. 1890. The freight train was allowed to run only during night hours so as not to interfere with tramway traffic. Postcard. Courtesy of the Suna & İnan Kıraç Research Institute for Mediterranean Civilizations.

support and trust of the local business community, they took on the concessions previously granted to Barker, Charnaud, and Guarracino and acquired all the shares to become the sole owners of the Smyrna Quay Company. The revised contract and the takeover by the Dussaud Brothers allowed the completion of the quay in 1875. In addition, the full involvement of the Dussaud Brothers, an esteemed international firm, provided more local support for the works, particularly among promoters of French interests. After the Dussaud takeover several newspapers began to praise the project for making Izmir "the first city in the empire to enjoy such progress."[46]

This change in the perception and the merit of the project was not unanimous as the Dussaud enterprise faced mounting difficulties in enforcing the stipulations of the contract, and their takeover did not eliminate antagonism against the works. In 1872, three years after the project began, the Quay Company met with landowners' resistance to filling in the land or paying for its cost. Months after the official expropriation of their land, coffee-shop owners and other small businesses refused to give up their establishments and vacate the premises. Forced expropriation produced not only discontent and delaying tactics among owners, but also a heightened level of opportunism. Business owners, knowing that they ultimately had to vacate their properties, no longer bothered to maintain their structures. On at least one occasion this led to a tragic accident. On February 9, 1873, at around ten o'clock in the evening, a coffee shop known as Kivoto, built on piles off shore, gave way suddenly during an acrobatic performance, and the audience was thrown into the deep water, causing the loss of one hundred lives (see Figure 3.7).[47] Six weeks before the disaster, the Dussauds had officially purchased Kivoto. They had ordered the owner to vacate the premises because the structure was in a dangerous condition and it was necessary to demolish it to facilitate the quay works.[48] Although central authorities sent two orders for taking down such structures, all remained unheeded until the grievous event forced local authorities to demolish all other wooden coffee shops running out into the sea.

The layout of the sewers was another site of friction. In 1872 government approval of the sewer lines was pending. Meanwhile, the company put off the filling in of reclaimed land and started building the outer wall of the quay, which was their priority in order to fulfill the terms of the contract.[49] The process of construction produced long and stagnant water pools between the old shore and the new quay walls (Figure 3.12). In the spring of 1872 the foul smell around the quay walls alarmed many people, particularly waterside residents and foreign consuls, whose houses were near this wet zone. The formation of wet zones

FIGURE 3.12. The construction of the quay showing the landfill along the bay front, ca. 1870. Courtesy of the Suna & İnan Kıraç Research Institute for Mediterranean Civilizations.

stimulated the anxiety that mounted in seasons of rain and extreme heat about sewers and public health. The sight and stench of sewers was not only unpleasant to the eyes and the noses, but also dangerous. In summer months Frank Street and its vicinity were "little better than cesspools, whose nephitic exhalations placed the health of the residents in direct jeopardy."[50] Shops were sometimes closed because "sewers spread such an infection."[51] Before the quay works, streets and houses bordering the water had small private sewers flowing freely into the sea, with discharge washed off by sea currents. During the works, however, these sewers emptied into a narrow pool that no longer had a connection to the open sea. All sorts of deposits accumulated, and neither the company nor the authorities took effective measures to alleviate this unhygienic situation. Twelve consuls of Izmir sent an official note to their respective embassies in Istanbul to protest against the company's leaving sewers open during hot weather thus poisoning the atmosphere.[52] For lack of sufficient study or by omission there was no clear agreement between local authorities and the company about the tasks related to the sewer lines and embankment works. The only stipulation was that the company should be bound to establish drains down to the sea within the limits of its works.[53] In the note, the consular body decried the threats that the project presented to the health of the city and to the commercial interests of all nations. Their hope was to urge the Sublime Porte to delay the quay wall until all landfill was completed. The consular note also demanded that the company relieve the town of the noxious discharges by building temporary conduits that connected the unhealthy water pools to the sea.

Meanwhile, the governor, Hamdi Pasha, asked Margossian Efendi, the chief engineer of the province of Aydın, and W. Williamson, municipal engineer, to draft a detailed report on how to improve urban hygiene.[54] Initially the company's scheme provided thirteen sewer lines to the sea. The municipal engineers rejected the scheme and suggested instead a hierarchical web with one main collector sewer along Parallel Street, thirty-one branch sewers connecting the main sewer to the sea, and smaller private sewers from the waterside buildings connecting to these thirty-one sewers (Map 3.5).[55] Margossian and Williamson made further suggestions, proposing digging out the ancient galleries that connected the old crusader castle near the shore to the sea and thus developing a "large and magnificent sewer." Their report advocated modern urban planning techniques based on a rational and comprehensive underground web for the entire city. Invoking the methods and the practices used in European cities, the two engineers conceived a triple duct system including the sewer, water, and gas conduits. The sewer plan proposed by the engineers provided the basis for later negotiations with the Quay Company. It also revealed local authorities' determination in having the company execute a modern infrastructure system suited to the second city of the empire.

Although the company recognized the importance of a collector sewer along Parallel Street as the engineers proposed, it refused to build the scheme or to provide any public or private sewers outside the scope of the contract unless the government provided additional compensation for the work. The Quay Company acknowledged, but was not bound to, a notion of public utility. It defined its responsibilities based on the conditions of the contract and on the desire to build up a profitable business. The Dussauds went to Istanbul to negotiate new terms with the Porte and received an extension on their contract in return for developing the public and private sewers from the old shore to the sea and completing the landfill in conjunction with the quay walls. By the close of the negotiations the Public Works Ministry decided that it was the responsibility of individual owners to improve their property and make the necessary connection between street sewers and private lots. Future construction sites on the shore, except the projected streets, were privately owned either by new waterside proprietors or by the company, which became a major property owner on the shore and had to abide by the common rights that regulated these properties. If proprietors refused to improve their lot, the company had the right to perform the necessary work and charge property owners according to the length of their street facade.[56]

The problem of drainage exhibited the difficulty of reconciling the requirements of a private enterprise with those of a public endeavor. This conflict between private pursuits and public purposes can be further traced within the controversial position of some of the parties involved in the project. Richard Van Lennep, the consul of the Dutch community and an established merchant in Izmir, was also the local director of the quay enterprise. Van Lennep's name appeared in the diplomatic note that the consular body sent to Istanbul to deplore

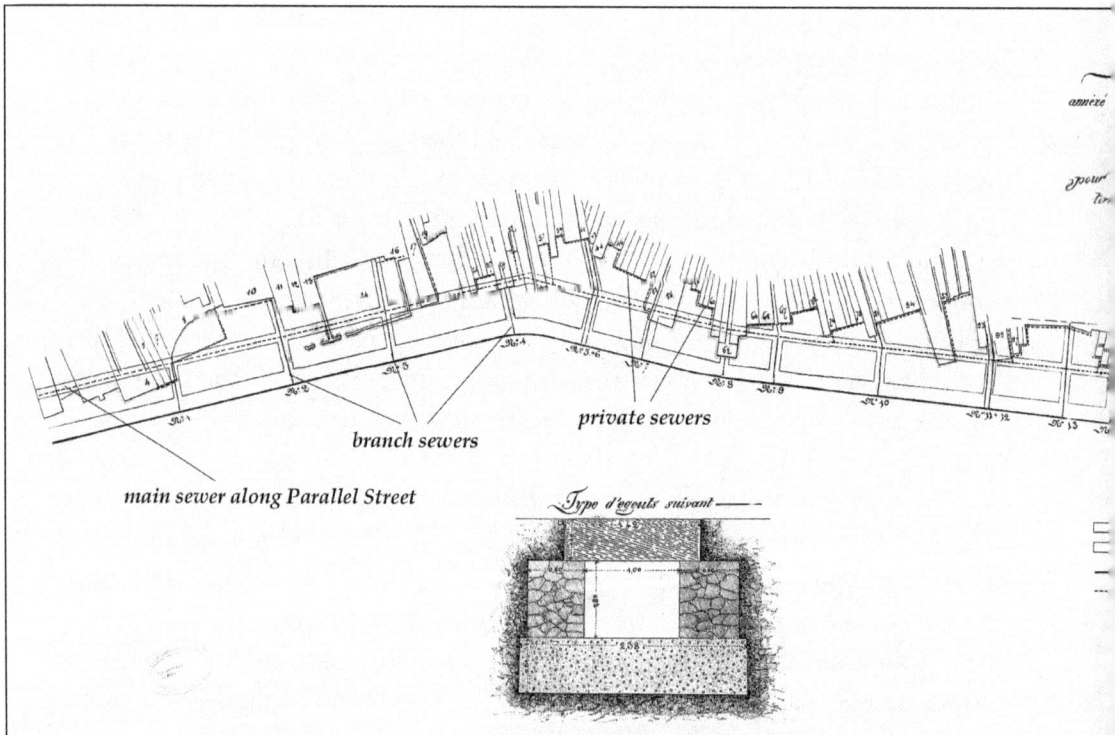

MAP 3.5. Sewer lines proposed by C. Margossian and W. Williamson (BOA, BEO, A. AMD. MV. 112/44 [1872/1288]). Courtesy of Başbakanlık Ottoman Archives.

the state of the water pools and ask for official intervention.⁵⁷ In his dealings with Ottoman authorities, however, Van Lennep defended the actions of the Quay Company. In his response to the report of the municipal engineers and to the imperial commissioner, Nihad Efendi, he attenuated the harm caused by the stagnant water pools and dismissed on "scientific" grounds that they constituted a threat to public health.

In 1880, a few years after the completion of the works, *La Turquie* approvingly reprinted a long article from Izmir's French newspaper, *La Réforme*. The article glorified the quay works for considerably improving urban hygiene and bringing about changes in the habits of the population. The reporter drew on standard views that tied physical order and social improvement, linking "new streets, new quarters, new buildings" to "broad-minded ideas, elegance, and comfort" and assessing that "straighter, wider, better paved, and better ventilated streets inevitably lead the mind to seek betterment."⁵⁸ Such optimistic portrayal, however, glossed over some persistent resentment that continued to mar the project, even after the major parts of the works were completed. In 1874, for example,

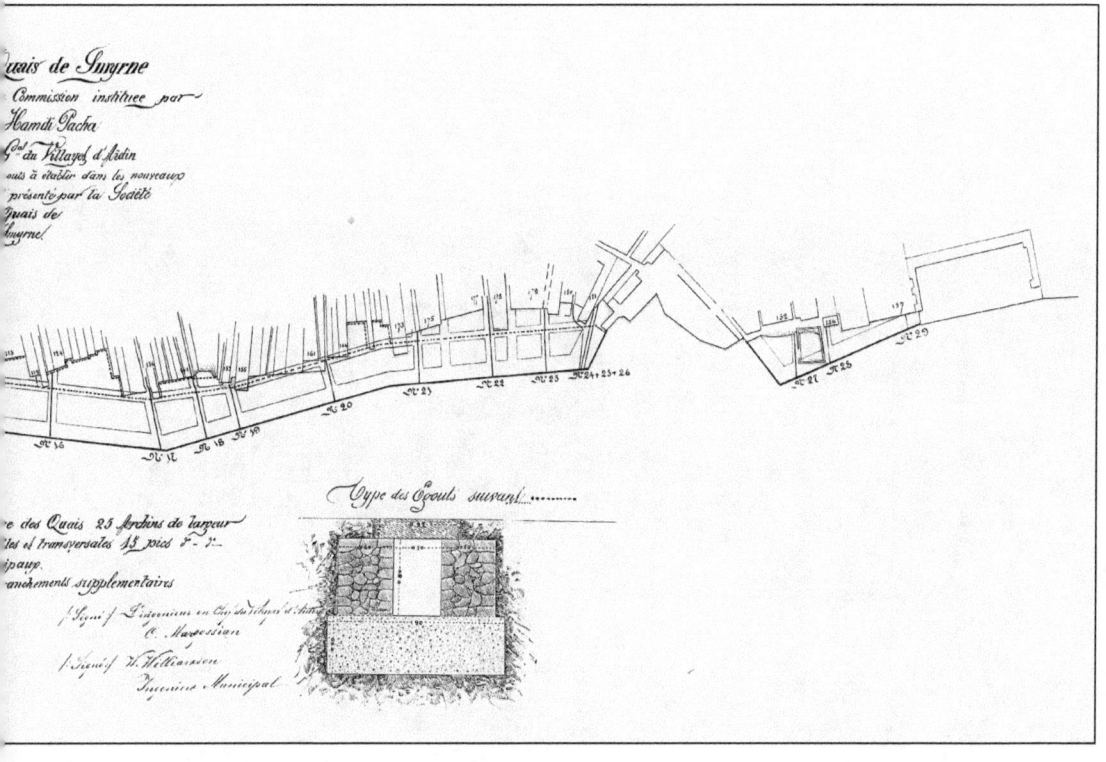

opposition came from new shore owners. As building constructions were to begin soon a group of proprietors sent a petition to Istanbul to complain about the "uniform plan" that the Dussaud Brothers imposed on buildings along the quay. More than the uniformity of the plan, however, it was having to give up land for a two-meter footpath that produced strong resentment. The street along the quay was to be eighteen meters broad. Considering that a tramway was laid down about five meters from the sea, the remainder was insufficient for the construction of a suitable footpath. The Dussaud Brothers proposed building an arcade, asking all owners to give two meters of ground in exchange for which they would be allowed to extend their second floor for four meters over the arcade (Figure 3.13).[59] According to the Dussauds, the proprietors would in the end lose nothing while the quay would be endowed with a regular arcade and gas lamps attached at every four pillars as well as sufficient space for pedestrian circulation. Landowners, who were reluctant to incur extra expense, however, resented the plan, attacking its regimented aesthetic. The arcade was never built, and the casual canvass awnings of stores and cafés provided shade to pedestrians.

FIGURE 3.13. Arcade proposed by the Dussaud Brothers. Courtesy of İzmir Büyükşehir Belediyesi Kent Kitaplığı; original in Başbakanlık Ottoman Archives.

After the completion of the contracted works, the question of the one hundred pics free area was again brought to the fore. The free zone left around the customs house did not entirely resolve the problem of wharf dues, and throughout the execution of the works, the business community, particularly British merchants, maintained a fierce opposition against wharf dues.[60] On their part, the Dussaud Brothers wanted to extend the quay works in front of the customs house and abolish the one hundred pics free zone to be able to apply uniform taxation on the quay. The space around the customs house was also disagreeable to those who perceived it as a remnant of the old shore that needed to be improved. In 1874, Dr. Borg, the public health officer and physician at the Ottoman hospital, had addressed a report to the governor about the dangers caused by "the heaps of refuse accumulating around those coffeehouses, which are built on piles in the immediate vicinity of the customhouse."[61] In 1876, a new round of negotiations

FIGURE 3.14. Boatmen loading and unloading in front of the new customs house, ca. 1880. Courtesy of the Suna & İnan Kıraç Research Institute for Mediterranean Civilizations.

started between Ottoman authorities, merchants, and the company. The Dussaud Brothers proposed giving merchants a considerable reduction in quay dues and providing important urban improvements in the city if they agreed to forfeit their rights of landing goods at the customs house free of quay dues.[62] In return they received a ten-year extension on the privilege of operating the installations. On this basis, a mixed commission of experienced local merchants, including J. E. Psiachi, J. B. Patterson, P. Aliotti, A. Farkoa, Abrahamoğlu Enriquez, Yenişehirlizade Ahmed Efendi, and Evliyazade Mehmed Efendi, developed a new reduced tariff.[63] The issue, however, would not be entirely settled for another decade.

Taxation on the quay agitated not only merchants but also more modest, yet not less indispensable segments of quay users. In 1874, when the quay works were mostly completed, the government decided to impose a monthly tax of fifteen piastres per month on the boatmen who plied between the ships and the shore (Figure 3.14). Once they were informed of their tax liability, the boatmen protested by drawing up a petition to the Porte. Their demand did not seem to be heard since a new order was received, enjoining that the tax should be levied and that the boatmen had to pay additionally ninety piastres as six-month arrears. As the boatmen did not consent to such terms, and were not permitted to continue their task until they had paid the required arrears, they went on strike. All work in the port was suspended that day, and passengers who had to embark on that day were obliged to pay the ninety piastres tax in addition to their usual fare. In the meantime quarrels between the boatmen and the police and mounting turmoil led to the granting of delays that allowed the boatmen to resume their work.[64]

Izmir's public sphere emerged from deliberations, contests, and compromises over the shaping of the physical city and the construction of its modern infrastructure, and especially the quay. Such issue-based debates galvanized disparate groups into action, providing points of convergence that transcended people's primary religious, ethnic, or professional affiliations. These alliances were neither ideological nor consistent nor long lived, but rather driven by business and personal interests. Sometimes one individual, as in the case of Richard Van Lennep, could be involved in two opposite ends of the same debate, or the same newspaper could advocate different views, as *La Turquie* did, depending on which parties were involved and the specific concern at hand. In sum, the exchanges and transactions that defined Izmir's public sphere were fluid and open to continual remaking and redefinition through lived experience.

The building of Izmir's quay also illustrates how different players mobilized rival yet equally novel and modern definitions of the public good, which they variously equated with tax revenues, economic growth and robust trade, a dependable real-estate market, or rights to healthy and orderly environments. To rally support for their argument, opposing parties frequently cast the "public good" as antagonistic to "private interest," implying that the pursuit of one would inevitably mean the violation of the other. Newspapers and governmental policies further reified this divide. In practice, however, appealing to the public good more often than not was used as a legitimizing rhetoric. As various private aspirations were couched in terms of public good, it was difficult to neatly separate the public good that a given project promised from the private interests it served. At a more general level, the negotiations detailed in this chapter suggest some broader directions for analyzing urban modernization in cities across the globe. Viewing city-building processes in relation to the constitution of a modern public sphere and competing notions of the public good foregrounds the actors and their actions. By drawing attention to who negotiates with whom, how, and why, it helps uncover the messy, compromised, and uncertain context of everyday life, thereby opening new possibilities for reconstituting the rich texture of urban experiences that over the long haul transform cities.

Up until now, I have explored the production of a modern urban landscape through property and tax regimes, municipal restructuring, and the provision of services and infrastructure, underscoring both interventions and setbacks. In the following chapter, I will turn to more ephemeral yet not less powerful practices that further expose how the interactions between urban dwellers and their material surroundings shaped Izmir's physical landscape and its residents' view of their place in it.

4

Performing Community
Rituals and Identity

ON MAY 27, 1842, *ÉCHO DE L'ORIENT* ran a long report describing the extraordinary pomp surrounding the Corpus Christi procession in Izmir.[1] That year, for the first time, Antonio Mussabini, the archbishop of Izmir, had moved the procession from the private precinct of the church into the streets of Izmir's Frank quarter. Buildings along the itinerary had been lavishly decorated several days in advance. On the morning of the ceremony, squads of soldiers in uniform were stationed along the parade route to keep the crowd in check, and a Muslim guard of honor escorted the procession. In order to ensure a peaceful event, Governor Salih Pasha personally inspected the area several times. The regular and secular (lay) clergy[2] and scores of students from various Catholic institutions cleared the way for the archbishop, who headed the procession, walking under a grand canopy and holding the Eucharist. The French consul—considered "the protector of the Catholics of the Orient"—followed the archbishop along with dignitaries from other Catholic European nations.[3] The solemn procession moved amid the sounds of hymns and the intense smell of incense. It passed an ethnically and religiously diverse crowd, packed in the narrow confines of the streets, reverently watching the event, as gun salutes fired from French, Sardinian, and Austrian warships that stationed in the harbor echoed in the air.

Although non-Muslim feasts and holidays were an integral part of communal expression, and had historically boosted Izmir's reputation as a permissive and liberal place, the 1842 procession departed dramatically from the city's established festive customs.[4] The choice of a public venue for the procession itself broke with the practices of local Catholic churches, whose activities, while protected by extraterritorial agreements, were generally confined to the private precinct of the church. More importantly, the range of participants and spatial strategies deployed by the organizers reveal highly complex and unprecedented political agendas that far transcended the character of a conventional public devotion. For nearly two decades, the empire's Roman Catholic subjects (*Latin râyası*) had been bidding for millet status that would give them an organizational structure comparable to the autonomous Greek Orthodox, Armenian Gregorian, and Jewish millets within the empire.[5] Catholics were small compared to the empire's major non-Muslim communities, but a recent increase in missionary offerings and expanding international trade networks gave these groups more prominence in major commercial centers. Hence, not only did the procession help Archbishop Mussabini solidify his power base by promoting the newly expanded schools and institutions of his church; it also offered local Catholics a unique opportunity to claim centrality in the city and legitimacy within the changing Ottoman constitutional order. In other words, the image of an influential and unified Catholic community, presented by the procession, helped realize ritually what local Catholics lacked in constitutional terms.

Moreover, these efforts at communal self-definition were intimately intertwined with shifting international dynamics. The French consul, for example, used the feast to polish the image of his country as the protector-in-chief of local Catholics. Although France had historically claimed this privilege in the Ottoman Empire, interruptions in missionary support since the 1789 revolution had given the upper hand to the Holy See and Austria. As a matter of fact, the rise of Antonio Mussabini to the rank of archbishop was a sign of the erosion of French dominance. Unlike his immediate predecessors, who were sent from France, Mussabini was born in Izmir and was of Syrian origin. Trained by the Italian clergy, he maintained a close relationship to Rome, which often irritated the French consul.[6] Equally significant, this overt display of Catholicism was a timely event for Ottoman authorities. The Gülhane Edict, promulgated three years earlier, had promised to create a more egalitarian polity by abolishing the constitutional differences between Muslims and non-Muslims and by extending the same freedoms and securities to all imperial subjects.[7] The public enactment of the procession under Ottoman license offered international audiences tangible proof of Tanzimat promises, while helping counter prevailing arguments about the Porte's unequal treatment of its national minorities. Consequently, the significance of the 1842 Corpus Christi procession extended beyond the locality, engaging power balances and realignments of international scale.

Feasts and ceremonies are temporary but forceful collective creations. They perpetuate and sustain a sense of identity and belonging just as permanent structures do. They also advance new social visions and offer political propaganda, particularly during times of major social and political transformations.[8] This chapter highlights the architecture of spectacle—that is, the material and experiential qualities that render ideologies and worldviews tangible. As I illustrate in the following pages, Izmir's mid-nineteenth-century public rituals only gain their full sociopolitical significance when examined in relation to their spatial and sensory dimensions. Like other aspects of social and political life, public feasts and spectacles were space contingent. The permanent qualities of Izmir's landscape created opportunities and set constraints, which in turn structured the format and experience of these events. While the presence of a harbor and coastline had long made marine displays an integral and popular component of Izmir's public celebrations, the reconfiguration of the waterfront in the mid-1870s gave additional splendor to these spectacles. Further, Izmir's dense and irregular layout as well as the social character of its thoroughfares and open spaces placed limitations on the festive format and on the range of permissible ritual practices, driving event sponsors to fashion their events accordingly. At the same time, as Mona Ozouf puts it in her analysis of festivals during the French Revolution, the power of public performances and their effectiveness in conveying their intended message depended on a "judicious arrangement of space."[9] The way Izmir's streets and public spaces were made to look, sound, and smell, the patterns of movement carved through them, and the spatial relations created within them significantly shaped how these events were understood and remembered. Event sponsors often instilled values, shaped norms of behavior, and validated particular sentiments and attachments through ephemeral, yet tactical, reorganizations of outdoor spaces. These material interventions helped local groups and actors imagine and define themselves within larger social constellations, facilitating the formation of new types of group identification and solidarity.

Religious rituals have long shaped the spatial and temporal patterns of socialization in Izmir. Following a brief outline of the ebbs and flows of festive seasons, I first examine the choreography of the 1842 Corpus Christi along with other comparable religious performances in Izmir to expound on how social groups used the material city to forge new political meanings and shape identity processes at various scales, from communal to imperial and transnational. Next, I turn to various spectacles of statehood—foreign national holidays, diplomatic protocols, and Ottoman imperial feasts—in which both the Tanzimat state and various European powers competed to carve for themselves spheres of influence in the city and assert their sovereignty vis-à-vis one another and the Smyrniot audience. The concurrence, in the same physical terrain, of these public rituals and displays attests to the multivalence of Izmir's urban spaces, which lent themselves to the tactical appropriation of diverse actors and their divergent agendas.

Festive Cycles of a Plural City

The most prominent manifestations of religious diversity in Izmir were the ritual celebrations based on different calendars. All major Muslim, Jewish, and Christian—Catholic and Orthodox—holy days were regularly observed. Throughout the nineteenth century, these rituals temporally organized public life. They connected time and space in distinctive ways, providing what Anthony Giddens called "socio-spatial markers" that shaped the flow of time and the pace of economic and administrative life.[10] Although each community celebrated its own holy days, many observances were made known to all because of their implications for the daily life of the entire city. Businesses and shops owned by Muslims, Jews, and Christians were closed on Fridays, Saturdays, and Sundays, respectively, which pressed other groups to make their provisions accordingly and left only four workdays for the entire city.[11] Until 1873, government agencies in Izmir closed during the entire month of Ramadan, and official transactions were either suspended or conducted at night.[12] When Greek Orthodox and Roman Catholic Lent overlapped with Ramadan, as they did in 1860, the festive mood engulfed the entire city. This led to an overall slowing down of business, but at the end of the period of abstinence, it also brought about an exceptionally colorful holiday season with the *bayram* (Muslim feast) and Easter falling together.[13]

Excursions to the countryside were an indispensable component of holy day celebrations for all classes of people. Despite the incipient push for expansion, in the 1840s, Izmir was still fundamentally a walking city. As mentioned earlier, its streets were narrow, its outdoor spaces were cramped, and its shore was largely privatized. In contrast, vast orchards surrounded the city. Many well-to-do Smyrniots also owned large estates in neighboring villages. When weather permitted, city dwellers took walks along the Meles River, had picnics in nearby orchards, and made mass pilgrimages to neighboring sites of religious significance. By the 1860s the Izmir Railway Company organized special excursion trains to take people to neighboring villages during the bayram. Similarly, the annual Armenian festival held in honor of the Virgin Mary or *panayır* regularly drew thousands of people to Ephesus, the alleged site of her house.[14] On the Tuesday following Easter, the company also provided additional services to transport crowds of elites and commoners to the large open field of Cumaovası in Buca to watch the annual spring horse race organized by the Smyrna Jockey Club.

Organized by Izmir's enterprising British residents and generously sponsored by the imperial Ottoman government, the event provided public entertainment to broader segments of the population, creating a venue for mixed sociability.[15]

By the mid-nineteenth century, as the size and power of mercantile groups grew ever more rapidly, sumptuous parties and social events announced the climax of the festive season. Regularly publicized in Izmir's press, these lavish events enriched the festive season. They provided a parallel realm of celebration to outdoor public entertainment, allowing elite groups to socialize in their own protected environment. Following Easter, balls and philanthropic activities were held in the large halls of the European, Levantine, and Greek clubs to provide annual funds to charities, community hospitals, and schools, expanding the scope and scale of the holidays. Likewise, musical and dramatic soirees, hosted by leading merchant families in their private mansions at Buca or Burnabat, provided diversion to a broad-ranging elite. Ottoman governors, military commanders, and higher state functionaries often appeared on the list of distinguished guests, and their participation was repeatedly reported as a source of great pride and an indication of the official recognition given to the events.

Quartier St. Jean pendant les Fêtes de Pâques Smyrne.

FIGURE 4.1. Easter decoration in the neighborhood of St. John, ca. 1900. Courtesy of Orlando Carlo Calumeno and Birzamanlar Yayıncılık.

Most significantly for the purpose of this study, religious feasts transformed the physical spaces of the city and created a temporary reconfiguration of public life. On these occasions people refashioned select streets and other outdoor spaces to house or otherwise mark these events. They hung flags, banners, flowers, and lanterns on designated buildings and structures and, at times, temporarily covered the streets with canopies stretched between buildings (Figure 4.1). On Muslim feast days (Ramazan and Kurban feasts) and holy evenings *(kandil gecesi)*, the illuminations of mosques and minarets with colored lanterns (and later gas lamps) transformed the experience of the nightly city. Other sensory displays including fireworks, gun salutes fired from the sea and the barracks, street decorations, and ships at harbor decked with banners created a lavish spectacle that distinguished these occasions from ordinary days.[16] Moreover, the sights and sounds of vendors selling holiday candy and desserts, people strolling through the city, and the stirring sound of drums and band music filling the streets also marked such special occasions. During Easter season, Orthodox Greeks carried their processions through several busy streets.[17] They attended mass at major churches within and near the city center, while on Easter eve large crowds gathered in the courtyard of the major church of St. Photini, the belfry of which was illuminated top to bottom as fireworks were set off and firearms discharged (Figures 4.2, 4.3, 4.4). Other Christian saints' days were also kept up till long after midnight. Festive groups assembled for nocturnal celebrations in neighborhood coffeehouses, which were allowed by authorities to remain open till dawn.[18] Such practices were clearly deemed indispensable by festive groups. Despite their ephemerality, they provided specially conceived environments that expanded the performance beyond its immediate participants and announced its significance to all of the city's inhabitants.

Religious feasts also produced more spontaneous transformations of the city's spaces. Holy days could be provocative, fueling latent prejudices, reifying the social boundaries between neighborhoods, and rendering visible the power inequalities among them. At the height of some festivities, casual incidents could be blown out of all proportion, producing anxiety and making neighborhoods, which were ordinarily more porous, exclusive by religion. For example, Jews considered it unsafe to be seen near working-class Greek neighborhoods before Passover as unsubstantiated rumors that Jews kidnapped Christian children for religious rites regularly resurfaced every year.[19] If a Christian child indeed disappeared around that time, Greek and Armenian rioters rushed to Jewish neighborhoods, harassing passersby or breaking into stores. Such periodic rise of suspicions conferred a sense of Greekness or Jewishness on particular neighborhoods—albeit temporarily.

FIGURE 4.2. Entrance to the Church of St. Photini with its monumental belfry in the background, 1900. Courtesy of Orlando Carlo Calumeno and Birzamanlar Yayıncılık.

FIGURE 4.3. Fireworks during Easter celebration in the courtyard of St. Photini. Photographer unknown. From *Üç İzmir* (Istanbul: Yapı Kredi Yayınları, 1992), 161.

Similarly, the common practice of discharging firearms on the streets during the Greek Orthodox Easter eve celebrations produced a temporary geography of fear. The festivities, which marked the culmination of Holy Week, began in the evening, lasted till dawn, and were accompanied by joyful firing of pistols into the air. But accidents were not uncommon, and casualties during the season could be as high as a few dozen injuries and several deaths.[20] Before Holy Week, news about the purchase of unusually large amounts of gunpowder and firearms would flare rumors of conspiracies being hatched by or against Greeks. They also increased the fear that the already eventful Holy Week festivities could turn into mayhem.[21] Such rumors were usually unfounded, but they kept Ottoman authorities on alert during the Easter season. On those occasions, the sight of an increased police force, patrolling the streets with greater frequency, further charged an already tense atmosphere. These events raised awareness about religious boundaries and forced people to abide by temporary territorial limits. They created provisional, but powerful, markings that identified certain urban areas as sites of potential danger and turbulence to be avoided. Consequently cultural differences that may have gone unnoticed in everyday life could become more foreboding and visible.

FIGURE 4.4. Greek carnival costumes, ca. 1900. Postcard. Courtesy of the Suna & İnan Kıraç Research Institute for Mediterranean Civilizations.

Conversely, the holy days could also help thaw the ice between feuding communities, releasing existing tensions. In Izmir, it was not uncommon for larger international conflicts to affect intercommunal relations in the city, particularly in the second half of the nineteenth century. During the Serbo-Ottoman War in 1876, for example, the arrival of large numbers of irregular armed forces from inland regions to be sent to the front triggered weeks of hostility between local Muslims and Christians. The French consul reported the state of anarchy on Izmir's streets and the mounting sense of alarm among local populations, underlining that "Turks are actively exchanging news, reading Istanbul papers, translating everything that appear in Greek, Armenian, or French and even European newspapers."[22] However, two weeks later, the sight of Muslims in holiday clothes strolling in the Frank quarter during the bayram that year received a particularly enthusiastic coverage from the local press, as it was seen as a sign of friendly relations and the ultimate imperviousness of local communities to tensions elsewhere in the empire.[23] In sum, not only established patterns of acceptance and deep-seated prejudices, but also the ebbs and flows of current political events shaped the boundaries between Izmir's diverse constituencies. At times, the cycle of religious rituals served as a reminder of social boundaries, at others it facilitated crossing boundaries that were ordinarily more impervious. This mutual process of checking and repositioning was vital to the functioning of this fluid world and its ever-changing political moods.

Performing a Transnational Catholic Community

The decision by Archbishop Mussabini to move the Corpus Christi procession to the streets carried more profound meanings than met the eye. Although Catholics were small compared to the empire's major non-Muslim communities, they were as diverse as the entire Ottoman society put together. They shared an allegiance to the Holy See but followed different rites and were divided by language, ethnic origins, and legal status.[24] This might explain why Catholics never constituted a single millet on a par with Orthodox Greeks, Gregorian Armenians, or Jews. Until the nineteenth century, Catholic subjects eluded easy classification within the Ottoman constitutional hierarchy. Unlike other non-Muslim subjects, whose spiritual heads combined both secular and religious authority over their communities, Catholics fulfilled their fiscal obligations toward the state through the fold of one of the Christian millets. For religious exercises, however, those of the Eastern rite kept to their autonomous churches, while those of the Latin rite (or Roman Catholics) congregated in missionary churches protected by the capitulations granted to France or Austria.[25]

The first decades of the nineteenth century ushered in important developments in the organization of Catholic communities within the empire. In 1818 Pope Pius VII restructured the territorial jurisdiction of the Latin church in Asia Minor and established the archdiocese of Smyrna that gave Izmir an uninterrupted sequence of archbishops in control of all Latin Catholics in the greater part of Asia Minor.[26] These interventions elevated Izmir to the center of Catholicism in the region while also suggesting that the area had a sizable Latin Catholic population to warrant the erection of a full-fledged archdiocese. Papal restructuring also coincided with Ottoman Catholics' struggle for communal self-definition within the empire. In 1831 Catholic Armenians were the first to form a separate millet *(Katolik milleti)* under an Armenian Catholic archbishop that the Ottoman state recognized as the civil and religious leader of the community.[27] Meanwhile, other Catholics, of both Eastern and Latin rites, continued in their efforts to claim millet status, but the process of subdividing and formalizing these communities proved to be a challenge as it lacked clearly established procedures and precedents.

In the case of Latin Catholics, the largest Catholic group in Izmir, being under the direct ecclesiastical jurisdiction of the pope precluded the possibility of classifying them as a local autonomous church that could be absorbed within the Ottoman structure. This prompted the central government to devise a new solution. Eventually, the Porte appointed a civil delegate (known as *nazır* or *vekil*) to head the secular affairs of the community in Istanbul.[28] Soon afterwards, Mahmud II officially recognized the Latin community *(Latin milleti)*, and by 1836, new suboffices, such as the Office des Latins Sujets Ottomans à Smyrne, were created in localities with large Latin Catholic populations (Figure 4.5).[29] The resulting Latin milleti was an arrangement that was unprecedented in its hybrid organization, simultaneously embodying the characteristics of a religious community and the secular administrative structure of a modern state.

In light of these multifaceted realignments, the 1842 Corpus Christi procession helped both to consolidate the leadership of the Latin Catholic Church over the empire's variegated Catholic populations and to reinforce the political recognition of its members within the institutional structure of Izmir and the empire. Staging the procession on the streets of Izmir was a delicate matter considering the internal divisions among local Catholic missions, their latent religious tensions with non-Catholics, and the competition between the European powers that protected them. Consequently, the event had to be carefully choreographed so as to be inclusive and to honor the diverse constituencies that Archbishop Mussabini wanted to draw under his umbrella without antagonizing any of them in the process. To accomplish this, Mussabini creatively tailored what was a universal

FIGURE 4.5. Seal of Izmir's Office of Latin Catholic Ottoman Subjects, 1845. Courtesy of Centre des Archives Diplomatique de Nantes.

Catholic tradition to Izmir's social and physical landscape, judiciously selecting the itinerary, the stops along the way, and the participants.

First, to create a distinctively Catholic experience, Mussabini had the outdoor space of Rose and Frank Streets decorated with festive and religious imagery for the procession. Rose Street in the 1840s was primarily residential, lined with regular rows of houses occupied by indigenous families of Greek Orthodox, Maltese, and Armenian origin. In contrast, Frank Street was one of the most animated and busiest commercial thoroughfares that epitomized Izmir's social and cultural diversity. In preparation for the procession, organizers covered building facades on both streets with tapestries, cloths, and banners and adorned them with pictures, foliage, and lanterns. They placed small altars, decorated with flowers and statuettes of the Virgin Mary, on street corners and stretched canvas tents between buildings to provide shade for the crowd.[30] Such interventions created a sense of enclosure and interiority far different from Frank Street's usual appearance (Figure 4.6). During the procession, sights, sounds, and smells that produced a church-like quality in the outdoors reinforced this sense of interiority, temporarily transforming the street into a sacred enclosure. The spectacle of clergymen in full regalia, nuns in their distinctive headdress, hundreds of young girls in white dresses, Catholic brotherhoods carrying banners and torches, consular representatives in their official costumes, and uniformed Ottoman soldiers, bearing arms and integrated into a larger disciplined body directed by Mussabini, conferred to Frank Street a deeply religious and ceremonial character (Figures 4.7, 4.8). Altar boys scattering flowers and spreading incense, a choir of artists chanting religious hymns, the sound of various musical instruments, and periodic gun salutes transformed the experience of the otherwise bustling commercial street. In short, the Corpus Christi procession gave Izmir's Catholics temporary control over the city's space.

Second, Mussabini carefully marked the itinerary of the procession with selected buildings and establishments that demonstrated the centrality of the Latin Catholic community to Izmir's historical heritage and honored the constituencies that he deemed critical for a Catholic coalition. The procession began

FIGURE 4.6. Reconfiguration of street space during a parade on Reşidiye Avenue in the Armenian quarter, 1907. Typically, tapestries and banners were displayed from every window and hung on the walls and over doors. Courtesy of Orlando Carlo Calumeno and Birzamanlar Yayıncılık.

at the prominent Catholic College of the Propaganda, established only a decade earlier, and ended at the oldest standing Catholic church in Izmir, the Capuchin Church of St. Polycarp (Map 4.1). While the college represented the prosperity and most recent achievement of Izmir's Latin Catholics, the Church of St. Polycarp, dedicated to a highly celebrated second-century local martyr, symbolized their long history (Figure 4.9).[31] Together these two buildings did more than delineate the physical boundaries of the procession. They gave the event a historical

FIGURE 4.7. Priests and nuns in regalia during a funeral procession at the French hospital in Izmir, ca. 1890. From Jean-Baptiste Piolet, ed., *Les missions catholiques françaises au XIXe siécle,* vol. 1, *Missions d'Orient* (Paris: Librairie Armand Colin, 1901).

FIGURE 4.8. Official costumes of consular guards *(cavass)*, ca. 1865. Courtesy of the Suna & İnan Kıraç Research Institute for Mediterranean Civilizations.

dimension that reinforced the legitimacy of Izmir's Latin Catholic community. Because both institutions were officially under French protection and thus flew the tricolor flag, they also made visible the continuous support France had given to Izmir's Catholics.

Along Frank Street the procession made four ceremonial stops where the archbishop gave his blessing to the large crowd in attendance. Most strikingly, the first stop on the way was a secular institution, the Levantine Club, which was the center of the commercial and social life of a largely Catholic elite, who also supported Catholic establishments. At the request of Mussabini, the Sisters of Charity with the support of club members erected an altar at its entrance. The altar temporarily pulled a mundane club into the religious realm, proclaiming the importance of the Levantine elite, of which Mussabini was a prominent member, to Izmir's Catholic life. Next, the procession stopped at two institutions run by French missions: the church of the Sacred Heart, adjacent to the Lazarist School,

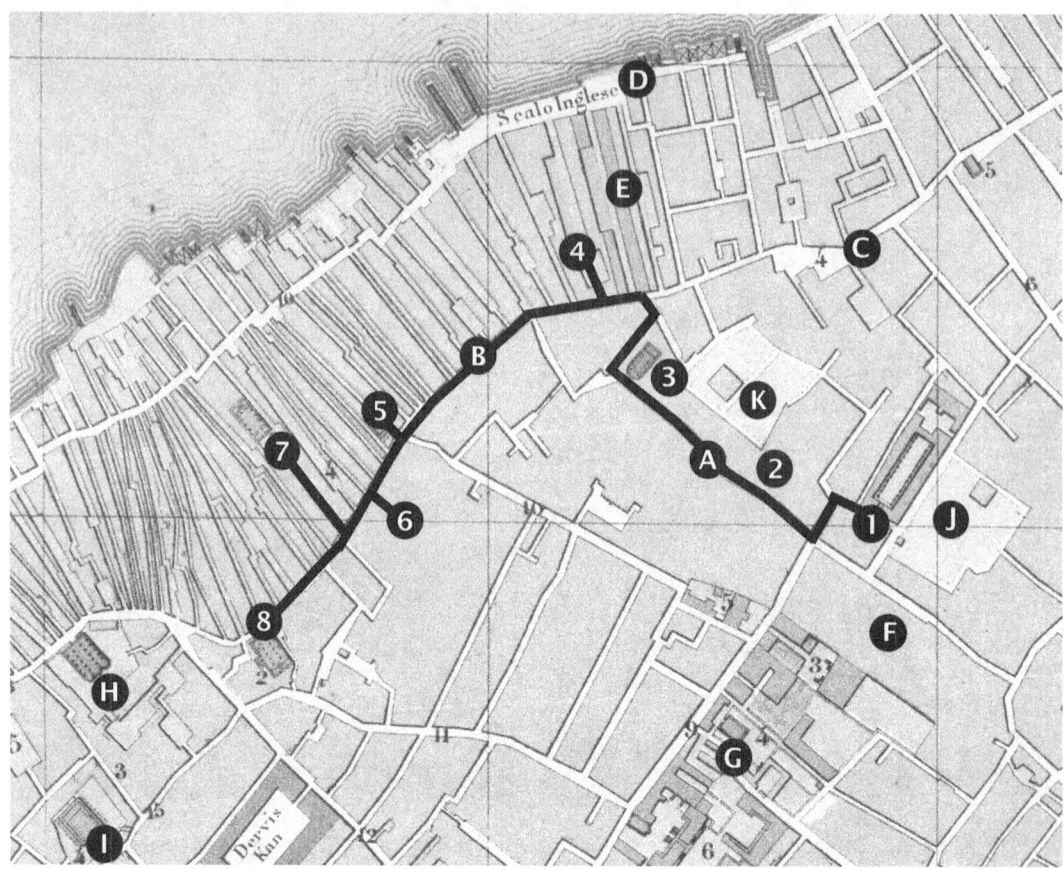

MAP 4.1. Path of the 1842 Corpus Christi procession, based on the plan by Storari (Map 2).

LEGEND: 1. College of the Propaganda; 2. Christian Brothers Boys' School; 3. Euterpe Theater; 4. Levantine Club; 5. Lazarist Church (Sacré Cœur); 6. Establishment of the Sisters of Charity (Maison de la Providence); 7. St. Mary; 8. St. Polycarp; A. Rose Street; B. Frank Street; C. Fasula Place; D. English Pier; E. English Consulate and Chapel; F. Deaconesses (Girls) Institute; G. Hospitals; H. St. Photini (Greek Orthodox); I. St. George (Greek Orthodox); J. Site of future Cathedral of St. John (Catholic); K. Site of future Cammarano Theatre.

and the private chapel of the Sisters of Charity. Due to the rising popularity of free Lazarist education *(école gratuite)* the school's enrollments had tripled from one hundred students in 1839 to three hundred in 1841.[32] As a result, in 1841 the Christian Brothers and the Sisters of Charity were brought in to assist the mission and instigate "recognition and appreciation of Christianity and of France."[33] The former ran a boys' school and the latter a convent for young girls in addition to a hospital for the poor. These two establishments epitomized the recent success of Catholic missions and their ability to provide not only for Catholics, but for all who needed assistance. Finally, the march stopped at the Franciscan Church of St. Mary, which had been rededicated in 1818 as a cathedral and placed under Austrian protection. Here the Austrian consul and his staff greeted the procession, signaling the active role his country played in the protection of local Catholics.

The itinerary stitched together these discrete institutions and their respective facilities to reinforce the appearance of a seamless Latin Catholic space and publicize the extent of the social, educational, and religious infrastructure that Catholicism had provided for the city. In reality, however, Latin Catholic missions and institutions had tangled and thorny histories that set them apart. Skirmishes between Capuchins and Reformed Franciscans were all too common; so were clashes over the decisions related to the administration of Catholic schools and hospitals and the populations that Latin missions were to serve.[34] Moreover,

FIGURE 4.9. Plaque erected during the rededication of the Church of St. Polycarp in 1820. Photograph by author.

Catholic institutions had no definite national affiliation, depending instead on a supranational network of logistical alliances, which further complicated their relations. They received official support or "protection" from rival nations, France and Austria, and allowances from diverse sources, including Rome, France, Austria, and the Italian states of Sardinia, Tuscany, and Naples, in addition to the contributions made by local Catholic communities. Hence, the College of the Propaganda, although under official French protection, was largely supported by the Sacred Congregations for the Propagation of the Faith in Rome (or *Propaganda Fide*), after which it was named. Similarly, the Church of St. Polycarp may have been protected by France, but it had been run by Italian Capuchins since France abolished its Capuchin order in 1802. Meanwhile, the Franciscan Church of St. Mary served primarily indigenous Catholics of highly diverse origins but was under Austrian protection.

To be sure, these complex and ambiguous affiliations made Catholic institutions supple enough to survive and thrive through shifting political climates. But they also resulted in frequent tensions and internal divisions as diverse sponsors and users imposed specific requirements, criteria, and obligations on these institutions, and their interests were not necessarily local.[35] In a carefully choreographed moment of Catholic pride, however, the Corpus Christi performance masked these schisms. Instead, it produced a powerful spatial imagery that symbolically united these groups under the banner of a single and harmonious Catholic community. Such displays provided tangible reference points that helped local Catholic groups imagine themselves as a unified community.

Beyond constructing a cohesive Latin Catholic identity, the Corpus Christi performance staged the complex political position of Izmir's Catholics within international and local spheres. As mentioned earlier, Izmir's Latin Catholics depended for their spiritual legitimacy on the church of Rome. But for local dealings and transactions they relied on the Ottoman state's recognition of their status as millet and also on European protections that gave them important privileges. Mussabini carefully selected the participants and prescribed their order in the procession to play up Ottoman and European support. He also walked a fine line so as not to cause friction between these powers. Hence at the head of the procession, Governor Salih Pasha's guards *(cavass)* alternated with those of the consulates of European powers. The Ottoman squad at the end of the procession provided a counterpart to the staff and dragomans of European consulates. Mussabini asked European consuls to participate in the procession but as "dignitaries of Catholic countries" rather than political representatives of their respective states. In turn, the French consul invited Governor Salih Pasha and higher functionaries of the government to watch the event from a privileged position—the balcony of the archbishop's palace, overlooking Frank Street.[36] Careful diplomacy permeated the entire organization of the event to present the appearance of a balanced power distribution between Ottoman and European sovereignties.

The competition between European nations, all of which wanted to use the occasion to proclaim their superiority over the others, further complicated matters. Although in the eyes of the Ottoman state France had long been the de facto protector of the Catholics, Austrians and Italians had been challenging the primacy of France on this matter.[37] Mussabini resolved this problem through a cautious orchestration that conferred distinctive duties to the top representatives of each state. The archbishop's grand canopy—the centerpiece of the procession—rested on the shoulders of two French and two Austrian merchants.[38] The consuls followed the archbishop according to a strategic ranking that expressed international political hierarchies. Thus the French consul and the commander of the French corvette in the harbor came first, followed by the consuls of Sardinia and Tuscany, and then the acting consul of Naples. When the Austrian government refused to have its consul take second place after the French, an impasse that could only be resolved through diplomatic compromise arose. Rather than participating in the procession, the Austrian consul decided to play host at his church and received the procession at the door during Mussabini's ceremonial benediction.[39] Creative maneuvers diffused potential diplomatic confrontation between France and Austria, providing each power a unique position that eluded comparison, and ultimately offering the governor the honor of watching the procession from a highly privileged location. Not only did the structure of the procession mediate these diverse political demands; it also positioned the celebrants in a clever and skillful manner vis-à-vis the powers that shaped their world. French and Austrian support provided Izmir's Latin Catholics international recognition, while official Ottoman presence confirmed the status that local Catholics were claiming for themselves as equal participants in the reformed empire free to practice their religion.

In addition, the procession asserted the place of Izmir's Catholics in relation to the recognized ethnoreligious structure of the city, particularly the Greek Orthodox community that constituted the majority of its Christian population. The general sense of distrust and antagonism, which prevailed among Catholic and Orthodox clergy, was periodically ignited when, for instance, local Christians violated the canonical banning of marriages across sects.[40] In publicizing the event to a broader readership, *Écho de l'Orient* placed great emphasis on the respect shown by non-Catholic audiences. It detailed the lavish decorations along the predominantly Greek Rose Street and the enthusiasm exhibited by Greek Orthodox, Jewish, and even Muslim businesses that adorned their storefronts on Frank Street. The article also extolled the level of religious tolerance, mutual respect, and civility attained in Izmir on that day, which for the reporter far surpassed the conditions found in Europe, where "nonbelievers continuously hindered such performances."[41] It is clear from these reports that the comportment of non-Catholics, which helped stage a harmonious coexistence, was as critical as the design of the procession itself.

The quiet demeanor of Izmir's Muslims was equally significant considering that in 1841 the procession had to be postponed due to flaring tensions and prejudices between Muslims and Christians following insurrections on the islands of Samos and Crete. Read against this background, *Écho de l'Orient*'s statement about the sight of "Muslims watching the event reverently" was as much a political commentary on the recent shifts in intercommunal and international relations as it was about a sense of Catholic pride and a eulogy to the Catholic Church for arousing exemplary feelings in a multireligious city.[42] In short, the careful choreography of the procession was both attuned to the political realities of the time and capable of producing and validating new realignments at local, national, and international scales.

Religious Rituals and State Spectacles

The Corpus Christi performance provides clues about the range of permissible ceremonial practices and available symbolic tools in mid-nineteenth-century Izmir. Indeed, to secure official support for a public performance, Mussabini had cleverly manipulated familiar tools and practices. To justify his request, he had tapped into a repertoire of rituals that belonged to the time-honored calendar of fixed feasts and holy days and cited other overtly sanctioned Christian festivals including Catholic rituals in Istanbul and Greek Orthodox feasts in Izmir.[43] In the Ottoman Empire, Christian feasts *(yortu)* were well-known observances, long in practice. They were recognized by ancient usage and permitted in various parts of the empire. As a major feast in the Roman Catholic calendar, Corpus Christi was a suitable contender to receive official sanction. Moreover, to back up Mussabini's demand, the French consul had claimed that the practice was performed on the streets until a century earlier, providing a direct precedent for this feast in Izmir and additional grounds for performing the event in public.[44]

In many ways, however, the format and choreography of the 1842 Corpus Christi procession trumped and transcended conventional religious rituals. To convey the authority and prestige of Izmir's Catholic churches, Mussabini employed symbols and concepts that resonated with performances of state power rather than those ordinarily associated with communal religious celebrations. A royal twenty-one-gun salute—the standard show of military power used in rendering the highest honors to sovereign states—accompanied the archbishop's blessings. French and Austrian national flags, the visible expressions of international status, flew over the Catholic institutions located on the itinerary. Foreign consuls and their staffs, military commanders in elaborate official uniforms, and the Ottoman honor guard presenting arms further confirmed the stately significance of the event.

In the course of the nineteenth century, as western European powers acquired their highly centralized and bureaucratic forms, flags and banners, uniforms and military parades, and gun salutes and honor guards standing at attention came to constitute the staples of modern state ceremonials.[45] They symbolized sovereign power both within the country's geographic borders and in relation to other sovereign entities. As evidenced in official records and local newspapers, these tools were also deployed in Istanbul and prominent provincial centers to honor the national anniversaries of friendly nations and commemorate such events as the royal accession and birthday of their sovereigns. In Izmir, where sixteen different countries—Austria-Hungary, Belgium, Britain, Denmark, France, Germany, Greece, Italy, the Netherlands, Persia, Portugal, Russia, Spain, Samos, Sweden and Norway, and the United States—had official representation in the 1870s, national days (or *yevm-i mahsus*) were regularly observed through a range of formal and informal events (Map 4.2). Foreign colonies held special religious services and dinners at the consulate and set up street parties and theatrical performances to display national loyalties. In addition to social events, they performed diplomatic protocols appropriate to the size and prestige of the local colony. Generally, official celebrations began with an exchange of the royal twenty-one-gun salute in the morning hours, followed by consulates hoisting their flags and receiving greetings from local Ottoman government officials and members of the consular corps.

In its ceremonial procedures, the 1842 Corpus Christi shared some striking similarities with national feasts, which on the whole made the performance a cross between a religious festival and a state ceremony. The choreography married the explicit religiosity of the former and the political character of the latter, expanding and infusing a familiar devotional rite with the authority and symbolism of state sovereignty. Significantly, the unusual character of the newly conjured Latin millet within the Ottoman constitutional hierarchy enabled Mussabini to

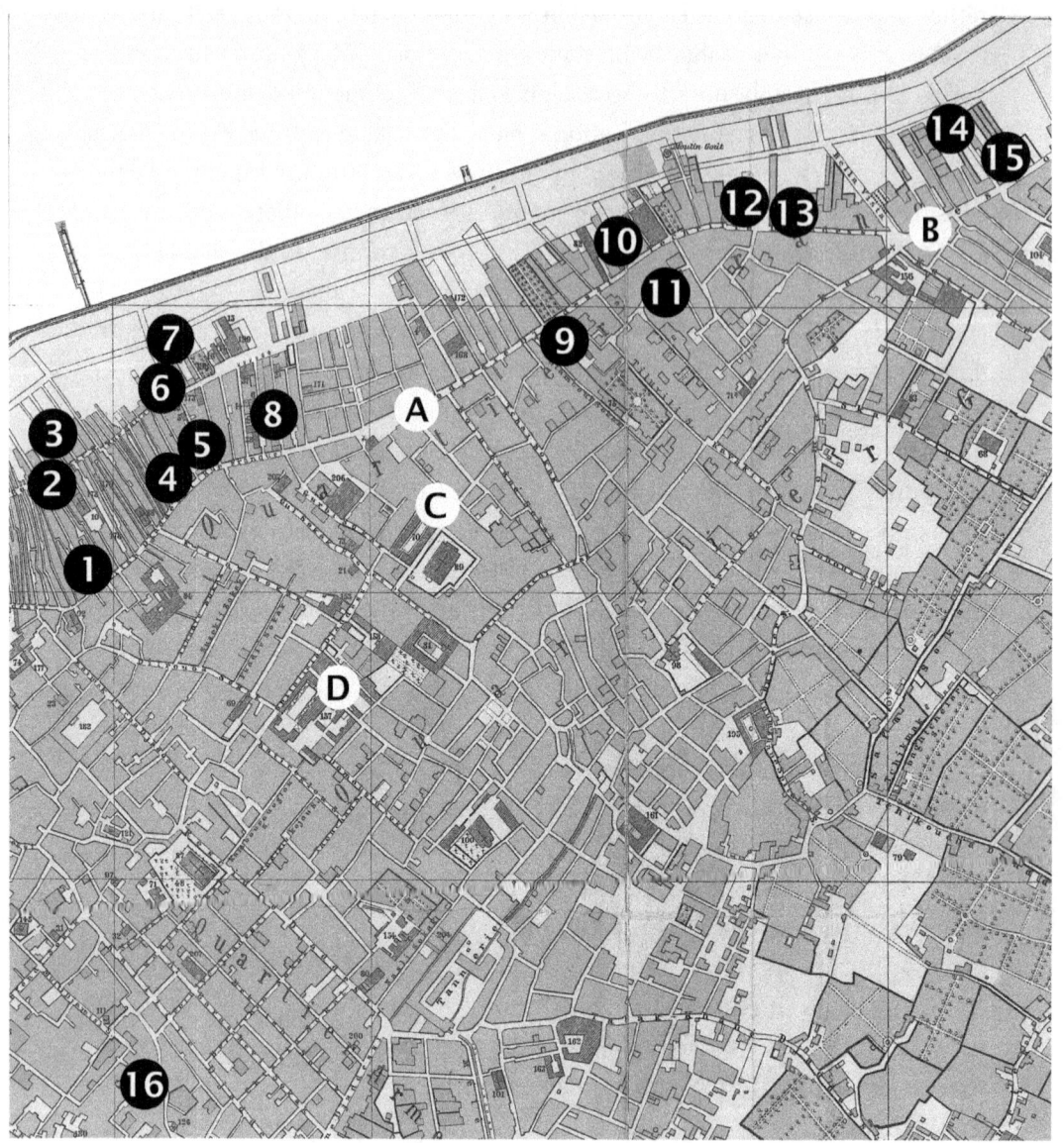

MAP 4.2. Location of foreign consulates, ca. 1880, based on the plan by Saad (Map 3).

LEGEND: 1 = Sweden and Norway; 2 = Samos; 3 = Italy; 4 = the Netherlands; 5 = Austria-Hungary; 6 = Portugal; 7 = Spain; 8 = Britain; 9 = France; 10 = Greece; 11 = United States; 12 = Russia; 13 = Belgium; 14 = Germany; 15 = Denmark; 16 = Persia; A = Fasula Place; B = Bella Vista; C = College of the Propaganda; D = hospitals.

creatively exploit available performative tools and augment the prestige of the Catholic Church, while defusing the possibility of interpreting the event as an explicit political threat.

The confluence of religious symbols and political displays fit well with established practices in the Ottoman Empire. Secular authority had long been part of the religious. Unlike present-day perspectives that construe these realms as deeply separate, the temporal and the spiritual were neither mutually exclusive nor even clearly distinguishable categories. As mentioned earlier, personal status was defined through membership in a religious community, and the exigencies of civic and political life were largely met through religious institutions, as were city services. This overlap was also the basis of the privileges and separate status accorded to non-Muslim communities in the empire. Despite Tanzimat statesmen's efforts at separating these spheres by proclaiming equality of all subjects or creating new secular courts, the religious and the civic remained intensely intertwined in everyday life. The newly built churches, missionary schools, and hospitals that served different confessional groups and punctuated Izmir's nineteenth-century urban landscape were salient markers of a society in which the civic was inextricably linked to the religious.

Although religious feasts had long been an important part of communal life, in the nineteenth century these enactments took on a new significance, offering non-Muslim subjects rich and unique opportunities for communal self-definition. In many cities with large Christian populations, Tanzimat freedoms were greeted with the ringing of church bells, parades, and religious processions on the streets.[46] In Izmir, familiar acts of public devotion lent themselves to a range of innovative practices and purposes and were reworked beyond the spiritual realm to respond to the political exigencies of the day. Whereas the Corpus Christi procession revealed Catholic efforts at forging for themselves a new institutional category, Greek Orthodox feasts illustrated how an existing institutional category could be expanded and compounded with new loyalties and attachments. The establishment of an independent Greek Kingdom in 1832 fostered new national feelings and sympathies that compounded with and complicated the various attachments of Greek Orthodox Ottoman subjects.[47] The enthusiastic blend of religious and nationalistic themes that characterized Orthodox Easter celebrations in the second half of the nineteenth century is well known. Local news reports commonly made references to spirited midnight Easter ceremonies attended by thousands of people holding lit candles in the courtyard of St. Photini and chanting hymns alongside "national marches and nondescript selections" (see Figure 4.3).[48] Similarly, European observers of Izmir's street life made note of the "half-religious, half-patriotic" character of Easter, celebrated under the protection of "Muslim *zaptiehs* [gendarmes], who paid honors to the Metropolitan."[49]

The repurposing of the festival of St. George into the onomastic day of King George of Greece was yet another manifestation of how a conventional religious festival acquired new political symbolism. After King George came to power in 1863, St. George's day became not only a religious holy day in the Greek Orthodox calendar, but also a national day *(yevm-i mahsus)* observed in the Ottoman Empire. Already in 1864 it was celebrated in Izmir with gun salutes, consulates hoisting their flags, and other diplomatic protocols.[50] On the same feast in 1867, the Greek and Russian consuls and their full staffs attended the church service during which the names of the Greek king, the Russian emperor, and Sultan Abdülaziz were memorialized "openly and freely."[51]

Whether the Greek king and the Russian emperor represented Orthodox leaders or sovereign rulers in this context is unclear. It is precisely such ambiguity and the complex layering of religious and secular allegiances it afforded that facilitated the incorporation of new norms into the existing panoply of festive practices. News reports through the long reign of King George indicate the endurance of such ambiguous interplays. Similarly, in a highly evocative, although idealized, depiction of the St. George's holiday in late nineteenth-century Izmir, novelist Kozmas Politis provides a glimpse of how the event was remembered and inscribed in the collective memory of the Greek nation years later. He describes streets decorated with the blue and white Greek flags; guards of the Greek club and consulate wearing their national costume; the consul of Greece walking at the side of the metropolitan in his three-cornered hat, medallions, and a sword hanging by his side; and crowds hailing "Long live the Metropolitan!" "Long live the Grand Sultan!" and "Long live our grand King."[52] These images powerfully capture the commingling of these symbols in the city's spaces. They reveal how a temporary reconfiguration of physical space together with collective action helped link and layer the different sources of political allegiance that were available to Izmir's Greek Orthodox community.

While it appears that this was an expression of allegiance to mainland Greece, the interests of the Greek Kingdom and those of the Ottoman polities that shared affinities with it did not overlap neatly. To be sure, consular authorities made concerted campaigns for winning the allegiance of Ottoman Greeks. Diplomatic events in honor of the Greek king extended into public banquets that large numbers of enthusiasts joined.[53] In addition, the sales of Hellenic passports to Ottoman Christians offered a targeted strategy for claiming members of the Orthodox millet.[54] But protests against the Greek consul were far from unusual. In one instance, a group of local artisans and shopkeepers holding Hellenic passports made a mass assault on the consulate when the Greek consul represented their interests poorly.[55] Political instability in mainland Greece, as in the years leading to the overthrow of King Otto of Greece in 1862, also strained the relation between local communities and the consul. In one instance, it influenced a group of Greek Orthodox to hoist the Greek national flag upon the spire of the cathedral of St. Photini in support of Greek revolutionaries, to the apprehension of the consul, who was forced to seek the assistance of the governor and Ottoman police forces.[56] When read in light of these day-to-day struggles, religious feasts and holidays appear as deliberate creations rather than inevitable manifestations of a preordained national solidarity espoused by the polity at the time.

Despite obvious differences in the pretext of their staging, their participants, and the spatial tactics they employed, rituals like Corpus Christi, St. George's festival, or Easter reveal how fundamental innovations can be wrapped into tradition. These performances may be best characterized as rituals of modern times, or in Eric Hobsbawm's terms, invented traditions, in that they helped forge and express patently modern communal identities and also presented themselves as old.[57] "Invented traditions," however, are not fabricated from scratch, as the phrase may suggest. Rather, they occur within a pre-existing framework of collective loyalties and identities. As in the case of Izmir's public performances, they resonate with the familiar and draw their license and popular appeal from longstanding traditions. The availability of a ritual format facilitates their sanctioning while also creating venues for innovative forms of identity politics.

The Delicate Dance of Diplomacy

In the mid-nineteenth century, not only was the self-definition of the empire's myriad communities in flux, but so was the world's geopolitical realignment given the contested ascendance of the nation-state as the primary unit of political organization. Diplomatic protocols and their corresponding repertoire of visual and material expressions were quintessential means through which states cultivated "will to nationhood," preserved legitimacy, and asserted their claims for recognition in the international arena.[58] By moving politics from the documentary to the spectacular, they gave a concrete character to diplomatic activity. Already in 1815, the Congress of Vienna explicitly recognized the importance of diplomatic conduct by prescribing standard rules to prevent the frequent controversies that occurred over the rank and precedence of states in the world order. But the rivalry for prestige and authority remained integral to diplomatic exchange through the nineteenth century. As a busy port city in which all European powers had representation but none had managed to establish dominance, nineteenth-century Izmir provides a particularly rich environment for examining how protocols and honors were open to opportunistic appropriations. Contending nations deployed diplomatic events to assert their sovereignty and stake out various claims for superiority over one another. Above all, the miscellaneous ceremonial events they staged incorporated the city's public spaces into this international competition.

In this context of heightened awareness of competition and increasing ceremonial codification, seemingly minor symbolic transactions could become expressions of national pride and rivalry. The importance attached to national flags during diplomatic ceremonies was a case in point. National flags were more than pragmatic props that identified foreign ships at harbor and buildings under foreign protection. In Izmir, they had long been powerful tools to jockey for power and visibility in a multinational city. That France and Austria relentlessly flew their flags over two contiguous sections of the same Franciscan complex, the former over the archbishop's house and the latter atop the adjacent Church of St. Mary, is a good illustration of the competing claims these states made over the protection of the complex.[59] In a low-rise cityscape that visitors and foreign dignitaries approached primarily from the water, flags were meant to be seen from afar (Figure 4.10). Like minarets and church towers, they organized the skyline and they stood against it as prominent statements of power.

In the course of the second half of the nineteenth century, however, raising the national flag during diplomatic enactments became an essential device of political communication. Precisely because they lent themselves to quick changes, flag displays were effective indicators of the constant fluctuations in international politics as they happened. For example, on the coronation of Napoleon III in 1852, which was officially celebrated in Izmir, all consulates, with the exception of those of Austria, Prussia, Russia, and the United States, were reported to have raised their flags to honor France—although the Austrian and Prussian consuls presented their personal regrets for having to refrain from attending on the grounds that France had not yet accredited the minister of their governments in Paris.[60] Similarly, in the years following the reunification of a large part of the Italian peninsula by King Victor-Emmanuel, only the consulates of governments that recognized the new Italian Kingdom hoisted their flag on the king's birthday.[61] And when the Spanish consulate did not raise its flag on Queen Victoria's birthday, the British consul refused to give his colleague the customary honors presented to diplomatic representatives when he came on the British ship in harbor.[62] In sum, the sheer amount of consular and newspaper reports on this matter

The Port of Smyrna.

FIGURE 4.10. View of flags from the shore, ca. 1850. Flags were an important aspect of Izmir's panorama. On special occasions, foreign flags were hoisted on consular buildings while the Ottoman flag crowned Kadifekale. From William Harrison De Puy, *People's Cyclopedia of Universal Knowledge* (New York: Phillips and Hunt, 1883).

reveals the extent to which flags and corresponding honors were the means of choice for broadcasting adversarial or friendly messages between states.

Diplomatic enactments were also choice occasions for foreign missions to earn the sympathies of local populations and for local expatriates to express their allegiances to their home countries. On the birth of a male heir to the French throne in 1856, the French ship at harbor, the batteries on shore, and the Ottoman station-ship exchanged a rare 101 imperial gun salute, and all consulates hoisted their flags. A detachment of French, Ottoman, and British squads marched in line through the streets, presenting an extravagant military feast, while the French consulate, illuminated for two nights, offered a glowing spectacle. Moreover, the consular gate and vestibule were decked with the French, Ottoman, and British flags and banners, shaped like trophies and topped with the imperial eagle.[63] "Through the streets leading to the College and from the consulate to the French Church, one heard only good wishes and congratulations for the illustrious offspring of the great emperor," rejoiced the reporter to the *Journal de Constantinople/Écho de l'Orient*. The successful alliance of France, Britain, and the Ottoman

Empire during the Crimean War (1853–56), which had repercussions in many areas of cultural production, may have served as a point of cross-cultural exchange in this regard. Similar spectacles became increasingly more common—during the visits of important foreign dignitaries such as the duchess of Edinburgh in 1876, for the jubilee of Queen Victoria in 1887, as well as for the Bastille Day celebrations from the early 1880s onward. These events were reported in great detail and with great pride to the respective Foreign Offices of home governments, particularly on account of the crowd they drew and the good order and respect they instilled. Such enactments helped expatriate colonies display their allegiance and patriotism toward their home countries. In return, they created opportunities for these governments to advance their interests and extend their cultural hegemony over Ottoman communities.

To be sure, Ottoman statesmen were not indifferent to such displays on their land. In a world that was increasingly organized around the principles of modern diplomacy, they were quick to adopt new procedures in line with European norms for diplomatic receptions. Through these new principles, they claimed diplomatic equivalence and reciprocity, which were paramount for the expression of Ottoman sovereignty. They also banned diplomatic shows and military displays that could potentially undercut their sovereignty and make them look inferior on their own turf. For example, in 1859 central authorities informed provincial governors that the celebrations of allied sovereigns were limited to one day per year, on either their onomastic or coronation day.[64] They also prescribed the use of international codes regarding the use of flags, gun salutes, and other military honors on ceremonial occasions. Since international maritime laws of the period considered all sovereign states equal, gun salutes no longer suggested superiority of one state or the submission of others. Instead, they were purely courteous acts that indicated cordial relations and could be reciprocated either with an equal salute from sea or a similar salute from land in the absence of comparably sized vessels in harbor.[65] To comply with these new standards, the central government also proscribed Ottoman vessels of less than ten cannons from reciprocating salutes made by foreign warships, requiring instead that the honors be returned either by salutes from the shore or simply by raising the Ottoman flag on the citadel.

Similarly, an 1870 circular abolished the ostentatious custom of displaying military honors to new consuls arriving to an Ottoman port city. Instead, it restricted the honors to the raising of national flags over the consulate in question and the local citadel, thereby bringing local practices in line with recent changes in Europe.[66] Furthermore, new regulations enacted in the following years sought to streamline the ceremonial honors accorded to ambassadors and diplomatic agents in light of the stipulations of the Congress of Vienna, although such actions drew vehement protests from heads of foreign missions who maintained that the Ottoman Empire had not been a signatory in the Congress of Vienna.[67] Whether or not these procedures could be entirely implemented in Izmir, they illustrate the extent to which Ottoman statesmen turned the new tools of diplomatic conduct to their advantage.

On occasion, diplomatic controversies erupted over the propriety of displaying the national flags on local institutions—despite general rules that restricted these displays to embassies and consulates. In 1862, for example, the display of the Austrian flag on the building of the Armenian Mechitarist mission in the neighboring city of Aydın became a bone of contention between local authorities, foreign representatives, and the local mission. The deputy governor *(kaymakam)* prohibited the mission from using a foreign flag as was ordinarily done in Izmir. Although the mission received Austrian support, the governor argued that the practice was unacceptable since both the missionaries and the congregation consisted of Ottoman subjects.[68] In assuming a direct correlation between a state's national flag and the allegiances of the body of citizens on its territories, local officials shrewdly used the logic of modern territorial sovereignty against Austria to counter its efforts at staking claims over Ottoman subjects.

Admittedly, Izmir's particular situation afforded more latitude for ceremonial innovations and expression. The semiofficial press frequently decried the conspicuous breach of international norms in Izmir. "In every country of the world the national flag is privileged over foreign flags. In Turkey, it is different," scathingly noted an Izmir correspondent to the *Journal de Constantinople*. "Foreign flags are favored at the expense of the national one."[69] Nevertheless, local authorities' stance toward a specific event and the risk of diplomatic or intercommunal friction placed explicit and implicit limits on how such events should be performed in Izmir. There were, for instance, important constraints over the design of the 1842 Corpus Christi procession, discussed earlier in this chapter. As the long deliberations between Mussabini and the consuls of France indicate, the priority of the Catholic Church and its missions was to assert themselves as a recognized community, while that of the French consul was to avoid potential diplomatic confrontations. Securing the governor's support loomed large on the consul's agenda. Only recently had France signed on to the 1840 Treaty of London, which formally inducted the Ottoman Empire into Europe's international political system and offered guarantees to its sovereignty and territorial integrity.[70] Despite the Catholic clergy's determination to perform Corpus Christi publicly in 1841 and 1843, the French consul withdrew his support from the procession because the governor could not provide his military squad to escort the procession. When the clergy asked to have French marine officers protect the procession, the consul refused on the basis that this would conflict with the religious character of the event, the very grounds on which Ottoman officials would permit the procession in the first place.[71] Ultimately, the procession could not be performed in both years, but resumed again in 1844. The backing of the authorities was necessary to prevent potential flare-up and to add to the pomp of the event. These careful maneuvers attest in large part to the divergence between French interests and those of local Catholic missions. Above all, they indicate the importance of finding an acceptable ceremonial format without infringing overtly on Ottoman sovereignty.

Formalism of the Modern State

The sensitivities on display in the design of the 1842 Corpus Christi were symptomatic of broader changes taking place in the tools and conduct of diplomacy within the empire. In the first decades of the nineteenth century, the significant rise in the level and importance of diplomatic transactions in Istanbul culminated in what has rightly been called the "era of embassies" or "devr-i süfera."[72] In the 1840s, Ottoman reformers expanded and reorganized the ancient office of the chief scribe *(reis-ül kittab)* into a specialized ministry of foreign affairs. In the provinces, they established local offices to deal with the problems incurred with consular representatives.[73]

In conjunction with changes in diplomacy, Ottoman officials introduced their own protocols that both affirmed the empire's sovereignty over its domestic constituencies and asserted its rightful place within the emerging international system. During Abdülmecid's reign (1839–61), the central government in Istanbul encouraged celebrations of imperial power on occasions such as the anniversary of the sultan's accession to the throne *(cülus-u hümayun)* and his birthday *(veladet-i padişah)*. These celebrations were not new, but they acquired a new dimension as public events celebrated on an annual basis throughout the empire. Significantly, while they previously structured the rhythms of courtly life in Istanbul almost exclusively, in the course of the second half of the nineteenth century, they gradually spilled out to other provinces to organize time and space across the empire.[74]

In Izmir, imperial events and most remarkably the visits of two consecutive sultans to the city—Abdülmecid in 1850 and Abdülaziz in 1863—eclipsed in size and scope all other displays.[75] Communal and diplomatic events were played out in clearly demarcated areas of the city. In contrast, imperial celebrations took over the entire city to convey a sense of all-inclusiveness. Street decorations and nighttime illumination overrode everyday divisions and boundaries, reinforcing the appearance of a unified populace. On these occasions, every government building and consulate put out flags and illuminations. The residences of the Greek and Armenian patriarchs and the Jewish rabbi, the mansions of local notables and merchants across communities were adorned and similarly illuminated as were the lavishly decked vessels at harbor. Major thoroughfares such as Frank Street and Kemeraltı Street (the ring road around the bazaar) also had their shops and houses festooned with myrtle and evergreens.

Imperial celebrations went beyond temporarily appropriating the city's existing public spaces to convey a message. They brought about permanent changes in the urban fabric. The arrival of Sultan Abdülmecid, for example, prompted the governor to repave all major streets and add an ornamental iron balustrade to the Caravan Bridge—the gateway to the city from its hinterland.[76] Most notably, the increased importance given to imperial ceremonies was an important factor in the wholesale revamping of Izmir's governmental quarters. In the 1860s, the old timber-framed Kâtipzade mansion that served as the governor's palace or Konak could no longer sustain the pomp and circumstance that these festivities required.[77] On official days, most large-scale social events such as balls and receptions had to be carried out on board ships. Eventually, the reconstruction of the Konak between 1868 and 1872 and the creation of a formal public square between the palace and the imperial barracks—which in turn opened onto the Cordon that ran the entire length of the city—radically transformed the area (see Map I.6). Cumulatively, the Konak and the public buildings around it offered an imposing panorama from the water. They outweighed the consular buildings to the north that had long dominated the image of the city from the bay and announced the presence and prestige of the modern state to local and international audiences simultaneously (see Figures I.13, I.14, 4.11). At the same time, the new Konak's neoclassical style, in line with institutional developments elsewhere, inscribed Izmir within a broader international geography of nineteenth-century urban modernization, further anchoring the city's role as a regional capital of distinction.

While this physical reorganization made the area more fit for stately ceremonial exercises, it also established the centrality of state ceremonies as instruments of social cohesion. In the following years, the displays created on imperial celebrations acquired a more sumptuous character. On one occasion, it was reported that specially made braziers, displaying "Maşallah" (a word of praise, literally "God willed it") when lit, were placed on every alley and thoroughfare; that fireworks

FIGURE 4.11. Konak Square, showing the governor's palace and the military barracks to the right. The clock tower was added in 1901 to mark the twenty-fifth anniversary of Abdülhamit's accession to the throne. Postcard. Courtesy of the Suna & İnan Kıraç Research Institute for Mediterranean Civilizations.

were kept up from sunset till midnight; and that sightseers in small boats glided back and forth to admire the continuous line of illumination overlooking the harbor.[78] After most consulates moved from Frank Street to the new quay, on festive days the first Cordon was turned into a protocol strip (Figure 4.12). Framed on one side by the consulates, cafés, and businesses raising their flags and on the other by steamers of different nations anchored in the harbor and flying colorful bunting, the Cordon turned into a festive showcase.

To forge a cohesive polity was central to Tanzimat ideology and Ottomanist policies. Like other heterogeneous empires facing the challenges of national states, Ottoman statesmen engaged in campaigns that enacted multiconfessionalism under one political umbrella. They gave a broader base and a new orientation to state ceremonials by including the non-Muslim groups in the empire. Until then, Muslim religious feasts had prevailed as official state celebrations. But the new imperial feasts enlisted the participation of all non-Muslim heads of millets, in addition to civil and military chiefs and Muslim dignitaries. Over the second half of the nineteenth century, these feasts were increasingly codified to include processions of various groups of officialdom to the governor's palace, the presentation of congratulations, and public speeches. In 1864, Governor Kayserili Ahmed Pasha, dressed in full regalia and wearing his *Osmaniye* decoration, was reported to have responded with heartfelt words to the speeches delivered by the Greek archbishop and the Armenian bishop for the occasion.[79] Afterward, students of Ottoman, Greek, Armenian, and Jewish schools came to the main hall of the governor's palace and delivered speeches in praise of the sultan. These codified actions, performed according to rank and precedence, indicate a rewiring of the Ottoman constitutional system and hierarchies under a new paradigm. They sought to define shared symbols to facilitate integration and social harmony and stem potential conflict within the social whole.

That these new imperial feasts aimed at forging a broader sense of loyalty to the state by including the empire's multireligious polity is already evident in reports dating back to the 1840s. On Sultan Abdülmecid's birthday in 1844, *Écho de l'Orient* recounted with great enthusiasm how the delegations of every

FIGURE 4.12. View of the Cordon during ceremonies for the accession to the throne, 1909. Postcard. Courtesy of the Suna & İnan Kıraç Research Institute for Mediterranean Civilizations.

community gathered at their respective places of worship to observe the occasion according to their own rituals. Following the service at the Armenian church, Bishop Matteos made a short speech, followed by chants of "Long Live the Sultan!" After attending ceremonies at the synagogue, the local Jews marched through the bazaar to the sound of Amen chants performed by students in their holiday attire. In the words of the reporter "all the mosques, Greek and Armenian churches, and synagogues resounded with hymns addressed to the Almighty for the sultan's long life."[80]

The actual effectiveness of imperial feasts in creating a new Ottoman allegiance is difficult to assess. By the later part of the nineteenth century, news reports featured in greater detail the lavish decorations put up on mansions, local businesses, and firms. Some described how, in several locations within the city, the sultan's portrait wreathed in flowers occupied the place of honor in the decorations.[81] Others dedicated a special issue that enumerated all the mansions, hotels, theaters, coffee shops, stores, and taverns that had been decorated and illuminated for the event as *Hizmet,* the local Turkish-language newspaper, did on a yearly basis.[82] Clearly, for local groups in Izmir, these feasts became instruments for jockeying for power within the locality via the imperial reference. Extravagant expressions of allegiance in the form of displays and illuminations garnered attention as advertisement, prompting people to lavish energy regardless of their actual loyalty to the state.

Imperial events also had a second related function. They provided opportunity for the Ottoman state to demand the reciprocation of diplomatic honors parallel to the ones it offered European states with diplomatic representation on its lands. After the governor announced an upcoming feast, consuls and the consular offices had to conform to a set repertoire of requirements. For example, they had to decorate and illuminate the consulate for the duration of the festivities. They had to hoist their flag to reciprocate Ottoman gun salutes fired several times throughout the day. Consuls and their staff also had to take part in person in the official ceremonies. In the morning hours, they were the first group to present their congratulations to the governor. Their participation in ceremonial uniform *(büyük üniforma)* and in company of their dragomans was integral to the new Ottoman ceremonial conventions.

Ceremonial uniforms and illuminations were considerable expenses that reveal the extent of the demands the Ottoman state made from foreign legations. Ottoman ceremonial codes prescribed full uniforms and medals to be worn during all diplomatic visits. Ceremonial uniforms represented the status and authority of the bearer and indicated the level of honor accorded to the receiving party.

The profound political meaning attributed to uniforms in Izmir is most explicitly captured in the objections of Edward Stephen Offley, the American consul at Izmir, to the U.S. secretary of state when the consular uniform was revoked in 1853 to be replaced with the simple dress of the American citizen: "This regulation cannot be put in practice without some inconvenience particularly in the intercourse between the consulate and the local authorities, as they generally attach more importance to external distinctions than to anything else."[83] Similarly, illuminations of consular buildings presented a considerable expense and an additional chore that required the consulate to request additional funds from their home country. The repeated justifications that the consulates had to provide their home countries were revealing. Not only did they indicate the extent to which the Ottoman Empire could enforce diplomatic honors, as a sovereign entity, beyond the limits of its capital; they also attest to Izmir's increasing prominence as an arena for displays of international diplomacy.

The festive practices detailed in this chapter show how public rituals helped forge a sense of community and nationhood during a formative period in Ottoman history, just before the paradigm of modern-state territoriality crystallized and gained general acceptance. Diverse constituencies organized feasts and celebrations in the city to promote their respective agendas—their actions often prompting counteractions by other interested parties, and eventually resulting in a fluid context of identity politics at both the local and the international levels. In an effort to stem the tide of secessionist movements and create a cohesive polity that transcended ethnic and religious affiliations, Tanzimat bureaucrats gave imperial rituals a lavish and more overarching character in Izmir. European consuls, for their part, put on ostentatious celebrations of their national holidays to best represent the interests of their respective states in the empire and expand their influence in the city. As Izmir's consular legations engaged in increasingly more elaborate diplomatic protocols, Ottoman officials responded by imposing more stringent checks over such activities to shore up their authority at home and abroad. Meanwhile, non-Muslim communities sought to claim a recognizable place within the city's decision-making mechanisms. They retooled their religious rituals, invented themselves new political roles, and took advantage of both the empire's newly recalibrated administrative hierarchies and foreign powers' expansionist designs. It is the interplay between these symbolic assertions that effectively brings to light the uncertainties of national and communal realignments in the Tanzimat era as well as the challenges the Ottoman government faced in creating a unified polity.

Feasts and ceremonies animate the history of Ottoman urban communities, which are too often portrayed in neatly delineated religious, ethnic, and national categories. Cumulatively, these ephemeral events bring to life the moods and rhythms of a plural society. They expose the ever-fluctuating communal boundaries that otherwise go unacknowledged in historical narratives and yet, at the time, were crucial in defining and sustaining the Ottoman modus vivendi. Above all, festive practices direct attention to the physical landscape and to the ways it can be used to shape, reinforce, or undercut political ideology—be it state sanctioned or community based. The carefully designed choreography of these events, their relative positioning of celebrants, and their unfolding in time and space indicate that communal and national identities were far from being given. Rather they continually had to be reinvented and reinscribed through performative actions, grounded in built form. Last but not least, festive practices allowed people to tap into familiar repertoires of action to convey new meanings. As mechanisms that concretized hierarchies, they were instrumental in mapping out emerging ideas of community and belonging, which we now take for granted.

Epilogue

The View from Izmir

DURING THE MID-NINETEENTH-CENTURY DECADES, the transformations in Izmir's physical form, institutional structures, and patterns of civic engagement became particularly intensified. Focusing on the city's property regime, street services, waterfront and shipping facilities, and public rituals, this book has exposed the closely intertwined and mutually reinforcing nature of these transformations. Neither social or spatial processes alone nor a direct causality between them can satisfactorily account for these dynamic changes. The ever-shifting and contingent nature of this formative period is revealed in the complicated histories of committees that were constituted, dissolved, and reconstituted; laws and ordinances that were never fully put into practice; projects that remained on the drawing board; and ceremonies that were adopted with great fanfare only to be abandoned soon thereafter. Importantly, these instabilities point to the lacunae left by histories that focus on outcome as opposed to process and possibility. As crucial as end results might have been in determining the course of future developments, the potential paths, roadblocks, and stakes associated with each trial are far more significant in understanding the lived experience of historical actors, the complex world they inhabited, and the choices they made within its constraints. In his study of early European exploration of Australia, Paul Carter reconstructs the imaginative universe of social actors, highlighting the relevance of the paths both taken and abandoned and of the history of possibilities they engender. This book shares this approach insofar as it takes into account, to borrow Carter's evocative phrase, the "roads, footprints, trails of dust, and foaming wakes" and "the haze which preceded clear outlines" to unpack a pivotal moment in the history of the Ottoman Empire and in the making of a modern city.[1]

Although for narrative purposes the book is organized around specific aspects of the material environment, at no point did local actors experience or deal with these in isolation. Considering that the developments explored in the chapters unfolded concurrently, controversies spawned by one issue informed others, further entangling the interests and questions addressed in each chapter. If disputes over the quay project's aims and goals affected the workings of the municipal council, then policies to restrain diplomatic displays intersected with efforts to keep non-Ottoman subjects' property rights under check. Moreover, several local transactions were played out simultaneously on both the national and international planes. Centrally enacted legislations and policies may have determined the scope of Ottoman reforms, but their implementation relied heavily on the ability to adapt and adjust them to local circumstances and power structures. Similarly, what foreign states could or could not do in Ottoman territory hinged as much on the nature of their extraterritorial agreements as on how their local agents could leverage them through concrete, on-the-ground politics. At the same time, state functionaries, whether Ottoman or foreign, did not develop measures and policies in the abstract. Often, the opportunistic actions and resistance of local actors trickled up to inform the issues that the state took up and fought over. At times, seemingly innocuous disputes over property transactions triggered international confrontations and, at others, the delicate balance of power among states affected the status and rights of local subjects or the format of ephemeral events like parades or celebrations.

Collectively and cumulatively, the stories told in this book support and complicate many overarching issues inherent in worldwide modernization processes. In particular, they address three interrelated themes: the assertion of state sovereignty, the emergence of a citizen-subjectivity, and the constitution of a modern public, demonstrating in each case how these processes were bound up with the city's material resources and assets. In what follows, I will briefly pull together these themes to consider their articulation in Izmir from a broader global standpoint.

The increasing territorialization of state rule is one of the most salient trends outlined in this book. Claiming exclusive control over a physical terrain and over the people living, conducting business, and investing in it; standardizing citizenship, property rights, and taxation regimes; overseeing the movement of goods and people; and regulating ceremonial conduct are telltale signs of a state territorializing its sovereignty. It is the adoption of these practices as routine that effectively establishes modern-state territoriality, which we now take for granted. As the foregoing chapters illustrate, nineteenth-century Izmir provides an exceptionally useful case study for understanding both the introduction of these practices and the challenges associated with them. Historically, the Ottoman state had used group-based privileges and exemptions to attract diverse groups to live and work within the empire, benefitting, in turn, from their economic activities. But these exemptions were becoming increasingly disruptive for the centralizing Ottoman state and were undermining its position within the emerging international system of states. The 1867 protocol—signed with foreign powers and formally recognizing non-Ottoman subjects' property rights—demanded, in exchange, subjection to Ottoman laws in all matters related to real estate, seeking to bring highly differentiated groups more evenly under state jurisdiction. Ottoman bureaucrats also established new ground rules for representation in municipal committees and directly tied local political participation to Ottoman nationality, hence advancing a new understanding of citizenship. Moreover, by standardizing customs tariffs and procedures and providing more supervision over the waterfront, the Tanzimat government strove to control more effectively state revenues and keep tighter tabs on imported and exported merchandise through its ports. At the same time, the government formalized and placed restrictions on diplomatic displays and ceremonial honors, bringing them in conformity with international standards to shore up its sovereignty in the domestic and international spheres.

Evidently, Ottoman state interventions were incomplete and underfunded. Their effect was diffused and undercut by existing structures, laws, and practices, which their newly introduced counterparts rarely phased out. Efforts to standardize and fix Ottoman subjecthood were undertaken in the face of a resilient extraterritorial regime and increased opportunities for changing personal status. Nizamiye courts were introduced into an already complex regime of overlapping legal structures. For instance, new provisions that protected public rights of way associated with streets and easements coexisted with rules privileging private property rights, sometimes contradicting them. New millets were formed and old ones were restructured at the same time as Ottoman bureaucrats were trying to create a more integrated polity. Measures to territorialize state rule were developed by compromise and accretion, in fitful starts and stops, rather than following a linear path without detours. Despite the unevenness of their implementation, their collective impact on the experience of urban life was hard to ignore as they made the presence of the state in people's lives more palpable. From the increased surveillance of the port and the streets to the new legal and bureaucratic practices at the provincial and international levels, Ottoman state interventions signaled incipient shifts from a permeable, imperial territorial regime, based on accommodative state practices, to a modern-state territoriality premised on more exclusionary practices.

Modern citizenship subjectivity—the second theme that runs through the various chapters—is closely related to but not entirely dependent on modern state processes. Although citizenship models derived in the context of nation-states tend to consider primarily the legal rights and obligations assigned by a given state, the exercise of agency—whereby individuals understand themselves as actors who can effect change—is equally important in generating a sense of citizenship. When the practices and exchanges developed in this book are viewed together, modern citizen-subjectivity emerges as a two-way process, an interplay between state-initiated actions and grassroots engagement, enacted through the city's material resources by granting or restricting access to them, or appropriating them. On the one hand, a number of state-driven processes had begun to stress individual rights and duties over collective ones. For example, the new property and income tax transformed what had largely been a communal responsibility into an individual one. Similarly, new property registration procedures laid emphasis on individual national status rather than membership in an ethno-religious community. Most saliently, the Ottoman Nationality Law affirmed individual citizenship status as the primary basis of a person's political and property rights, even if communal affiliation continued to define other privileges and duties.

On the other hand, a growing number of individuals from across religious and ethnic lines were finding new ways of asserting themselves in Izmir's socio-economic life and actively participating in major decision-making processes, including the shaping of the city's built environment. Savvy and well-tuned to developments in Izmir and beyond, these individuals invented new identities for themselves as urban actors and carved new channels of legitimate action. Businessman and newspaper owner Anthony Edwards reframed the taxpayer and resident status of local foreign subjects to justify their demands for urban improvements from the Ottoman government. Archbishop Antonio Mussabini appointed himself to a religious-political role, choreographing not only a spiritual feast, but also diplomatic protocols, simultaneously affirming Catholics' centrality to the city and honoring the support of Ottoman and foreign governments without appearing to favor one over the other. Consul and director of the Smyrna Quay Company Richard Van Lennep adopted widely incongruous views about the dangers of stagnant water collecting in the bay as a result of the quay construction, at once to defend the company's actions and to argue for the interests of those he represented as consul. And for every governor or civil servant leery about reforms and their effectiveness, there were many enterprising bureaucrats, such as Ali Nihad Efendi, who used the new authority given to them by the reformist government to devise ways to mediate between the exigencies of the modernizing state and a resistant context. To be sure, the rise of new ways of cultivating the self, especially in cosmopolitan, multiethnic, and polyglot centers like Izmir, significantly contributed to both transforming individuals' self-perception as free agents and making them advocates of change. The emergence of a wide range of players—from technocrat and engineer Margossian Efendi to well-travelled newspapermen, and polyglot merchants, civil servants, and dragomans, as well as countless humbler cultural brokers capable of functioning in more than one language—suggests that a growing number of individuals were investing in educating themselves through either formal schooling or other life activities. Although such resources were not available to everyone equally, there was a palpable expansion of opportunities, especially for ambitious individuals. Certainly, this is not to say that individuals lacked agency before. Rather, it is to underscore the growing shift in the modalities through which such agency was expressed, from a mediated representation, generally through communal leaders, to a more direct participation in public life.

Izmir's dynamic public sphere—the third and main theme that undergirds the various chapters—emerged at the intersection of the modernizing Ottoman state and the fashioning of new urban identities. The presence of discursive arenas outside the immediate community and the state for debating public concerns and forming public opinion, a participatory political culture with some degree of free association among a diverse citizenry, and a sense of rational, critical argumentation based on the separation of private and public interests are constitutive elements of the modern public sphere. It is the actions, contestations, alliances, and negotiations, both verbal and physical, in relation to issues of mutual interest that constantly remake public space and redefine the public sphere. The battles examined in this book bring into sharp focus a public sphere in the making as various stakeholders and local institutions vied to sway public opinion and steer the course of urban development. They also highlight the role of the built environment as a locus around which notions of the public good and public nuisance were forged and legitimated, exposing, at the same time, the inherently unsettled and contingent nature of such notions.

Although religious and communal institutions, which had historically offered urban services, continued to expand, rapid urban growth in the mid-nineteenth century required new types of services and larger-scale infrastructural provisions that could no longer be delivered through these discrete communal structures. The city's perceived shortcomings, coupled with an awareness of developments taking place in the capital and elsewhere in Europe, propelled merchants and prominent residents to demand improvements. Their appeals and criticisms also went beyond specific services and provisions to the administrative structures associated with them. Local stakeholders exploited various channels to engage in public discussion and constitute themselves as agents capable of political judgment and, when necessary, intervention. They used the empire's burgeoning newspaper industry to lobby for a particular railway terminal location; to object to more development along the waterfront; or to praise or evaluate the choice of an appointed Ottoman official, the effectiveness of a committee, or the conduct of a consul. Moreover, they drafted collective petitions to local or state authorities to demand the adoption of measures about a range of issues, from street safety to marsh draining, at times forwarding these formal requests to newspapers to ensure broader circulation. And, for example, when the central government began to question the legitimacy of foreign subjects' property rights, they produced an elaborate pamphlet in which they laid out a counterargument to secure the support of foreign states. These venues and actions did not necessarily bring about the anticipated result. But they focused the attention of the central government, delineated what is worthy and legitimate for public consideration, and importantly allowed locals to define the issues in their own terms. In addition to print media, Smyrniots also used voluntary associations to engage with questions of broader common interest. They formed social and commercial clubs, committees, and temporary bodies outside the realm of state-defined political participation. In times of crisis, notably fires and epidemics, Izmir's leading citizens joined efforts to bring relief to the various classes of the urban population as in the case of the Committee for Hygiene and Relief initiated in 1865 to block the spread of cholera. Seasoned governors and bureaucrats were also quick in forming ad hoc coalitions with consuls or religious leaders to more effectively enforce good order and maintain security in an increasingly diverse urban society, divided by legal status.

The debates and exchanges taking place in these venues repeatedly invoked the city's general welfare, stressing its separation from discrete private interests. Although the social standing of the individuals making the pronouncements still mattered, their arguments now emphasized rational decision-making processes. The medical reports used in opposing the construction of the quay or the statements of receipts and expenditures periodically published in defense of the cadastral commission indicate the increasing credibility given to facts and scientific evidence as sources of objective judgment. This rhetoric reinforced the authority and legitimacy of a given argument by tying it, morally and functionally, to the interests of a larger constituency, often conveniently masking the personal interests vested in it. In the nineteenth century, when rapidly growing cities across the modernizing world were facing increased pressure on their finite physical resources—be it clean air, roads, water access, or safety—the use of such discursive tools became central to generating and validating public decisions. In Izmir, these tools produced an animated public sphere in which actors with divergent stakes simultaneously deployed competing characterizations of the public good, laying bare the flexibility and multivalence of such concepts.

Although holders of economic and cultural capital dominated this incipient public sphere, bureaucrats and officials too played an active role in it by subsidizing or censuring newspapers and by forging alliances with or seeking to control local stakeholders. Notably, the dynamics of this sphere and the coalitions and factions it engendered were issue- and interest-based as opposed to being primarily driven by national or ethnoreligious ideology. In the end, the debates and exchanges spawned by this burgeoning public sphere had a conspicuous impact on how the city's problems and prospects were formulated and acted upon. They informed the shape of the city, the direction of its development, and the functioning of the waterfront. In turn, ensuing regulations about building encroachment, circulation, safety, and hygiene; decisions about which neighborhoods and streets received amenities; or designation of certain areas for specific public displays and rituals articulated new types of social hierarchies, divisions, and inclusions and new rules of propriety in the city's public domain.

Above all, examining the increasing territorialization of sovereignty, the changes in the definition of citizenship, and the rise of a public sphere reveals unmistakable parallels between the experiences of Izmir and those of contemporary cities across the globe, whether in Europe, America, or the colonial world. It brings into relief a process that, much like its counterparts elsewhere, offered no preconceived path for becoming modern, but rather consisted of incremental and often contentious efforts to reconfigure taxation, create public works, delineate municipal jurisdictions, and define the rights and duties of citizens at home and abroad. Despite variations in their geographies, resources, and other specifically local conditions, many mid-nineteenth-century cities grappled with similar urban pressures and demands and developed comparable, if distinct, solutions. The formation of Izmir's cadastral commission as a municipal corporation in the 1850s, followed by subsequent attempts to establish a modern municipality, took place at about the same time British, French, Italian, and German cities were going through similar processes of incorporating themselves as modern municipalities and constituting their respective city councils. Likewise, Izmir's police department, quarantine facilities, and public-health regulations were coeval with the emergence of such institutions and policies in many fast-growing urban centers, from San Francisco and Chicago to Calcutta and Shanghai, concurrently seeking solutions to rampant crime rates and epidemics.

Beyond shared experiences and parallel processes, in the mid-nineteenth century states often found themselves entangled in overlapping jurisdictions, negotiating the boundaries of modern sovereignty collectively. This became particularly noticeable in formulating the rules of modern diplomatic conduct as evidenced in the planning and staging of ceremonial displays in Izmir. The same was true for establishing definitions of citizenship and nationality as exemplified in the much debated "Koszta affair"—an international row over the identity of Martin Koszta, a Hungarian rebel domiciled in Izmir.[2] In 1849, following the failed Hungarian revolution, Koszta first fled to the Ottoman Empire, which granted him asylum, then took up residence in the United States where he even declared his intention to become an American citizen. But in 1853, when he returned to Izmir in search of better business prospects, the Austrian consul had him arrested for repatriation, claiming Austria's extraterritorial jurisdiction over its own subjects in the Ottoman Empire. An international crisis erupted when an American captain in harbor threatened to attack the Austrian ship carrying Koszta, eventually securing his release to the United States. As a symptomatic—if unusual—anecdote, the Koszta case raised questions about whether a declaration of intention without residence entitled the bearer to American citizenship, whether such declaration was a renouncement of the original Austrian nationality, and how such issues were to be handled in a third-party territory, such as the Ottoman Empire. Significantly, the case illustrated not only how all the countries involved were simultaneously testing their respective definitions of modern citizenship and residency rights, but also the degree to which these definitions were mutually constituted and interdependent.

Pulling away from Izmir's specificities to look at the surrounding world-historical context from this vantage point reveals the polycentric and interrelated patterns of modernization with their myriad local articulations. Such a view fundamentally calls into question the default categories and models of historical analysis we traditionally use. Despite the considerable work that has gone into uncovering the shared histories of modernity through comparative studies, the making of the modern city continues to be seen as, to borrow Timothy Mitchell's framing, "a process begun and finished in Europe, from where it has been exported across ever-expanding regions of the non-West" and against which "all other histories must establish their significance."[3] The view from Izmir, presented in this book, foregrounds the "milieu of accidents and contingencies" in which people live and the improvisation they make to address problems that may be similar to but never exactly the same as those encountered elsewhere.[4] This approach emphasizes permeability, tentativeness, and fluidity among social groups and actors and their modernizing agendas on a variety of scales, rather than a constant dissemination of ideas generated by a single group with preassigned roles and identities. This is not to deny that in mid-nineteenth-century Izmir various urban stakeholders borrowed and adapted emerging institutions, legal codes, and administrative structures to address specific challenges, advance new visions, and carve out a place for themselves in a rapidly changing world. My purpose is, rather, first to stress that neither Smyrniots nor their counterparts in other cities had a self-evident, coherent, and fully crystallized model that had gained general acceptance prior to their actions. It is to underscore that invention and adaptation were shared experiences unfolding simultaneously in different places. Second, it is to point out that, despite the obvious asymmetry of power between the Ottoman state and its European counterparts, the resolution of a significant number of problems depended on reciprocal exchange and leveraging. In sum, this book is as much a history of mid-nineteenth-century Izmir as it is an effort to interrogate how we construe the narrative of modernization at large.

Acknowledgments

Writing *Ottoman Izmir* has been an illuminating immersion into a world whose opportunities and constraints force us to rethink contemporary notions of identity and belonging. A book this long in the making incurs, along the way, many debts to institutions and people far and wide. It is a pleasure to acknowledge them here, even if it is impossible to mention each and every one by name. I thank them all for their support for and contributions to this project.

I was fortunate to do the doctoral work on which this book is based at the University of California at Berkeley, a stimulating and intellectually spacious environment. I owe my deepest appreciation to my mentors there, who provided inspiration for the intellectual routes taken here. In particular, I thank the members of my dissertation committee: the late Allan Pred, Kathleen James-Chakraborty, and my advisor, Dell Upton, whose probing questions and incisive comments challenged and guided me as I shaped this work. I am tremendously grateful to my external reader, Reşat Kasaba from the University of Washington, who unreservedly shared his extensive knowledge of Izmir.

In rethinking and recasting this book, I was supported by fellowships from the National Endowment for the Humanities and the Aga Khan Program for Islamic Architecture at the Massachusetts Institute of Technology, as well as a semester research leave and summer research grants from the College of William and Mary. Without these generous awards and the time they gave me to expand my research and write, this book would not have been possible in its present form.

Ottoman Izmir's international connections have led me to libraries and archives scattered across Turkey, Europe, and the United States. I thank the helpful staffs of the Başbakanlık Ottoman Archives, the Istanbul University Library, the Atatürk Library, and the French Institute of Anatolian Studies in Istanbul; and the National

Library and the Turkish Historical Institute in Ankara. I greatly appreciate the courtesy of the staff at the Izmir National Library, who accommodated me even as the collection was undergoing reorganization, and the diligence of the staffs at the Centre des Archives Diplomatiques in Nantes and at the National Archives in Kew, who enabled me to accomplish a great deal in a short time. I owe debts to several fine librarians at UC Berkeley and Harvard University, especially the research staff at the Widener Library for their patience and assistance. My sincere thanks go to Christopher Winters of the Regenstein Library in Chicago and to Osman Köker at Birzamanlar Publishing for helping me procure visuals; to Orlando Carlo Calumeno, Petros Mechtidis, and the Suna & İnan Kıraç Research Institute for Mediterranean Civilizations for sharing their postcard collections; and to Alex and Becky Bloom and Lina Davidian for assisting me with Greek and Armenian texts.

Many people have, at various stages of research and writing, offered their insights on the project and the period. Their guidance and direction were paramount. I particularly thank Sibel Bozdoğan, Edhem Eldem, and Leslie Peirce for their constructive and generous feedback on earlier drafts; Eleni Bastea, Cânâ Bilsel, Shirine Hamadeh, Marie-Carmen Smyrnelis, and Salim Tamari for providing a much-needed sounding board for my ideas; and Engin Akarlı and Cemal Kafadar for sharing with me their immense expertise in Ottoman history. I greatly benefited from the pertinent comments I received during presentations at Brown University, the University of Virginia, and MIT, and I thank Evelyn Lincoln, the Thomas Jefferson Chapter of the Society of Architectural Historians, and Nasser Rabbat, respectively, for organizing these venues. I was privileged to write parts of this book during my research leave in Cambridge, Massachusetts, in the company of congenial and astute colleagues, among whom I thank especially, for their friendship and intellectual camaraderie, Ralph Bodenstein, Emine Fetvacı, Ilham Khuri-Makdisi, Dana Sajdi, Ali Yaycıoğlu, and İpek Yosmaoğlu.

Two long-term friends warrant special thanks for making the writing process exceptionally enriching. Over the years, Zeynep Kezer and Jessica Sewell have shared my excitement and trials, listened to every idea I ran by them, read and commented on numerous iterations of this project, and helped me pull through several impasses. Their pointed observations and comprehensive vision provoked my best efforts and significantly improved the content of this study.

Colleagues and friends in Williamsburg, Virginia, deserve my utmost gratitude for their unwavering support and encouragements, which saw me through the completion of this manuscript. Convivial and always rewarding discussions with my wonderful colleagues, including Bruce Campbell, Maryse Fauvel, Rachel

DiNitto, Catherine Levesque, Giulia Pacini, Gül Özyeğin, Ron Schechter, and Alan Wallach, considerably helped my thinking about the entire project. Thanks also to Najla Kurani and Ute Schechter for keeping me in good humor while I was finalizing the project.

If producing a final draft is one big thing, turning it into a finished book is another. Pieter Martin's support at the University of Minnesota Press played a crucial role in guiding the manuscript through the review process. His enthusiastic endorsement of this project came when I needed it most, for which I warmly thank him. Kristian Tvedten has been a sharp and tireless editorial assistant. I thank him and my copy editor, Deborah A. Oosterhouse, for their painstaking work in seeing the book through to publication. I am also grateful to the anonymous reviewers for the University of Minnesota Press, who offered perceptive and stimulating comments that helped crystallize my arguments and made this book much better. Needless to say, any errors and shortcomings in the final version remain my own.

My research trips to Turkey would not have been as fulfilling if not for the warmth and generosity of friends and family members. I thank my brother Cemil, who offered me a home base in Izmir and responded to my many research requests over the years, and Ayfer Bartu, the Coptys, Ahmet Ersoy, and the Sayeks for their support and generous hospitality during my extended stays in Istanbul. I greatly cherish the congenial times I shared with Deniz Kutay and the late Barış Eyikan; they were indispensable in easing my occasional bouts of anxiousness, and they remain invaluable.

My most heartfelt thanks go to Jack Farraj, who accompanied me through this project from start to finish, patiently enduring the evenings I spent trying to get these pages together. His never-failing sense of humor and unselfishness sustained and anchored me through it all.

This book has been as much a journey of intellectual pursuit as one of self-discovery. I save my final and deepest appreciation for my parents for giving me unconditional support, for putting up with me and without me over the years, and above all for introducing me to this rich but ebbing "world in flux." I dedicate this work to them.

Notes

Introduction

1. For population estimates of the 1840s, see Kütükoğlu, "Izmir Şehri Nüfüsu Üzerine Bazı Tesbitler"; for Ottoman census data of 1881/82, see Karpat, *Ottoman Population, 1830–1914*, 122–23. I discuss population estimates in notes 44–45 below.

2. Rolland, *La Turquie contemporaine*, 78.

3. Studies in a variety of fields have built on the inextricability of spatial forms and social life first theorized by geographers and sociologists, such as Agnew and Duncan, *Power of Place*; Gottdiener, *Social Production of Urban Space*; Gregory and Urry, *Social Relations and Spatial Structures*; Jackson, *Maps of Meaning*; Lefebvre, *Production of Space*; Soja, *Postmodern Geographies*. In the interdisciplinary field of cultural landscape studies, scholars have used this conceptual framework to look more closely at the built environment. See, among others, Dear and Wolch, *Power of Geography*; Groth and Bressi, *Understanding Ordinary Landscapes*; Hayden, *Power of Place*; Low, *On the Plaza*; Upton, "The City as Material Culture"; Zukin, *Landscapes of Power*.

4. Hobsbawm, *Nations and Nationalism Since 1780*, 23.

5. The problem of growth in nineteenth-century cities has long been a subject of profound interest among urban historians. For more recent scholarship on North American and European cities, see, among others, Agostoni, *Monuments of Progress*; Allen, *Cleansing the City*; Barnes, *Great Stink of Paris*; Peterson, *Birth of City Planning in the United States*; Scobey, *Empire City*; Taylor, *The Environment and the People in American Cities*; Upton, *Another City*. Recent works on colonial urban landscapes include Archer, "Paras, Palaces, Pathogens"; Chattopadhyay, *Representing Calcutta*; Glover, *Making Lahore Modern*; Hosagrahar, *Indigenous Modernities*; Scriver and Vikramaditya, *Colonial Modernities*; Yeoh, *Contesting Space*.

6. An ever-growing body of scholarship is examining urban transformations from a comparative and world-historical perspective. See, among others, Fawaz and Bayly, *Modernity and Culture*; Nasr and Volait, *Urbanism*; Prakash and Kruse, *Spaces of the Modern City*; Ewen and Saunier, *Another Global City*. Scholars are also reconsidering the transformation

of nineteenth- and twentieth-century European cities within a global context of imperial connections and colonial expansion. See, for example, Driver and Gilbert, *Imperial Cities*; Jacobs, *Edge of Empire*; Crane, "Digging Up the Present in Marseille's Old Port"; Rabinow, *French Modern*.

7. Economic historians have devoted considerable attention to this question. See, among others, Issawi, *Economic History of Turkey*; Issawi, *An Economic History of the Middle East and North Africa*; Owen, *The Middle East in the World Economy*; İslamoğlu-İnan, *The Ottoman Empire and the World-Economy*; Pamuk, *The Ottoman Empire and European Capitalism*; Kasaba, Keyder, and Tabak, "Eastern Mediterranean Port Cities and Their Bourgeoisies."

8. For a concise history of the treaty, see Kütükoğlu, "Ottoman-British Commercial Treaty of 1838"; for an insightful analysis of the treaty in a comparative perspective, see Kasaba, "Treaties and Friendships"; for its impact on Izmir, see Frangakis-Syrett, "Implementation of the 1838 Anglo-Turkish Convention on Izmir's Trade."

9. On the practices of modern statecraft in the Ottoman Empire, see, for example, Rogan, *Frontiers of the State in the Late Ottoman Empire*; İslamoğlu-İnan, "Property as a Contested Domain"; İslamoğlu-İnan, "Politics of Administering Property"; Güran, "Nineteenth Century Temettuat (Revenue) Censuses"; Behar, "Ottoman Population Statistics and Modernization after 1831."

10. "Cadastre et impôt de la ville de Smyrne et de ses environs," *Journal de Constantinople,* November 10, 1856.

11. For comparable seaports, see, for example, Anastassiadou, *Salonique, 1830–1912*; Hanssen, *Fin de Siècle Beirut*; Ilbert, *Alexandrie, 1830–1930*; Lafi, *Une ville du Maghreb entre ancien régime et réformes ottomanes*; Reimer, *Colonial Bridgehead*; Yerolympos, *Urban Transformations in the Balkans.* For the imperial seat, see Çelik, *Remaking of Istanbul*; Rosenthal, *Politics of Dependency.*

12. For examples of this growing scholarship, see Hanssen, Philipp, and Weber, *Empire in the City*; Rogan, *Outside In on the Margins of the Modern Middle East*; Weber, *Damascus*; Kırlı, "Struggle Over Space"; Chalcraft, *Striking Cabbies of Cairo*; Fahmy, "The Police and the People in Nineteenth-Century Egypt"; Khuri-Makdisi, *The Eastern Mediterranean and the Making of Global Radicalism.*

13. Space and place—the built environment and the experiences it engenders—have become central to discussions of identity formation. On the construction and negotiation of social identity through spatial practices, see, among others, De Certeau, *Practice of Everyday Life*; Hall and Du Gay, *Questions of Cultural Identity*; Hillier and Rooksby, *Habitus*; Carter, Donald, and Squires, *Space and Place.* On space and identity politics, see, for example, Gupta and Ferguson, "Beyond 'Culture'"; Keith and Pile, *Place and the Politics of Identity.*

14. For a critical analysis of the millet construct, see, among others, Braude, "Foundation Myths of the Millet System"; Goffman, "Ottoman Millets in the Early Seventeenth Century." On the historiographic problems raised by the use of these categories, see, for example, Todorova, "Ottoman Legacy in the Balkans"; Barbir, "Memory, Heritage and History"; Kasaba, "Izmir 1922."

15. Recent academic inquiries on the subject include Berber, *Sancılı Yıllar—İzmir 1918–1922*; Berber, *Yeni Onbinlerin Gölgesinde bir Sancak*; Georgelin, *La fin de Smyrne*; Kasaba, "Izmir 1922." Publications on the tragedy run the gamut from works that portray the events

as Turkish atrocities visited upon Greeks and Armenians to those that present Turks as victims of fleeing Greek armies; see, among others, Dobkin, *Smyrna 1922*; Horton, *Blight of Asia*; Lowry, "Turkish History"; *Greek Atrocities in the Vilayet of Smyrna (May to July 1919)*. More recent additions to this debate, however, transcend factional divides. See, for example, Clark, *Twice a Stranger*; Hirschon, *Crossing the Aegean*; Milton, *Paradise Lost*; Kolluoğlu Kırlı, "Modern Spaces," Neyzi, "Remembering Smyrna/Izmir."

16. *Murray's Hand-book for Travellers in the Ionian Islands, Greece, Turkey, Asia Minor, and Constantinople*, 280.

17. Broughton, *A Journey through Albania*, 2:618; MacFarlane, *Constantinople et la Turquie en 1828*, 1:69; Michaud and Poujoulat, *Correspondance d'Orient, 1830–1831*, 1:204.

18. According to historian Tuncer Baykara, the phrase goes back to Tamerlane's 1402 chronicles and was reused by the eighteenth-century Ottoman traveler Evliya Çelebi; see Baykara, *İzmir Şehri ve Tarihi*, 21–22. Nineteenth-century European travelers and missionaries repeatedly remarked on this designation, imbuing it with further significance.

19. Rolleston, *Report on Smyrna*, 20. Emphasis mine.

20. On the fluidity of the Levantine/Mediterranean world, see, for example, Goffman, *Izmir and the Levantine World*; Greene, *A Shared World*; Benbassa and Rodrigue, *Sephardi Jewry*.

21. Cadoux, *Ancient Smyrna*, 291–92, n. 1; *Murray's Handbook for Travellers in Turkey in Asia*, 258. For a concise summary of Izmir's ancient history, see also Oikonomos, *Étude sur Smyrne*; Nezih, *İzmir Tarihi*; Rolleston, *Report on Smyrna*, 15–20.

22. Izmir's continual recovery from calamities is often attributed to its commercial vibrancy enabling it to recover rapidly; see, for example, Oikonomos, *Étude sur Smyrne*; Frangakis-Syrett, *Commerce of Smyrna in the Eighteenth Century*, 43–74; Kasaba, "İzmir."

23. Murray et al., *Encyclopædia of Geography*, 274.

24. Hughes, *A Manual of European Geography*, 290.

25. Historian Daniel Goffman, *Izmir and the Levantine World*, 25–26, explains this growth through a combination of internal events and structural changes in world trade. Rural rebellions (known as *Celâli*) in seventeenth-century Anatolia drove the dispossessed to seek refuge in protected towns like Izmir. Concurrently, changing world trade routes made Izmir a strategic location for immigrants in search of economic opportunity.

26. Wood, *A History of the Levant Company*, 73.

27. Rolleston, *Report on Smyrna*, 12; on mixed Jewish and Muslim neighborhoods, see Kütükoğlu, "İzmir Şehri Nüfusu Üzerine Bazı Tesbitler."

28. Functional sorting of trade in the bazaar helped sustain occupational solidarities and networks, while also keeping all parties informed of the actual value of any article at any given time. The separation of residence from workplace was a common pattern throughout the Middle East and has generally been explained by the need to separate private and public spaces based on a combination of Islamic and pragmatic criteria. See, for example, Abu-Lughod, "The Islamic City"; Eickelman, *The Middle East*, 277–94.

29. Faroqhi, "Izmir." See also Anderson, *An English Consul in Turkey*, 3–4; Goffman, "Izmir," 94–95.

30. French sources refer to the street as Rue Franque or Rue des Francs. On Frank Street in the seventeenth century, see Anderson, *An English Consul in Turkey*, 2 and passim; see

also Bruyn, *Voyage au Levant;* D'Arvieux, *Mémoires du chevalier d'Arvieux;* Tournefort, *Relation d'un voyage du Levant, fait par ordre du roy,* vol. 2.

31. The name suggests that Maltese migrants were the predominant group occupying the shops and rooms in the area. The city's different linguistic groups often used different designations to refer to the same street and urban landmarks. Although, for administrative purposes, all major commercial arteries were given Turkish names after the 1850s, Greek and European designations continued to be simultaneously recognized in city plans and insurance maps. See, for example, Goad, *Plan d'assurance de Smyrne (Smyrna).*

32. Fasula Place is named after the green-bean fields formerly located in the area.

33. D'Estourmel, *Journal d'un voyage en Orient,* 1:199. See also Valon, *Une année dans le Levant,* 492–94.

34. *Journal de Constantinople/Écho de l'Orient,* September 6, 1860.

35. Smyrnelis, *Une société hors de soi.* See also Th. Bargigli, "Letter to the Editor," *Écho de l'Orient,* March 15, 1845.

36. Smyrnelis, "Colonies europénnes et communautés ethnico-confessionnelles à Smyrne."

37. Rolleston, *Report on Smyrna,* 49–50.

38. Valon, *Une année dans le Levant,* 48.

39. Kasaba, *The Ottoman Empire and the World Economy,* 89, table 4. According to this estimate (based on Georgiades, *Smyrne et l'Asie Mineure,* and Issawi, *Economic History of Turkey*) total imports rose from 14.5 million francs in 1839–43 to 90.2 million francs in 1874–78. See also Martal, *Değişim Sürecinde İzmir'de Sanayileşme,* 84–86.

40. Martal, *Değişim Sürecinde İzmir'de Sanayileşme,* 87; see also Scherzer, *La province de Smyrne,* 223–25.

41. Total exports rose from 32.9 million francs in 1839–43 to 103.4 million francs in 1874–78. Kasaba, *The Ottoman Empire and the World Economy,* 89, table 4. See also, Martal, *Değişim Sürecinde İzmir'de Sanayileşme;* Scherzer, *La province de Smyrne.*

42. During the period under consideration, Izmir's population increased by 2 percent yearly, about twice the average growth rate estimated for the empire; see Kasaba, *The Ottoman Empire and the World Economy,* 97, 151 n. 15. On average population growth within the Ottoman Empire in the second half of the nineteenth century, see Issawi, *Economic History of Turkey,* 18; Karpat, *Ottoman Population, 1830–1914,* 18–44. In Izmir, migration and the significant slowing of epidemics after the 1830s were significant in boosting demographic growth.

43. Ottoman counts from the 1830s and 1840s, undertaken for tax and conscription purposes, often generated local resistance yielding estimates of varied reliability. See Kütükoğlu, "İzmir Şehri Nüfüsu Üzerine Bazı Tesbitler." For a summary of travelers' estimates, see Beyru, *19. Yüzyılda İzmir'de Yaşam,* 50, table 3 and 53, table 4.

44. Between the 1840s and 1890 the relative breakdown of the various ethnic groups in relation to the total urban population changed as follows: Muslims from 45–55 percent to 44 percent; Orthodox Greeks from 25–35 percent to 26 percent; Armenians from 4–10 percent to 3 percent; Jews from 4–10 percent to 8 percent; and foreign subjects from 4–10 percent to 19 percent. The 1840s percentages are averages based on Beyru's tables (see previous note). The 1890 percentages are from Cuinet, *La Turquie d'Asie,* 3:440. Similar estimates are

found in Ottoman records; see *Aydın Vilâyetine Mahsus Salname* (1307 M/1890-91). The 1890 percentages represent the population of the city proper. With neighboring villages included, the proportion of foreign subjects rises to 23 percent of the total population.

45. The breakdown of foreign subjects by religion suggests that the Greek Orthodox population constitutes the overwhelming majority of foreign subjects. See Cuinet, *La Turquie d'Asie*.

46. Th. Bargigli, "Letter to the Editor," *Écho de l'Orient*, March 15, 1845.

47. Thomas Graves's 1836 map shows the stream, and in the 1840s Charles Texier mentions its presence. In Storari's 1856 map, however, Boyahane Street replaces the Boyacı Stream.

48. Texier, *Asie mineure*, 308.

49. In 1842, Jean Mathon, a French subject, built a silk-winding factory that he later transferred to Auguste Cousinéry; see *Murray's Handbook for Travellers in Turkey in Asia*, 256. On other industrial establishments built in the mid- to late nineteenth century, see Martal, *Değişim Sürecinde İzmir'de Sanayileşme*, 121–59.

50. On the urban expansion, see Smyrnelis, *Une société hors de soi*, 257. On the Provincial Council's request for draining of the marshes in 1868, see BOA, I. ŞD, no. 614, also cited in Serçe, *Tanzimat'tan Cumhuriyet'e İzmir'de Belediye*, 53.

51. From the mid-eighteenth century to its removal in 1864, the castle walls enclosed rooms and lodging for Muslim populations, and a guardhouse flanked one of its outer walls; see Rolleston, *Report on Smyrna*, 8–9. On the Genoese and Rhodian origins of the castle, see ibid., 19; Baykara, *İzmir Şehri ve Tarihi*, 28–29. On its 1607 reconstruction by Izmir's magnates, see Goffman, *Izmir and the Levantine World*, 135.

52. Rougon, *Smyrne*; Scherzer, *La province de Smyrne*.

53. Geary, *Through Asiatic Turkey*, 299.

54. Playfair, *Handbook to the Mediterranean*, 91.

55. Beyru, *19. Yüzyılda İzmir'de Yaşam*, 211–12, 218; Kupferschmidt, "Who Needed Department Stores in Egypt?" On the rise of a modern consumer culture in the Ottoman Empire, see, among others, Kupferschmidt, *European Department Stores and Middle Eastern Consumers*; Micklewright, "London, Paris, Istanbul, and Cairo"; Quataert, *Consumption Studies and the History of the Ottoman Empire*.

56. Travelers and guidebooks repeatedly talked about Izmir's casinos. For early mentions, see MacFarlane, *Constantinople in 1828*, 97–98; Arundell, *Discoveries in Asia Minor*, 395; Hervé, *A Residence in Greece and Turkey*, 326–47. The European casino was also known as *cercle levantin*, and the Greek casino as *cercle commercial*. By the 1890s, Izmir had several additional clubs, including the Sporting Club, the Hunter's Club, the New Club, and Sailor's Home.

57. The Cammarano Theater, also known as Théâtre de Smyrne, burned down in 1884. On the history of Izmir's nineteenth-century theaters, see Sevinçli, *İzmir'de Tiyatro*; Solomonides, *To Theatro ste Smyrne*; Stamatopoulou-Vasilakou, "Greek Theater in Southeastern Europe and the Eastern Mediterranean from 1810 to 1961," 272–74.

58. *Journal de Constantinople*, June 12 and 21, 1865.

59. Home to the empire's first newspaper in 1826, Izmir sustained a dynamic press. In the late 1840s, even after the Ottoman government had lured *Journal de Smyrne* and *Écho*

de l'Orient to Istanbul, Izmir continued to be home to several papers in different languages—including *L'Impartial*, published for a while in English, then in French; *Amalthea* in Greek; *Archalonis* (Aurora) in Armenian; and *Chaka-Misrah* (Eastern Aurora) in Hebrew. See Çağlar and Groc, *La presse française de Turquie de 1795 à nos jours*; Lagarde, "Note sur les journaux français de Smyrne à l'époque de Mahmoud II"; Koloğlu, *Osmanlı'dan Günümüze Türkiye'de Basın*; Ubicini, *Letters on Turkey*, 246–53. The Turkish-language press of Izmir began in 1869 with the official bulletin *Aydın*, followed by two short-lived nonofficial papers, *İntibah* and *İzmir*, and eventually by *Hizmet* in 1886. See Arıkan, *İzmir Basın Tarihi*.

60. Bouquet Deschamps founded *Journal de Smyrne*; Th. Bargigli, consul general of Tuscany, established *Écho de l'Orient* in 1838; in the 1840s Anthony Edwards founded *L'Impartial*, S. Samiotaki the *Amalthea*, and Luc G. Balthazar the *Archalonis*. See PRO, FO, 195/610, Balthazar to Consul Blunt, October 15, 1860; and Samiotaki to Consul Blunt, October 25, 1860. Arteshas Oskanian launched *La Réforme* in 1868. Among the editors of *Hizmet* was the distinguished novelist Halid Ziya Uşaklıgil. See Çağlar and Groc, *La presse française de Turquie de 1795 à nos jours*, 121, 129–30, 180–81.

61. See, for example, Kırlı, *Sultan ve Kamuoyu*. For a more general discussion on newspapers and the formation of a public sphere, see Habermas, *Structural Transformations of the Public Sphere*; Calhoun, *Habermas and the Public Sphere*; Warner, "The Mass Public and the Mass Subject."

62. Former functions that had to be relocated included soap manufactories *(sabunhane)* and boarding rooms for Jewish residents *(yahudhane)*. On the construction of the barracks and the original plan of the structure, see Ülker, "İzmir Sarıkışlanın Yapım Çalışmaları." On the size of the barracks, see Cuinet, *La Turquie d'Asie*, 3:449.

63. Storari's map indicates seven guardhouses. Thirty years later, the *Aydın Vilâyeti Salname* (1303M/1886–87) identifies eighteen gendarme and seven police guardhouses within Izmir. See Serçe, *İzmir ve Çevresi Resmi, Özel Binalar İstatistiği 1918*, 49.

64. Local magnates assumed power under different titles. *Voyvodalık* was the particular form that this governorship took in Izmir. On the Voyvoda system, see Çadırcı, *Tanzimat Döneminde Anadolu Kentleri'nin Sosyal ve Ekonomik Yapıları*, 29–32 and passim.

65. For an overview of the âyân system and the broader administrative changes introduced by the central government, see McGowan, "The Age of the Ayans, 1699–1812," 658–79.

66. On the construction of the Kâtipzade mansion and the various additions to the square, see Eyüce, "Konak Square."

67. According to Rougon the hospital was erected in 1846. For its use as a British medical headquarters during the Crimean War, see Rolleston, *Report on Smyrna*, 71; Nicol, *Ismeer, or Smyrna, and Its British Hospital in 1855*, 85–86. For an overview of Izmir's various communal hospitals, see Rolleston, *Report on Smyrna*, 57–73; Rougon, *Smyrne*, 58–63; Scherzer, *La province de Smyrne*, 54–59; De Andria and Timoni, *Indicateur des professions commerciales et industrielles de Smyrne, de l'Anatolie* (1895), 25–66 passim.

68. On the use of architecture as an instrument of Ottoman self-redefinition and legitimation, see Çelik, *Empire, Architecture, and the City*; Deringil, *Well-Protected Domains*, chaps. 6, 7; Ersoy, "On the Sources of the 'Ottoman Renaissance.'"

69. The permanent transfer of the provincial government to Izmir took place during the governorship of Halil Pasha in 1850; see PRO, FO, 195/350, Consul Brant to Ambassador Canning, March 1, 1850.

70. On the treasury's sale of property, see Berber, *Yeni Onbinlerin Gölgesinde bir Sancak*, 9, n. 21.

71. On late nineteenth-century Ottoman administrative quarters, see Çelik, *Empire, Architecture, and the City*, chap. 4.

72. For a brief overview of the major spheres of reforms, see Findley, "The Tanzimat"; Quataert, "The Age of Reforms, 1812–1914." For a more in-depth treatment of the reforms and their eighteenth-century origins, see Hanioğlu, *A Brief History of the Late Ottoman Empire*; Quataert, *The Ottoman Empire*; Zürcher, *Turkey: A Modern History*.

73. Smyrnelis, *Une société hors de soi*, 55–56; D'Egremont, "Rapport du 21 juillet 1864," 588. On judicial reforms in Ottoman cities, see Çadırcı, *Tanzimat Döneminde Anadolu Kentleri'nin Sosyal ve Ekonomik Yapıları*, 268–72; on the reformed Ottoman judiciary structures, see Young, *Corps de droit ottoman*, 1:159–303.

74. These mechanisms were akin to what James Scott calls "state simplifications," *Seeing Like a State*, 77–83. For a comparable understanding of modernity and state processes, see also Anthony Giddens's "expert system" and "disembedding" mechanisms, *Consequences of Modernity*, 21–29.

75. The only exceptions were the Specialized (İhtisas) Commission, which continued to include Ottoman and foreign subjects.

76. Geographers and social theorists have extensively theorized about space as both expressive and formative of social relations. Seminal works include Soja, *Postmodern Geographies*; Harvey, *Condition of Postmodernity*; Massey, *Space, Place, and Gender*.

1. Defining Citizenship

1. For a concise introduction to the distinctive aspects of the Ottoman legal system, see Schacht, *An Introduction to Islamic Law*, 89–93; Akarlı, "Gedik," 172–74. For an insightful analysis of the Hanafi/Islamic legal tradition that prevailed in Ottoman territories, see Johansen, *Contingency in a Sacred Law*, 1–76. On non-Muslim courts, see Gradeva, *War and Peace in Rumeli*.

2. I use real property in a broader sense to mean both freehold property (mülk) and various kinds of leasehold property (such as *gedik* and *vakıf*) that by the 1840s had become akin to freehold, permitting exchange, transfer, and inheritance. On the transformation of gedik property in large commercial centers, see Akarlı, "Gedik"; Anastassiadou, *Salonique, 1830–1912*. On the transformation of vakıf property, see Barnes, *An Introduction to Religious Foundations in the Ottoman Empire*.

3. On the administrative and legal autonomy granted to non-Muslim communities, see, among others, Braude and Lewis, "Introduction"; Keyder, "The Ottoman Empire"; Keyder, "Law and Legitimation in Empire"; Göçek, "Legal Recourse of Minorities in History."

4. Taxable property comprised both mülk and gedik property. In 1854, the value of such property held by foreigners amounted to 82,250,821 piastres (PRO, FO, 195/720, "Valuation of property held by foreigners in Smyrna," Consul Blunt to Ambassador Bulwer, August 2, 1862) while total taxable property in Izmir was assessed at 194,000,000 piastres

(PRO, FO, 195/447, "Report of July 13, 1854 meeting," Consul Brant to Ambassador de Redcliffe, July 20, 1854). These were cadastral values, recorded by the Emlak office for tax purposes. According to British consul Charles Blunt they were not representative of the actual value of the property, as for tax purposes each property had been assessed systematically at about one third of its market value.

5. Foreigners could hold real property in their name only on the rare occasion that they were equipped by a special order *(firman)* from the sultan. On foreigners' right to hold real estate prior to the 1867 protocol, see Aliotti, *Des Français en Turquie*, 118–34; Collas, *Turquie en 1861*, 80.

6. For an in-depth treatment of diplomatic and consular protection, see Rey, *De la protection diplomatique et consulaire dans les échelles du Levant et de Barbarie*, 244–450. On the expansion of the protégé status, see also Arminjon, "La protection en Turquie et en Égypte"; Brown, *Foreigners in Turkey*, 92–97; Susa, *Capitulatory Régime of Turkey*, 93–102. For anecdotal accounts on consular protections, see Stephens, *Incidents of Travel in Greece, Turkey, Russia and Poland*, 189.

7. This question has received sustained scholarly attention for over a decade. For example, see Holston and Appadurai, "Introduction: Cities and Citizenship"; Işın, *Democracy, Citizenship, and the Global City*. See also Işın, "Introduction: Cities and Citizenship in a Global Age" and other contributions to the special issue; Staeheli, "Cities and Citizenship" and other contributions to the special issue; Painter and Philo, "Spaces of Citizenship: An Introduction," and other contributions to the special issue.

8. I borrow the notions of appropriation and participation from Henri Lefebvre's *Le droit à la ville* (The right to the city) where he imagines citizens *(citadins)* to have two main rights: the right to *appropriate* urban space (that is, to live in and occupy urban space in a particular city) and the right to *participate* in urban space (that is, to take part in decision making surrounding the production of space). See also Lefebvre's *Writings on Cities,* particularly 172–73, 179. For a concise analysis of Lefebvre's notion of the right to the city, see Purcell, "Citizenship and the Right to the Global City."

9. The notion of legal pluralism is garnering attention across a range of law-related fields, including legal anthropology and legal sociology and most recently in comparative law and world history. For a historical overview, see Benton, *Law and Colonial Cultures;* Merry, "Legal Pluralism." For a discussion on the historical and present relevance of the concept, see Tamanaha, "Understanding Legal Pluralism."

10. On personal law in Muslim lands, see Liebesny, *Law of the Near and Middle East*, 8–11; Susa, *Capitulatory Régime of Turkey,* 15–33; Pélissié du Rausas, *Le régime des capitulations dans l'empire ottoman*, 1:21–24.

11. Islamic jurists have generally attributed the origins of zimmi protections to the Pact of Umar, concluded with the conquered people of the book, and enumerating the obligations and restrictions that applied to them in Muslim lands. For a version of the pact, see Stillman, *Jews of Arab Lands,* 157–58. For a concise discussion on the topic, see Goddard, *A History of Christian–Muslim Relations.*

12. On the articulation of the concept of zimmi in the Ottoman Empire, see Steen de Jehay, *De la situation légale des sujets ottomans non-musulmans;* Ubicini, *Letters on Turkey,* 134–66; Bozkurt, *Alman-İngiliz Belgelerinin ve Siyasi Gelişmelerin Işığı Altında Gayrimüslim*

Osmanlı Vatandaşlarının Hukuki Durumu; Van den Boogert, *The Capitulations and the Ottoman Legal System.*

13. Susa, *Capitulatory Régime of Turkey,* 39, n. 12; Van den Boogert, *The Capitulations and the Ottoman Legal System.*

14. For a concise discussion of the origin of *ahdnames,* see Goffman, "Negotiating with the Renaissance State." For an in-depth treatment, see Van den Boogert, *The Capitulations and the Ottoman Legal System,* 19–61. Like their Byzantine predecessors, early Ottoman sultans had been granting special privileges to Venetian, Genoese, and other merchant communities living in their domains. After their alliance in 1535, Süleyman the Magnificent and Francis I drafted a more comprehensive treaty that provided a basis for renewals, confirmations, and expansion of its clauses in 1740, 1802, 1838, and 1861. For a text of these treatises, see Noradounghian, *Recueil d'actes internationaux de l'empire ottoman;* Pélissié du Rausas, *Le régime des capitulations dans l'empire ottoman,* vol. 1; Schopoff, *Les réformes et la protection des chrétiens en Turquie.*

15. The term "capitulations" comes from *capitula,* the Latin word for a treaty written under articles. For an overview of the Ottoman capitulatory regime, see Amar, *Capitulations en Turquie, dans le Levant et en Extrême-orient;* Essad, *Du régime des capitulations ottomanes;* Susa, *Capitulatory Régime of Turkey.* On Ottoman perceptions of the capitulations, see Ahmad, "Ottoman Perceptions of the Capitulations."

16. On the ancient origins of extraterritorial jurisdictions, see Kassam, "Extraterritorial Jurisdiction in the Ancient World"; for a concise treatment of "the personality of the law" in the medieval world, see Liebesny, "Comparative Legal History," 38–41. There is a rich literature on the evolution of extraterritorial jurisdictions and nineteenth-century treaty-systems between expanding Europe and older Eurasian states. For a comparative treatment, see, for example, Horowitz, "International Law and State Transformation in China, Siam, and the Ottoman Empire during the Nineteenth Century."

17. On non-Muslims' use of the kadı court, see Göçek, "Legal Recourse of Minorities in History"; Al-Qattan, "Dhimmis in the Muslim Court." Even matters concerning personal status, divorce and marriage, which are generally imagined to remain within the domain of each community, could provide a reason for crossing jurisdictional boundaries. For example, Christians who wanted to circumvent such matrimonial restrictions placed by their church as marrying a second wife or a relative, or secure the legitimacy of children born from such a union, voluntarily contracted marriages at the kadı court; see Pantazopoulos, *Church and Law in the Balkan Peninsula during the Ottoman Rule,* 91–112.

18. While Islamic law *(şeriat)* and its elaborate system of legal thought *(fıkh)* provided the principal source of jurisprudence, kadı courts also drew from complementary legal traditions. Ottoman state law *(kanuns),* enacted by the sovereign powers of the sultans, offered a body of regulations that supplemented the precepts of Islamic law. Moreover, a variety of local customs *(örf* and *âdet),* although usually unwritten, were also recognized as binding precedent.

19. On Ottoman kadı court practices and their course of justice, see, for example, Jennings, "Kadi, Court, and Legal Procedure in 17th C. Ottoman Kayseri"; Doumani, "Palestinian Islamic Court Records"; Gerber, *State, Society, and Law in Islam;* Peirce, *Morality Tales;* Ergene, *Local Court, Provincial Society, and Justice in the Ottoman Empire.*

20. See article 26 of the 1740 capitulation with France; cited in Aliotti, *Des Français en Turquie*, 83–84.

21. On the rationale of third-party ownership, see CADN, FC, Smyrne no. 50, "Note de la Commission pour la Défense de la Propriété," February 3, 1872 (a thirteen-page printed pamphlet, signed by twenty-one delegates representing nine foreign nationalities, and written in response to the circular of Server Pasha, the minister of foreign affairs); NA, DUSCS, "Memorial to the Honorable Hamilton Fish, Secretary of State of the United States of America from the American residents at Smyrna, Turkey," July 20, 1872. See also Collas, *Turquie en 1864*, 127–29; McCoan, *Our New Protectorate*, 2:195. Although McCoan notes that Izmir was exceptional in that foreigners had even acquired permission to own property in their own names, the real-estate disputes consulted for the present study show that property held in trust via a female relative was by far the most common strategy in Izmir.

22. Smyrnelis, *Une société hors de soi*, 291.

23. Van Dyck, *Report on the Capitulations*, 56. Different transfer strategies were used in different localities. For example, in Damascus a foreign lessee purchased a building through an indefinite lease of possession, under which the former proprietor could regain the property only on repayment of the money advanced to him. See Reilly "Status Groups and Propertyholding in the Damascus Hinterland," 524.

24. This was, at least, the case until the 1869 Ottoman Nationality Law brought more definition to the status of râya women marrying foreigners. By stating that such women could regain their Ottoman nationality within three years of the husband's death, the new law implied that these women lost their Ottoman nationality upon marriage (article 7 of the 1869 Ottoman Nationality Law). For the full text of the law, see Aristarchi Bey, *Législation ottomane*, 1:67; Young, *Corps de droit ottoman*, 2:226–29. For a discussion of the status of râya women marrying foreigners, see Aliotti, *Des Français en Turquie*, 13–28.

25. The consular archives contain numerous court cases on the topic. See PRO, FO, 78/1787, "Tenure of Property by Female Foreigners," 1861–63.

26. Until the creation of a new land registry in the 1850s, title deeds for mülk were prepared at the kadı court in the presence of the parties. Long-term leases for vakıf property were drafted by endowment administrators *(mütevelli)* and then delivered to the kadı court to complete the transaction.

27. PRO, FO, 78/1787, Judge Logie to Governor Osman Pacha, August 2, 1861. A significant number of wives declared the property their own and appealed to the kadı court for protection from what they saw to be a wrong done by the consular court. These cases, however, were not always resolved to the advantage of the bankrupt and the female proprietor. The kadı court could rule against the registered proprietress and auction off the property to the benefit of the creditors. See Marcozade's bankruptcy in 1832 where the kadı court ordered the seizure of the property registered to his mother-in-law, PRO, FO, 195/241, Consul Brant to Ambassador Wellesley, November 30, 1846.

28. CADN, FC, Smyrne no. 42, Consul Béchard to Ambassador Bourqueney, January 8, 1847, annexes 4, 8, and 9. Suzon de Hochepied Guys's ownership rights in the property in question were based on a private contract dated April 7, 1841, and signed at the Dutch consulate, where Sara de Hochepied and her three other children, Jean Edmond, Frederic Pierre, and Annette Marie de Hochepied, agreed to give the property to their sister

Suzon in order to make up for the unequal share she received from her father's inheritance in 1824.

29. CADN, FC, Smyrne no. 46, Consul Mure de Pélanne to Ambassador Moustier, October 1, 1862. The dispute was between Suzon Guys and Sara Karcher. Guys had mortgaged her house for a debt her husband owed to the Manchester firm of d'Heauregard that Mr. Karcher represented in Izmir. She had the option of repurchase within a period of three years during which she would continue to live in the house as a tenant. By the end of the period, the debt in question not having been settled, the wife of Karcher brought the case to court.

30. On the discrepancies among consular court procedures, see CADN, FC, Smyrne no. 42, Consul Béchard to Ambassador Bourqueney, January 8, 1847.

31. PRO, FO, 195/389, C. Fisher to Consul Brant, April 30, 1853. On the case *Fisher v. Kramer*, see also PRO, FO, 195/389, Consul Brant to Ambassador de Redcliffe, May 2, 1853.

32. PRO, FO, 195/389, Âli Pasha to Ambassador Canning, memorandum dated December 10, 1851, regarding the case of *Hripsima v. Vapopoulo*, attached to Consul Brant to Ambassador Canning, December 18, 1852. See also PRO, FO, 195/389, Âli Pasha to Colonel Rose, July 28, 1852/Şevval 11, 1268.

33. CADN, FC, Smyrne no. 42, Consul Béchard to Ambassador Bourqueney, January 8, 1847. Emphasis mine.

34. Mecelle or Mecelle-i Ahkam-ı Adliye was issued between 1867 and 1876 under the guidance of Ahmed Cevdet Pasha and was a codification of the treatises of jurists of the Hanafi school, the official school of law in Ottoman territories. For an overview and a transcription of the Mecelle to modern Turkish, see Öztürk, *Osmanlı Hukuk Tarihinde Mecelle*.

35. For an overview of nizamiye courts, see Findley and Inalcık, "Mahkama." For an in-depth account of procedural changes, see Young, *Corps de droit ottoman*, 1:159–238. On legal reforms in Izmir, see Smyrnelis, *Une société hors de soi*, 55–57.

36. For an in-depth study of nizamiye courts, see Rubin, "Ottoman Modernity"; and Rubin, "Legal Borrowing and Its Impact on Ottoman Legal Culture in the Late Nineteenth Century." On the relationship between kadı and nizamiye courts, see Miller, "Apostates and Bandits."

37. This was the case when the burden placed on the private proprietor by the easement exceeded the benefits it gave to other owners. Hence an owner whose property was adjacent to a dead-end street or was crossed by an easement could block the passageway and prevent others from using it. I further discuss these questions in chapter 2, at notes 101–4.

38. "Ionian" refers to subjects of the British Ionian Islands, located west of present-day mainland Greece. Initially under Venetian protection, the islands came under British rule in 1815 and were eventually transferred to independent Greece in the early 1860s. As a result, Ionians who lived in Izmir generally claimed British (and later Hellenic) protections.

39. The arguments of the parties are recorded in CADN, FC, Smyrne no. 45, Cousinéry to Ambassador Thouvenel, January 18, 1858; consul to Ambassador Thouvenel, March 1, 1858; *L'Impartial*, February 22, 1858; PRO, FO, 195/610, Governor Mustafa Pasha to Consul Blunt, April 9, 1858; Consul Blunt to Governor Mustafa Pasha, April 17, 1858. See also petitions by the members of the Zadé family, May 17, 1858, and by residents living nearby the disputed drain enclosed in PRO FO, 195/610, Consul Blunt to Ambassador Alison, May 21,

1858. The case of *Cousinéry v. Zadé* (also spelled Sadé or Sade) was further complicated by the personal status of the litigants, resulting in the involvement of an unusually large number of legal authorities, including members of the municipal council, the kadı, the Greek Orthodox clergy, and the French and British consular judges.

40. I borrow the term "forum shopping" from Keebet von Benda-Beckmann's analysis of disputes in the legally plural arena of Indonesia; see "Forum Shopping and Shopping Forums," 117. For more recent applications of her concept, see Rouveroy van Nieuwaal and Zips, *Sovereignty, Legitimacy, and Power in West African Societies*; Merry, "Legal Pluralism."

41. While in theory both Muslims and non-Muslims could be employed as consular staff and agents, hence obtain consular protection, in practice non-Muslim Ottoman subjects constituted the bulk of consular protégés.

42. On the variations among consular practices, see Steen de Jehay, *De la situation légale des sujets ottomans non-musulmans*; Rey, *De la protection diplomatique et consulaire dans les échelles du Levant et de Barbarie*. For an in-depth analysis on foreigners' property inheritance, see Aliotti, *Des Français en Turquie*.

43. The *askeri* (or the military) was the ruling class and included officers of the court and the army, civil servants, and the ulema. The râya comprised everyone else: peasants, urban craftsmen and merchants, and nomads, who paid taxes but had no part in the government; see İnalcık "Nature of Traditional Society."

44. Office-based privileges were a major aspect of Ottoman governance. On the parallels between the protégé concept and office-based privileges, see Pélissié du Rausas, *Le régime des capitulations dans l'empire ottoman*, 2:33. Similarly, tax exemptions were granted to people who performed services to the Ottoman state, from Janissaries and non-Muslim communal leaders to villagers who repaired roads and guarded dangerous passes.

45. On the protégé system, see Sonyel, "The Protégé System in the Ottoman Empire"; Masters, "The Sultan's Entrepreneurs"; Reilly, "Status Groups and Propertyholding in the Damascus Hinterland"; Bağış, *Osmanlı Ticaretinde Gayri Müslimler*; Van den Boogert, *The Capitulations and the Ottoman Legal System*.

46. See note 6 above.

47. For most of the nineteenth century, liberal theorists debated the rights of national minorities in multinational states. For a historical overview and critique, see Kymlicka, *Multicultural Citizenship*, chap. 4.

48. PRO, FO, 195/241, Consul Brant to Ambassador Wellesley, November 30, 1846. For a complete account of the case, see PRO, FO, 195/288, "Consul Brant's Remarks on a Paper received from the Embassy," June 24, 1847.

49. On the difficulty of sorting out these groups in Ottoman income censuses, see Kütükoğlu, "Izmir Temettü Sayımları ve Yabancı Tebaa," 38–42. Izmir's 1844/45 income census estimates a foreign population slightly below ten thousand. The 1881/82 Ottoman general census counts fifty thousand foreigners (out of a total population of slightly over two hundred thousand). See Karpat, *Ottoman Population, 1830–1914*, 122–23. The extent of the protégé problem can only be gleaned from incidental evidence. For instance, the 1841 general census showed that half of the three hundred thousand individuals who claimed Hellenic nationality in the Ottoman Empire had been born in Ottoman territories and from parents who were Ottoman subjects; see Engelhardt, *La Turquie et le Tanzimât*, 1:64; 2:102.

See also Rey, *De la protection diplomatique et consulaire dans les échelles du Levant et de Barbarie,* 244–305. Political events gave greater momentum to these claims. For example, King George's accession to power in Greece in 1863 resulted in several Ottoman Greeks insisting on their Hellenic nationality; see *Journal de Constantinople,* April 22 and June 30, 1864.

50. Ahmed Vefik Pasha had to make such decisions as to whether Maltese should produce rapports in proof of their origin and whether provisional terms of protection granted to Ionians should be accepted; see PRO, FO, 195/241, Consul Brant to Ambassador Canning, October 12, 1844.

51. See BOA, I. MVL, no. 2379/1. Also cited in Kütükoğlu, "Izmir Temettü Sayımları ve Yabancı Tebaa," 757, nn. 9 and 10.

52. On the effect of the 1863 decree, see Pélissié du Rausas, *Le régime des capitulations dans l'empire ottoman;* Steen de Jehay, *De la situation légale des sujets ottomans non-musulmans;* Brown, *Foreigners in Turkey.*

53. Memorandum of the Sublime Porte, dated April 1869/Muharrem 1286 in Testa, Testa, and Testa, *Recueil des traités de la Porte ottomane avec les puissances étrangères,* 7:542–45.

54. NA, DUSCS, Consul Smithers to G. H. Boker, minister resident at Constantinople, September 6, and Consul Smithers to secretary of state, October 24, 1873.

55. Transcript of the Congress of Paris in PRO, FO, 78/1787, enclosed in Erskine to Ambassador Russell, November 12, 1862.

56. Memorandum cited in Pélissié du Rausas, *Le régime des capitulations dans l'empire ottoman,* 36. The memorandum had repercussions across the empire. For its impact in Aleppo and Damascus, see Rafeq, "Ownership of Real Property by Foreigners in Syria."

57. See the cases collected in PRO, FO, 78/1787.

58. PRO, FO, 78/1902, official announcement of *L'Impartial,* July 14, 1862, enclosed in George Lee (proprietor in Izmir) to Ambassador Russell, July 26, 1862.

59. PRO, FO, 195/720, Consul Blunt to Ambassador Bulwer, August 2, 1862.

60. PRO, FO, 78/1787, Pisani to Ambassador Bulwer, November 5, 1861.

61. Ibid. The omission of last names in the title deeds as a strategy for transferring property in the name of foreign women is also noted in CADN, FC, Smyrne no. 50, "Note de la Commission pour la Défense de la Propriété," February 3, 1872; PRO, FO, 78/1787, Ambassador Bulwer to Judge Hornby, November 13, 1861; *Levant Herald,* July 16, 1862.

62. *Levant Herald,* July 16, 1862.

63. PRO, FO, 78/1787, memorandum of foreign ambassadors (including British Bulwer, French Marquis de Moustier, Austrian Prokesh-Oster, Russian Sohanov) to Âli Pasha, February 15, 1862.

64. The 1867 decree formalized the exchange of rights and obligations already formulated in the Hatt-ı Hümayun, article 17, which admitted property rights to all inhabitants in return for subjection to the laws of the country. Accordingly, foreigners' ownership rights were granted throughout the empire, except for the province of Hicaz. For the official text, see BOA, I. MMS, no. 1417 (1284/1867) and Aristarchi Bey, *Législation ottomane,* 1:19–25. On the consequences of the law on foreign proprietors, see Aliotti, *Des Français en Turquie,* 118–34.

65. This pattern constituted a major concern for the Ottoman central government. See "Memorandum of the Sublime Porte to Foreign Legations in Response to Attacks Waged

against Ottoman Nationality Law," dated April 1869/Muharrem 1286, in Testa, Testa, and Testa, *Recueil des traités de la Porte ottomane avec les puissances étrangères*, 7:543. Also see the further confirmation of this measure in articles 5 and 6 of the 1869 Ottoman Nationality Law in ibid., 7:526–27.

66. In 1869, Britain, France, Austria, and the Netherlands had signed the protocol. Russia, Greece, and Italy, who had the largest numbers of protégés, followed more reluctantly. In 1874 Prussia and the United States also joined the signatories. See Susa, *Capitulatory Régime of Turkey*, 83–84, n. 39.

67. The Ottoman state followed the general principle that, regardless of the category of the land, the nature of the dispute, or the legal action needed to resolve it, foreigners would be considered Ottoman subjects in relation to property. In contrast, foreign missions insisted that their subjects should only be tried in Ottoman nizamiye courts, as opposed to kadı courts, although both courts shared competence over real property until 1880.

68. *La Turquie*, June 6, 1871.

69. On Ottoman fiscal reforms, see Çadırcı, *Tanzimat Döneminde Anadolu Kentleri'nin Sosyal ve Ekonomik Yapıları*; Heidborn, *Manuel de droit public et administratif de l'empire ottoman*, vol. 2; Akyıldız, *Tanzimat Dönemi Osmanlı Merkez Teşkilâtında Reform*; Davison, *Reform in the Ottoman Empire*.

70. The central government and local authorities repeatedly underscored the principle of equality before the tax and its universal application. See PRO, FO, 195/177, memorandum of the Sublime Porte to Ambassador Ponsonby, July 19, 1841; CADN, FC, Smyrne no. 41, memorandum of the Municipal Council (Şura) to Consul Challaye, July 2, 1841 (the memorandum was signed by Governor Osman Pasha; Treasurer (Muhassıl) Abdul Nihad Efendi; Molla Muhammed Hilmi; Müftü Seyyid Ahmet Soflu; and members Seyyid el-Hac İbrahim, Süleyman el-Nehbi, Seyyid Raşid, Theodoraki, Yanako veled-i Spiro, and Aghasar, Salomon). See also the following memoranda in CADN, FC, Smyrne no. 41: January 24, 1843/Zilhicce 23, 1258 enclosed in dispatch January 31, 1843; May 13, 1843/Rebiülakhir 15, 1259 enclosed in dispatch May 16, 1843; September 17, 1843/Şaban 22, 1259 enclosed in dispatch September 19, 1843; and October 21, 1834/Ramazan 27, 1259 enclosed in dispatch October 23, 1843.

71. According to the Hanafite rite of Islamic law, one's home was exempt from any dues. See Belin, *Étude sur la propriété foncière en pays musulman*, 66, article 133. For a discussion of the state's transgression of this law, see ibid., 21, article 31. On the *resm-i dukhan* (hearth tax) found in some regions, see ibid., 148, article 348. Belin's study is based on the Multeka, the sixteenth-century code of Ottoman laws compiled by İbrahim Halebi and commented upon by Mehmet Mevkufati. On the principle of the tax exemption of the residence, see also Heidborn, *Manuel du droit public et administratif de l'empire ottoman*, 1:320–22.

72. The real-estate tax law of 1303/1886 *(emlak ve akar vergisi)* eventually fixed the tax to a percentage of the value of the building. Accordingly, all revenue-generating commercial and residential buildings were to pay 1 percent; owner-occupied buildings of a value above 20,000 piastres were to pay 0.8 percent; and similar buildings of a value below 20,000 piastres were to pay 0.5 percent. See Padel and Steeg, *De la législation foncière ottomane*, 334–35; Young, *Corps de droit ottoman*, 6:119–23.

73. Salzmann, "Citizens in Search of a State," 42.

74. CADN, FC, Smyrne no. 39, Consul Challaye to chargé d'affaire Varennes, July 19, 1832 and September 7, 1832.

75. CADN, FC, Smyrne no. 39, Consul Challaye to chargé d'affaire Varennes, August 18, 1832. According to Consul Challaye, the tax rate was set at 4 percent of the assessment. Considering that the rental value of the property was 10–12 percent of its capital value, the tax represented 40–50 percent of the revenues.

76. In the Ottoman Empire cadastral lists had been in use since the sixteenth century to assess the collective tax burden of specific localities. But the new system was more thorough and systematic, thus expanding the boundaries of the state in new ways. On the *temettuat* (income) registers, see Aydın and Hayashi, *The Ottoman State and Societies in Change*; Güran, "Nineteenth Century Temettuat (Revenue) Censuses"; İslamoğlu-İnan, "Politics of Administering Property."

77. In Izmir, in the absence of an official valuation of the tax base, it proved impossible to calculate separately income tax and property tax, precluding fairness in individual tax obligation. Thus, the 1,200,000 piastres lump sum generated from the outset much resistance among foreign parties liable for the tax who saw it as being "an arbitrary contribution to the Porte," "not a fair tax paid upon landed property." See PRO, FO, 195/177, petitions of British proprietors (R. B. Abbott, John Werry, George Perkins) to Consul Brant, June 21, 1843.

78. Report of the meeting of the delegates of French proprietors (A. Cousinéry, Ch. Salzani, G. Amie) with Governor Salih Pasha, CADN, FC, Smyrne no. 41, March 19, 1843.

79. On the difficulties of codifying property ownership, see İslamoğlu-İnan, "Property as a Contested Domain" and other contributions in that same volume.

80. BOA, I. MVL, no. 2379/2 (dated Receb 9, 1265/May 31, 1849); BOA, I. MVL, no. 4104/1 (dated Şaban 10, 1265/July 1, 1849); PRO, FO, 195/288, Consul Brant to Ambassador Canning, May 19, 1849.

81. CADN, FC, Smyrne no. 43, Consul Pichon to General Aupick, May 19, 1850.

82. *Journal de Constantinople*, November 10, 1856.

83. BOA, I. MVL, no. 5865/4. Also mentioned in Rolland, *La Turquie contemporaine*, 79–82. These strategies are akin to modern state efforts at increasing the legibility of local landscapes and societies. For an excellent discussion, see Scott, Tehranian, and Mathias, "Production of Legal Identities Proper to States."

84. Luigi Storari, a former major in the artillery at Rome who fled to Izmir in the aftermath of the 1848 revolutions, worked with Ali Nihad Efendi between 1851 and 1854. Storari was also active in Istanbul, where he implemented the first grid street pattern in 1856 after the fire in the Aksaray neighborhood. See Klay, *Daring Diplomacy*, 47, 77. On Luigi Storari's work in Istanbul, see Ergin, *Mecelle-i Umûr-i Belediyye*, 9:1244. On his work in Izmir and Istanbul, see Yerasimos, "Quelques éléments sur l'ingénieur Luigi Storari."

85. Accordingly, all registered property was to yield a tax of 800,000 piastres and all taxable income (from local trade and retail) was to produce 400,000 piastres. Article 2 of the 1856 regulation underscores that these two taxes have different bases and that each tax should be levied with impartiality, regardless of the amount a person may have paid toward either one of these taxes.

86. Report of the meeting of the delegates of French proprietors with Governor Salih Pasha, CADN, FC, Smyrne no. 41, March 19, 1843.

87. For example, already in 1841, a firman announced new procedures whereby members of the local corporations *(esnafs)*, Muslim and non-Muslim alike, would vote en masse to elect delegates, who would in turn choose the municipal council members. These members would serve on a one-year basis. See *Écho de l'Orient*, October 9, 1841. On the formation of modern municipal councils during the Tanzimat, see Çadırcı, "Osmanlı İmparatorluğunda Eyalet ve Sancaklarda Meclislerin Oluşturulması."

88. For an Ottoman Turkish and French version of the regulation, see "Izmir ve Muzafatı Vergisinin Tevzi ve Tesviyesine dair Nizamname" and "Réglement concernant la répartition de l'impot de la ville de Smyrne et de ses dependences," dated October 21, 1856/Sefer 22, 1273, in PRO, FO, 195/527. The French version also appeared in *Journal de Constantinople*, November 10, 1856. For an interpretation of the 1856 regulation, see CADN, FC, Smyrne no. 50, "Note de la Commission pour la Défense de la Propriété," February 3, 1872, 4–5.

89. *Journal de Constantinople/Écho de l'Orient*, April 30, 1857.

90. Cadastral records between 1855 and 1860 confirm the wide discrepancy in the ability to exact income taxes as opposed to property taxes. While the cadastral office collected 81 percent of the property taxes it assessed, it could only levy 23 percent of the income taxes it imposed. Percentages are based on amounts recorded in *Journal de Constantinople/Écho de l'Orient*, November 27, 1861 (reprinted from *L'Impartial*). On government complaints about income-tax arrears, see BOA, BEO, A. MKT. MVL 3426/143/15 (1278/1860–61).

91. *Levant Herald*, September 17, 1862.

92. *Journal de Constantinople/Écho de l'Orient*, March 14, 1861, excerpt from *L'Impartial*, February 22, 1861.

93. Objections against gas lighting escalated because of a general conviction that the cadastral commission favored the British company's interest. In June 1864, the mixed committee that studied the question included Süleyman Bey Kanzıbanoğlu, Abro Efendi, George Pappa, Polycarpe Barry, and Robert Wilkin. The commission lowered the initial price of 1,300 piastres to 850 piastres, but the latter price was still believed to leave a considerable margin of profit to the British company. For a detailed report of the gas question, see *Journal de Constantinople/Écho de l'Orient*, August 4, 1864, and *Levant Herald*, December 4, 1867.

94. *Journal de Constantinople/Écho de l'Orient*, February 9, 1859.

95. PRO, FO, 195/910, Governor Ismail Pasha to Consul Cumberbatch, May 30/June 11, 1868.

96. PRO, FO, 195/943, Âli Pasha to Ambassador Elliot, March 11, 1869.

97. On the invitations sent to individual proprietors, see PRO, FO, 195/943, Consul Cumberbatch to Ambassador Elliott, July 8, 1869. For a sample invitation sent to John Fisher, see PRO, FO, 1995/943, 18/30 June, 1869. On the controversy about the term *mixed*, see the report of the meeting with Süreyya Pasha (signed by Alex Bonnal, J. H. Belhomme, and Ch. Salzani) enclosed in dispatch March 6, 1874, and response from ambassador to Consul Burggraff, March 19, 1874.

98. On proprietors' resistance, see PRO, FO, 195/943, petition dated September 5, 1870, and signed by over sixty property owners. Reprinted in *Levant Herald*, March 16, 1872. See also CADN, FC, Smyrne no. 50, "Note de la Commission pour la Défense de la Propriété," February 3, 1872.

99. NA, DUSCS, "Memorial to the Honorable Hamilton Fish, Secretary of State of the United States of America from the American residents at Smyrna, Turkey," July 20, 1872, 11.

100. *La Turquie*, January 16, 1872; emphasis mine. The memorandum was drafted on the occasion of the Porte's sending informants (or *jurnalcıs*) to assess the general needs and complaints in the provinces. See also *La Turquie*, January 30, March 16, April 9, and August 20, 1872.

101. The concept of nationality or *tabiyet* had been acknowledged in the Ottoman Empire since the Tanzimat edict of 1856 and was officially adopted with the 1869 Ottoman Nationality Law; see Heidborn, *Manuel du droit public et administratif de l'empire ottoman*, 1:122–31.

102. They further complained that the municipality was no more than an administrative bureau that took no input from taxpayers: *La Turquie*, August 20, 1872.

2. Ordering the Streets

1. *Journal de Constantinople/Écho de l'Orient*, January 9, 1861.
2. *Journal de Constantinople/Écho de l'Orient*, December 19, 1856.
3. On the silk-winding factory, see Introduction, note 49. On the history of the factory, see CADN, FC Smyrne 45, Cousinéry to Thouvenel, January 18, 1858.
4. For example, the popular Greek neighborhoods of Choriat-Alan (Village Place), Keratochori (Village of Horns), and Mana-Perivoli (Mother Orchard), laid out in the 1840s, suffered in summer months from stagnant waters and in winter from inundation; see Th. Bargigli, "Letter to the Editor," *Écho de l'Orient*, March 15, 1845.
5. See, for example, Kayserili Ahmed Pasha's printed instructions, posted in public places across Izmir, that prescribed proper public conduct and listed the punishments that would be inflicted on offenders. PRO, FO, 195/758, enclosed in dispatch April 18, 1863.
6. The kadı's assistants included a chief of police (*subaşı*) who oversaw public order; a chief of guilds and markets (*ihtisab ağası*), responsible for public morality, market control, and tax collection; and a chief architect (*mimarbaşı*), charged with pulling down dangerous buildings, maintaining sidewalks, and sometimes mediating disputes over property in the city. On the functions of chief architects, see Orhonlu, *Osmanlı İmparatorluğunda Şehircilik ve Ulaşım Üzerine Araştırmalar*, 21. For a concise summary of Ottoman municipal institutions, see Lewis, *Emergence of Modern Turkey*, 393–400; Rosenthal, *Politics of Dependency*, 29–34; Tümerkan, *Türkiye'de Belediyeler*. For an in-depth treatment of premodern municipal institutions in the capital, see Mantran, *Istanbul dans la seconde moitié du XVIIe siècle*. A good primary source is Ergin, *Mecelle-i Umûr-i Belediyye*.
7. Osman Nuri Ergin, the prominent municipal historian, distinguished two modes of urban government that coexisted in the pre-Tanzimat era, one based on individualism (*ferdiyet*) that relied on individual donors and another on the community of believers (*cemaat*); see Ergin, *Türk Tarihinde Evkaf, Belediye ve Patrikhaneler*, 4–76. See also Ergin, *Türkiye'de Şehirciliğin Tarihi İnkişafı*.
8. See Introduction, note 5.

9. In the 1870s, arson was not uncommon. See, for example, cases reported in *Levant Herald,* November 12, 1873; June 3, 1874; July 1, 1874; August 11, 1875; and *La Turquie,* June 3, 1874.

10. The losses were reported to be 3,050 houses in Muslim neighborhoods, 500 large houses for 1,500 families in Jewish neighborhoods, 157 houses in Greek neighborhoods, 17 houses in Armenian neighborhoods, 2 Greek public schools, 15 khans, 7 bathhouses, 17 bakeries and mills, 12 large mosques, 30 small mosques, 22 religious schools, 5 public schools, 7 synagogues, 1 Jewish hospital, 5 *tekke* (dervish lodges), and 2,437 shops. *Écho de l'Orient,* August 14, 1841.

11. The fire destroyed the English, Dutch, Catholic, and Greek hospitals, located in the same neighborhood. According to one report, it spared only forty houses in the Armenian quarter, destroying eight hundred; see *Écho de l'Orient/Journal de Smyrne,* July 9, 1845.

12. This injunction, traced to Islamic law, was generally followed in the empire; see Gibb and Bowen, *Islamic Society and the West,* 2:208. In some cases, the Porte also allowed new churches; see Bozkurt, *Alman-İngiliz Belgelerinin ve Siyasi Gelişmelerin Işığı Altında Gayrimüslim Osmanlı Vatandaşlarının Hukuki Durumu,* 22.

13. *Journal de Constantinople/Écho de l'Orient,* January 19, 1858.

14. BOA, C. BLD, no. 5078 (1261/1845). One *pic* or *arşın* or *zira-i mimariye* is equal to 2.5 feet.

15. *Écho de l'Orient,* July 17, 1845.

16. *Journal de Constantinople/Écho de l'Orient,* February 2, 1859.

17. *Journal de Constantinople/Écho de l'Orient,* September 6, 1860.

18. Panzac, *La peste dans l'empire ottoman.*

19. Dağlar, *War, Epidemics and Medicine in the Ottoman Empire.*

20. NA, DUSCS, Vice-consul Griffith to Secretary of State N. H. Seward, September 23, 1865.

21. On the environmental disasters (fires, earthquakes, epidemics), see Introduction, note 22.

22. PRO, FO, 195/797, "Raport du Comité d'Hygiène et de Secours," October 19, 1865.

23. For an overview on quarantines and lazarettos in the Ottoman Empire, see Panzac, *La peste dans l'empire ottoman;* Panzac, *Quarantaines et lazarets.*

24. PRO, FO, 195/288, "Report on the State of the Quarantine Establishment at Smyrna," March 1, 1847.

25. Although sanitary measures stated that lazarettos had to be located at least four hundred pics from residences, in 1864, some proprietors, including Hacı Ragıb Bey, the director of the quarantine office, erected their new country cottages on the southwestern coastline not far from the lazaretto. See *Journal de Constantinople,* July 21, 1864. The municipal commission was forced to sell the site to procure funds to relocate the facilities at a more appropriate distance from the city. See *La Turquie,* April 6, 1866.

26. Committee members included consular agents Count de Bentivoglio, M. Guérin, R. Cumberbatch, Baron Baüm, J.-B. d'Egremont, J. Griffith, Palamides, R. J. Van Lennep, B. Berio, Baron Bulow, C. Mostras, F. La Fontaine; sanitary doctors Borg, Japhet, Mustafa Bey, J. Chasseaud, Kaliga, J. McCraith, A. Masgana, Von Eichstroff, Matheyss, Caracoussi; and H. J. Hanson, Barker, and Calligaki. See PRO, FO, 195/797, "Raport du Comité d'Hygiène et de Secours," October 19, 1865, 18.

27. The formation of the committee led to the resignation of several Ottoman officers working for the sanitary department, who saw such proceedings as outright examples of foreign interference in local affairs. PRO, FO, 195/797, Consul Cumberbatch to Ambassador Bulwer, August 28, 1865. As soon as the epidemic receded the governor abolished the commission. *La Turquie,* June 5, 1868.

28. On theories of medical disease, see Corbin, *The Foul and the Fragant;* Delaporte, *Disease and Civilization.* Similar definitions were deployed in Izmir; see Rolleston, *Report on Smyrna,* 58.

29. *Levant Herald,* September 7, 1870.

30. *La Turquie,* July 15, 1874.

31. PRO, FO, 195/797, "Raport du Comité d'Hygiène et de Secours," October 19, 1865, 5–9.

32. BOA, I. DH, no. 41301 (1286/1869–70); CADN, FC, Smyrne no. 46, Consul Bentivoglio to Ambassador Moustier, July 28, 1865; NA DUSC, Vice-consul Griffith to secretary of state, dispatch, October 18, 1865.

33. *Levant Herald,* October 23, 1967.

34. BOA, I. DH, no. 41301 (1286/1869–70). The relocation of the British cemetery turned into a major controversy. PRO, FO, 195/797, Consul Cumberbatch to Lord Stanley, secretary of state, October 8, 1866.

35. Letters to the Editor, *Levant Herald and Eastern Express,* February 6, 1884, and February 27, 1884.

36. Tales of brigandage and highwaymen, especially the activities of the gangs of Yörük Osman and Captain Andrea, were frequently reported in the local press and consular documents. On banditry in the region of Izmir, see Yetkin, *Ege'de Eşkiyalar.*

37. The gang's assaults had repercussions far beyond Izmir. On these assaults and the subsequent police repression, see response letters dated April 7 and 25, 1851, to the articles published in *Malta Mail,* in CADN, FC, Smyrne no. 43.

38. PRO, FO, 195/389, December 9, 1852. Signed by thirty-three British residents in Izmir.

39. Ibid.

40. *Levant Herald,* October 18, 1876. According to international treaties, foreign nationals could not be detained in Ottoman prisons. Generally consulates had their own detention rooms for keeping sailors who troubled public order.

41. *Levant Herald,* September 20, 1871.

42. *Levant Herald,* September 19, 1878. The term *palikaraki* holds several meanings, including a young, handsome, and courageous boy; a hero; a mercenary enlisted in the Greek army in the nineteenth century; or a knife wielder.

43. In 1862 the movement of armed *zeybek* troops to Montenegro was done through Izmir. Similarly, during the Ottoman–Russian War in 1876–77 waves of volunteer army forces passed through the city. See, for example, *La Turquie,* August 30, 1876; July 18, 1877; August 21, 1877; and *Levant Herald,* August 2 and 9, 1876.

44. For Halil Pasha's memorandum, see PRO, FO, 195/350, March 27, 1850 and CADN, FC, Smyrne no. 43, March 27, 1850. Consuls were asked to notify their subjects on such measures. In addition, *Journal de Constantinople/Écho de l'Orient* often reiterated the regulation; see, for example, February 28, 1862.

45. On the pledge of commitment of Burnabat, Buca, Seydiköy, and Kokluca residents, see PRO, FO, 195/389, "Acte de promese et d'engagement," enclosed in Governor Ali Mehmed Emin Pasha to Consul Brant, March 25, 1853.

46. *Journal de Constantinople/Écho de l'Orient,* October 20, 1860.

47. *Levant Herald,* September 17, 1862.

48. *Levant Herald,* August 9, 1876.

49. *La Turquie,* February 1, 1881. On the achievements of Midhad Pasha in Izmir, see Midhat, *Midhat-Pacha: sa vie, son oeuvre;* Arıkan, "Midhat Paşa'nın Aydın Valiliği." See also NA, DUSCS, Consul Duncan to secretary of state, no. 48, May 17, 1881.

50. PRO, FO, 195/610, Consul Blunt to Ambassador Alison, June 2, 1858. Accordingly, policemen had to wear a distinctive uniform and receive yearly one suit and one pair of shoes; each would be enrolled for five years and would be punished for desertion from the corps in the same manner as in the army; and policemen were not to be employed as servants by any of the officers of the corps.

51. See, for example, Halil Pasha's 1850 memorandum and Kayserili Ahmed Pasha's 1863 order, PRO, FO, 195/758, enclosed in dispatch April 18, 1863.

52. *Levant Herald,* September 17, 1862.

53. A first-order house paid six piastres per month, while a second-order house paid three piastres. *La Turquie,* April 18, 1866.

54. On street lighting, see Zandi-Sayek, "Public Space and Urban Citizens," chap. 3.

55. In the Ottoman context, *ihtisab* refers to the practice of applying public morals to commercial transactions, for example by fixing market prices to prevent profiteering and by controlling weights and quality of merchandise to prevent fraud. On the historical development of the *ihtisab* institution, see Kazıcı, *Osmanlılarda İhtisab Müessesesi.*

56. For a concise treatment of street regulations, see Kostof, *The City Assembled,* 200–212. On modern urban norms and public spaces, see, for example, Ogborn, *Spaces of Modernity;* Wilson, *The Sphinx in the City.*

57. On the memorandum establishing the new commission, see Rosenthal, *Politics of Dependency,* 39. On Istanbul's municipal reforms, see ibid.; Çelik, *Remaking of Istanbul;* Gül and Lamb, "Mapping, Regularizing and Modernizing Ottoman Istanbul." On the application of the Galata model in other cities of the empire, particularly in the Balkan provinces, see Ortaylı, *Tanzimat'tan Cumhuriyet'e Yerel Yönetim Geleneği,* 164–70.

58. "The Municipalities in Turkey," *Levant Herald,* January 25, 1865.

59. *Écho de l'Orient,* March 15, 1845.

60. *Journal de Constantinople/Écho de l'Orient,* September 6, 1860.

61. *Journal de Constantinople,* December 9, 1864.

62. Serçe, *Tanzimat'tan Cumhuriyet'e İzmir'de Belediye,* 53.

63. According to the gas company, however, the price asked in Izmir was considerably lower than what the city of Istanbul paid for street lighting or the French company that lit Alexandria and Cairo charged the Egyptian government; see *Levant Herald,* July 18, 1866. On the committee negotiating on behalf of the city, see chapter 1, note 93. See also *La Turquie,* April 18, 1866.

64. See the petition addressed to Grand Vizier Mehmed Reşid Pasha, December 14, 1859, enclosed in PRO, FO, 195/447, Consul Blunt to Ambassador Bulwer, February 17, 1860.

65. *Journal de Constantinople/Écho de l'Orient,* February 22, 1860 (reprinted from *L'Impartial*).

66. BOA, Ayniyat, no. 817, 28–29. Also cited in Serçe, *Tanzimat'tan Cumhuriyet'e İzmir'de Belediye,* 54. Municipality translates to Turkish as *belediye* deriving from *beled,* a versatile geographical unit, which may mean city, town, village, or country. In the early years of the Tanzimat, belediye referred specifically to the office in charge of streets and other public affairs in a city or town. In the following decades, the meaning of belediye was broadened in accordance with definitions used in Europe. In *Mecelle-i Umûr-i Belediyye,* Osman Nuri Ergin defined belediye as "the capacity of townspeople to come together and manage affairs concerning the common interest and mutual needs of the town, within the limits and rights defined by state law, and by means of commonly elected representatives."

67. "La Municipalité de Smyrne: réponse verbale de son Exc. Hourchid Pacha," *La Turquie,* March 17, 1876.

68. On the question of rental contract fees, see ibid. On the municipal revenues and diverted market taxes, see Serçe, *Tanzimat'tan Cumhuriyet'e İzmir'de Belediye,* 70; *Hizmet,* July 21, 1888.

69. "La Municipalité de Smyrne: réponse verbale de son Exc. Hourchid Pacha," *La Turquie,* March 17, 1876.

70. "La Municipalité de Smyrne: rapport des membres Européens de la municipalité à S. Exc. Hourchid Pacha," *La Turquie,* March 17, 1876.

71. İsmail Pasha identified three competing constituencies: the Hellenic community "antagonistic to all governmental activities" and desiring to establish majority in the council; a group of foreign merchants, who viewed the projected regularization of the harbor as an imminent danger to their capitulatory rights; and those who pressured for the development of a new quay. BOA, ŞD Aydın, no. 1375/15, also cited in Serçe, *Tanzimat'tan Cumhuriyet'e İzmir'de Belediye,* 55.

72. The first municipal council consisted of twenty-four elected members: six Muslim subjects, eight non-Muslim subjects, and eight foreigners. Eight of these councilors were appointed as permanent members: Leblebicizade Mehmed Bey (Muslim), Evliyazade Mehmed Efendi (Muslim), Martiroz Tatakian (Armenian), Hacı Tsiro Nicoli (Greek Orthodox), Anastas Ağa Papazoğlu (Greek Orthodox), J. Christofidis (Hellenic), J. G. B. d'Andria (Italian), Ch. Moraitini (Austrian). For a complete list of councilors, see CADN, FC, Smyrne no. 48, enclosed in dispatch July 1, 1868. On the shortfalls of the municipal council, see *Levant Herald,* October 4, 1869.

73. *Levant Herald,* September 9, 1869.

74. *Levant Herald,* August 7, 1869; see also Serçe, *Tanzimat'tan Cumhuriyet'e İzmir'de Belediye,* 57.

75. *La Turquie,* July 17, 1868.

76. The 1864 Provincial Code was first tested in the Danubian Provinces, before being implemented widely. See, among others, Ortaylı, *Tanzimat'tan Cumhuriyet'e Yerel Yönetim Geleneği;* Tümerkan, *Türkiye'de Belediyeler.*

77. BOA, Ayniyat, no. 817, 28–29, also cited in Serçe, *Tanzimat'tan Cumhuriyet'e İzmir'de Belediye,* 55 n. 146. The cadastral commission and the Galata municipality were obvious precedents for this principle. The Galata Municipal Regulation required a minimum of ten years of residency *(mutavattın)* in the city as a primary qualification for election as council

member; see, for example, Akgündüz, *Osmanlı Devleti'nde Belediye Teşkilâtı ve Belediye Kanunları*, 543; Rosenthal, *Politics of Dependency*, 54.

78. "Ce qu'on dit être 'l'opinion publique' en Turquie," *Journal de Constantinople/Écho de l'Orient*, November 4, 1861.

79. *La Turquie*, March 26, 1879 (reprinted from *L'Impartial*). On the 1877 Provincial Code, see Ortaylı, *Tanzimat'tan Cumhuriyet'e Yerel Yönetim Geleneği*, 170–74.

80. Bilget, *Son Yüzyılda İzmir Şehri*, 23.

81. The division into two municipal districts was informed by the stipulations of the Provincial Code that allowed settlements of forty thousand inhabitants to create a municipal council. In 1889 the two districts were eventually merged in an effort to overcome financial problems, a decision precipitated by the central government asking to have all market taxes, formerly used as municipal funds, directly sent to the central treasury, thus further crippling the already underfunded municipal budget. On the central government's request, see *Hizmet*, July 21, 1888.

82. Emin Bey and Ragıb Bey served as mayors of the first and second municipal districts respectively. Each municipal council consisted of nine members, salaried officers, a head secretary, an accountant, a translator, a treasurer, a contracts secretary, a doctor, an engineer, a commissioner, a market supervisor, and an architect; see *Aydın Vilâyetine Mahsus Salname*, 1 (1307M/1890–91), 100. In 1880 the ratio of Muslim to non-Muslim was six to four in the first district, and three to six in the second district; see *Salname-i Vilâyet-i Aydın* (1297H/1879–80), 56–57.

83. PRO, FO, 185/1240, undated newsclip from *La Réforme* enclosed in dispatch, April 28, 1879.

84. *Hizmet*, May 1, 1888.

85. BOA, I. MMS, no. 3175; Arıkan, "Midhat Paşa'nın Aydın Valiliği," 145–46.

86. *Salname-i Vilâyet-i Aydın* (1296H/1878–79), 76.

87. *Levant Herald*, July 18, 1866.

88. *Levant Herald*, September 10, 1873.

89. *Hizmet*, December 16, 1890.

90. PRO, FO, 195/1161, petition to Governor Hamdi Pasha, signed by forty-one representatives of the British community, October 24, 1878.

91. According to the 1858 Land Code (Arazi Kanunnamesi), *arazi-i metruke* could also include mosque spaces and courtyards, spaces assigned for marketplaces and fairs, areas within or on the fringe of cities for storing carts and animals, and pastures given for the use of a community. On the Ottoman land regime, see Tute, *Ottoman Land Laws*, 88–96; Rougon, *Smyrne*, 203. For a detailed discussion of the reformed Land Code, see Padel and Steeg, *De la législation foncière ottomane*. For a discussion of the pre- and postreform land regime, see Heidborn, *Manuel du droit public et administratif de l'empire ottoman*, 1:320–46. For a comprehensive compilation of reformed Ottoman land codes, see Young, *Corps de droit ottoman*, 6:45–83.

92. On absolute versus negotiated property boundaries, see Yerasimos, "À propos des réformes urbaines des Tanzimat," 26–27. See also Brunschvig, "Urbanisme médiéval et droit musulman"; Hakim, *Arabic-Islamic Cities*, 26–27.

93. For example, although article 1213 states that an owner cannot build bridges over a public way, it also declares that if such a bridge exists and does not obstruct circulation, it

cannot be removed. Öztürk, *Osmanlı Hukuk Tarihinde Mecelle*, 318; Young, *Corps de droit ottoman*, 6:342.

94. Article 1215 allows an owner who fixes his house to use a portion of the street to prepare his mortar as long as it does not restrict the public's right of passage, and article 1217 allows a person to purchase an unessential portion of the street from the treasury to add to his house. See Ibid.

95. See the case of *Cousinéry v. Zadé* in chapter 1.

96. Article 1220 of the Mecelle confirms the semiprivate status of the dead-end street. Article 1223 allows the public entry into private ways whenever there is congestion in public ways. See Öztürk, *Osmanlı Hukuk Tarihinde Mecelle*, 319. Young, *Corps de droit ottoman*, 6:343.

97. I borrow the expression from Janet Abu-Lughod, "The Islamic City," n. 44 who, unlike orientalist scholars such as Jean Sauvaget or Gustav von Grünebaum, does not regard such privatization as a form of "degeneration" or "decay."

98. For example, the 1848 Building and Road Code distinguishes three categories of street: large avenues *(büyük cadde)* at ten pics, regular avenues *(âdi cadde)* at eight pics, and other streets *(sair sokak)* at six pics. See Ergin, *Mecelle-i Umûr-i Belediyye*, 2:1044.

99. The Penal Code detailed the penalties of littering and endangering public health. Article 254 imposed a fine on innkeepers who encumber public ways, leaving miscellaneous items on them, failing to sweep them, or creating circumstances that could harm passersby. Article 264 imposed a fine on anyone who created damage or encroached on public ways and other spaces intended for common use. See Young, *Corps de droit ottoman*, 7:52–54. For a summary of the Penal Code, see also Heidborn, *Manuel du droit public et administratif de l'empire ottoman*, 1:354–441.

100. Although Mecelle article 1216 makes a general provision that private property can be expropriated by imperial order and with fair compensation, the 1856 law of eminent domain brought greater definition to the clause by making public utility a prerequisite for such expropriation.

101. *Écho de l'Orient*, March 15, 1845.

102. *Journal de Constantinople/Écho de l'Orient*, March 28, 1862.

103. *La Turquie*, July 26, 1866 (reprinted from *L'Impartial*).

104. *La Turquie*, January 16, 1872.

105. *Hizmet*, October 29, 1889.

106. *La Turquie*, May 24, 1866.

107. *La Turquie*, April 4, 1866.

108. See Kayserili Ahmed Pasha's printed instructions in PRO, FO, 195/758, enclosed in dispatch April 18, 1863.

109. Reprinted in *La Turquie*, February 5, 1875.

110. According to article 254 of the Ottoman Penal Code, five days after the publication of the order offenders were liable to a fine, and in case of continual offense the fine would be doubled according to article 8 of the same code; see *Levant Herald*, April 17, 1878.

111. On such networks of solidarities and how they helped wholesale grocers, butchers, and other provision dealers circumvent official market controls, see *La Turquie*, May 24, 1866.

112. On the differential treatment of peddlers and grocers, see *Hizmet,* October 19 and 22, 1889. These issues have resonance in nineteenth-century urban contexts beyond the Ottoman world. See, among others, Upton, "Another City"; Bluestone, "'The Pushcart Evil.'"

113. *La Turquie,* April 4, 1866. That butchers were the target of scathing criticism was probably no coincidence as for over a decade the high price of meat and the monopoly butchers enjoyed had been a contentious issue, repeatedly brought up in the press; see *Journal de Constantinople/Écho de l'Orient,* March 5, 1857, and March 8, 1860, and *Levant Herald,* March 8, 1865.

114. For this case, see CADN, FC, Smyrne no. 50, Consul Aubaret to Aubert, charge d'affaires, August 17, 1872; Consul Aubaret to Governor Sadık Pasha, August 20, 1872; Consul Aubaret to Aubert, charge d'affaires, August 20, 1872.

115. CADN, FC, Smyrne no. 50, Sublime Porte to Aubert, charge d'affaires, undated.

116. CADN, FC, Smyrne no. 52, Governor Hamdi Pasha to Consul Pélissier, April 7/19, 1880.

117. On the inviolability of domicile, see Brown, *Foreigners in Turkey,* 90–92.

118. Several such disputes erupted between governors and consuls. On the case of the American merchant Joseph Langdon, see NA, DUSCS, Consul E. S. Offley to secretary of state, January 7 and 17, and February 13, 1851. On the case of the British merchant Benjamin Barker, see PRO, FO, 195/350, Barker to Governor Halil Rıfat Pasha, January 14, 1851. Some of these cases received press coverage beyond the Ottoman Empire, creating further tensions and reactions in Izmir. See, for example, note 37 above.

119. Susa, *Capitulatory Régime of Turkey,* 80.

120. In Izmir, the criminal court was composed of five Muslim members, including the president, and of three non-Muslim Ottoman members (one Greek, one Armenian, and one Jewish). See PRO, FO, 195/350, Consul Brant to Ambassador Canning, March 7, 1851.

121. PRO, FO, 195/1075, Governor Sabri Pasha to the consular corps, October 14/26, 1876. For a similar note by his predecessor Hurşid Pasha to the consular corps, see *La Turquie,* April 19, 1876 (reprinted from *L'Impartial*).

122. PRO, FO, 195/720, Consul Blunt to Ambassador Bulwer, June 30, 1862. According to a story told by Deli Ahmed, Kayserili Ahmed Pasha, who was concerned that criminals evaded justice by bribing parties in charge of the prison, disguised himself one night as a murderer and was in jail with other criminals, where he learned that Dayı Christo, the main spy in the service of the chief of police Hamid Bey, was the actual individual who received bribes and assisted with the liberation of prisoners. Although Dayı Christo was arrested and exiled soon after, he was eventually recalled after the departure of Kayserili Ahmed Pasha.

123. *Levant Herald,* September 19, 1878. Complaints about the use of Albanian irregulars appear repeatedly; see, for example, PRO, FO, 195/720, June 30, 1862.

124. PRO, FO, 195/610, Consul Blunt to Ambassador Alison, June 2, 1858.

125. On Sabri Pasha's reorganization, see *Levant Herald,* October 18, 1876; September 19, 1878; October 26, 1878.

126. *Levant Herald and Eastern Express,* February 7, 1887.

127. *La Turquie,* April 19, 1876.

3. Shaping the Waterfront

1. Elie Dussaud (1821–99) and his brothers, Elzéar, Louis, Joseph, and Auguste, established the Dussaud Brothers in 1853. By the time they undertook the works in Izmir, the company had already developed the Port de la Joliette and Pont Napoléon in Marseilles, the docks in Algiers, and the military port in Cherbourg. When the Suez Canal was dug, they also built a dry dock for Messageries Maritimes and the jetties in Port Said. Later, they built the Porto Nuovo in Trieste, collaborated on the port of Genoa, worked on the jetties of Toulon and Sète, and built the port of Talcahuano in Chile. See Roman d'Amat, *Dictionnaire de biographie française,* 12:866–67. See also Caty, Richard, and Echinard, *Les patrons du second empire.*

2. The competition between French and British imperial interests in Izmir has received much attention. See, among others, Kurmuş, *Emperyalizm'in Türkiye'ye Girişi,* 201–04; Issawi, *Economic History of Turkey,* 167–72; on the unfolding of these interests in relation to the quay project, see Georgiades, *Smyrne et l'Asie Mineure,* 154–63; Frangakis-Syrett, "Concurrence commerciale et financière entre les pays ocidentaux à Izmir," 117–27; Thobie, *Intérêts et impérialisme français dans l'empire ottoman;* Kütükoğlu, "İzmir Rıhtımı İnşaatı ve İşletme İmtiyazı"; Oberling, "Quays of Izmir"; Korkut, *Belgelerle İzmir Rıhtım İmtiyazı.*

3. On the Tanzimat restructuring of imperial endowments, see Meier, "Wakf"; Barnes, *An Introduction to Religious Foundations in the Ottoman Empire.*

4. The system of icareteyn, used since the late sixteenth century, became the standard way of leasing vakıf property in the eighteenth century. On the origins of the icareteyn system, see Barnes, *An Introduction to Religious Foundations in the Ottoman Empire,* 50–66. For an overview of icareteyn and mukataa contracts, see Akarlı, "Gedik." For a concise treatment of vakıf property in the Ottoman empire, see, for example, Padel and Steeg, *De la législation foncière ottomane,* 228–70.

5. For comparable analyses of waterfront speculation beyond the Ottoman Empire, see, for example, Hartog, *Public Property and Private Power,* esp. chap. 5; Delgado, *Gold Rush Port;* Upton, "New Orleans."

6. PRO, FO, 195/720, Judge Logie to Consul Blunt, November 15, 1862.

7. The case was eventually resolved in her favor with the involvement of Anthony Edwards, editor of *Journal de Constantinople/Écho de l'Orient,* and Ovannes Dilbérian, influential merchant and honorary dragoman to the U.S. consulate. See BOA, I. MMS, no. 801 (1276/1859) for the various petitions sent by Aliotti, the official reports, and the letter of Edwards to Grand Vizier Âli Pasha.

8. On the appointment of a new Evkaf director, see BOA, I. DH, no. 27850 (1275/1858).

9. According to one count, the price of one square pic (14 sq ft) of land rose from five piastres in 1833 to twenty piastres in the late 1850s. See Texier, *Asie mineure,* 308.

10. For descriptions of the old shore, see Rolleston, *Report on Smyrna,* 8–9; *Murray's Handbook for Travellers in Turkey in Asia,* 262–63; Finnie, *Pioneers East,* 22–23.

11. BOA, I. MMS, no. 1317/57 (1284/1867), also cited in Korkut, *Belgelerle İzmir Rıhtım İmtiyazı,* 29–31.

12. On notions of common property, see chapter 2.

13. On central government deliberations about the development, see BOA, I. MVL, no. 21555 (1279/1862). The initial scheme consisted of a dock on rafts with iron balustrades and controlled entrances that would prevent smuggling and reduce the number of watchmen. Although the government gave serious consideration to this proposal, it was concerned that the structure would be unstable in rough seas. A second scheme, proposed by a local builder named Yanako, consisted of a continuous, nine-pic-wide and nine-pic-deep dock on piles that ran the entire front of the city, but his cost estimate was found too high. The government requested alternative schemes.

14. *Journal de Constantinople*, February 16, 1857.

15. Among the signatories were Ottoman and foreign subjects—including the leading British merchants J. B. Patterson and F. Whittall; the Gout brothers, who ran steamboat companies; the ship chandler G. Mitchell; and Vernazza, one of Patterson's local agents—many of whom would later oppose the project. On the 1865 petition, see *Levant Herald*, February 15, 1868.

16. *Levant Herald*, August 17, 1864.

17. On the origins of modern boulevards and their interpretation across world cities, see, among others, Girouard, *Cities and People*; Kostof, *The City Assembled*, 249–76; Wilson, *The City Beautiful Movement*; Wright, *Politics of Design in French Colonial Urbanism*. On the ways boulevards institutionalize modernity, civility, and a novel sense of public life, see, among others, Berman, *All That Is Solid Melts into Air*; Clark, *Painting of Modern Life*, 23–78; Sennett, *Fall of the Public Man*; Scobey, "Anatomy of the Promenade."

18. *Journal de Constantinople*, August 29, 1860.

19. Ibid.

20. On the distinction between a through and a dead-end street, see chapter 2.

21. *Journal de Constantinople*, August 29, 1860.

22. BOA, BEO, A. MKT. MVL 3426/143/15 (1278/1860–61).

23. Warner, "The Mass Public and the Mass Subject," 381.

24. See, for example, *Levant Herald* refusing to publish Whittall's letter of objection to the quay scheme, "Letter from the Editor," February 15, 1868.

25. *Journal de Constantinople*, February 16, 1857.

26. *Journal de Constantinople*, January 22, 1864.

27. *Levant Herald*, August 17, 1864.

28. Ibid.

29. BOA, I. MMS, no. 1317/57 (1284/1867).

30. For the original text of the contract between the ministry of commerce and public works and John Charnaud, Alfred Barker, and George Guarracino, see BOA, I. MVL, no. 26094. The contract was reprinted in *Levant Herald*, January 8, 1868.

31. Thobie, *Intérêts et impérialisme français dans l'empire ottoman*.

32. *Levant Herald*, December 18, 1867. From the outset, the hundred preference shares produced resentment as they limited the number of shareholders and thus of potential beneficiaries.

33. Thobie, *Intérêts et impérialisme français dans l'empire ottoman*.

34. Articles 4, 7, and 10 of the contract, *Levant Herald*, January 8, 1868. The law of expropriation for public utility was passed in 1856, providing a legal basis for the acquisition of private lands for public use.

35. *La Turquie*, July 2, 1868.

36. Ibid.

37. Article 15, *Levant Herald*, January 8, 1868.

38. Beginning on January 1, 1873, the Dussaud enterprise started charging wharf dues on the completed part of the works. The commercial body felt aggrieved because former methods of shipping by means of lighters were much less costly than the fees. A petition signed by thirteen foreign consuls tried, with no success, to urge the government to extend the one hundred pics to five hundred; see *Levant Herald*, January 22, 1873.

39. A committee of fifteen local merchants, protected by their respective consuls and presided over by John Honischer, signed the letter. The committee included Italian delegate Pierre Aliotti, British delegates James Whittall and Robert Hadkinson, Austro-Hungarian delegates J. Schiffmann and P. Boscovich, Russian delegate N. Kalomiraki, French delegates Alex Bonnal and A. Farkoa, American delegates E. J. Davee and Alexander Sidi, German delegates Bernard Kuhn and E. Schmidt, Greek delegates J. Christofidhi and A. A. Dalta, and Belgian delegate L. De Vries. See letter to the editor of *La Turquie*, dated December 23, 1872, and reprinted in *La Turquie*, January 16, 1873.

40. *La Turquie*, April 1, 11, and 15, 1868, and May 7 and 14, 1868.

41. *La Turquie*, April 11, 1868.

42. Ibid.

43. *La Turquie*, January 16, 1873.

44. Article 12 of the contract, *Levant Herald*, January 8, 1868.

45. *La Turquie*, April 15, 1868.

46. *La Réforme* reprinted in *La Turquie*, March 23, 1880.

47. *Levant Herald*, February 19, 1873.

48. *La Turquie*, February 15, 1873.

49. The contract specified that the twenty-five-pic-wide quay was mandatory *(mecbur)* while landfill was optional *(muktedir, salahetli)* for accomplishing the works. This point was reiterated in later negotiations; see the letter of Richard J. Van Lennep (administrator of the Quay Company) to Nihad Efendi (imperial commissary of the Quay Company) on March 28, 1872, in BOA, BEO, A. AMD. MV. 112/44 (1872/1288).

50. *Levant Herald*, September 7, 1870.

51. *La Turquie*, July 15, 1874.

52. See note addressed to Governor Hamdi Pasha and a copy of the note sent to the embassies in Istanbul in BOA, BEO, A. AMD. MV. 112/44 (1872/1288). The official note carried the signatures of the consuls of Great Britain, Spain, the Netherlands, France, Italy, Greece, Austria-Hungary, Germany, Portugal, Belgium, Denmark, and Russia.

53. Article 18 of the contract, *Levant Herald*, January 8, 1868.

54. Margossian Efendi had studied at the École des Ponts et Chaussée in Paris and had been recently appointed as chief engineer; see *La Turquie*, April 18, 1871.

55. "Rapport sur les égouts de la ville de Smyrne," in BOA, BEO, A. AMD. MV. 112/44 (1872/1288).

56. See report of the Public Works Ministry, "Égouts de la ville débouchant à ses quais et comblement du vide restant entre le rivage et les quais," in BOA, BEO, A. AMD. MV. 112/44 (1872/1288).

57. BOA, BEO, A. AMD. MV. 112/44 (1872/1288).

58. *La Réforme* reprinted in *La Turquie,* March 23, 1880.

59. *Levant Herald,* November 25, 1874. In the nineteenth century, arcades had become a standard tool for creating visual uniformity along major streets. On contemporaneous writings on arcaded streets, see the collection of short essays compiled in Davis et al., *The Great Streets of the World.*

60. On the continued antagonism of British merchants, see Georgiades, *Smyrne et l'Asie Mineure,* 154–63; Kütükoğlu, "İzmir Rıhtımı İnşaatı ve İşletme İmtiyazı"; Korkut, *Belgelerle İzmir Rıhtım İmtiyazı;* Thobie, *Intérêts et impérialisme français dans l'empire ottoman.*

61. *Levant Herald,* September 2, 1874.

62. *Levant Herald,* March 3, 1877. The company would reduce the tariff by 30 percent, transfer the customs house, join the two lines of the railway with the quay by means of a tramway, build stores for the wares embarked or disembarked, give a bonus of 50 percent on the reduced tariff to merchants whose ships do not use the quay, repair the streets, and supervise the sewage of the town.

63. *La Turquie,* March 24, 1880.

64. *Levant Herald,* September 3, 1874.

4. Performing Community

1. The Corpus Christi procession was a medieval Catholic ceremony that first appeared in the context of mid-thirteenth-century Europe. Part of the rite was generally performed out of doors as a public event and consisted of carrying the Eucharist across town. During the nineteenth century the ritual was still alive throughout the Catholic world but was frequently under attack in places where the influence of the French Enlightenment and secularization had made itself most felt. On the history of the ritual, see Rubin, *Corpus Christi,* 243.

2. Unlike the regular clergy, who were sent by their respective missions, the secular clergy were generally recruited among locals, native to the country, and did not belong to a specific religious order. In 1842, the Catholic clergy counted about fifty members in Izmir, fifteen of whom were secular. The catholic missions active in the city at the time were the Franciscan-Récollets (or Reformed Franciscans), the Capuchins, the Lazarists (or Vincentians) who replaced the Jesuits, and the Dominicans. In 1845 the Mechitarist (or Catholic Armenians) joined in. See CADN, FC, Smyrne no. 41, "Notes sur les Établissements Religieux de Smyrne," Soulange Bodin to Consul Ségur-Montaigne, April 29, 1843; see also San Lorenzo, *Saint Polycarpe et son tombeau,* 321–51.

3. *Écho de l'Orient,* May 27, 1842.

4. On the diversity of religious rites and practices in seventeenth-century Izmir, see Anderson, *An English Consul in Turkey,* 8–9; Goffman, *Izmir and the Levantine World.*

5. Since the mid-1820s, Roman Catholics had been asking to be removed from the fold of other Christian millets and be granted their own appointed delegate; see, for example, their 1826 petition in Ahmed Lütfi, *Vak'anüvis Ahmed Lütfi Efendi Tarihi,* 1:172–73; see also Steen de Jehay, *De la situation légale des sujets ottomans non-musulmans,* 320. On the

constitutional differences of Roman Catholic subjects of the empire, see Ubicini, *Letters on Turkey*; Engelhardt, *La Turquie et le Tanzimât*; Bozkurt, *Alman-İngiliz Belgelerinin ve Siyasi Gelişmelerin Işığı Altında Gayrimüslim Osmanlı Vatandaşlarının Hukuki Durumu*; Steen de Jehay, *De la situation légale des sujets ottomans non-musulmans*, 306–27; Frazee, *Catholics and Sultans*.

6. On the record, Mussabini was under French protection and received a pension from France, as were all other former archbishops. His politics, however, often conflicted with the official policies of France in Izmir. See CADN, FC, Smyrne no. 41, "Notes sur les Établissements Religieux de Smyrne," Soulange Bodin to Consul Ségur-Montaigne, April 29, 1843.

7. For the text of the Edict promulgated in 1839, see Aristarchi Bey, *Législation ottomane*, 2:14–22.

8. On public rituals and parades as instruments of identity formation, see among others, Davis, *Parades and Power*; Fortier, "Re-Membering Places and the Performance of Belonging(s)"; Ryan, "The American Parade"; Sanders, *Ritual, Politics, and the City in Fatimid Cairo*; Slyomovics, "New York City's Muslim World Day Parade"; Waldstreicher, "Rites of Rebellion, Rites of Assent." For the Ottoman imperial context, see, for example, Necipoğlu, *Architecture, Ceremonial, and Power*; Terzioğlu, "Imperial Circumcision Festival of 1582"; Deringil, *Well-Protected Domains*; Karateke, *Padişahım Çok Yaşa!*

9. Ozouf, *Festivals and the French Revolution*, 127.

10. Giddens, *Consequences of Modernity*, 17.

11. Dursun, *İzmir Hatıraları*, 3.

12. Governor Süreyya Pasha abolished the practice in 1873, requiring government agencies to work during the daytime. See *Levant Herald*, October 22, 1873.

13. *Journal de Constantinople*, March 14, 1860.

14. *Levant Herald*, May 21, 1873.

15. The Smyrna Jockey Club, established in the late 1850s, received an annual grant from the sultan. The yearly races were regularly reported in the *Levant Herald* and later in *Hizmet* as highly animated and joyful celebrations. On the history of the Smyrna Jockey Club, see Cuinet, *La Turquie d'Asie*, 3:466–67; Gardey, *Voyage du sultan Abd-ul-Aziz de Stamboul au Caire*, 250–53.

16. On pyrotechnics in the Ottoman context, see Faroqhi, *Subjects of the Sultan*, 162–84.

17. CADN, FC, Smyrne no. 41, Consul Ségur-Montaigne to Ambassador Bourqueney, June 2, 1842.

18. On nocturnal celebrations during the festival of St. John, see PRO, FO, 195/610, Consul Blunt to Ambassador Bulwer, September 12, 1860.

19. Such incidents were repeated in 1864, 1872, 1874, 1888, 1890, 1896, 1901, and 1921. On the "calamity of the ritual murder" in Izmir, see, for instance, Galanté, *Histoire des juifs d'Anatolie*, 2:183–99.

20. During one Easter eve celebration, for example, a total of thirty-seven injuries and four deaths were reported in various parts of town, including the neighborhoods of St. Photini, St. Dimitri, and St. Catherine, along the Street of the Great Taverns; see *La Turquie*, April 26, 1876.

21. CADN, FC, Smyrne no. 41, Consul Challaye to ambassador, April 23, 1840.

22. CADN, FC, Smyrne no. 50, Consul Burggraff to Ambassador de Vogüe, October 11, 1876.

23. *La Turquie,* October 24, 1876.

24. For example, Izmir's Catholics spoke predominantly Italian and French but also Greek, Armenian, Turkish, and Arabic. Some were originally from France, Austria, and Sardinia; but many were râyas or European protégés, comprising Armenians from Persia and Anatolia, Syrian Arabs, Maltese, and Sciotes. On Catholics in the Ottoman Empire, see Frazee, *Catholics and Sultans.* On Izmir's Catholics, see Missir Reggio Mamachi di Lusignano, *Épitaphier des grandes familles latines de Smyrne;* Smyrnelis, *Une société hors de soi;* Schmitt, *Les Levantins;* Ter Minassian, "Les Arméniens."

25. Eastern Catholics paid allegiance to the pope, but preserved the liturgical, theological, and devotional practices of the autonomous churches (whether Chaldean, Melchite, Syrian, Armenian, Coptic, Serbian, or Bulgarian Catholics) with which they were associated.

26. In the nineteenth century, the Latin see of Smyrna (originally established in 1346 by Pope Clement VI) had administrative powers stretching to Mesopotamia, Syria, and Constantinople. Following the restructuring of the see, Luigi M. Cardelli (1818–30), Don Emanuel Balladur (1830–32), Julien M. Hillereau (1832–34), Pierre Marcelin Bonamil (1834–37), Antonio Mussabini (1838–61), Vincenzo Spaccapietra (1862–78), and Andrea Policarpo Timoni (1879–1904) served as archbishops. See Rougon, *Smyrne,* 32–35; Herbermann, *Catholic Encyclopedia,* 14:60.

27. On the schism of the Armenian community and the formation of various Catholic millets, see Ubicini, *Letters on Turkey,* 246–341; Steen de Jehay, *De la situation légale des sujets ottomans non-musulmans,* 244–65.

28. According to Ahmed Lütfi in 1826 a *nazır* (overseer) was appointed for the Roman Catholics living in the provinces of Cezair-i Bahr (Aegean Islands) and Rumeli as well as in Izmir and Istanbul. Ahmed Lütfi, *Vak'anüvis Ahmed Lütfi Efendi Tarihi.*

29. On the firman of Mahmud II, see Steen de Jehay, *De la situation légale des sujets ottoman non-musulmans,* 320. Similar offices were created in Edirne, Trabzon, and Chios. On the organization of the Latin millet, see ibid., 306–27, and Ubicini, *Letters on Turkey,* 375–92.

30. CADN, FC, Smyrne no. 41, Consul Ségur-Montaigne to Ambassador Bourqueney, June 2, 1842; *Écho de l'Orient,* May 27, 1842.

31. St. Polycarp (70–155 CE), a direct pupil of the apostle John, served as the bishop of the church at Smyrna and was recognized as one of the earliest combatants of Christian heresies. On the history of St. Polycarp, see San Lorenzo, *Saint Polycarpe et son tombeau.*

32. CADN, FC, Smyrne no. 45, Consul Pichon to Comte de Salvandy, secretary of public instruction, September 28, 1847.

33. Schlicht, *Frankreich und die Syrischen Christen,* 158. For an overview of Izmir's Catholic institutions, see San Lorenzo, *Saint Polycarpe et son tombeau,* 321–51; Piolet, *Les missions catholiques françaises,* 1:142–47; Pierre, *Constantinople, Jérusalem et Rome,* 182–88.

34. For example, the administration of the Hospital of St. Roch, rebuilt after the fire of 1845, was the subject of great controversy that pitted these missions against one another. Following protracted debates over who should run the establishment, who should be admitted, and whether the institution had to have its own Catholic chapel and chaplain, the

management was eventually abandoned to the Ottoman (Armenian) Catholic millet under the supervision of the archbishop, to the dissatisfaction of the French colony. On the St. Roch controversy, see *Journal de Constantinople/Écho de l'Orient,* February 3, 1858; July 10, 1858; February 16, 1859; and September 3, 1859. See also Rougon, *Smyrne,* 62.

35. For instance, when Capuchins proposed to merge their small hospital with the large hospital of St. Antoine run by Reformed Franciscans in order to serve more effectively local constituencies, the mission head in Constantinople opposed the merger, accusing the Capuchins of alienating mission property. See CADN, FC, Smyrne no. 41, "Notes sur les Établissements Religieux de Smyrne," Soulange Bodin to Consul Ségur-Montaigne, April 29, 1843.

36. CADN, FC, Smyrne no. 41, Consul Ségur-Montaigne to Ambassador Bourqueney, June 2, 1842.

37. Ferragu, "Église et diplomatie au Levant au temps des capitulations."

38. *Écho de l'Orient,* May 27, 1842.

39. CADN, FC, Smyrne no. 41, Consul Ségur-Montaigne to Ambassador Bourqueney, June 2, 1842.

40. See Zandi-Sayek, "Orchestrating Difference and Performing Identity."

41. *Écho de l'Orient,* May 27, 1842.

42. Ibid.

43. CADN, FC, Smyrne no. 41, Mussabini to Consul Ségur-Montaigne, February 4, 1843.

44. CADN, FC, Smyrne no. 41, Consul Devoize to Ambassador Bourqueney, June 12, 1841.

45. On the material culture of modern states, see Cannadine, *Ornamentalism;* Harvey, *Hybrids of Modernity;* Hobsbawm and Ranger, *Invention of Tradition;* Anderson, *Imagined Communities;* Smith, *Ethnic Origins of Nations,* chap. 7. For an insightful analysis of British ceremonial in nineteenth-century Shanghai, see Goodman, "Improvisations on a Semicolonial Theme."

46. See, for example, Ma'oz, *Ottoman Reform in Syria and Palestine,* 190.

47. On Ottoman Greek subjects after Greek independence, see Augustinos, *Greeks of Asia Minor;* Clogg, "Greek Millet"; Clogg, "Mercantile Bourgeoisie."

48. *Levant Herald,* April 28, 1877.

49. Deschamps, *Sur les routes d'Asie,* 152–53. Deschamps visited Izmir in 1887.

50. *Journal de Constantinople,* May 11, 1864.

51. *Amalthea,* April 28, 1867; cited in Augustinos, *Greeks of Asia Minor,* 242 n. 23.

52. Politis, *Yitik Kentin Kırk Yılı,* 72.

53. PRO, FO, 195/758, Consul Blunt to Ambassador Bulwer, November 11, 1863.

54. PRO, FO, 195/758, Consul Blunt to Ambassador Erskine, December 10, 1863.

55. CADN, FC, Smyrne no. 43, Consul Pichon to General Aupick, September 20, 1849.

56. PRO, FO, 195/720, Consul Blunt to Ambassador Bulwer, April 11, 1862.

57. Hobsbawm, "Introduction: Inventing Tradition."

58. On the will to nationhood, see Renan, *Qu'est-ce qu'une nation?* = *What Is a Nation?* On the role of protocols in assertions of sovereignty, see Langhorne, "History and Evolution of Diplomacy."

59. CADN, FC, Smyrne no. 46, Consul Mure de Pélanne to Ambassador Moustier, September 6, 1862.

60. CADN, FC, Smyrne no. 44, Consul Pichon to Ambassador Lavalette, December 22, 1852.

61. *Journal de Constantinople,* March 23, 1864.

62. PRO, FO, 195/1075, Spanish viceconsul to British acting consul, May 27, 1876.

63. The ceremony was held in honor of the birth of Eugène Louis Jean Joseph, son of Napoleon III. See *Journal de Constantinople/Écho de l'Orient,* March 31, 1856.

64. "Instructions relatives au cérémonial à suivre par les bâtiments de guerre Ottomans et par les forts et forteresses de L'Empire les jours de fêtes des souverains amis tracées conformément au règlement transmis en date du 29 Chaban 1275 [April 3, 1859] et du 27 Rédjeb 1279 [January 18, 1863], aux autorités civiles du littoral de l'empire"; see Aristarchi Bey, *Législation ottomane,* 4:22–24. These and similar instructions were periodically sent to diplomatic missions and their consulates. See, for example, PRO, FO, 195/720, Consul Blunt to Ambassador Erskine, December 2, 1862; CADN, FC, Smyrne no. 46, Consul Mure de Pélanne to Ambassador Moustier, February 28, 1863.

65. Testa, *Le droit public international maritime,* 118.

66. "*Circulaire* du Ministère des Affaires Etrangères en date du 12 Rédjeb 1287 [October 8, 1870]"; see Aristarchi Bey, *Législation ottomane,* 4:24.

67. Young, *Corps de droit ottoman,* 3:41.

68. CADN, FC, Smyrne no. 46, Consul Mure de Pélanne to Ambassador Moustier, September 6, 1862.

69. *Journal de Constantinople,* July 21, 1860.

70. The Treaty of London (the result of British Foreign Minister Lord Palmerston's effort to settle the Egyptian question) was initially signed by Britain, Russia, Austria, and Prussia on July 15. France joined the signatories later, in 1841. See Neff, "The Ottoman Empire and Europe."

71. On consular deliberations about allowing the procession, see CADN, FC, Smyrne no. 41, Consul Devoize to Ambassador Bourqueney, June 3, 7, and 12, 1841; Mussabini to Consul Ségur-Montaigne, February 4, 1843; and Consul Ségur-Montaigne to Bourqueney, June 11, 1844.

72. Karateke, *Padişahım Çok Yaşa!* 147.

73. On the creation of the ministry, see Findley, *Bureaucratic Reform in the Ottoman Empire,* chap. 5. A foreign affairs director *(vilayet hariciye müdürü)* and interpreter *(vilayet tercümanı)* were assigned to each province and placed under the orders of local governors; see ibid., 189.

74. On imperial celebrations in the capital, see Karateke, *Padişahım Çok Yaşa!;* Deringil, *Well-Protected Domains.*

75. For a detailed account of Abdülaziz's visit to Izmir, see Gardey, *Voyage du sultan Abd-ul-Aziz de Stamboul au Caire.*

76. CADN, FC, Smyrne no. 43, Consul Pichon to General Aupick, June 28, 1850.

77. *Levant Herald,* July 5, 1865.

78. *Levant Herald,* July 9, 1873.

79. *Journal de Constantinople,* February 4, 1864.

80. *Écho de l'Orient,* June 15, 1844.

81. *Levant Herald,* September 7, 1891.

82. *Hizmet* ran long reports on the special decorations appearing on buildings across the city, including government institutions in the Konak-Sarıkışla area, Kemeraltı Street and the bazaar, prominent buildings along the quay (customs houses and warehouses, shipping companies, hotels, cafés, banks, beer gardens, clubs, and theaters), as well as numerous private houses and business scattered across town. See *Hizmet,* April 5, 1890.

83. NA, DUSCS, Consul Offley to secretary of state, August 5, 1853.

Epilogue

1. Carter, *Road to Botany Bay,* xxi–xxii.

2. On the "Koszta affair," see, for example, Klay, *Daring Diplomacy;* Schroeder, "Bruck versus Buol"; Walker, *A Manual of Public International Law,* 67–68; NA, DUSCS, consul to secretary of state, July 5, 1853.

3. Mitchell, *Questions of Modernity,* 1, 7.

4. Upton, "Starting from Baalbek," 464.

Bibliography

Archives

Başbakanlık Ottoman Archives (BOA), Istanbul
   Ayniyat Defterleri, Anadolu Valiliklerine (Ayniyat)
   Bab-ı Ali Evrak Odası (BEO)
      Sadaret, Mektubi Kalemi, Meclis-i Vala (A. MKT. MVL)
      Sadaret, Amedi Kalemi, Meclis-i Vükela (A. AMD. MV)
   Cevdet Belediye (C. BLD)
   İrade Dahiliye (I. DH)
   İrade Meclis-i Mahsus (I. MMS)
   İrade Meclis-i Vala (I. MVL)
   İrade Şura-i Devlet (I. ŞD)
   Şura-i Devlet, Aydın (ŞD Aydın)
Bibliothèque nationale de France, Paris
Centre des Archives Diplomatique de Nantes (CADN), Nantes
   Fonds Constantinople, Séries D, Correspondance Consulaire: Smyrne (FC Smyrne)
Istanbul University, Rare Books Library, Istanbul
National Archives, Public Records Office (PRO), Kew
   Foreign Office (FO)
National Archives (NA), Washington, D.C.
   Despatches from United States Consuls in Smyrna (DUSCS)

Periodicals

Newspapers

Amalthea
Aydın
Écho de l'Orient
Hizmet
L'Impartial

Journal de Constantinople
Journal de Constantinople/Écho de l'Orient
Levant Herald
Levant Herald and Eastern Express
Le Monde Illustré
La Réforme
La Turquie

Salnames [Yearbooks] of the Province of Aydın

Salname-i Vilâyet-i Aydın. Aydın: Vilâyet Matbaası, 1296 H/1878–79.
Salname-i Vilâyet-i Aydın. Aydın: Vilâyet Matbaası, 1297 H/1879–80.
Salname-i Vilâyet-i Aydın. Aydın: Vilâyet Matbaası, 1300 H/1882–83.
Aydın Vilâyeti Salnamesi. Aydın: Vilâyet Matbaası, 1303 M/1886–87.
Aydın Vilâyeti Salnamesi. Aydın: Vilâyet Matbaası, 1306 M/1889–90.
Aydın Vilâyetine Mahsus Salname. 2 vols. Aydın: Vilâyet Matbaası, 1307 M/1890–91.

Commercial Directories

De Andria, Jacob, and Joseph Nalpas. *Annuaire des commerçants de Smyrne et de l'Anatolie.* Smyrna, 1893.
De Andria, Jacob, and G. Timoni. *Indicateur des professions commerciales et industrielles de Smyrne, de l'Anatolie.* Smyrna: Imprimerie commerciale Timoni, 1894.
De Andria, Jacob, and G. Timoni. *Indicateur des professions commerciales et industrielles de Smyrne, de l'Anatolie.* Smyrna: Imprimerie commerciale Timoni, 1895.
Fardhoulis, Panaghiotis. *Indicateur Français de Smyrne et Anatolie.* Smyrna: Imprimerie Amalthée, 1900.

Books, Dissertations, and Articles

Abensur-Hazan, Laurence. *Smyrne: Évocation d'une échelle du Levant, XIXe–XXe siècles.* Saint-Cyr-sur-Loire: A. Sutton, 2004.
Abu-Lughod, Janet L. "The Islamic City: Historic Myth, Islamic Essence, and Contemporary Relevance." *International Journal of Middle East Studies* 19, no. 2 (1987): 155–76.
Adanır, Fikret. "Religious Communities and Ethnic Groups under Imperial Sway: Ottoman and Habsburg Lands in Comparison." In *The Historical Practice of Diversity: Transcultural Interactions from the Early Modern Mediterranean to the Postcolonial World*, edited by Dirk Hoerder, Christiane Harzig, and Adrian Shubert, 54–86. New York: Berghahn, 2003.
Agnew, John. *Globalization and Sovereignty.* Lanham, Md.: Rowman & Littlefield, 2009.
———. "The Territorial Trap: The Geographical Assumptions of International Relations Theory." *Review of International Political Economy* 1, no. 1 (Spring 1994): 53–80.
Agnew, John A., and James S. Duncan. *The Power of Place: Bringing Together Geographical and Sociological Imaginations.* Boston: Unwin Hyman, 1989.
Agostoni, Claudia. *Monuments of Progress: Modernization and Public Health in Mexico City, 1876–1910.* Calgary: University of Calgary Press; Boulder: University Press of Colorado, 2003.

Ahmad, Feroz. "Ottoman Perceptions of the Capitulations 1800–1914." *Journal of Islamic Studies* 11, no. 1 (2000): 1–22.

Ahmed Lütfi. *Vak'anüvis Ahmed Lütfi Efendi Tarihi*. 8 vols. Istanbul: Yapı Kredi Yayınları, 1999.

Akarlı, Engin. "Gedik: A Bundle of Rights and Obligations for Istanbul Artisans and Traders, 1750–1840." In *Law, Anthropology, and the Constitution of the Social: Making Persons and Things*, edited by Alain Pottage and Martha Mundy, 166–200. Cambridge: Cambridge University Press, 2004.

Akgündüz, Ahmet. *Osmanlı Devleti'nde Belediye Teşkilâtı ve Belediye Kanunları*. Istanbul: Osmanlı Araştırmaları Vakfı, 2005.

Aktepe, Münir. "İzmir Hanları ve Çarşıları Hakkında Ön Bilgi." *Tarih Dergisi* 25 (March 1971): 105–54.

Aktüre, Sevgi. *19uncu Yüzyıl Sonunda Anadolu Kenti Mekansal Yapı Çözümlemesi*. Ankara: O.D.T.Ü. Mimarlık Fakültesi, 1978.

Akyıldız, Ali. *Tanzimat Dönemi Osmanlı Merkez Teşkilâtında Reform, 1836–1856*. Istanbul: Eren, 1993.

Akyüz, Vecdi, and Seyfettin Ünlü. *İslam Geleneğinden Günümüze: Şehir ve Yerel Yönetimler*. Istanbul: Ilke, 1996.

Alemdar, Korkmaz. *İstanbul, 1875–1964: Türkiye'de Yayınlanan Fransızca bir Gazetenin Tarihi*. Ankara: Ankara İktisadi ve Ticari İlimler Akademisi, 1978.

Alfred, Bruneel. *Notes et souvenirs*. Ghent: Ferdinand Vanderhaeghen, 1869.

Aliotti, Ange. *Des Français en Turquie; Spécialement au point de vue de la proprieté immobilière et du régime successoral*. Paris: Marchal & Billard, 1900.

Allen, Michelle Elizabeth. *Cleansing the City: Sanitary Geographies in Victorian London*. Athens: Ohio University Press, 2008.

Amar, Isaac A. *Les capitulations en Turquie, dans le Levant et en Extrême-orient*. Geneva, 1922.

Annales de la propagation de la foi, Recueil périodique. Lyon, France: chez l'éditeur des annales, 1841, 89–120.

Anastassiadou, Meropi. *Salonique, 1830–1912*. Leiden, The Netherlands: Brill, 1997.

And, Metin. *Tanzimat ve İstibdat Döneminde Türk Tiyatrosu, 1839–1908*. Ankara: Türkiye İş Bankası Kültür Yayınları, 1972.

Anderson, Benedict. *Imagined Communities: Reflections on the Origin and Spread of Nationalism*. London: Verso, 1983.

Anderson, James. "The Shifting Stage of Politics: New Medieval and Postmodern Territorialities?" *Environment and Planning D: Society and Space* 14, no. 2 (1996): 133–53.

Anderson, Sonia P. *An English Consul in Turkey: Paul Rycaut at Smyrna, 1667–1678*. Oxford: Clarendon Press, 1989.

Archer, John. "Paras, Palaces, Pathogens: Frameworks for the Growth of Calcutta, 1800–1850." *City and Society* 12, no. 1 (Spring 2000): 19–54.

Arıkan, Zeki. *İzmir Basın Tarihi, 1868–1923*. İzmir: Ege Üniversitesi Basımevi, 2006.

———. "Midhat Paşa'nın Aydın Valiliği (Ağustos 1880–Mayıs 1881)." In *Uluslararası Midhat Paşa Semineri: Bildiriler ve Tartışmalar, Edirne, 8–10 Mayıs 1984*, 127–64. Ankara: Türk Tarih Kurumu Basımevi, 1986.

Aristarchi Bey, Grégoire. *Législation ottomane ou Recueil des lois règlements ordonnances traités capitulations et autres documents officiels de l'empire ottoman.* 7 vols. Constantinople: Frères Nicolaïdes, 1873.

Arminjon, Pierre. "La protection en Turquie et en Égypte." *Revue du droit public et de la science politique* 16 (1901): 5–44.

Arundell, Francis Vyvyan Jago. *Discoveries in Asia Minor.* London: Richard Bentley, 1834.

Atay, Çınar. *19. Yüzyıl İzmir Fotoğrafları.* Istanbul: Suna & İnan Kıraç Akdeniz Medeniyetleri Araştırma Enstitüsü, 1997.

———. *İzmir'in İzmir'i.* Izmir: Ege Sanayicileri ve İşadamları Derneği, 1993.

———. *Osmanlı'dan Cumhuriyet'e: İzmir Planları.* Ankara: Ajans Türk, 1993.

———. *Tarih İçinde Izmir.* Izmir: Tifset Basım ve Yayın Sanayii, 1978.

Augustinos, Gerasimos. *The Greeks of Asia Minor: Confession, Community, and Ethnicity in the Nineteenth Century.* Kent, Ohio: Kent State University Press, 1992.

Aydın, Mahir, and Kayoko Hayashi, eds. *The Ottoman State and Societies in Change: A Study of the Nineteenth Century Temettuat Registers.* London: Kegan Paul, 2004.

Bağış, Ali İhsan. *Osmanlı Ticaretinde Gayri Müslimler: Kapitülasyonlar, Avrupa Tüccarları, Beratlı Tüccarlar, Hayriye Tüccarları, 1750–1839.* Ankara: Turhan Kitabevi, 1983.

Balibar, Etienne. *Race, Nation, Class: Ambiguous Identities.* London: Verso, 1991.

Barbir, Karl K. "Memory, Heritage and History: The Ottomans and the Arabs." In *Imperial Legacy: The Ottoman Imprint on the Balkans and the Middle East,* edited by L. Carl Brown, 100–114. New York: Columbia University Press, 1996.

Barkan, Ömer Lütfi. "Osmanlı İmparatorluğu'nda bir İskan ve Kolonizasyon Metodu olarak Vakıflar ve Temlikler." *Vakıflar Dergisi* 2 (1942): 279–386.

———. *Türk Toprak Hukuku Tarihinde Tanzimat ve 1274 (1858) Tarihli Arazi Kanunnamesi.* Istanbul: Maarif Matbaası, 1960.

Barkey, Karen. *Empire of Difference: The Ottomans in Comparative Perspective.* Cambridge: Cambridge University Press, 2008.

Barrell, George. *Letters from Asia.* New York: A.T. Goodrich, Elliott & Bellamy, 1819.

Barnes, David S. *The Great Stink of Paris and the Nineteenth-Century Struggle against Filth and Germs.* Baltimore: Johns Hopkins University Press, 2006.

Barnes, John Robert. *An Introduction to Religious Foundations in the Ottoman Empire.* Leiden, The Netherlands: Brill, 1987.

Baykal, Hülya. *Türk Basın Tarihi, 1831–1923: Tanzimat, Mesrutiyet, Millî Mücadele Dönemleri.* Istanbul: Afa Matbaacilik, 1990.

Baykara, Tuncer. *İzmir Şehri ve Tarihi.* Izmir: Ege Üniversitesi Matbaası, 1974.

———. *Son Yüzyıllarda Izmir ve Batı Anadolu Sempozyumu Tebliğleri.* Izmir: Akademi Kitabevi, 1994.

Bayly, C. A. *The Birth of the Modern World, 1780–1914: Global Connections and Comparisons.* Malden, Mass.: Blackwell, 2004.

Behar, Cem. "Ottoman Population Statistics and Modernization after 1831." In *Osmanlı Devletinde Bilgi ve İstatistik = Data and Statistics in the Ottoman Empire,* edited by Halil Inalcik and Şevket Pamuk, 63–72. Ankara: T. C. Başbakanlık Devlet Istatistik Enstitüsü, 2000.

Belin, M. François-Alphonse. *Étude sur la propriété foncière en pays musulman, et spécialement en Turquie (rite Hanéfite)*. Paris, 1862.

Bellows, Henry Whitney. *The Old World in Its New Face*. New York: Harper & Brothers, 1869.

Benbassa, Esther, and Aron Rodrigue. *Sephardi Jewry: A History of the Judeo-Spanish Community, 14th-20th Centuries*. Berkeley: University of California Press, 2008.

Benda-Beckmann, Keebet von. "Forum Shopping and Shopping Forums: Dispute Settlement in a Minangkabau Village in West Sumatra." *Journal of Legal Pluralism* 19 (1981): 117–60.

Benhabib, Seyla. "Models of Public Space: Hannah Arendt, the Liberal Tradition, and Jürgen Habermas." In *Habermas and the Public Sphere*, edited by Craig J. Calhoun, 73–98. Cambridge, Mass.: MIT Press, 1992.

Benton, Lauren. *Law and Colonial Cultures: Legal Regimes in World History, 1400–1900*. Cambridge: Cambridge University Press, 2002.

Berber, Engin. *Sancılı Yıllar — İzmir 1918-1922: Mütareke ve Yunan İşgali Döneminde İzmir Sancağı*. Ankara: Ayraç Yayınevi, 1997.

———. *Yeni Onbinlerin Gölgesinde bir Sancak*. Istanbul: Türkiye Ekonomik ve Toplumsal Tarih Vakfı, 1999.

Berman, Marshall. *All That Is Solid Melts into Air: The Experience of Modernity*. New York: Simon & Schuster, 1982.

Beyru, Rauf. *18. ve 19. Yüzyıllarda İzmir*. Izmir, 1973.

———. *19. Yüzyılda İzmir'de Sağlık Sorunları ve Yaşam*. Izmir: İzmir Büyükşehir Belediyesi Kültür Yayını, 2005.

———. *19. Yüzyılda İzmir'de Yaşam*. Istanbul: Literatür, 2000.

Bickers, Robert. "Shanghailanders: The Formation and Identity of the British Settler Community in Shanghai 1843-1937." *Past and Present*, no. 159 (1998): 161–211.

Bilget, Adnan. *Son Yüzyılda İzmir Şehri: 1849-1949*. Izmir: Mesher Basımevi, 1949.

Bilsel, Câna F. "Cultures et fonctionnalité: évolution morphologique de la ville de Izmir au XIXe et au début du XXe siècles." PhD diss., Université de Paris X, 1996.

Blomley, Nicholas K., David Delaney, and Richard Thompson Ford. *The Legal Geographies Reader*. Oxford: Wiley-Blackwell, 2001.

Bluestone, Daniel M. "'The Pushcart Evil': Peddlers, Merchants, and New York City's Streets, 1890–1940." *Journal of Urban History* 18, no. 1 (November 1, 1991): 68–92.

Blumi, Isa. *Rethinking the Late Ottoman Empire: A Comparative Social and Political History of Albania and Yemen, 1878–1918*. Istanbul: Isis Press, 2003.

Böke, Pelin. *İzmir, 1919-1922: Tanıklıklar*. Istanbul: Tarih Vakfı Yurt Yayınları, 2006.

Bora, Siren. *İzmir Yahudileri Tarihi: 1908-1923*. Istanbul: Gözlem Gazetecilik Basın ve Yayın, 1995.

Bouillet, Marie Nicolas. *Dictionnaire universel d'histoire et de géographie*. Paris: Hachette, 1858.

Bozdoğan, Sibel. *Modernism and Nation Building: Turkish Architectural Culture in the Early Republic*. Seattle: University of Washington Press, 2002.

Bozkurt, Gülnihâl. *Alman-İngiliz Belgelerinin ve Siyasi Gelişmelerin Işığı Altında Gayrimüslim Osmanlı Vatandaşlarının Hukuki Durumu (1839-1914)*. Ankara: Türk Tarih Kurumu Basımevi, 1989.

Braude, Benjamin. "Foundation Myths of the Millet System." In *Christians and Jews in the Ottoman Empire: The Functioning of a Plural Society,* edited by Benjamin Braude and Bernard Lewis, 1:69–88. New York: Holmes & Meier, 1982.

Braude, Benjamin, and Bernard Lewis. "Introduction." In *Christians and Jews in the Ottoman Empire: The Functioning of a Plural Society,* edited by Benjamin Braude and Bernard Lewis, 1:1–34. New York: Holmes & Meier, 1982.

Brewer, Josiah. *A Residence at Constantinople in the Year 1827.* New Haven, Conn.: Durrie & Peck, 1830.

Broughton, John Cam Hobhouse. *A Journey through Albania, and Other Provinces of Turkey in Europe and Asia, to Constantinople, during the Years 1809–1810.* Vol. 2. London: J. Cawthorn, 1813.

Brown, Philip. *Foreigners in Turkey: Their Juridical Status.* Princeton, N.J.: Princeton University Press, 1914.

Brunschvig, Robert. "Urbanisme médiéval et droit musulman." *Revue des études Islamiques* 5 (1947): 127–55.

Bruyn, Cornelis de. *Voyage au Levant: c'est-à-dire, dans les principaux endroits de l'Asie Mineure, dans les isles de Chio, Rhodes, Chypre, &c., de même que dans les plus considérables villes d'Egypte, Syrie, & Terre Sainte; enrichi d'un grand nombre de figures en taille-douce: où sont representées les plus célébres villes, païs, bourgs, & autres choses dignes de remarque, le tout dessiné d'après nature.* Vol. 1. Paris: J.-B.-C. Bauche le fils, 1725.

Burns, Jabez. *Help-book for Travellers to the East.* London: Thomas Cook, 1870.

Burton, Albert de. *Ten Months' Tour in the East.* London: F. Bowyer Kitto, 1870.

Butenschøn, Nils A., Uri Davis, and Manuel S. Hassassian. *Citizenship and the State in the Middle East: Approaches and Applications.* Syracuse, N.Y.: Syracuse University Press, 2000.

Çadırcı, Musa. "Osmanlı İmparatorluğunda Eyalet ve Sancaklarda Meclislerin Oluşturulması, 1840–1864." In *Yusuf Hikmet Bayur'a Armağan,* 257–77. Ankara: Türk Tarih Kurumu Basımevi, 1985.

———. *Tanzimat Döneminde Anadolu Kentleri'nin Sosyal ve Ekonomik Yapıları.* Ankara: Türk Tarih Kurumu Basımevi, 1991.

Cadoux, Cecil John. *Ancient Smyrna: A History of the City from the Earliest Times to 324 A.D.* Oxford: Blackwell, 1938.

Çağlar, İbrahim, and Gérard Groc. *La presse française de Turquie de 1795 à nos jours: histoire et catalogue.* Istanbul: Isis Press, 1985.

Çakmak, Zafer. *İzmir ve Çevresinde Yunan İşgali ve Rum Mezalimi, 1919–1922.* Istanbul: Yeditepe, 2007.

Calhoun, Craig J., ed. *Habermas and the Public Sphere.* Studies in Contemporary German Social Thought. Cambridge, Mass.: MIT Press, 1992.

Camp, Maxime Du. *Souvenirs et paysages d'Orient.* Paris: Arthus Bertrand, 1848.

Cannadine, David. *Ornamentalism: How the British Saw Their Empire.* Oxford: Oxford University Press, 2001.

Canpolat, Emin. *İzmir Kuruluşundan Bugüne Kadar.* Istanbul: İTÜ, Mimarlık Fakültesi, Pulhan Matbaası, 1953.

Carter, Erica, James Donald, and Judith Squires, eds., *Space and Place: Theories of Identity and Location.* London: Lawrence & Wishart, 1993.

Carter, Paul. *The Road to Botany Bay: An Exploration of Landscape and History.* Chicago: University of Chicago Press, 1987; reprint, Minneapolis: University of Minnesota Press, 2010.

Caty, Roland, Eliane Richard, and Pierre Echinard. *Les patrons du second empire.* 5 vols. Paris: Picard, 1991.

Çelik, Zeynep. *Displaying the Orient: Architecture of Islam at Nineteenth-Century World's Fairs.* Berkeley: University of California Press, 1992.

———. *Empire, Architecture, and the City: French-Ottoman Encounters, 1830-1914.* Seattle: University of Washington Press, 2008.

———. *The Remaking of Istanbul: Portrait of an Ottoman City in the Nineteenth Century.* Seattle: University of Washington Press, 1986.

Cevat, Sami, and Hüseyin Hüsnü. *İzmir 1905.* Edited by Erkan Serçe. Izmir: İzmir Büyükşehir Belediyesi Kültür Yayını, 2000.

Çeviker, Turgut. *Tanzimat İmzasız Karikatürler Antolojisi.* Istanbul: Adam, 1986.

Chalcraft, John T. *The Striking Cabbies of Cairo and Other Stories: Crafts and Guilds in Egypt, 1863-1914.* Albany: State University of New York Press, 2004.

Chandler, Dean. *Outline of History of Lighting by Gas.* London: Chancery Lane Printing Works, 1936.

Chandler, Richard, and Nicholas Revett. *Travels in Asia Minor and Greece.* Oxford: Clarendon Press, 1825.

Chattopadhyay, Swati. *Representing Calcutta: Modernity, Nationalism, and the Colonial Uncanny.* London: Routledge, 2005.

Clancy-Smith, Julia. "Marginality and Migration: Europe's Social Outcasts in Pre-Colonial Tunisia, 1830-81." In *Outside In on the Margins of the Modern Middle East,* edited by Eugene L. Rogan, 149-81. London: I. B. Tauris, 2002.

Clark, Bruce. *Twice a Stranger: The Mass Expulsions that Forged Modern Greece and Turkey.* Cambridge, Mass.: Harvard University Press, 2006.

Clark, Timothy. *The Painting of Modern Life: Paris in the Art of Manet and His Followers.* New York: Knopf, 1985.

Clarke, Hyde. *The Imperial Ottoman Smyrna and Aidin Railway, Its Position and Prospects.* Constantinople: Koehler Brothers, 1861.

———. *Report on the Traffic of Smyrna: With Statistics of Trade, &c.* London: Nissen & Parker, 1860.

Clogg, Richard. "The Greek Millet." In *Christians and Jews in the Ottoman Empire: The Functioning of a Plural Society,* edited by Benjamin Braude and Bernard Lewis, 1:185-207. New York: Holmes & Meier, 1982.

———. "The Mercantile Bourgeoisie: Progressive or Reactionary?" In *Balkan Society in the Age of Greek Independence,* edited by Richard Clogg, 85-110. Totowa, N.J.: Barnes & Noble, 1981.

Cochran, William. *Pen and Pencil in Asia Minor; or, Notes from the Levant.* New York: Scribner & Welford, 1888.

Collas, M. B. C. *La Turquie en 1864.* Paris: E. Dentu, 1864.

Conder, Josiah. *The Modern Traveller.* Boston: Wells & Lilly; Phialdelphia: Thomas Wardle, 1830.

Cook, Ian, ed. *Cultural Turns/Geographical Turns: Perspectives on Cultural Geography.* Harlow, England: Prentice Hall, 2000.

Cooper, Frederick. *Colonialism in Question: Theory, Knowledge, History.* Berkeley: University of California Press, 2005.

Corbin, Alain. *The Foul and the Fragrant: Odor and the French Social Imagination.* Cambridge, Mass.: Harvard University Press, 1986.

Crane, Sheila. "Digging up the Present in Marseille's Old Port: Toward an Archaeology of Reconstruction." *Journal of the Society of Architectural Historians* 63, no. 3 (2004): 296–319.

Cronin, Stephanie. *Subalterns and Social Protest: History from Below in the Middle East and North Africa.* London: Routledge, 2008.

Cuinet, Vital. *La Turquie d'Asie: géographie administrative.* Vol. 3. Paris: E. Leroux, 1894.

D'Arvieux, Laurent. *Memoires du Chevalier d'Arvieux . . . contenant ses voyages à Constantinople, dans l'Asie, la Syrie, la Palestine, l'Egypte et la Barbarie.* Vol. 1. Paris: J. B. Labat, 1735.

D'Egremont, J. B. "Rapport du 21 juillet 1864." *Recueil consulaire belge* 10 (1864): 573–88.

D'Estourmel, Comte Joseph. *Journal d'un voyage en Orient.* Vol. 1. Paris: Imprimerie de Crapelet, 1844.

Dagenais, Michèle, Irene Maver, and Pierre-Yves Saunier, eds. *Municipal Services and Employees in the Modern City: New Historic Approaches.* Aldershot, England: Ashgate, 2003.

Dağlar, Oya. *War, Epidemics, and Medicine in the Late Ottoman Empire (1912–1918).* Haarlem, Turkey: Sota, 2008.

Davis, Diane E., and Nora Libertun de Duren, eds. *Cities and Sovereignty: Identity Politics in Urban Spaces.* Bloomington: Indiana University Press, 2011.

Davis, Richard Harding, Andrew Lang, Francisque Sarcey, William Wetmore Story, Henry James, Paul Lindau, and Isabel Florence Hapgood. *The Great Streets of the World, 1844–1912.* New York: C. Scribner's Sons, 1892.

Davis, Susan G. *Parades and Power: Street Theatre in Nineteenth-Century Philadelphia.* Philadelphia: Temple University Press, 1986.

Davison, Roderic. *Nineteenth Century Ottoman Diplomacy and Reforms.* Istanbul: Isis Press, 1999.

———. *Reform in the Ottoman Empire, 1856–1876.* Princeton, N.J.: Princeton University Press, 1963.

De Certeau, Michel. *The Practice of Everyday Life.* Berkeley: University of California Press, 1984.

Dear, Michael, and Jennifer Wolch. *The Power of Geography: How Territory Shapes Social Life.* Boston: Unwin Hyman, 1989.

Defrance, Eugène. *Histoire de l'éclairage des rues de Paris.* Paris: Imprimerie nationale, 1904.

Delaporte, François. *Disease and Civilization: The Cholera in Paris, 1832.* Cambridge, Mass.: MIT Press, 1986.

Delgado, James P. *Gold Rush Port: The Maritime Archaeology of San Francisco's Waterfront.* Berkeley: University of California Press, 2009.

Dennis, Richard. *Cities in Modernity: Representations and Productions of Metropolitan Space, 1840–1930.* Cambridge: Cambridge University Press, 2008.

Deringil, Selim. *The Well-Protected Domains: Ideology and the Legitimation of Power in the Ottoman Empire, 1876–1909.* London: I. B. Tauris, 1998.

Deschamps, Gaston. "En Turquie—Smyrne." *Revue des deux mondes* 117 (1893): 281–320.
———. *Sur les routes d'Asie*. Paris: A. Colin, 1894.
Dobkin, Marjorie Housepian. *Smyrna 1922: The Destruction of a City*. London: Faber, 1972.
Dorr, Benjamin. *Notes of Travel in Egypt, the Holy Land, Turkey, and Greece*. Philadelphia: J. B. Lippincott, 1856.
Doumani, Beshara. "Palestinian Islamic Court Records: A Source for Socioeconomic History." *MESA Bulletin* 19, no. 2 (1985): 155–72.
Driver, Felix, and David Gilbert, eds. *Imperial Cities: Landscape, Display and Identity*. Manchester: Manchester University Press; New York: St. Martin's Press, 1999.
Dursun, M. Kâmil. *İzmir Hatıraları*. Edited by Ünal Şenel. Izmir: Akademi Kitabevi, 1994.
Eickelman, Dale F. *The Middle East: An Anthropological Approach*. Englewood Cliffs, N.J.: Prentice-Hall, 1981.
Elliott, Charles Boileau. *Travels in the Three Great Empires of Austria, Russia, and Turkey*. Philadelphia: Lea & Blanchard, 1839.
Engelhardt, Ed. *La Turquie et le Tanzimât, ou, histoire des réformes dans l'empire ottoman depuis 1826 jusqu'à nos jours*. 2 vols. Paris: A. Cotillon, 1882.
Ergenç, Özer. "Osmanlı Şehirlerindeki Yönetim Kurumlarının Niteliği Üzerinde Bazı Düşünceler." Paper presented at the VIII. Türk Tarih Kongresi, Ankara 1981.
———. "Osmanlı Şehrindeki Mahalle'nin İşlev ve Nitelikleri Üzerine." *Osmanlı Araştırmaları* 4 (1984): 69–88.
Ergene, Boğaç A. *Local Court, Provincial Society, and Justice in the Ottoman Empire: Legal Practice and Dispute Resolution in Çankırı and Kastamonu (1652–1744)*. Leiden, The Netherlands: Brill, 2003.
Ergin, Osman Nuri. *Mecelle-i Umûr-i Belediyye*. 9 vols. Istanbul: İstanbul Büyükşehir Belediyesi Kültür İşleri Daire Başkanlığı, 1995.
———. *Türk Tarihinde Evkaf, Belediye ve Patrikhaneler*. Istanbul: Türkiye Basımevi, 1937.
———. *Türkiye'de Şehirciliğin Tarihi İnkişafı*. Istanbul: Istanbul Üniversitesi Yayını, 1936.
Ersoy, Ahmet A. "On the Sources of the 'Ottoman Renaissance': Architectural Revival and Its Discourse during the Abdülaziz Era (1861–76)." PhD diss., Harvard University, 2000.
Ersoy, Bozkurt. *Izmir Hanları*. Ankara: Atatürk Kültür, Dil ve Tarih Yüksek Kurumu, 1991.
Eryılmaz, Bilal. *Osmanlı Devletinde Gayrimüslim Teb'anın Yönetimi*. Istanbul: Risale, 1990.
———. *Tanzimat ve Yönetimde Modernleşme*. Istanbul: Işaret, 1992.
Essad, Mahmoud. *Du régime des capitulations ottomanes: leur caractère juridique d'après l'histoire et les textes*. Istanbul: S. A. de Papeterie et d'Imprimerie, Fratelli Haim, 1928.
Ewen, Shane, and Pierre-Yves Saunier, eds. *Another Global City: Historical Explorations into the Transnational Municipal Moment, 1850–2000*. New York: Palgrave Macmillan, 2008.
Exertzoglou, Haris. "The Cultural Uses of Consumption: Negotiating Class, Gender, and Nation in the Ottoman Urban Centers during the 19th Century." *International Journal of Middle East Studies* 35, no. 1 (2003): 77–101.
Eyüce, Özen. "Konak Square: From Past to Present in Pictures." *Ege Mimarlık* 35, no. 3 (2000): 4–8.
Fahmy, Khaled. *All the Pasha's Men: Mehmed Ali, His Army, and the Making of Modern Egypt*. Cambridge: Cambridge University Press, 1997.

———. "The Police and the People in Nineteenth-Century Egypt." *Die Welt des Islams*, n.s. 39, no. 3 (November 1999): 340–77.

Faroqhi, Suraiya. "Izmir." In *The Encyclopaedia of Islam, Second Edition*, edited by P. Bearman, Th. Bianquis, C. E. Bosworth, E. van Donzel, and W. P. Heinrichs. Online edition. Leiden, The Netherlands: Brill, 2002.

———. *Subjects of the Sultan: Culture and Daily Life in the Ottoman Empire*. London: I. B. Tauris, 2005.

Faroqhi, Suraiya, Halil İnalcık, and Donald Quataert. *An Economic and Social History of the Ottoman Empire*. 2 vols. Cambridge: Cambridge University Press, 1997.

Fawaz, Leila Tarazi. *Merchants and Migrants in Nineteenth-Century Beirut*. Cambridge, Mass.: Harvard University Press, 1983.

Fawaz, Leila Tarazi, and C. A. Bayly, eds. *Modernity and Culture: From the Mediterranean to the Indian Ocean*. New York: Columbia University Press, 2002.

Fellows, Sir Charles. *A Journal Written during an Excursion in Asia Minor*. London: J. Murray, 1839.

Ferragu, Gilles. "Église et diplomatie au Levant au temps des capitulations." *Rives méditerranéennes*, no. 6 (2000). http://rives.revues.org/document67.html.

Findley, Carter. *Bureaucratic Reform in the Ottoman Empire: The Sublime Porte, 1789–1922*. Princeton, N.J.: Princeton University Press, 1980.

Findley, Carter, and Halil Inalcık. "Mahkama." In *The Encyclopaedia of Islam, Second Edition*, edited by P. Bearman, Th. Bianquis, C. E. Bosworth, E. van Donzel, and W. P. Heinrichs. Online edition. Leiden, The Netherlands: Brill, 2002.

Findley, Carter Vaughn. "The Tanzimat." In *The Cambridge History of Turkey*. Vol. 4, *Turkey in the Modern World*, edited by Reşat Kasaba, 11–37. Cambridge: Cambridge University Press, 2008.

Finnie, David H. *Pioneers East: The Early American Experience in the Middle East*. Cambridge, Mass.: Harvard University Press, 1967.

Fortier, Anne-Marie. "Re-Membering Places and the Performance of Belonging(s)." *Theory, Culture and Society* 16, no. 2 (1999): 41–64.

Frangakis-Syrett, Elena. *The Commerce of Smyrna in the Eighteenth Century (1700–1820)*. Athens: Centre for Asia Minor Studies, 1992.

———. "Concurrence commerciale et financière entre les pays ocidentaux à Izmir, XIXe–début XXe siècles." In *Enjeux et rapports de force en Turquie et en méditerranée orientale*, edited by Jacques Thobie, Roland Perez, and Salgur Kançal, 117–27. Paris: L'Harmattan, 1996.

———. "The Economic Activities of the Greek Community of Izmir in the Second Half of the Nineteenth and Early Twentieth Centuries." In *Ottoman Greeks in the Age of Nationalism: Politics, Economy, and Society in the Nineteenth Century*, edited by Dimitri Gondicas and Charles Philip Issawi, 17–44. Princeton, N.J.: Darwin Press, 1999.

———. "The Greek Mercantile Community of Izmir in the First Half of the Nineteenth Century." In *Les villes dans l'empire ottoman: Activités et sociétes*, edited by Daniel Panzac, 1:391–416. Paris: CNRS, 1991.

———. "Implementation of the 1838 Anglo-Turkish Convention on Izmir's Trade: European and Minority Merchants." *New Perspectives on Turkey* 7 (1992): 91–112.

———. *Trade and Money: The Ottoman Economy in the Eighteenth and Early Nineteenth Centuries.* Istanbul: Isis Press, 2007.

Frazee, Charles A. *Catholics and Sultans: The Church and the Ottoman Empire, 1453–1923.* Cambridge: Cambridge University Press, 1983.

Galanté, Abraham. *Histoire des juifs d'Anatolie: les juifs d'Izmir (Smyrne).* Vol. 1. Istanbul: Imprimerie M. Babok, 1937.

Gardey, Louis. *Voyage du sultan Abd-ul-Aziz de Stamboul au Caire.* Paris: E. Dentu, 1865.

Gavillot, J. C. Aristide. *Essai sur les droits des européens en Turquie et en Égypte: les capitulations et la réforme judiciaire.* Paris: E. Dentu, 1875.

Geary, Grattan. *Through Asiatic Turkey.* London: S. Low, Marston, Searle & Rivington, 1878.

Georgelin, Hervé. *La fin de Smyrne: du cosmopolitisme aux nationalismes.* Paris: CNRS, 2005.

Georgeon, François, Paul Dumont, and Meropi Anastassiadou, eds. *Vivre dans l'empire ottoman: sociabilités et relations intercommunautaires (XVIIIe–XXe siècles).* Paris: L'Harmattan, 1997.

Georgiades, Demetrios. *Smyrne et l'Asie Mineure au point de vue économique et commercial.* Paris: Chaix, 1885.

Gerber, Haim. *State, Society, and Law in Islam: Ottoman Law in Comparative Perspective.* Albany: State University of New York Press, 1994.

Gerçek, Selim Nüzhet. *Türk Gazeteciliği, 1831–1931: Yüzüncü Yıl Dönümü Vesilesile.* Istanbul: Devlet Matbaası, 1931.

Gibb, H. A. R. Sir, and Harold Bowen. *Islamic Society and the West: A Study of the Impact of Western Civilization on Moslem Culture in the Near East.* 2 vols. Oxford: Oxford University Press, 1950.

Giddens, Anthony. *The Consequences of Modernity.* Stanford: Stanford University Press, 1990.

Girouard, Mark. *Cities and People: A Social and Architectural History.* New Haven, Conn.: Yale University Press, 1985.

Glover, William J. *Making Lahore Modern: Constructing and Imagining a Colonial City.* Minneapolis: University of Minnesota Press, 2007.

Goad, Charles E. *Plan d'assurance de Smyrne (Smyrna).* London: C. E. Goad, 1905.

Göçek, Fatma Müge. "The Legal Recourse of Minorities in History: Eighteenth Century Appeals to the Islamic Court of Galata." In *Minorities in the Ottoman Empire,* edited by Molly Greene, 47–69. Princeton, N.J.: Markus Wiener, 2005.

Goddard, Hugh. *A History of Christian–Muslim Relations.* Chicago: New Amsterdam Books, 2000.

Goffman, Daniel. *Izmir and the Levantine World, 1550–1650.* Seattle: University of Washington Press, 1990.

———. "Izmir: From Village to Colonial Port City." In *The Ottoman City Between East and West: Aleppo, Izmir, and Istanbul,* edited by Edhem Eldem, Daniel Goffman, and Bruce Alan Masters, 79–133. Cambridge: Cambridge University Press, 1999.

———. "Negotiating with the Renaisance State: The Ottoman Empire and the New Diplomacy." In *The Early Modern Ottomans: Remapping the Empire,* edited by Virginia H. Aksan and Daniel Goffman, 61–74. Cambridge: Cambridge University Press, 2007.

———. "Ottoman Millets in the Early Seventeenth Century." *New Perspectives on Turkey* 11 (1994): 135–58.

Gondicas, Dimitri, and Charles Philip Issawi, eds. *Ottoman Greeks in the Age of Nationalism: Politics, Economy, and Society in the Nineteenth Century.* Princeton, N.J.: Darwin Press, 1999.

Goodman, Bryna. "Improvisations on a Semicolonial Theme, or, How to Read a Celebration of Transnational Urban Community." *Journal of Asian Studies* 59, no. 4 (November 2000): 889–926.

Gottdiener, Mark. *The Social Production of Urban Space.* Austin: University of Texas Press, 1985.

Gradeva, Rositsa. *War and Peace in Rumeli: 15th to the Beginning of 19th Century.* Istanbul: Isis Press, 2008.

Greek Atrocities in the Vilayet of Smyrna (May to July 1919) Inedited Documents and Evidence of English and French Officers: First Series. Lausanne, Switzerland: Permanent Bureau of the Turkish Congress at Lausanne, 1919.

Greene, Molly. *A Shared World: Christians and Muslims in the Early Modern Mediterranean.* Princeton, N.J.: Princeton University Press, 2000.

Gregory, Derek, and John Urry. *Social Relations and Spatial Structures.* New York: St. Martin's Press, 1985.

Groth, Paul Erling, and Todd W. Bressi, eds. *Understanding Ordinary Landscapes.* New Haven, Conn.: Yale University Press, 1997.

Guide to the Eastern Mediterranean Including Greece and the Greek Islands, Constantinople, Smyrna, Ephesus, etc. London: Macmillan, 1904.

Gül, Murat, and Richard Lamb. "Mapping, Regularizing and Modernizing Ottoman Istanbul: Aspects of the Genesis of the 1839 Development Policy." *Urban History* 31, no. 3 (2005): 420–36.

Gunn, Simon, and Robert John Morris, eds. *Identities in Space: Contested Terrains in the Western City Since 1850.* Aldershot, England: Ashgate, 2001.

Gupta, Akhil, and James Ferguson. "Beyond 'Culture': Space, Identity, and the Politics of Difference." *Cultural Anthropology* 7, no. 1 (February 1992): 6–23.

Güran, Tevfik. "Nineteenth Century Temettuat (Revenue) Censuses." In *Osmanlı Devletinde Bilgi ve İstatistik = Data and Statistics in the Ottoman Empire,* edited by Halil İnalcık and Şevket Pamuk, 179. Ankara: T. C. Başbakanlık Devlet İstatistik Enstitüsü, 2000.

———. *Osmanlı Malî İstatistikleri Bütçeleri, 1841–1918: Ottoman Financial Statistics Budgets.* Ankara: T. C. Başbakanlık Devlet İstatistik Enstitüsü, 2003.

———. *Tanzimat Döneminde Osmanlı Maliyesi: Bütçeler ve Hazine Hesapları (1841–1861).* Ankara: Türk Tarih Kurumu Basimevi, 1989.

Habermas, Jürgen. *The Structural Transformations of the Public Sphere: An Inquiry into a Categorie of Bourgeois Society.* Translated by Thomas Burger with Frederick Lawrence. Cambridge, Mass.: MIT Press, 1989.

Hacikyan, Agop Jack, Gabriel Basmajian, and Edward S. Franchuk. *The Heritage of Armenian Literature: From the Eighteenth Century to Modern Times.* Detroit: Wayne State University Press, 2005.

Hakim, Besim S. *Arabic-Islamic Cities: Building and Planning Principles.* London: Kegan Paul, 1986.

Hall, John. "In Search of Civil Society." In *Civil Society: Theory, History, Comparison*, edited by John A. Hall, 1–31. Cambridge: Polity, 1995.

Hall, Stuart, and Paul Du Gay, eds. *Questions of Cultural Identity*. London: Sage, 1996.

Hamilton, William John. *Researches in Asia Minor, Pontus and Armenia: With Some Account of Their Antiquities and Geology*. London: J. Murray, 1842.

Hanioğlu, M. Şükrü. *A Brief History of the Late Ottoman Empire*. Princeton, N.J.: Princeton University Press, 2008.

Hanley, Will. "Grieving Cosmopolitanism in Middle East Studies." *History Compass* 6, no. 5 (2008): 1346–67.

Hanssen, Jens. *Fin de Siècle Beirut: The Making of an Ottoman Provincial Capital*. Oxford: Clarendon Press, 2005.

Hanssen, Jens, Thomas Philipp, and Stefan Weber, eds. *The Empire in the City: Arab Provincial Capitals in the Late Ottoman Empire*. Würzburg, Germany: Ergon in Kommission, 2002.

Hartog, Hendrik. *Public Property and Private Power: The Corporation of the City of New York in American Law, 1730–1870*. Chapel Hill: University of North Carolina Press, 1983.

Harvey, David. *The Condition of Postmodernity*. Oxford: Blackwell, 1989.

Harvey, Penelope. *Hybrids of Modernity: Anthropology, the Nation State and the Universal Exhibition*. London: Routledge, 1996.

Hatcherian, Garabed. *Smyrne 1922: entre le feu, le glaive et l'eau, les épreuves d'un médecin Arménien*. Paris: L'Harmattan, 2000.

Hayden, Dolores. *The Power of Place: Urban Landscapes as Public History*. Cambridge, Mass.: MIT Press, 1995.

Heidborn, A. *Manuel de droit public et administratif de l'empire ottoman*, 2 vols. Vienna: C. W. Stern, 1909.

Herbermann, Charles G., ed. *The Catholic Encyclopedia*. Vol. 14. New York: Encyclopedia Press, 1912.

Hervé, Francis. *A Residence in Greece and Turkey*. London: Whittaker, 1837.

Hillier, Jean, and Emma Rooksby, eds. *Habitus: A Sense of Place*. Aldershot, England: Ashgate, 2002.

Hirschon, Renee. *Crossing the Aegean: An Appraisal of the 1923 Compulsory Population Exchange between Greece and Turkey*. New York: Berghahn, 2003.

Hobsbawm, E. J. "Introduction: Inventing Tradition." In *The Invention of Tradition*, edited by E. J. Hobsbawm and T. O Ranger. Cambridge: Cambridge University Press, 1992.

———. *Nations and Nationalism Since 1780: Programme, Myth, Reality*. Cambridge: Cambridge University Press, 1992.

Hobsbawm, E. J., and T. O Ranger, eds. *The Invention of Tradition*. Cambridge: Cambridge University Press, 1992.

Hoexter, Miriam, S. N. Eisenstadt, and Nehemia Levtzion, eds. *The Public Sphere in Muslim Societies*. Albany: State University of New York Press, 2002.

Holston, James, and Arjun Appadurai. "Introduction: Cities and Citizenship." In *Cities and Citizenship*, edited by J. Holston, 1–20. Durham, N.C.: Duke University Press, 1999.

Horner, Gustavus Richard Brown. *Medical and Topographical Observations upon the Mediterranean*. Philadelphia: Haswell, Barrington, & Haswell, 1839.

Horowitz, Richard S. "International Law and State Transformation in China, Siam, and the Ottoman Empire during the Nineteenth Century." *Journal of World History* 15, no. 4 (2004): 445–86.

Horton, George. *The Blight of Asia: An Account of the Systematic Extermination of Christian Populations by Mohammedans and of the Culpability of Certain Great Powers, with the True Story of the Burning of Smyrna.* Indianapolis: Bobbs-Merrill, 1926.

Hosagrahar, Jyoti. *Indigenous Modernities: Negotiating Architecture, Urbanism, and Colonialism in Delhi.* Milton Park, England: Routledge, 2005.

Hughes, William. *A Manual of European Geography.* London: Longman, Green, Longman, & Roberts, 1861.

Ilbert, Robert. *Alexandrie, 1830–1930: Histoire d'une communauté citadine.* Cairo: Institut français d'archéologie orientale, 1996.

İnalcık, Halil. "The Nature of Traditional Society: Turkey." In *Political Modernization in Japan and Turkey,* edited by Robert Edward Ward and Dankwart Rustow, 42–63. Princeton, N.J.: Princeton University Press, 1964.

Işın, Engin F. *Being Political: Genealogies of Citizenship.* Minneapolis: University of Minnesota Press, 2002.

———, ed. *Democracy, Citizenship, and the Global City.* Innis Centenary Series. London: Routledge, 2000.

———. "Introduction: Cities and Citizenship in a Global Age." *Citizenship Studies* 3 (1999): 165–72.

İslamoğlu-İnan, Huri, ed. *The Ottoman Empire and the World-Economy.* Cambridge: Cambridge University Press and Maison des sciences de l'homme, 1987.

———. "Politics of Administering Property: Law and Statistics in the Nineteenth-Century Ottoman Empire." In *Constituting Modernity: Private Property in the East and West,* edited by Huri İslamoğlu-İnan, 276–320. London: I. B. Tauris, 2004.

———. "Property as a Contested Domain: A Reevaluation of the Ottoman Land Code of 1858." In *New Perspectives on Property and Land in the Middle East,* edited by Roger Owen, 3–61. Cambridge, Mass.: Harvard University Press, 2000.

İslamoğlu-İnan, Huri, and Peter C. Perdue, eds. *Shared Histories of Modernity: China, India and the Ottoman Empire.* London: Routledge, 2009.

Issawi, Charles Philip. *An Economic History of the Middle East and North Africa.* New York: Columbia University Press, 1982.

———. *The Economic History of Turkey, 1800–1914.* Chicago: University of Chicago Press, 1980.

Jackson, Peter. *Maps of Meaning: An Introduction to Cultural Geography.* London: Unwin Hyman, 1989.

Jacobs, Jane M. *Edge of Empire: Postcolonialism and the City.* London: Routledge, 1996.

Jennings, R. C. "Kadi, Court, and Legal Procedure in 17th C. Ottoman Kayseri." *Studia Islamica* 48 (1978): 133–72.

Johansen, Baber. *Contingency in a Sacred Law: Legal and Ethical Norms in the Muslim Fiqh.* Leiden, The Netherlands: Brill, 1999.

Karateke, Hakan T. *Padişahım Çok Yaşa! Osmanlı Devletinin Son Yüz Yılında Merasimler.* Istanbul: Kitap Yayınevi, 2004.

Karpat, Kemal. *An Inquiry into the Social Foundations of Nationalism in the Ottoman State: From Social Estates to Classes, from Millets to Nations.* Princeton, N.J.: Center of International Studies, Princeton University, 1973.

———. *Ottoman Population, 1830–1914: Demographic and Social Characteristics.* Madison: University of Wisconsin Press, 1985.

Kasaba, Reşat. "İzmir." In *Doğu Akdeniz'de Liman Kentleri, 1800–1914,* edited by Çağlar Keyder, Y. Eyüp Özveren, and Donald Quataert, 1–22. Istanbul: Tarih Vakfı Yurt Yayınları, 1994.

———. "Izmir 1922: A Port City Unravels." In *Modernity and Culture: From the Mediterranean to the Indian Ocean,* edited by Leila Tarazi Fawaz and C. A. Bayly, 204–29. New York: Columbia University Press, 2002.

———. *The Ottoman Empire and the World Economy: The Nineteenth Century.* Albany: State University of New York Press, 1988.

———. "Treaties and Friendships: British Imperialism, the Ottoman Empire, and China in the Nineteenth Century." *Journal of World History* 4, no. 2 (1993): 215–41.

Kasaba, Reşat, Çağlar Keyder, and Faruk Tabak. "Eastern Mediterranean Port Cities and Their Bourgeoisies: Merchants, Political Projects and Nation-States." *Review* 10, no. 1 (1986): 121–35.

Kassam, Shalom. "Extraterritorial Jurisdiction in the Ancient World." *American Journal of International Law* 29, no. 2 (April 1935): 237–47.

Kazıcı, Ziya. *Osmanlılarda İhtisab Müessesesi: Osmanlılarda Ekonomik, Dini, ve Sosyal Hayat.* Istanbul: Kültür Basın Yayın Birliği, 1987.

Keating, Ann Durkin Tarr, Eugene P. Moehring, and Joel A. Tarr. *Infrastructure and Urban Growth in the Nineteenth Century.* Chicago: Public Works Historical Society, 1985.

Keith, Michael, and Steve Pile, eds. *Place and the Politics of Identity.* London: Routledge, 1993.

Kenanoğlu, Macit. *Osmanlı Millet Sistemi: Mit ve Gerçek.* Istanbul: Klasik, 2004.

Kévorkian, Raymond H. *Les Arméniens dans l'empire ottoman à la veille du génocide.* Paris: Éditions d'art et d'histoire, 1992.

Keyder, Çağlar. "Law and Legitimation in Empire." In *Lessons of Empire: Imperial Histories and American Power,* edited by Craig J. Calhoun, Frederick Cooper, and Kevin W. Moore, 116–31. New York: New Press distributed by W. W. Norton, 2006.

———. "The Ottoman Empire." In *After Empire: Multiethnic Societies and Nation-Building; The Soviet Union and the Russian, Ottoman, and Habsburg Empires,* edited by Karen Barkey and Mark Von Hagen, 30–44. Boulder, Colo.: Westview Press, 1997.

Khuri-Makdisi, Ilham. *The Eastern Mediterranean and the Making of Global Radicalism, 1860–1914.* Berkeley: University of California Press, 2010.

Kırlı, Cengiz. "The Struggle Over Space: Coffeehouses of Ottoman Istanbul, 1780–1845." PhD diss., State University of New York at Binghamton, 2002.

———. *Sultan ve Kamuoyu: Osmanlı Modernleşme Sürecinde "Havadis Jurnalleri," 1840–1844.* Istanbul: Türkiye İş Bankası Kültür Yayınları, 2009.

Klay, Andor. *Daring Diplomacy: The Case of the First American Ultimatum.* Minneapolis: University of Minnesota Press, 1957.

Knight, Charles. *The English Cyclopaedia.* London: Bradbury, Evans, 1867.

Kolluoğlu Kırlı, Biray. "Modern Spaces: Cityscapes and Modernity; Smyrna Morphing into Izmir." In *Ways to Modernity in Greece and Turkey: Encounters with Europe, 1850–1950*, edited by Anna Phrankoudake and Çağlar Keyder, 217–35. London: I. B. Tauris, 2007.

Koloğlu, Orhan. *Osmanlı'dan Günümüze Türkiye'de Basın*. Istanbul: İletişim Yayınları, 1992.

Kontente, Léon. *Smyrne et l'occident: de l'Antiquité au XXIème siècle*. Montigny-le-Bretonneux, France: Yvelinédition, 2005.

Korkut, Cevat. *Belgelerle İzmir Rıhtım İmtiyazı: Örnek bir Yap-İşlet-Devret Modeli*. Izmir: Dağaşan Ofset, 1992.

Kostof, Spiro. *The City Assembled: The Elements of Urban Form through History*. Boston: Little, Brown, 1992.

Kupferschmidt, Uri M. *European Department Stores and Middle Eastern Consumers: The Orosdi-Back Saga*. Istanbul: Ottoman Bank Archive and Research Centre, 2007.

———. "Who Needed Department Stores in Egypt? From Orosdi-Back to Omar Effendi." *Middle Eastern Studies* 43, no. 2 (March 2007): 175–92.

Kurdakul, Necdet. *Tanzimat Dönemi Basınında Sosyo-Ekonomik Fikir Hareketleri*. Ankara: T. C. Kültür Bakanlığı, 1998.

Kurmuş, Orhan. *Emperyalizm'in Türkiye'ye Girişi*. Istanbul: Bilim Yayınları, 1974.

Kütükoğlu, Mübahat. "İzmir Rıhtımı İnşaatı ve İşletme İmtiyazı." *Tarih Dergisi* 32 (March 1979): 495–553.

———. "İzmir Şehri Nüfüsu Üzerine Bazı Tesbitler." In *İzmir Tarihinden Kesitler*, 11–33. Izmir: İzmir Büyükşehir Belediyesi Kültür Yayını, 2000.

———. "İzmir Temettü Sayımları ve Yabancı Tebaa," *Belleten* 63, no. 238 (1999): 755–82.

———. "The Ottoman-British Commercial Treaty of 1838." In *Four Centuries of Turco-British Relations: Studies in Diplomatic, Economic and Cultural Affairs*, edited by William M. Hale and Ali Ihsan Bağış, 53–61. North Humberside: Eothen Press, 1984.

Kymlicka, Will. *Multicultural Citizenship: A Liberal Theory of Minority Rights*. Oxford: Clarendon Press; New York: Oxford University Press, 1995.

Lafi, Nora. *Une ville du Maghreb entre ancien régime et réformes ottomanes: genèse des institutions municipales à Tripoli de Barbarie, 1795–1911*. Paris: L'Harmattan; Tunis: Institut de recherche sur le Maghreb contemporain, 2002.

Lagarde, L. "Note sur les journaux français de Smyrne à l'époque de Mahmoud II." *Journal Asiatique* 238 (1950): 103–44.

Langhorne, Richard. "History and Evolution of Diplomacy." In *Modern Diplomacy*, edited by Jovan Kurbalija, 147–62. Malta: University of Malta, 1998.

Launay, Louis de. *La Turquie que l'on voit*. Paris: Hachette, 1913.

Lefebvre, Henri. *Le droit à la ville*. Paris: Anthropos, 1968.

———. *The Production of Space*. Oxford: Blackwell, 1991.

———. *Writings on Cities*. Edited by Eleonore Kofman and Elizabeth Lebas. Oxford: Blackwell, 1996.

Lewis, Bernard. *The Emergence of Modern Turkey*. New York: Oxford University Press, 1961.

Lieberman, Victor B., ed. *Beyond Binary Histories: Re-imagining Eurasia to c.1830*. Ann Arbor: University of Michigan Press, 1999.

Liebesny, Herbert J. "Comparative Legal History: Its Role in the Analysis of Islamic and Modern Near Eastern Legal Institutions." *American Journal of Comparative Law* 20, no. 1 (Winter 1972): 38–52.

———. *The Law of the Near and Middle East: Readings, Cases, & Materials.* Albany: State University of New York Press, 1975.

Littre, E. "Auguste Comte a Smyrne." *La Philosophie positive* 22–23 (1879): 313.

Lorenz, Daniel Edward. *The Mediterranean Traveller.* New York: F. H. Revell, 1905.

Low, Setha M. *On the Plaza: The Politics of Public Space and Culture.* Austin: University of Texas Press, 2000.

Lowry, Heath W. "Turkish History: On Whose Sources Will It Be Based? A Case Study on the Burning of Izmir." *Osmanlı Araştırmaları* 9 (1988): 1–29.

MacFarlane, Charles. *Constantinople et la Turquie en 1828.* Trans. A. F. Nettement. Vol. 1. Paris: Moutardier, 1829.

———. *Constantinople in 1828.* London: Saunders & Otley, 1829.

———. *Turkey and Its Destiny.* Philadelphia: Lea & Blanchard, 1850.

Ma'oz, Moshe. *Ottoman Reform in Syria and Palestine, 1840–1861: The Impact of the Tanzimat on Politics and Society.* Oxford: Clarendon Press, 1968.

Mantran, Robert. *Istanbul dans la seconde moitié du XVIIe siècle: Essai d'histoire institutionnelle, économique et sociale.* Paris: A. Maisonneuve, 1962.

Marcus, Abraham. *The Middle East on the Eve of Modernity: Aleppo in the Eighteenth Century.* New York: Columbia University Press, 1989.

Marcus, Alan. *Plague of Strangers: Social Groups and the Origins of City Services in Cincinnati, 1819–1870.* Columbus: Ohio State University Press, 1991.

Martal, Abdullah. *Değişim Sürecinde İzmir'de Sanayileşme: 19. yüzyıl.* Izmir: Dokuz Eylül Yayınları, 1999.

Massey, Doreen. *Space, Place, and Gender.* Minneapolis: University of Minnesota Press, 1994.

Masters, Bruce. "The Sultan's Entrepreneurs: The Avrupa Tuccaris and the Hayriye Tuccaris in Syria." *International Journal of Middle East Studies* 24, no. 4 (1992): 579–97.

Mazower, Mark. *Salonica, City of Ghosts: Christians, Muslims, and Jews, 1430–1950.* New York: Knopf, 2005.

McCoan, James Carlile. *Our New Protectorate: Turkey in Asia; Its Geography, Races, Resources, and Government.* London: Chapman & Hall, 1879.

McGowan, Bruce. "The Age of the Ayans, 1699–1812." In *An Economic and Social History of the Ottoman Empire,* edited by Halil Inalcik and Donald Quataert, 2:637–758. Cambridge: Cambridge University Press, 1997.

Meier, Astrid. "Wakf." In *The Encyclopaedia of Islam, Second Edition,* edited by P. Bearman, Th. Bianquis, C. E. Bosworth, E. van Donzel, and W. P. Heinrichs. Online edition. Leiden, The Netherlands: Brill, 2002.

Meller, Helen. *European Cities 1890–1930s: History, Culture & the Built Environment.* Chichester, England: Wiley, 2001.

Melosi, Martin V. *The Sanitary City: Environmental Services in Urban America from Colonial Times to the Present.* Pittsburgh: University of Pittsburgh Press, 2008.

Merry, Sally Engle. "Legal Pluralism." *Law & Society* 22, no. 5 (1998): 869–96.

Michael, G. N., and Engin Berber. *İzmir 1920: Yunanistan Rehberinden İşgal Altındaki bir Kentin Öyküsü*. Izmir: Akademi Kitabevi, 1998.

Michaud, Joseph-François, and Baptistin Poujoulat. *Correspondance d'Orient, 1830–1831*. Vol. 1. Paris: Ducollet, 1833.

Michelsen, Edward Henry. *The Ottoman Empire and Its Resources*. London: W. Spooner, 1854.

Micklewright, Nancy. "London, Paris, Istanbul, and Cairo: Fashion and International Trade in the Nineteenth Century." *New Perspectives on Turkey* 7 (1992): 127–36.

Midhat, Ali Haydar. *Midhat-Pacha: sa vie, son oeuvre*. Paris: Stock, 1908.

Miller, Ruth A. "Apostates and Bandits: Religious and Secular Interaction in the Administration of Late Ottoman Criminal Law." *Studia Islamica* 97 (2003): 155–78.

Milton, Giles. *Paradise Lost: Smyrna, 1922; The Destruction of a Christian City in the Islamic World*. New York: Basic Books, 2008.

Missir Reggio Mamachi di Lusignano, Livio. *Épitaphier des grandes familles latines de Smyrne*. Brussels: Livio Missir, 1885.

Mitchell, Timothy, ed. *Questions of Modernity*. Minneapolis: University of Minnesota Press, 2000.

Moehring, Eugene P. *Public Works and the Patterns of Urban Real Estate Growth in Manhattan, 1835–1894*. New York: Arno Press, 1981.

Moralı, Nail. *Mütarekede Izmir: Önceleri ve Sonraları*. Istanbul: Tekin Yayınevi, 1976.

Morton, Graeme, R. J. Morris, and B. M. A. de Vries, eds. *Civil Society, Associations, and Urban Places: Class, Nation and Culture in Nineteenth-Century Europe*. Aldershot, England: Ashgate, 2006.

Muir, Edward. *Civic Ritual in Renaissance Venice*. Princeton, N.J.: Princeton University Press, 1981.

Mundy, Martha, and Richard Saumarez Smith, eds. *Governing Property, Making the Modern State: Law, Administration and Production in Ottoman Syria*. London: I. B. Tauris, 2007.

Murray, Hugh. *Historical Account of Discoveries and Travels in Asia*. Edinburgh: A. Constable, 1820.

Murray, Hugh, William Wallace, Robert Jameson, Sir William Jackson Hooker, William Swainson, and Thomas Gamaliel Bradford. *The Encyclopædia of Geography*. Philadelphia: Lea & Blanchard, 1839.

Murray's Hand-book for Travellers in the Ionian Islands, Greece, Turkey, Asia Minor, and Constantinople. London: John Murray, 1845.

Murray's Handbook for Travellers in Turkey in Asia including Constantinople, the Bosphorus, Plain of Troy, Siales of Cyprus, Rhodes, &c., Smyrna, Ephesus, and the Routes to Persia, Bagdad, Mosool, &c. London: John Murray, 1878.

Nahum, Henri. *Juifs de Smyrne: XIXᵉ–XXᵉ siècle*. Paris: Aubier, 1997.

Nasr, Joseph, and Mercedes Volait, eds. *Urbanism: Imported or Exported? Native Aspirations and Foreign Plans*. London: Academy Editions, 2003.

Necipoğlu, Gülru. *Architecture, Ceremonial, and Power: The Topkapi Palace in the Fifteenth and Sixteenth Centuries*. New York: Architectural History Foundation, 1991.

Neff, Thomas. "The Ottoman Empire and Europe." In *The Expansion of International Society*, edited by Hedley Bull and Adam Watson, 143–69. Oxford: Oxford University Press, 1984.

Newton, Charles Thomas, and Sir Dominic Ellis Colnaghi. *Travels & Discoveries in the Levant*. London: Day & Son, 1865.

Neyzi, Leyla. "Remembering Smyrna/Izmir: Shared History, Shared Trauma." *History and Memory* 20, no. 2 (Fall/Winter 2008): 106–27.

Nezih, Raif. *İzmir Tarihi*. Izmir: Bilgi Matbaası, 1927.

Nicol, Martha. *Ismeer, or Smyrna, and Its British Hospital in 1855*. London: James Madden, 1856.

Noradounghian, Gabriel Effendi. *Recueil d'actes internationaux de l'empire ottoman: Traités, conventions, arrangements, déclarations, protocoles, procès-verbaux, firmans, bérats, lettres patentes et autres documents relatifs au droit public extérieur de la Turquie*. 4 vols. Paris: F. Pichon, 1897.

Oberling, Pierre. "The Quays of Izmir." In *L'empire ottoman, la République de Turquie et la France*, edited by Hâmit Batu, Bacqué-Grammont, and Pierre Oberling, 315–25. Istanbul: Isis Press; Paris: Éditions d'Amérique et d'Orient, 1986.

Œconomos, Lysimachos. *The Martyrdom of Smyrna and Eastern Christendom; a File of Overwhelming Evidence, Denouncing the Misdeeds of the Turks in Asia Minor and Showing Their Responsibility for the Horrors of Smyrna*. London: G. Allen & Unwin, 1922.

Ogborn, Miles. *Spaces of Modernity: London's Geographies, 1680–1780*. New York: Guilford Press, 1998.

Oikonomos, Konstantinos. *Étude sur Smyrne*. Translated by Bonaventure F. Slaars. Smyrna: Imprimerie B. Tatikian, 1868.

Okurer, Mehmet. *İzmir: Kuruluştan Kurtuluşa*. Izmir: Ticaret Matbaacılık, 1970.

Ölçer, Nazan. *Images d'empire: Aux origines de la photographie en Turquie = Türkiye'de Fotoğrafın Öncüleri*. Istanbul: Institut d'études françaises d'Istanbul, 1993.

Olsen, Donald J. *The City as a Work of Art: London, Paris, Vienna*. New Haven, Conn.: Yale University Press, 1986.

Orhonlu, Cengiz. *Osmanlı İmparatorluğunda Şehircilik ve Ulaşım Üzerine Araştırmalar: Şehir Mimarları, Kaldırımcılık, Köprücülük, Su-Yolculuk, Kayıkçılık, Gemicilik, Nehir Nakliyatı, Kervan, Kervan Yolları*. Izmir: Ticaret Matbaacılık, 1984.

Örs, Ilay. "Beyond the Greek and Turkish Dichotomy: The Rum Polities of Istanbul and Athens." *South European Society & Politics* 11, no. 1 (2006): 79–94.

Ortaylı, İlber. *Hukuk ve İdare Adamı Olarak Osmanlı Devletinde Kadı*. Ankara: Turhan Kitabevi, 1994.

———. *Tanzimat'tan Cumhuriyet'e Yerel Yönetim Geleneği*. Istanbul: Hil Yayın, 1985.

———. *Tanzimattan Sonra Mahalli İdareler*. Ankara: Türkiye ve Orta Doğu Amme İdaresi Enstitüsü, 1974.

Owen, Roger. *The Middle East in the World Economy, 1800–1914*. London: Methuen, 1981.

Ozouf, Mona. *Festivals and the French Revolution*. Cambridge: Harvard University Press, 1988.

Öztürk, Osman. *Osmanlı Hukuk Tarihinde Mecelle*. Istanbul: İrfan Matbaası, 1973.

Padel, Wilhelm, and Louis Steeg. *De la législation foncière ottomane*. Paris: A. Pedone, 1904.

Painter, Joe, and Chris Philo, "Spaces of Citizenship: An Introduction," *Political Geography* 14 (1995): 107–20.

Pamuk, Şevket. *The Ottoman Empire and European Capitalism, 1820–1913: Trade, Investment, and Production*. Cambridge: Cambridge University Press, 1987.

Pantazopoulos, Nikolaos. *Church and Law in the Balkan Peninsula during the Ottoman Rule.* Thessaloniki, Greece: Institute for Balkan Studies, 1967.

Panzac, Daniel. *La peste dans l'empire ottoman, 1700–1850.* Collection Turcica. Leuven, Belgium: Peeters, 1985.

———. *Quarantaines et lazarets: L'Europe et la peste d'Orient, XVIIème–XXème siècles.* Aix-en-Provence, France: Edisud, 1986.

Papoutsy, Christos. *Ships of Mercy: The True Story of the Rescue of the Greeks; Smyrna, September 1922.* Portsmouth: Peter E. Randall, 2008.

Paul, Darel. "Sovereignty, Survival and the Westphalian Blind Alley in International Relations." *Review of International Studies* 25, no. 2 (1999): 217–31.

Peirce, Leslie P. *Morality Tales: Law and Gender in the Ottoman Court of Aintab.* Berkeley: University of California Press, 2003.

Pélissié du Rausas, G. *Le régime des capitulations dans l'empire ottoman.* 2 vols. Paris: A. Rousseau, 1902.

Penny Cyclopaedia of the Society for the Diffusion of Useful Knowledge. London: Charles Knight, 1841.

Peri, Oded. *Christianity under Islam in Jerusalem.* Leiden, The Netherlands: Brill, 2001.

Peterson, Jon A. *The Birth of City Planning in the United States, 1840–1917.* Baltimore: Johns Hopkins University Press, 2003.

Pierre (Abbé). *Constantinople, Jérusalem et Rome.* Paris: Michel Lévy, 1860.

Piolet, Jean-Baptiste, ed. *Les missions catholiques françaises au XIXe siècle.* Vol. 1. Paris: Librairie Armand Colin, 1901.

Playfair, Robert Lambert. *Handbook to the Mediterranean: Its Cities, Coasts, and Islands.* London: John Murray, 1882.

Politis, Kosmas. *Yitik Kentin Kırk Yılı: İzmir'in Hacı Frangu Semtinden.* Translated by Osman Bleda. Istanbul: Belge Yayıncılık, 1994.

Pottage, Alain, and Martha Mundy, eds. *Law, Anthropology, and the Constitution of the Social: Making Persons and Things.* Cambridge: Cambridge University Press, 2004.

Prakash, Gyan, and Kevin M. Kruse, eds. *The Spaces of the Modern City: Imaginaries, Politics, and Everyday Life.* Princeton, N.J.: Princeton University Press, 2008.

Pred, Allan. *Lost Words and Lost Worlds: Modernity and the Language of Everyday Life in Late Nineteenth-Century Stockholm.* Cambridge: Cambridge University Press, 1990.

———. *Making Histories and Constructing Human Geographies: The Local Transformation of Practice, Power Relations, and Consciousness.* Boulder, Colo.: Westview Press, 1990.

Purcell, Mark. "Citizenship and the Right to the Global City: Reimagining the Capitalist World Order." *International Journal of Urban and Regional Research* 27, no. 3 (2003): 564–90.

Qattan, Najwa, al-. "Dhimmis in the Muslim Court: Documenting Justice in Ottoman Damascus, 1775–1860." PhD diss., Harvard University, 1996.

Quataert, Donald, ed. *Consumption Studies and the History of the Ottoman Empire, 1550–1922: An Introduction.* Albany: State University of New York Press, 2000.

Quataert, Donald. "The Age of Reforms, 1812–1914." In *An Economic and Social History of the Ottoman Empire,* edited by Halil Inalcik and Donald Quataert, 2:759–946. Cambridge: Cambridge University Press, 1997.

———. *The Ottoman Empire, 1700–1922*. Cambridge: Cambridge University Press, 2000.

Rabinow, Paul. *French Modern: Norms and Forms of the Social Environment*. Cambridge, Mass.: MIT Press, 1989.

Rafeq, Abdul-Karim. "Ownership of Real Property by Foreigners in Syria." In *New Perspectives on Property and Land in the Middle East*, edited by Roger Owen, 175–239. Cambridge, Mass.: Harvard University Press, 2000.

Reclus, Elisée. *Nouvelle géographie universelle: La terre et les hommes*. Vol. 9. Paris: Hachette, 1884.

Reilly, James A. "Status Groups and Propertyholding in the Damascus Hinterland, 1828–1880." *International Journal of Middle East Studies* 21, no. 4 (1989): 517–39.

Reimer, Michael J. "Becoming Urban: Town Administrations in Transjordan." *International Journal of Middle East Studies* 37, no. 2 (2005): 189–211.

———. *Colonial Bridgehead: Government and Society in Alexandria, 1807–1882*. Boulder, Colo.: Westview Press, 1997.

———. "Ottoman-Arab Seaports in the Nineteenth Century: Social Change in Alexandria, Beirut and Tunis." In *Cities in the World-System*, 135–56. New York: Greenwood Press, 1991.

Renan, Ernest. *Qu'est-ce qu'une nation? = What Is a Nation?* Toronto: Tapir Press, 1996.

Rey, Francis. *De la protection diplomatique et consulaire dans les échelles du Levant et de Barbarie*. 2 vols. Paris: L. Larose, 1899.

Ripley, George, and Charles Anderson Dana. *The American Cyclopaedia*. New York: D. Appleton, 1876.

Rogan, Eugene L. *Frontiers of the State in the Late Ottoman Empire: Transjordan, 1850–1921*. Cambridge: Cambridge University Press, 1999.

———, ed. *Outside In on the Margins of the Modern Middle East*. London: I. B. Tauris, 2002.

Rolland, Charles. *La Turquie contemporaine*. Paris: Pagnerre, 1854.

Rolleston, George. *Report on Smyrna*. London: G. E. Eyre & W. Spottiswoode, 1856.

Roman d'Amat, ed. *Dictionnaire de biographie française*. Vol. 12. Paris: Letouzey et Ané, 1970.

Rosenthal, Steven T. *The Politics of Dependency: Urban Reform in Istanbul*. Westport, Conn.: Greenwood Press, 1980.

Roth, Ralf, and Marie-Noëlle Polino, eds. *The City and the Railway in Europe*. Aldershot, England: Ashgate, 2003.

Rougon, Firmin. *Smyrne: Situation commerciale et économique*. Paris: Berger-Levrault, 1892.

Rouveroy van Nieuwaal, E. Adriaan B. van, and Werner Zips, eds. *Sovereignty, Legitimacy, and Power in West African Societies: Perspectives from Legal Anthropology*. Hamburg: LIT, 1998.

Rubin, Avi. "Legal Borrowing and Its Impact on Ottoman Legal Culture in the Late Nineteenth Century." *Continuity and Change* 22, no. 2 (2007): 279–303.

———. "Ottoman Modernity: The Nizamiye Courts in the Late Nineteenth Century." PhD diss., Harvard University, 2006.

Rubin, Miri. *Corpus Christi: The Eucharist in Late Medieval Culture*. Cambridge: Cambridge University Press, 1991.

Ruggie, John Gerard. "Territoriality and Beyond: Problematizing Modernity." *International Organization* 47, no. 1 (Winter 1993): 139–74.

Ryan, Mary. "The American Parade: Representations of the Nineteenth-Century Social Order." In *The New Cultural History: Essays*, edited by Aletta Biersack and Lynn A. Hunt, 131–53. Berkeley: University of California Press, 1989.

Sakayan, Dora. *An Armenian Doctor in Turkey*. Montreal: Arod Books, 1997.

Salvatore, Armando, and Dale F. Eickelman, eds. *Public Islam and the Common Good*. Leiden, The Netherlands: Brill, 2004.

Salzmann, Ariel. "Citizens in Search of a State: The Limits of Political Participation in the Late Ottoman Empire." In *Extending Citizenship, Reconfiguring States*, edited by Michael P. Hanagan and Charles Tilly, 37–66. Lanham, Md.: Rowman & Littlefield, 1999.

San Lorenzo, Jean-Baptiste. *Saint Polycarpe et son tombeau: Notice historique sur la ville de Smyrne*. Constantinople: F. Loeffler, 1911.

Sanders, Paula. *Ritual, Politics, and the City in Fatimid Cairo*. Albany: State University of New York Press, 1994.

Schacht, Joseph. *An Introduction to Islamic Law*. Oxford: Clarendon Press, 1964.

Scherzer, Karl von. *La province de Smyrne, considérée au point de vue géographique, économique et intellectuel*. Vienna: Alfred Hölder, 1873.

Schickler, Baron F. de. *En Orient: Souvenirs de voyage, 1858–1861*. Paris: Michel-Lévy frères, 1863.

Schlicht, Alfred. *Frankreich und die Syrischen Christen, 1799–1861: Minoritäten und Europäischer imperialismus im Vorderen Orient*. Berlin: K. Schwarz, 1981.

Schmidt, Jan. *From Anatolia to Indonesia: Opium Trade and the Dutch Community of Izmir, 1820–1940*. Istanbul: Nederlands Historisch-Archaeologisch Instituut; Leiden: Nederlands Instituut voor het Nabije Oosten, 1998.

Schmitt, Oliver Jens. *Les Levantins: Cadres de vie et identités d'un groupe ethno-confessionnel de l'empire ottoman au "long" 19ème siècle*. Istanbul: Isis Press, 2007.

Schopoff, A. *Les réformes et la protection des chrétiens en Turquie, 1673–1904: Firmans, bérats, protocoles, traités, capitulations, conventions, arrangements, notes, circulaires, règlements, lois, mémorandums, etc.* Paris: Plon-Nourrit, 1904.

Schroeder, Paul W. "Bruck versus Buol: The Dispute over Austrian Eastern Policy, 1853–1855." *Journal of Modern History* 40, no. 2 (1968): 193–217.

Scobey, David M. "Anatomy of the Promenade: The Politics of Bourgeois Sociability in Nineteenth-Century New York." *Social History* 17, no. 2 (1992): 203–27.

———. *Empire City: The Making and Meaning of the New York City Landscape*. Philadelphia: Temple University Press, 2002.

Scott, James C. *Seeing Like a State: How Certain Schemes to Improve the Human Condition Have Failed*. New Haven, Conn.: Yale University Press, 1998.

Scott, James C., John Tehranian, and Jeremy Mathias. "The Production of Legal Identities Proper to States: The Case of the Permanent Family Surname." *Comparative Studies in Society and History* 44, no. 1 (January 2002): 4–44.

Scriver, Peter, and Prakash Vikramaditya, eds. *Colonial Modernities: Building, Dwelling and Architecture in British India and Ceylon*. London: Routledge, 2007.

Şener, Abdüllatif. *Tanzimat Dönemi Osmanlı Vergi Sistemi*. Istanbul: İşaret, 1990.

Sennett, Richard. *The Fall of Public Man.* New York: Vintage, 1978.
Serçe, Erkan, ed. *İzmir ve Çevresi Resmi, Özel Binalar İstatistiği 1918.* Izmir: Akademi Kitabevi, 1998.
———. *Tanzimat'tan Cumhuriyet'e İzmir'de Belediye, 1868-1945.* Izmir: Dokuz Eylül Yayınları, 1998.
Sevinçli, Efdal. *İzmir'de Tiyatro.* Izmir: Ege Yayıncılık, 1994.
Simmonds, P. L. "Statistics of Newspapers in Various Countries." *Journal of the Royal Statistical Society* 4 (1841): 111-36.
Sluglett, Peter, ed. *The Urban Social History of the Middle East, 1750-1950.* Syracuse, N.Y.: Syracuse University Press, 2008.
Slyomovics, Susan. "New York City's Muslim World Day Parade." In *Nation and Migration: The Politics of Space in the South Asian Diaspora,* edited by Peter van der Veer, 157-76. Philadelphia: University of Philadelphia Press, 1995.
Smith, Anthony D. *The Ethnic Origins of Nations.* Oxford: Blackwell, 1987.
Smyrnelis, Marie-Carmen. "Colonies europénnes et communautés ethnico-confessionnelles à Smyrne, coexistence et réseaux de sociabilité (fin du XVIIIe–milieu du XIXe siecle)." In *Vivre dans l'empire ottoman: sociabilités et relations intercommunautaires (XVIIIe–XXe siècles),* edited by François Georgeon, Paul Dumont, and Meropi Anastassiadou, 173-94. Paris: L'Harmattan, 1997.
———, ed. *Smyrne, la ville oubliée? Mémoires d'un grand port Ottoman, 1830-1930.* Paris: Autrement, 2006.
———. *Une société hors de soi: identités et relations sociales à Smyrne au XVIIIème et XIXème siècles.* Paris: Peeters, 2005.
———. *Une ville ottomane plurielle: Smyrne aux XVIIIème et XIXème siècles.* Istanbul: Isis Press, 2006.
Soja, Edward W. *Postmodern Geographies: The Reassertion of Space in Critical Social Theory.* London: Verso, 1989.
Solomonides, Christos. *To Theatro ste Smyrne, 1657-1922.* Athens: Typ. Ar. Mauride, 1954.
Sonyel, Salahi. *Minorities and the Destruction of the Ottoman Empire.* Ankara: Turkish Historical Society Printing House, 1993.
———. "The Protégé System in the Ottoman Empire." *Journal of Islamic Studies* 2, no. 1 (1991): 56-66.
Spencer, Edmund. *Travels in European Turkey, in 1850.* London: Colburn, 1851.
Staeheli, Lynn. "Cities and Citizenship." *Urban Geography* 24, no. 2 (2003): 97-102.
Stamatopoulou-Vasilakou, Chrysothemis. "Greek Theater in Southeastern Europe and the Eastern Mediterranean from 1810 to 1961." *Journal of Modern Greek Studies* 25, no. 2 (2007): 267-84.
Steen de Jehay, Frédéric Marie Joseph Ghislain van. *De la situation légale des sujets ottomans non-musulmans.* Brussels: O. Schepens, 1906.
Stephens, John Lloyd. *Incidents of Travel in Greece, Turkey, Russia and Poland, by the Author of "Incidents of Travel in Egypt, Arabia Petræa, and the Holy Land."* London: Wiley and Putnam, 1838.
Stillman, Norman A. *The Jews of Arab Lands: A History and Source Book.* Philadelphia: Jewish Publication Society of America, 1979.

Susa, Nasim. *The Capitulatory Régime of Turkey, Its History, Origin, and Nature.* Baltimore: Johns Hopkins University Press, 1933.

Tamanaha, Brian Z. "Understanding Legal Pluralism: Past to Present, Local to Global." *Sydney Law Review* 30 (2008): 375.

Taylor, Dorceta E. *The Environment and the People in American Cities, 1600-1900s: Disorder, Inequality, and Social Change.* Durham: Duke University Press, 2009.

Tekeli, İlhan. "Nineteenth-Century Transformation of Istanbul Metropolitan Area." In *Villes ottomanes à la fin de l'empire,* edited by Paul Dumont and François Georgeon, 33-45. Paris: L'Harmattan, 1992.

Ter Minassian, Anahide. "Les Arméniens: Le dynamisme d'une petite communauté." In *Smyrne, la ville oubliée? Mémoires d'un grand port Ottoman, 1830-1930,* edited by Marie-Carmen Smyrnelis, 79-91. Paris: Autrement, 2006.

Terzioğlu, Derin. "The Imperial Circumcision Festival of 1582: An Interpretation." *Muqarnas* 12 (1995): 84-100.

Testa, Carlos, and Adolphe Boutiron. *Le droit public international maritime: Principes généraux, règles pratiques.* Paris: G. Pedone-Lauriel, 1886.

Testa, Ignaz, Alfred Testa, and Leopold Testa. *Recueil des traités de la Porte ottomane avec les puissances étrangères, depuis le premier traité conclu en 1536, entre Suléyman I et François I jusqu'à nos jours.* 11 vols. Paris: Ernest Leroux, 1864.

Texier, Charles. *Asie mineure.* Paris: Firmin Didot, 1882.

Thobie, Jacques. *Intérêts et impérialisme français dans l'empire ottoman: 1895-1914.* Paris: Imprimerie nationale, 1977.

Todorova, Maria. "The Ottoman Legacy in the Balkans." In *Imperial Legacy: The Ottoman Imprint on the Balkans and the Middle East,* edited by L. Carl Brown, 45-77. New York: Columbia University Press, 1996.

Tournefort, Joseph Pitton de. *Relation d'un voyage du Levant, fait par ordre du roy: contenant l'histoire ancienne & moderne de plusieurs isles de l'archipel, de Constantinople, des cotes de la Mer Noire, de l'Armenie, de la Georgie, des frontieres de Perse & de l'Asie Mineure . . .* Vol. 2. Lyon: Chez Freres Bruysel, 1727.

Tümerkan, Sıddık. *Türkiye'de Belediyeler: Tarihi Gelişim ve Bugünkü Durum.* Istanbul. R. Zelliç Basımevi, 1946.

"Turquie: Incendie de Smyrne." In *Annuaire historique universel, ou, Histoire politique,* edited by Armand Fouquier and Charles-Louis Lesur, 153-54. Paris: A. Thoisnier-Desplaces, 1847.

Tute, Richard Clifford. *The Ottoman Land Laws, with a Commentary on the Ottoman Land Code of 7th Ramadan 1274.* Jerusalem: Greek Convent Press, 1927.

Ubicini, Abdolonyme. *Letters on Turkey.* Translated by Lady Easthope. New York: Arno Press, 1973.

———. *La Turquie actuelle.* Paris: L. Hachette, 1855.

Üç İzmir. Istanbul: Yapı Kredi Yayınları, 1992.

Ülker, Necmi. *XVII. ve XVIII. Yüzyıllarda Izmir Şehri Tarihi.* Izmir: Akademi Kitabevi, 1994.

———. "İzmir Sarıkışlanın Yapım Çalışmaları." In *X. Türk Tarih Kongresi, Ankara: 22-26 Eylül 1986; Kongreye Sunulan Bildiriler,* 2438-46, pls. 573-75. Ankara: Türk Tarih Kurumu Basımevi, 1994.

Umar, Bilge. *İzmir'de Yunanlıların Son Günleri*. Ankara: Bilgi Yayınevi, 1974.

Upton, Dell. "Another City: The Urban Cultural Landscape in the Early Republic." In *Everyday Life in the Early Republic, 1789-1828*, edited by Catherine E. Hutchins, 61-117. Winterthur, Del.: Winterthur Museum, 1994.

———. *Another City: Urban Life and Urban Spaces in the New American Republic*. New Haven, Conn.: Yale University Press, 2008.

———. "The City as Material Culture." In *The Art and Mystery of Historical Archaeology: Essays in Honor of James Deetz*, edited by Anne E. Yentsch and Mary C. Beaudry, 51-74. Boca Raton, Fla.: CRC Press, 1992.

———. "New Orleans: The Master of the World—the Levee." In *Streets: Critical Perspectives on Public Space*, edited by Zeynep Çelik, Diane G. Favro, and Richard Ingersoll, 277-86. Berkeley: University of California Press, 1994.

———. "Starting from Baalbek: Noah, Solomon, Saladin, and the Fluidity of Architectural History." *Journal of the Society of Architectural Historians* 68, no. 4 (2009): 457-65.

Vale, Lawrence J. *Architecture, Power, and National Identity*. New Haven, Conn.: Yale University Press, 1992.

Valon, Alexis de. "La Turquie sous Abdul-Medjid." *Revue des deux mondes* 6 (1844): 481-515.

Valon, Charles Marie Ferdinand Alexis (vicomte de). *Une année dans le Levant*. Paris: Jules Labitte, 1846.

Van den Boogert, Maurits H. *The Capitulations and the Ottoman Legal System: Qadis, Consuls, and Berats in the 18th Century*. Leiden, The Netherlands: Brill, 2005.

Van Dyck, Edward A. *Report on the Capitulations of the Ottoman Empire*. Washington, D.C.: Government Printing Office, 1881.

Waldstreicher, David. "Rites of Rebellion, Rites of Assent: Celebrations, Print Culture, and the Origins of American Nationalism." *Journal of American History* 82, no. 1 (June 1995): 37-61.

Walker, Thomas Alfred. *A Manual of Public International Law*. Cambridge: Cambridge University Press, 1895.

Warner, Michael. "The Mass Public and the Mass Subject." In *Habermas and the Public Sphere*, edited by Craig J. Calhoun, 377-401. Cambridge, Mass.: MIT Press, 1992.

Warner, Sam Bass. *The Private City: Philadelphia in Three Periods of Its Growth*. Philadelphia: University of Pennsylvania Press, 1987.

Watenpaugh, Keith David. *Being Modern in the Middle East: Revolution, Nationalism, Colonialism, and the Arab Middle Class*. Princeton, N.J.: Princeton University Press, 2006.

Weber, Stefan. *Damascus: Ottoman Modernity and Urban Transformation (1808-1918)*. 2 vols. Aarhus, Denmark: Aarhus University Press, 2009.

Weintraub, Jeff. "The Theory and Politics of the Public/Private Distinction." In *Public and Private in Thought and Practice: Perspectives on a Grand Dichotomy*, edited by Krishan Kumar and Jeff Alan Weintraub, 1-42. Chicago: University of Chicago Press, 1997.

Werry, Francis Peter. *Personal Memoirs and Letters of Francis Peter Werry, Edited by His Daughter (E. F. Werry)*. London: Charles J. Skeet, 1861.

Wilson, Elizabeth. *The Sphinx in the City: Urban Life, the Control of Disorder, and Women*. Berkeley: University of California Press, 1992.

Wilson, Sir Charles William, ed. *Handbook for Travellers in Asia Minor, Transcaucasia, Persia, etc.* London: John Murray, 1895.

Wilson, William H. *The City Beautiful Movement.* Baltimore: Johns Hopkins University Press, 1994.

Wood, Alfred Cecil. *A History of the Levant Company.* Oxford: Oxford University Press, 1935.

Wright, Gwendolyn. *The Politics of Design in French Colonial Urbanism.* Chicago: University of Chicago Press, 1991.

Yeoh, Brenda S. A. *Contesting Space: Power Relations and the Urban Built Environment in Colonial Singapore.* Oxford: Oxford University Press, 1996.

Yerasimos, Stéphane. "À propos des réformes urbaines des Tanzimat." In *Villes ottomanes à la fin de l'empire,* edited by Paul Dumont and François Georgeon, 17–32. Paris: L'Harmattan, 1992.

———. "Quelques éléments sur l'ingénieur Luigi Storari." In *Convegno "Architettura e architetti Italiani ad Istanbul tra il XIX e il XX secolo,"* 117–23. Istanbul: Istituto Italiano di Cultura, 1995.

———. "Tanzimat'ın Kent Reformları Üzerine." In *Modernleşme Sürecinde Osmanlı Kentleri,* edited by Paul Dumont and François Georgeon, 1–18. Istanbul: Tarih Vakfı Yurt Yayınları, 1999.

Yerolympos, Alexandra. *Urban Transformations in the Balkans (1820–1920): Aspects of Balkan Town Planning and the Remaking of Thessaloniki.* Thessaloniki, Greece: University Studio Press, 1996.

Yetkin, Sabri. *Ege'de Eşkiyalar.* Istanbul: Türkiye Ekonomik ve Toplumsal Tarih Vakfı, 1996.

Young, George. *Corps de droit ottoman; recueil des codes, lois, règlements, ordonnances et actes les plus importants du droit intérieur, et d'études sur le droit coutumier de l'empire ottoman.* Oxford: Clarendon Press, 1905.

Zandi-Sayek, Sibel. "Orchestrating Difference and Performing Identity: Urban Space and Public Rituals in Nineteenth-Century Izmir." In *Hybrid Urbanism: On the Identity Discourse and the Built Environment,* edited by Nezar AlSayyad, 42–66. Westport, Conn.: Praeger, 2001.

———. "Public Space and Urban Citizens: Ottoman Izmir in the Remaking, 1840–1890." PhD diss., University of California at Berkeley, 2001.

———. "Struggles Over the Shore: Building the Quay of Izmir, 1867–1875." *City and Society* 12, no. 1 (Spring 2000): 55–78.

Zukin, Sharon. *Landscapes of Power: From Detroit to Disney World.* Berkeley: University of California Press, 1991.

———. *Naked City: The Death and Life of Authentic Urban Places.* Oxford: Oxford University Press, 2009.

Zürcher, Erik Jan. *Turkey: A Modern History.* London: I. B. Tauris, 2004.

Index

Abbott, R. B., 215n77
Abdülaziz, 174, 180, 232n75
Abdülhamid II, 182; Hamidian era, 23
Abdülmecid, xiv, 120, 180, 181, 183
Abdul Nihad Efendi, 214n70
Abro, K., 135, 216n93
Aegean Islands, 11, 85, 230n28
Aghasar, Salomon, 214n70
Ahmed Cevdet Pasha, 211n34
Ahmed Vefik Pasha, 62, 213n50
Albanians: irregulars, 112, 224n123; migrants, 85
Aleppo, 11, 213n56
Alexandria, 5, 27, 53, 220n63
Ali Nihad Efendi, 69, 190, 215n84
Aliotti, Pierre, 148, 227n39
Aliotti, Polonie, 121, 123
Âli Pasha, 63, 64, 72
Amalthea (newspaper), 206n59-60
Amie, G., 215n78
Anatolia, 9, 203n25, 230n24; markets of, 10, 14; Western, 25, 85. *See also* Asia Minor
Andria, J. G. B. d', 221n72
Anglo-Ottoman commercial treaty, 5, 24
Apano Mahalle (neighborhood), 11
Armenians, 3, 7-8, 11, 25, 44, 51, 156, 162, 202n15, 204n44; bishop, 183; of Catholic faith, 161, 228n2, 231n34; cemetery, 85; church (*see* St. Stephen); community, 160, 230n24; festival, 154; hospices, 86; Mechitarist mission, 179, 228n2; patriarch, 181; quarter, 11, 12, 78-79, 81, 82, 98, 163, 218n10-11
Asia Minor, 1, 3, 7, 9, 10, 161
Au Bon Marché. *See* dry-goods stores
Au Louvre. *See* dry-goods stores
Austria, 151, 152, 160, 168, 169, 176, 179, 194, 214n66, 230n14, 232n70; Austria-Hungary, 171, 227n52; consul, 69, 167, 169, 176, 194; consular court, 55-56; consulate, 124; display of national flag, 171, 176, 179; protégés and protection, 61, 167-68; subjects, 55
Austrian Lloyd, 124, 128
âyân, 36
Aydın (newspaper), 109, 206n59
Aydın (province), 23, 25, 28, 38, 143, 179

Bahriye Street, 17, 18-19
Balkans, 25, 85, 87, 220n57
Balladur, Don Emanuel, 230n26
Balthazar, Luc G., 206n60
banditry, 88. *See also* brigandage
bankruptcy, 54-56, 61, 64, 210n27
Bargigli, Theodore, 91, 104, 206n60

Barker, Alfred, 117, 132, 133, 135, 141, 218n26
Barker, Benjamin, 224n118
barracks, 1, 26, 122, 126, 206n62; as expression of the modern state, 35–37, 39, 156, 181, 182. *See also* Sarıkışla
Barry, Polycarpe, 216n93
basmahane. See factories: calico
Basmahane Station, 26, 30, 88, 98, 100
bathhouses, 15, 218n10
Baüm, Baron, 218n26
bayram. *See* feasts: Muslim
bazaar: Ali Pasha fountain, 15; circulation in, 93; as commercial center, 8, 12, 14, 16, 79, 104, 233n82; customs houses, 123; festivities, 181, 184; gas lighting, 88, 100; and urban growth of, 15–17, 203n28
Beirut, 5
Belhomme, J. H., 216n97
Bella Vista: square, 16, 20, 25, 31, 89, 109, 116, 118, 126, 172; street, 17
Bentivoglio, Count de, 218n26
berat, 51, 60–61. *See also* protégé: as legal status
Berio, B., 218n26
Bezm-i Âlem Valide Sultan, 120
Blunt, Charles, 208n4
boatmen, 147; Greek and Maltese, 124; strike, 148
Bonamil, Pierre Marcelin, 230n26
Bonnal, Alex, 216n97, 227n39
Borg (sanitary doctor), 147, 218n26
Boscovich, P., 227n39
boulevards, 119, 129, 226n17. *See also* quay; promenade
Boyacı Stream, 25, 205n47
Boyahane Street, 19, 205n47
Brant, James, 61
brigandage, 78, 85, 219n36. *See also* banditry
Britain (England), 8, 24, 25, 91, 171, 177, 214n66, 227n52, 232n70; cemetery, 85, 219n27; chapel, 18–19, 105, 166; consul, 61, 84, 112, 176; consular court, 54, 61, 212n39; consulate, 56, 60, 122, 124, 125; display of national flag, 177; hospital, 9, 18–19; interests, 117, 225n2; language, 132, 206n59; merchants, 3, 118, 147, 224n118, 226n15, 228n60; protégés and protection, 58, 60–62, 135, 211n38; subjects, 25, 55, 56, 61, 85, 132
Buca (suburb), xiii, 27, 32, 83, 85, 154–55, 220n45; road to, 85; suburban line to, 29
Building and Road Code, 102, 223n98
Bulow, Baron, 218n26
Burnabat (suburb), xiii, 27, 83, 155, 220n45; Bay of, 126; road to, 32; suburban line to, 30
Bursa, 11
Büyük Vezir Khan, 18–19

cadastral commission, 69–73, 92–94, 98, 113, 197, 216n93, 221n77; records, 48, 208n4, 216n90; revenues, 71; surveys, 48, 69. *See also* land: registry
cafés (coffeehouses), 1, 75, 98; in bazaar, 15; at Bella Vista, 20; Captain Paolo's, 128; chantant, 17; control of, 87, 109; on the Cordon, 29, 115, 146, 182; expropriation of, 141; at Fasula, 20, 104; feasts and, 156, 184; Kivoto, 141, 128; raised on piles, 124, 128, 141, 147; and smuggling, 127; working-class, 17, 87
Cairo, 30
Cammarano Theater, 26, 32, 166, 205n57
capitulations. *See* extraterritorial agreements
Capuchins, 167, 168, 231n35
Caravan Bridge, xii, 11, 14, 25, 26, 75, 79, 85, 86, 181; road, 35, 82, 98
Cardelli, Luigi M., 230n26
carriages: dues on, 95; traffic, 105, 107, 128, 131
Carter, Paul, 187
casinos (clubs), 1, 8, 17, 30, 32, 98, 155, 192, 205n56; Greek, 124, 128, 174; Levantine, 165, 166. *See also* Smyrna Jockey Club

castle, old crusader's, 18–19, 26, 93, 143, 205n51; on Kadifekale, 11
Catholics, 20, 61, 151–52, 160–62, 164, 166–70, 190, 228n5, 230n24–25; administration of schools and hospitals, 167, 230n34; cemetery, 85, 86; churches, 151, 171; community, 85, 152, 160, 162, 165; hospitals, 79; missions, 161, 166, 167, 180, 228n2; prestige of the church, 161, 170, 173, 179. *See also names of individual churches, hospitals, and missions*
cavass, 165, 168
cemeteries, 14, 25, 82, 85, 86
charity, 83, 120–21, 155; balls, 32
Charnaud, John, 117, 132, 135, 141
Chasseaud, J. (sanitary doctor), 218n26
Chios, 11, 30, 63, 230n29
Christian Brothers, 166; Boys' School, 18–19, 166
Christofidis (Christofidhi), J., 221n72, 227n39
Çikudya (Izmir neighborhood), 25, 26, 86
citizenship: laws, 2, 23, 43, 48; and nationality, 49, 74, 188–90, 193–94; and property rights, 46, 49, 63, 66, 72; rights and duties of, 66, 72; and taxation, 71; urban, 49–50, 74. *See also* Ottoman Nationality Law; subjecthood
Civil Code, 57, 101, 211n34, 223n96, 223n100
cizye. *See* non-Muslims: and poll tax
College of the Propaganda, 18–19, 20, 164, 166, 168, 172
Commission for the Defense of Property, 73, 210n21
Committee of Hygiene and Relief, 84, 192
Committee of Ladies, 84
committees: ad hoc, 2, 35, 70, 133; mixed, 72, 127, 148, 216n93; representation in, 189; special, 94; voluntary, 73. *See also* cadastral commission
consuls: as diplomatic agents, 11, 46, 49, 51, 62, 65, 68, 144, 162, 171, 180, 184–85; jurisdictions of, 51, 53–54, 65, 111; as urban actors, 2, 69, 71–72, 93, 111–13, 141, 143, 174, 218n26, 227n38. *See also specific countries*
Cordon, 27, 29, 115; as commercial space, 139, 140; layout of, 118; as modern urban space, 31, 116, 117, 130, 131; and official ceremonies, 181, 182, 183. *See also* waterfront
Corpus Christi procession, 151–53, 160–61, 180, 228n1; choreography, 153, 162, 164–70; path of, 166; relation to other public feasts, 170–71, 173, 175, 179
courts: consular, 47, 54, 55, 64; criminal, 6, 224n120; ecclesiastical and rabbinical, 47; jurisdictional boundaries between, 53; kadı, 44, 52–56, 58, 209n17–19, 210n26–27, 211n36, 214n67; mixed commercial, 6, 42, 43, 57; nizamiye, 56, 58, 111, 189, 214n67
Cousinéry, Ange, 135
Cousinéry, Auguste, 58, 211–12n39, 215n78. *See also* factories: silk-winding
Coya Khan, 18–19
Crimean War, 91, 178, 206n67
Cumberbatch, Robert, 84, 218n26
customs houses, 115–16, 122, 134, 139; decoration of, 233n82; Frank, 16, 17, 123; loading/unloading at, 136–37, 147, 148; Ottoman, 39, 123

Dalta, A. A., 227n39
Damascus, 210n23
Darağaç, 17
Davee, E. J., 227n39
Deaconess Institute, 18–19, 20, 166
Değirmentepe, xii, 26, 36, 40, 41, 42
D'Egremont, J. B., 218n26
Demir Khan, 18–19
Deschamps, Bouquet, 206n60
De Vries, L., 227n39
difference: constitutional, 3, 44, 47, 100, 152; cultural and linguistic, 7, 32, 159; exploiting, 7; and interdependence, 3. *See also* identity

Dilbérian, Ovannes, 225n7
Dilruba Street, 17, 18–19
diplomacy: crisis, 111, 169, 179, 194; equivalence and reciprocity, 178, 180, 184, 188–89, 232n64; tools and conduct of, 171, 174–80, 185, 194
Dominicans, 122, 228n2
dragomans, 53, 56, 60, 64, 168, 184, 191
dry-goods stores, 30; Orosdi-Back, 30, 33; P. Xenopoulo & Cie., 30, 33; Salomon Stein, 30, 34
Dussaud Brothers, 117–18, 134–35, 140–41, 143, 146–48, 146, 225n1, 227n38
Dutch community. *See* Netherlands

earthquakes, 10
easement: conflict over, 47, 58, 189; private appropriation of, 101, 109–10, 211n37; for shore access, 126, 130–31
Easter. *See* feasts: Easter
Eastern Mediterranean: port cities, 5–6, 117, 178; region, 1, 9–10. *See also* Levantine
Écho de l'Orient (newspaper), 91, 151, 169–70, 183, 205n59, 206n60
Edwards, Anthony, 73, 190, 206n60, 225n7
England. *See* Britain
English pier, 16, 17, 118, 124, 125, 166
Enriquez, Abrahamoğlu, 148
epidemics, 4, 16, 78, 113, 194, 204n42, 219n27; cholera, 81, 83–85, 138, 192; plague, 10, 24, 81, 84
Ergin, Osman Nuri, 217n7, 221n66
ethnoreligious community (millet): Armenian Catholics as, 161, 230n27; boundaries of, 156, 159, 186; constitutional status of, 43, 44, 48, 51, 202n14; crossing/delimiting the boundaries of, 2–3, 6–8, 66, 160, 181, 209n17; and identity, 6, 45, 175, 185, 186, 190; institutions of, 1, 37, 77, 155, 19; leaders of, 3, 44, 51, 60, 174, 182, 191, 192, 212n44; membership in, 64, 173, 190; and nationhood, 2, 46, 175, 185;

realignment, 161, 185, 189; relief efforts, 83; Roman Catholics as, 152, 160–61, 168, 171, 228n5, 230n29; self-definition, 152, 161, 173, 179, 185
Euterpe Theater, 18–19, 26, 32, 166
Evkaf-ı Hümayun Nezareti, 120
Evliyazade Mehmed Efendi, 148, 221n72
exiles, 69; Hungarian and Italian, 25
extraterritorial agreements (capitulations): and the Catholic Church, 151, 160; history of, 16, 51–52, 209n15–16; and legal pluralism, 47, 56, 58; negotiated nature of, 113, 188; as obstacles to Ottoman sovereignty, 49, 62–63, 65, 71, 77, 111, 127, 189, 194

factories, 11, 76; calico, 76, 82; silk-winding, 18–19, 25, 26, 58, 59, 205n49. *See also* mills
Farkoa, A., 148, 227n39
Fasula: neighborhood, 26; place, 17, 20, 25, 93, 104, 106, 107, 118, 166, 172, 204n32; street, 17, 18–19, 74
feasts: Carnival, 159; cycle of, 154, 170; Easter, 154–56, 155, 158, 159, 173–75; of foreign states, 171, 174, 178; Greek Orthodox, 154, 170; Jewish, 154, 156, 229n19; Muslim, 154, 156, 160; Ottoman imperial, 171, 180, 182, 183, 183
fires, 2, 7, 10, 26, 45, 78–79, 81, 85, 120, 192, 218n10–11; arson, 78, 218n9; rebuilding after, 23, 79, 80, 82, 93, 104, 215n84
fireworks, 156, 158, 181
firman: on construction prohibition; 109–10; on the Latin millet, 230n29; on municipal councils, 216n87; on property tax, 68, 208n5
Fisher, C., 55, 211n31
Fisher, J. K., 55
foreign powers (states), 2, 4, 49, 61, 65–68, 73, 185, 188–89, 192
foreign subjects, 3, 20, 61, 226n15; claim status of, 49, 58, 61–62, 77, 93, 127, 211n38, 212n49; disputes between, 47;

and police measures, 112; and political representation, 43, 70–72, 97–98, 190, 207n75, 221n72; population, 25, 49, 204n44, 205n45, 212n49; and property, 48, 50, 53, 64–66, 68, 72, 73, 122, 192, 207n4, 208n5, 210n21, 213n64, 214n67; right to the city, 73; status, 16, 43, 51–52, 59–60, 111. *See also* protégé

forum shopping, 58

France, 8, 24, 61, 91, 152, 166, 177, 179, 214n66, 227n52, 230n24, 232n70; commercial and penal codes, 57, 102; consul, 57, 109, 151–52, 160, 168–70, 179; consular court, 55, 212n39; consulate, 18–19, 55, 118, 122, 124, 171, 172, 177; display of national flag, 165, 171, 176–77; hospital, 18–19, 20, 25, 59, 109, 110, 126, 164; imports, 24; interests, 117, 141, 180, 225n2; language, 9, 20, 66, 69, 109, 132, 206n59, 230n24; merchants, 3, 11, 135, 169; missions, 165; orphanage, 86; protégés and protection, 61, 160, 165, 168–69, 229n6; subjects, 54, 58, 70, 205n49, 215n78, 227n39

Franciscans, 167, 168, 176, 205n49, 228n2, 231n35

Frank quarter, 11, 12, 14; Corpus Christi procession, 151; gas lighting, 100; growth and expansion, 15–17; during Muslim holidays, 160; night patrols in, 88; post-fire reconstruction, 78, 104

Frank Street, 16, 18–23, 118, 203n30; congestion of, 74, 93, 104; evolution of, 17; feasts and processions, 162, 165, 166, 169, 181–82; modern stores and clubs on, 30, 32; police stations on, 35; sewers, 142

French hospital. *See* France: hospital

frenkhane, 12, 16–17, 55

Fuad Pasha, 136

gas lighting. *See* streets: and gas lighting
gasworks, 25, 26
Geary, Grattan, 27

gedik, 68, 207n2, 207n4
Geilinger & Blum, 54–55
gendarme, 88, 112, 206n63. *See also* police
Giddens, Anthony, 154, 207n74
Gout Brothers, 226n15
governor's palace. *See* Kâtipzade (mansion); Konak
Greco-Turkish war, 7
Greece (Kingdom of), 61, 173–75, 211n39, 214n66; consul, 174–75; consulate, 171, 172; display of national flag, 174–75; language, 9, 20, 25, 109, 206n59, 230n24; national day, 174; protections, 212n38; revolutionaries, 175; subjects, 25, 62, 175, 221n72
Greek Orthodox community. *See* Orthodox Greeks
Greek War of Independence, 23
Griffith, John, 218n26
guardhouses. *See* police: stations
guards, 134, 168; consular, 59, 60, 165, 174; of honor, 151, 171
Guarracino, George, 117, 132, 135, 141
Guérin, M., 218n26
Gülhane Edict, 4, 57, 67, 152. *See also* Tanzimat reforms
Gureba-i Müslümin. *See* Ottoman state: hospital
Guys, Firmin, 54–55
Guys, Suzon (née de Hochepied), 210n28, 211n29

Hadkinson, Robert, 227n39
Haliliye Avenue, 79, 82
Halil Pasha (governor), 87, 88, 207n69
Halkapınar, xii
Hamdi Pasha (governor), 73, 143
Hanson, H. J., 218n26
harbor, inner, 12–13, 15, 17
Hatt-ı Hümayun, 4, 213n64. *See also* Tanzimat reforms
Hillereau, Julien M., 230n26
Hisar or Ok castle, 16. *See also* castle: old crusader's

Hizmet (newspaper), 100, 105, 184, 205n59, 206n60
Hobsbawm, Eric, 4, 175
Hochepied, Sara de, 55, 201n28
Honischer, John, 227n39
hospitals: burial next to, 85; communal, 1, 37, 77, 78, 155, 166, 172, 173, 206n67; destroyed in fire, 218n11. *See also specific countries and communities*
Hospital Street, 18–19, 20
hotels, 1, 17, 27, 29, 98, 184, 233n82; Kraemer Palace, 31
Hripsima v. Vapopoulo, 56, 211n32
Hunter's Club, 205n56
Hurşid Pasha (governor), 95–96

icareteyn, 120, 225n4
identity: ambiguity of, 57–61, 168, 194; and belonging, 74, 152; and the built environment, 46, 50; communal/ethnoreligious, 7, 48, 74, 119, 185, 190; and difference, 3; dynamic nature of, 6–7, 9, 60, 148, 185–86; formation, 3, 6, 44–45, 66, 153, 168, 175, 190–91, 203n13, 229n8; linguistic, 63; national, 2, 168; Ottoman imperial, 44; religious, 50; state-sanctioned, 43, 74
illumination: citywide, 181, 184; consulates, 177, 181, 185; Cordon, 29, 182; mosques/minarets, 156
income: individual, 69–70; registers, 48; survey, 68, 212n49. *See also* taxation: income
İnebekoğlu, Abraham, 55
infrastructure, 26–27, 46; as battleground, 4, 96, 148–49; lack of, 25, 76, 191; as prestige projects, 143; as public/private good, 2, 4, 44, 99, 119, 128; and right to the city, 74; and social divisions, 100. *See also* Cordon; public works; streets: and gas lighting; waterfront
intercommunal dynamics, 42, 160, 170, 179
Ionian British Islands: subjects, 25, 58, 61–62, 211n38

Isfahan, 11
Islamic law, 47, 207n1; codification of, 57, 101; and consular jurisdiction, 60; flexibility of, 52, 57, 209n18; and foreigners, 51; and personal law, 50; and private property, 77, 102; and property transfer, 56, 58; and public space, 101–2; and state law, 101; and taxation, 214n71
İsmail Pasha (governor), 72, 94, 96, 221n71
Istanbul, 64, 68–69, 121, 132, 142, 144, 146, 161, 170, 171, 180; compared to Izmir, 10, 24, 26, 27, 53, 136; department stores, 30; gas lighting, 220n63; municipality, 71, 91, 220n57; press, 35, 65–66, 69, 71, 131–32, 160, 206n59, 215n84
Italy, 169, 176, 193, 214n66, 227n52; clergy, 152, 168; communities, 9, 51; consulate, 171, 172; delegates, 221n72, 227n39; exiles, 25, 69; language, 9, 20, 230n24; protégés, 61; states, 168
Izmir: as administrative capital, 23, 35–38, 39, 40–41, 207n69; demography, 1, 10–11, 24–25; fire and population exchange, 7–8; historiography of, 7; history of, 9–10; as international center, 2, 5, 23, 27, 29, 38, 42, 57, 61, 83, 92, 116, 169–70, 176, 181, 185, 189; modus vivendi in, 3, 78, 112, 186; as multilingual city, 8–9, 20, 32, 33–34, 45, 77, 84, 109, 160, 191, 230n24; periodical press, 32, 35; physical organization, 11, 14–16; urban expansion, 16–17, 16, 20, 23, 25–26

Janissary corps, 35, 76, 89, 120
Japhet (sanitary doctor), 218n26
Jesuits, 228n2
Jews, 3, 8–9, 11, 47, 154, 170, 206n62; cemetery, 13, 39, 85; community, 44, 51, 152, 160; hospital, 218n10; population, 25, 204n44; quarters, 11, 12, 78, 98, 100, 132, 156, 203n27, 208n10; rabbi, 51, 181
Journal de Constantinople (newspaper), 75, 81, 97, 129–30, 132, 179

Journal de Constantinople/Écho de l'Orient (newspaper), 177

Kabuli Mehmed Pasha (governor), 93
kadı, 47, 55, 76, 212n39, 217n6. *See also* courts: kadı
Kadifekale, xii, 11, 12, 25, 26, 81, 177
Kalomiraki, N., 227n39
Kanzıbanoğlu, Süleyman Bey, 216n93
Karcher, Sara, 55, 211n29
Kâtipzade (family), 37, 36
Kâtipzade (mansion), 36, 93, 181, 206n66
Katırcı Yanni, 85
Kaymak Pasha Street, 18–19
Kayserili Ahmed Pasha (governor), 88, 109, 133, 183, 217n5, 224n122
Kenourio Mahalle, 18–19, 20
khans, 15, 16, 18–19, 86; Cezayir, 37. *See also* frenkhane
Kızlarağası Khan, 18–19
Kızlar Street, 18–19
Kokluca (suburb), xiii, 83, 220n45
Konak, 26, 36, 38, 96, 112, 115, 181, 183; mosque, 39; and Sarıkışla area, 37–38, 39, 40, 233n82; square, 39, 40, 182. *See also* Kâtipzade (mansion)
Koszta, Martin, 194
Kuhn, Bernard, 227n39

La Fontaine, F., 218n26
land: expropriation, 35, 55, 85, 126, 141; registry (or cadastral office), 42, 43, 70, 96, 110, 130, 210n26, 216n90; speculation, 109–10, 121, 132, 225n5
Land Code, 48, 57–58, 102, 222n91
landownership. *See* property
Langdon, Joseph, 224n118
Launay, Louis de, 115
law: of expropriation for public utility, 102, 135, 223n100, 227n34; and jurisdictional boundaries, 50, 53, 56, 209n17; maritime, 178; partial overlap and conflict of, 4, 47, 53–54, 63, 77, 101, 173, 189, 194; personal, 50, 208n10, 209n16; plurality of, 4, 47, 50, 208n9; standardization of, 2, 5, 42–43, 48, 57, 67; territorial, 50, 52–54, 65, 111, 161, 189, 213n64. *See also* Ottoman Nationality Law; *names of individual law codes*
lazaretto, 84, 138, 218n25
Lazarists, 18–19, 104, 105, 122, 165, 166, 228n2
Leblebicizade Mehmed Bey, 221n72
Lefebvre, Henri, 208n8
legal pluralism. *See* law: plurality of
legal status, 2, 50, 60, 173, 209n17, 212n39; ambiguity of, 25, 43, 59–62; change of, 62–63, 189; and citizenship, 50; divides, 47–48, 77, 160, 192; of foreigners, 53, 59; and political participation, 97; of râya women, 53, 210n24; and social interaction, 53, 66; standardization of, 63, 72; and taxation, 43, 68. *See also* protégé
Levant Company, 11
Levant Herald (newspaper), 65, 87, 91, 97, 128, 226n24
Levantine, 9, 23, 165, 203n20
L'Impartial (newspaper), 73, 104, 205n59, 206n60
Liverpool, 27
Logie, Donald (consular judge), 54
London, 27, 93, 117, 134

Macropoderi, A. S., 63
Maltese, 14, 62, 162, 213n50, 230n24; migrants, 25, 204n31; street, 16, 17, 18–19. *See also* boatmen
Marcozade, 61–62, 210n27
Margossian Efendi, 143, 144, 191
Marseilles, 27, 124, 225n1
Masgana, A. (sanitary doctor), 218n26
Mathon, Jean, 205n49
Matteos (bishop), 184
McCraith, J. (sanitary doctor), 218n26
Mecelle-i Ahkam-ı Adliye. See Civil Code
Meles River, xii, 11, 25, 154
Messagerie Maritime, 124, 225n1
Midhad Pasha (governor), 88, 100, 220n49

migrants, 1, 3, 5, 85, 87, 203n25; diversity of, 25, 76; quarters, 20, 25, 76
millet. See ethnoreligious community
mills, 25, 26, 76, 218n10; steam-powered, 25, 18–19
Mitchell, G., 226n15
Mitchell, Timothy, 194
modernization: dynamics of, 4, 45–46; Ottoman state, 23, 35, 41, 45; as worldwide phenomenon, 4, 5, 44–46, 77, 90, 128, 149, 188, 193–94
modern state, 4, 37, 66, 161, 181, 190; ceremonies, 40, 44, 171, 181–82; instruments of, 5, 43, 69, 202n9, 215n83; territoriality, 49, 185, 188–89
Moraitini, Ch., 221n72
Morea, 11
Mostras, F., 218n26
Mount Pagus. *See* Kadifekale
Muammer Pasha (governor), 94
Muhammed Hilmi (molla), 214n70
mukataa, 120–21, 225n4
mülk (pl. emlak), 43, 58, 67–69, 207n2, 207n4, 210n26, 214n72
municipality, 39, 76–78, 109, 221n66; accountability of, 71, 74, 132; council, 43, 58, 94, 96, 101, 188, 212n39, 216n87, 221n72; districts, 98, 99, 222n81–82; duties of, 91; as modern city government, 1, 113; and political representation, 96–98; regulations, 6, 94, 96; relocation of, 95, 96; restructuring of, 46, 90–92, 94, 98, 113, 193; revenues, 94–95
Murtakya (neighborhood) 25, 26, 86
Murtakya khan. *See* Armenians: hospices
Muslims, 3, 8, 9, 24, 25, 160, 204n44, 205n51, 212n41; businesses, 154, 170; cemetery, 14, 14, 85, 86; charity, 121; corporations, 216n87; mosques, 1, 9, 11, 15, 85, 120, 184, 218n10; notables, 12, 122, 182; in police force, 112; quarters, 11, 12, 78, 98, 99, 100, 203n27, 218n10; refugees, 25; relations to non-Muslims, 44, 51–52, 57, 98, 152, 160, 170, 222n82

Mussabini, Antonio (archbishop), 151–52, 160–62, 165, 168–71, 179, 190, 229n6, 230n26
Mustafa Bey (sanitary doctor), 218n26

Naples, 168, 169. *See also* Italy
Napoleonic Wars, 23
national flag. *See* public display: of national flags
nationality: foreign, 62, 73; as a fungible category, 25; Ottoman, 66, 97–98, 189, 210n24, 217n101; and ownership rights, 66, 69. *See also* citizenship: and nationality; Ottoman Nationality Law
naturalization, 43, 59, 62, 65
Netherlands, 171, 214n66, 227n52; cemetery, 86; chapel, 105; community, 85; consul, 144; consular court, 55; consulate, 172, 210n28; hospital, 18–19, 20, 218n11; merchants, 3, 11; protégés, 55; subjects, 55
New Club, 205n56
newspapers: advertisement, 33–34; as critical voices, 72–73, 96–97, 112, 119, 126, 133, 137–38, 148–49; history in Izmir, 205–6n59; and the public good, 131–32; and the public sphere, 2, 23, 32, 35, 192
Nicoli, Hacı Tsiro, 221n72
nizam-ı cedid, 35
nizamiye. See courts: nizamiye
non-Muslims, 3, 8, 25, 30; autonomy of communities, 44, 48, 173, 207n3; corporations, 216n87; and European protection, 49, 59, 61, 62, 212n41; inclusion in state ceremonials, 182; under Muslim rule, 51, 208n11; and poll tax, 51, 52, 62, 67; proprietors, 122; quarters, 79. *See also* Muslims: relations to non-Muslims

Orosdi-Back, 30, 33
Orthodox Greeks, 3, 7–8, 25, 58, 60–61, 156, 159, 162, 170, 173–74, 203n16;

cemetery, 85; churches, 184 (see also names of individual churches); clergy, 212n39; community, 44, 51–52, 160, 169, 174; and Hellenic nationality, 174–75, 212–13n49; hospice, 86; hospital, 18–19, 20, 79, 218n11; metropolitan, 174, 181, 183; population, 25, 205n44–45; quarters, 11, 12–13, 20, 25, 78, 87, 98, 132, 156, 217n4, 218n10

Oskanian, Arteshas, 206n60

Osman Pasha (governor), 88, 214n70

Ottoman Nationality Law, 43, 60, 190, 210n24, 213n65, 217n101

Ottoman-Russian War, 219n43

Ottoman state: bureaucratic expansion, 1, 5, 35; censuses, 48, 62, 67, 201n1, 212n49; consolidation of power, 48–49, 63, 72, 189; diplomatic protocols, 174–75, 178, 185; ethnoreligious structure, 6–7, 44; hospital, 37, 39, 147; interment regulations, 85; and modern sovereignty, 5, 38, 41, 57, 63–67; municipal regulations, 6, 90–92, 94, 96, 97, 222n77; police organization, 35, 88, 89, 96, 112, 193, 206n63, 220n50; post-fire regulations, 79; territorial integrity, 4, 41, 179; treasury, 38, 67, 94, 95, 222n81. See also Tanzimat reforms

Ottoman subjects: foreign women passing as, 53–54, 64; passing as foreigners, 61–62, 65; relations with foreigners, 16–17, 60

palikaraki, 87

Panagia (neighborhood), 11

Papazoğlu, Anastas Ağa, 221n72

Pappa, George, 216n93

Patterson, J. B., 148, 226n15

Penal Code, 57–58, 102, 223n99, 223n110

Perkins, George, 215n77

Pisani, Etienne (dragoman), 64

Pius VII (pope), 161

Point, the (Punta), xvii, 17, 75, 87–88, 118, 133, 134; barracks and maneuver field,
26, 30, 35; gasworks at, 93; industrial plants at, 25; marshes at, 74; street lighting, 88; train station, 26, 29, 32

police: control/surveillance, 35, 87–88, 91, 101, 127, 159, 189; department, 88, 89, 96, 193; duties, 76; jurisdiction, 49, 63, 65, 77, 111–12; need for effective, 35, 74, 88; recruitment of, 112; shortcomings of the, 35, 71, 75, 77, 109, 111–12; stations, 18–19, 20, 59, 126, 205n51, 206n63. See also uniforms

Port Said, 117, 225n1

post offices, 1, 29

prison, 37, 39; and bribery, 112, 224n122; consular, 87, 219n40

promenade, 1, 20, 27, 29, 115, 128, 129, 140

property (real): and citizenship, 49, 66, 74, 190; customary rights to, 68, 73; disputes related to, 52, 54–58, 61, 188; and foreign subjects, 48, 50, 53–54, 57, 65–66, 68, 72, 188–89, 192, 208n5, 210n21, 214n67; ownership law, 2; registration, 53–54, 64, 112, 135, 190; and representation, 98; rights, 23, 43–44, 46, 49, 50, 52, 64, 73, 102, 110, 139, 213n64; taxation, 43, 49, 50, 67–72, 95–96, 136, 190, 215n77, 215n85, 216n90; and territorial jurisdictions, 47, 52; transfer, 47–48, 54–55, 64, 120, 213n61; values, 81, 99, 121, 133. See also mülk; vakıf; women: as property owners

protégé: as legal status, 59–62, 208n6, 212n44–45; as system, 60, 62–65, 68, 212n41, 212n49, 214n66, 230n24

Provincial Code, 91–92, 97–98, 221n76, 221n79

Prussia (Germany), 214n66; cemetery, 86; consulate, 124, 171, 172, 176; subjects, 85

Psiachi, J. E., 226n15

public display, 38, 40, 153, 176, 178, 194; of banners, 156, 162, 163, 171, 177; of national flags, 156, 165, 171, 174–79, 181–82, 184; of national/religious sentiments, 153, 156, 168, 171, 173, 178 public good: as economic welfare, 127–28; as flexible signifier, 4, 44, 46, 114, 119, 127, 138, 140, 149, 191, 193; newspapers and, 131–32, 192; and private rights, 27, 77; as public health, 129–30; public works and, 118–19, 126; as state interests, 127

public space: encroachment on, 74, 77, 92–93, 102, 104, 105, 107, 109, 193, 223n99; and festive format, 153, 176, 181; and nuisance, 44, 78, 101, 105, 107, 191; and the public sphere, 191; refashioning of, 44; regulation of, 35, 76–77, 84, 91, 113–14, 217n6, 219n40, 223n99; right to, 58, 78; and safety, 2, 4, 35, 77–78, 85, 87, 89, 104, 111–13, 193. *See also* streets

public sphere: and civic culture, 2, 3, 5, 187; constitution of, 74, 148–49, 191, 193; and newspapers, 35, 206n61

public works: ministry of, 134, 144, 226n30; as political arenas, 119; and private property, 136–37; projects, 26, 116, 193. *See also* infrastructure; urban improvements

quarantine, 74, 84, 89, 93, 193, 218n25. *See also* lazaretto

quay, 27, 29, 115, 182; access to water, 17, 118, 124, 126, 127, 133, 135, 137; construction of, 38, 46, 96, 114, 116–17, 119, 126–30, 133–41; project, 118, 134–35; sewers and public hygiene, 138, 141–43, 145, 147. *See also* Cordon; promenade

Queen Victoria, 176, 178

Ragıb Bey (Hacı), 218n25, 222n82
railway, 1, 26–27, 76, 116, 127, 154, 228n62; Izmir-Aydın, 26, 27, 28, 29, 85; Izmir-Kasaba, 26, 27, 28, 30, 85
Réforme, La (newspaper), 99, 145, 206n60
Reşidiye Avenue, 79, 82, 163
Reşid Pasha (governor), 84
rights and duties: of citizens, 4, 43, 49, 213n64; customary, 3, 52, 67, 77, 102; differentiated, 3, 44, 47, 189; of modern citizenship, 190, 193; related to property, 66–67, 72; related to public space, 77, 101

right to the city, 44, 73, 114, 208n8
Rolland, Charles, 2
Rolleston, George, 9
Rose Street, 18–19, 20, 162, 166, 170

Sabri Pasha (governor), 112
Sacré Cœur (church), 18–19, 165, 166. *See also* Lazarists
Sadık Pasha (governor), 110
Sailor's Home, 205n56
Salih Pasha (governor), 70, 151, 168, 215n86
salname, 25, 45
Salonika. *See* Thessaloniki
Salzani, Ch., 215n78, 216n97
Samaritaine, La. *See* dry-goods stores
Samiotaki, S., 206n60
sanitary office, 18–19, 123
Sardinia, 61, 168, 169. *See also* Italy
Sarıkışla, 35, 37–38, 39, 40, 41, 123, 134, 233n82
Schiffmann, J., 227n39
Schmidt, E., 227n39
Scio. *See* Chios
Scott, James, 207n74
Serbo-Ottoman War, 160
Server Pasha, 210n21
sewers: common, 100; and easement, 58, 59, 110; maintenance/improvement of, 74, 84, 89, 91, 100; as public good, 119; and public health, 75, 84, 142–43; for the quay project, 27, 116, 134, 141, 143, 144–45; vaulted, 100
Seydiköy (suburb), 220n45
Seyyid Ahmed Soflu, 214n70
Seyyid el-Hac İbrahim, 214n70
Seyyid Raşid, 214n70
ships (vessels), 5, 136, 178; as festive space, 151, 156, 178, 181–82; loading/unloading, 124, 127, 136, 148, 228n62; nationality of, 176; quarantine on, 84

Sidi, Alexander, 227n39
Sisters of Charity, 18, 165, 166
Sıvaslı Takvor, 109
slaughterhouses, xii, 84, 93, 101
Smyrna Gardens, 26, 32
Smyrna Gas Company, 93–94, 220n63
Smyrna Jockey Club, 32, 154, 229n15
Smyrna Quay Company, 117, 119, 134, 137–38, 141, 143, 145, 190, 227n49
sovereignty: assertion of, 5, 41, 52, 57, 153, 188–89; boundaries of, 194; and diplomacy, 169, 185, 231n58; expression of, 38, 171, 176, 178–80; and foreign subjects, 72; and property, 63–68; recognition of, 4
Spaccapietra, Vincenzo, 230n26
Sporting Club, 205n56
St. Antoine (hospital), 18, 79, 231n35
St. Catherine: church, 26; neighborhood, 229n20
St. Dimitri: church, 18–19, 26, 82, 86, 166; neighborhood, 20, 78, 81, 229n20
steamship lines, 1, 27, 76, 124, 128–29, 226n15
Stein store. *See* dry-goods stores
St. John: Catholic cathedral, 166; church at Apano Mahalle, 11; church near Bella Vista, 18–19, 59; feast of, 229n18; neighborhood, 155
St. George: church, 18–19, 79, 81, 82; feast of, 174–75; neighborhood, 78
St. Mary (church): at Apano Mahalle, 11; in Frank quarter, 18–19, 104, 166, 167–68, 176
Storari, Luigi, 69, 215n84
Storari (map) xiv, 18–19, 39, 59, 82, 166, 205n47, 206n63
St. Photini: belfry, 156, 157, 158, 175; church, 17, 18–19, 82, 105, 166, 173; neighborhood, 229n20
St. Polycarp: church, 17, 18–19, 20, 104, 164, 166, 167, 168; saint, 230n31
Street of the Great Taverns, 17, 18–19, 105, 229n20

streets: alignment, 92, 102; amenities/services, 1, 4, 46, 74, 89–92, 101, 113, 193; dead-end, 101–2, 130, 211n37, 223n96; and gas lighting, 26–27, 88, 89, 90, 94, 100, 119, 146, 156, 216n93, 220n63; and hygiene, 84, 102, 138, 193; and kerosene lamps, 27, 88, 94, 100; as public property, 77, 101–2; through, 101–2. *See also* easement; public space
St. Roch (hospital), 18–19, 79, 86, 230–31n34
St. Stephen (church), 19, 79, 80
St. Vukla (church), 86
subjecthood (Ottoman), 43, 44, 47, 60, 64, 189
suburbs, 1, 27; gangs in, 85; mansions, 76; police watch, 87. *See also* cemeteries; railway
Süleyman el-Nehbi, 214n70
Sultaniye Street, 18–19
Süreyya Pasha (governor), 63, 100, 216n97, 229n12
synagogues, 1, 12, 184, 218n10

Tanners Street, 18–19
tannery, 26, 82, 86
Tanzimat reforms, 4, 6–7, 23, 35–38, 41–44, 57, 64, 69, 111, 152, 173, 188; fiscal reforms, 50, 67–68; legal reforms, 44, 57, 88, 173; and localities, 5; and Ottomanism, 182; and provincial administration, 35, 38
Tatakian, Martiroz, 221n72
taverns (drinking places), 17, 20, 87, 123–24, 127, 184
taxation: arrears, 71, 92, 148, 216n90; communal, 51–52; income, 5, 43, 67, 70–71, 92, 190, 215n77, 215n85, 216n90; property, 5, 47, 49, 50, 52, 67–72, 95, 96, 136, 215n77, 216n90; standardization of, 2, 5, 188. *See also* wharf: dues
telegraph lines, 27
temettü. See taxation: income
Tepecik (neighborhood), 25, 26, 86

Teşrifiye Street, 18–19
theaters, 1, 98, 184, 233n82. *See also* Cammarano Theater; Euterpe Theater
Theodoraki (councilor), 214n70
Thessaloniki, 5, 11, 53, 61, 69
Tilkilik Avenue, 79, 82
Timoni, Andrea Policarpo, 230n26
train stations. *See* Basmahane Station; Point, the (Punta): train station
tramway, 27, 115, 117, 134, 139, 140, 146, 228n62
transportation: animal, 20, 102, 105, 107, 109; mix of old and new, 105; new modes of, 27, 76. *See also* carriages; railway; steamship lines; tramway
Trassa Street, 18–19
Treaty of London, 179, 232n70
Trieste, 27, 124, 225n1
Turkey, 9, 97, 179
Turks, 24–25, 160, 203n15. *See also* Muslims
Turquie, La (newspaper), 107, 109, 115, 136–39, 145, 148
Tuscany, 168, 169, 206n60. *See also* Italy
Tuzla Burnu, xii, 17. *See also* Point, the

uniforms: police, 40; significance of, 171, 184–85
urban anxieties: as impetus to improvements, 77–78, 93, 192; related to fires, 78–79; related to sanitation, 84–85, 138, 142, 145, 147, 190; related to security, 85, 87, 156, 159
urban governance: foreign interference in, 72; institutions/practices of, 4, 6, 40, 44; participatory, 43, 70, 73, 97; pre-Tanzimat, 76, 217n7; rationalization of, 113. *See also* municipality
urban growth, 5, 10; and congestion, 104–5, 113, 223n96; pressures of, 4, 45, 191. *See also* Izmir: urban expansion; urban anxieties
urban improvements: in the Armenian quarter, 81; and cadastral commission, 70–71; demands for, 73, 76, 91, 113, 119, 190–91; in exchange for taxes, 71, 148; funds for, 94, 100; and institutional structures, 4, 89–92, 94, 101, 114; obstacles to, 77–78, 101–2, 111–12; unevenness of, 88, 187. *See also* infrastructure
urban polity: diversity of, 2; foreigners' access to, 70, 73, 78, 97–98; membership in, 2, 44, 49, 74, 101
urban regulations, 2, 79, 83, 92, 193; building codes, 2, 36; building permits, 47, 96; power to enforce, 92, 130. *See also* public space: regulation of
Uşaklıgil, Halid Ziya, 206n60

vakıf (pl. evkaf), 58, 76, 120, 126; abuse of procedures, 121; administrator, 210n26; property, 58, 120, 207n2, 210n26, 225n4
Valon, Alexis de, 20
Van Lennep, Richard J., 144, 145, 148, 190, 218n26, 227n49
Vapopoulo, Manoli. *See Hripsima v. Vapopoulo*
Veli Pasha (governor), 94
Venetian colony, 3, 11, 209n14, 211n38
verhane (ferhane), 16, 17. *See also* frenkhane
Vernazza (merchant), 226n15
von Benda-Beckmann, Keebet, 212n40
Von Eichstroff (sanitary doctor), 218n26
voyvoda system, 206n64

warehouses, 1, 16–17, 29, 55, 56, 98, 116, 124, 127. *See also* frenkhane
war refugees, 25, 87
waterfront, 4, 27, 100, 115, 123, 126, 128, 138, 192–93; circulation along, 140; development of the, 46, 99, 126, 127, 132, 153, 187; land speculation, 121, 132, 225n5; lots, 132; promenade, 1, 27, 29; supervision over, 127, 189. *See also* Cordon; quay
water lots, 121–23, 130, 135
Werry, John, 215n77

wharf, 116, 127, 133; access to and control of, 127; dues, 119, 135–37, 147, 227n38; private, 16, 121
Whittall, F., 226n15
Whittall, James, 227n39
Wilkin, Robert, 216n93
Williamson, W., 143, 144
windmill, 126, 128. *See also* mills
women, 20, 29, 56, 85; foreign, 64, 210n25, 213n61; as property owners, 53–55, 64, 121–22, 210n21, 210n25, 210n27, 211n29; râya, 53–54, 210n24

Xenopoulo, P., & Cie. *See* dry-goods stores

Yanako veled-i Spiro, 214n70
Yenişehirlizade Ahmed Efendi, 148

Zadé, Constantino, 58, 59, 60, 212n39
zeybek, 85, 219n43
zimmi protections, 51, 208n11

SIBEL ZANDI-SAYEK is associate professor in the Department of Art and Art History at the College of William and Mary.

www.ingramcontent.com/pod-product-compliance
Lightning Source LLC
Chambersburg PA
CBHW060231240426
43671CB00016B/2907